American Vampire

AMERICAN

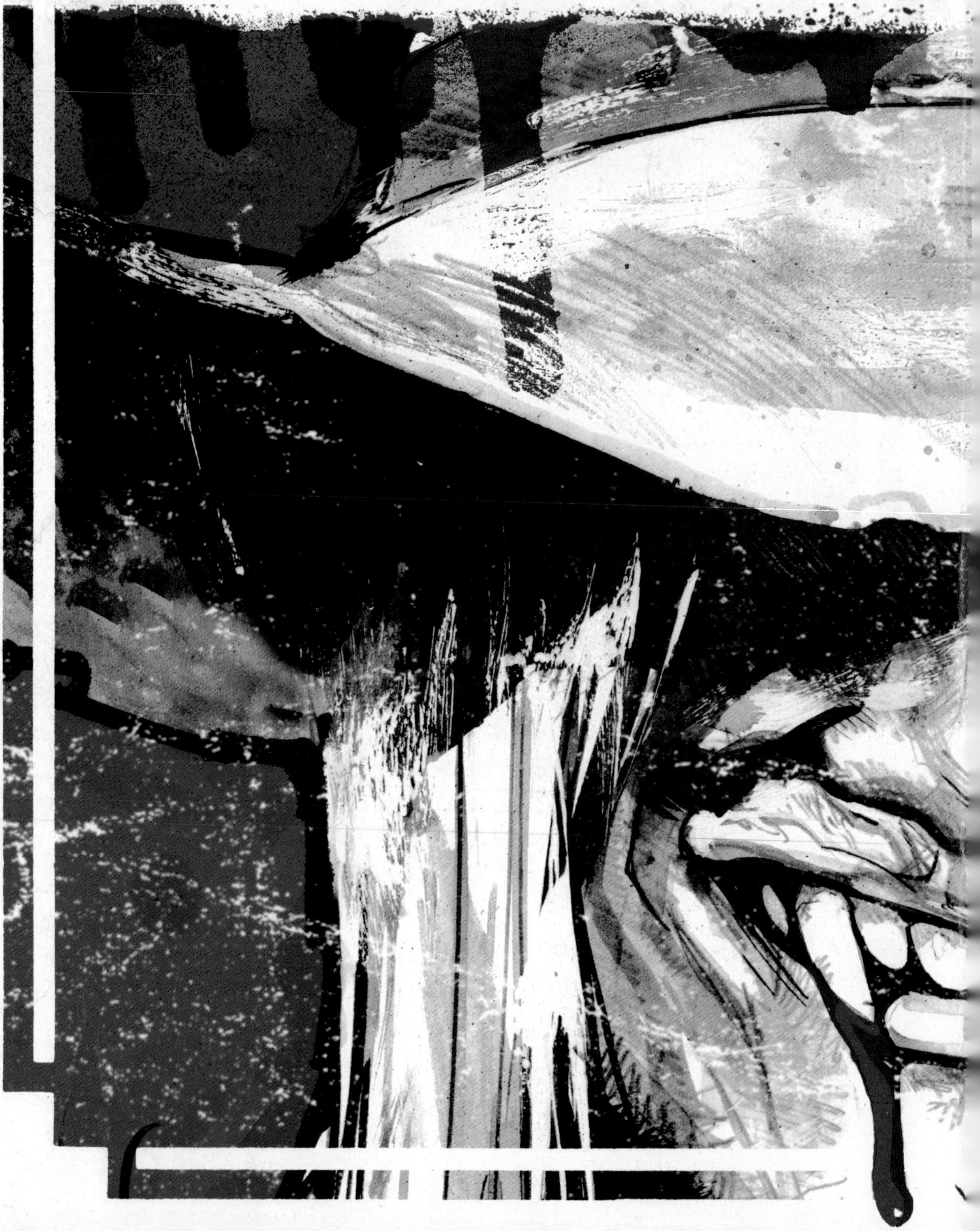

VAMPIRE

Scott Snyder Stephen King Writers
Rafael Albuquerque Artist
Dave McCaig Colorist
Steve Wands Letterer
American Vampire created by Scott Snyder

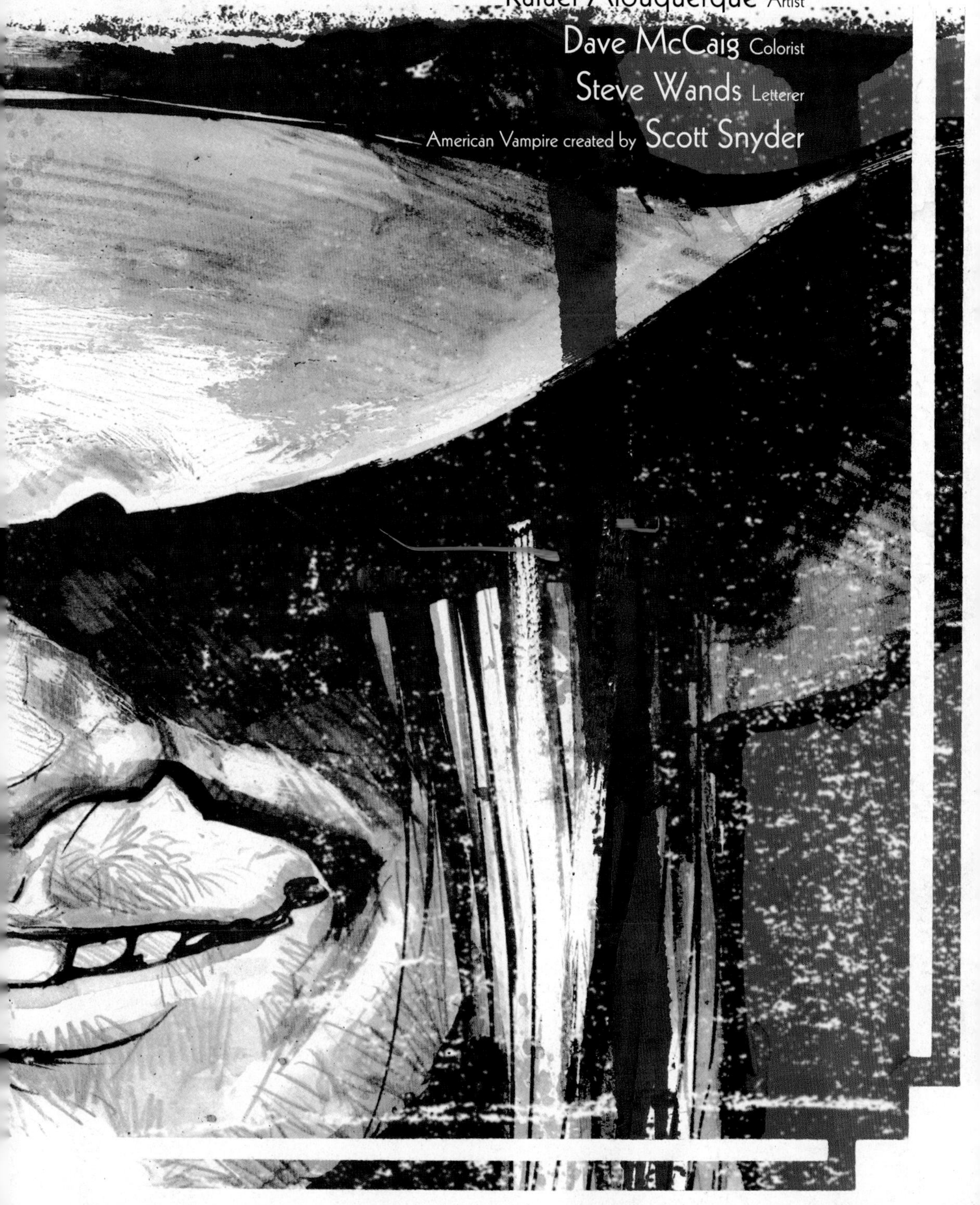

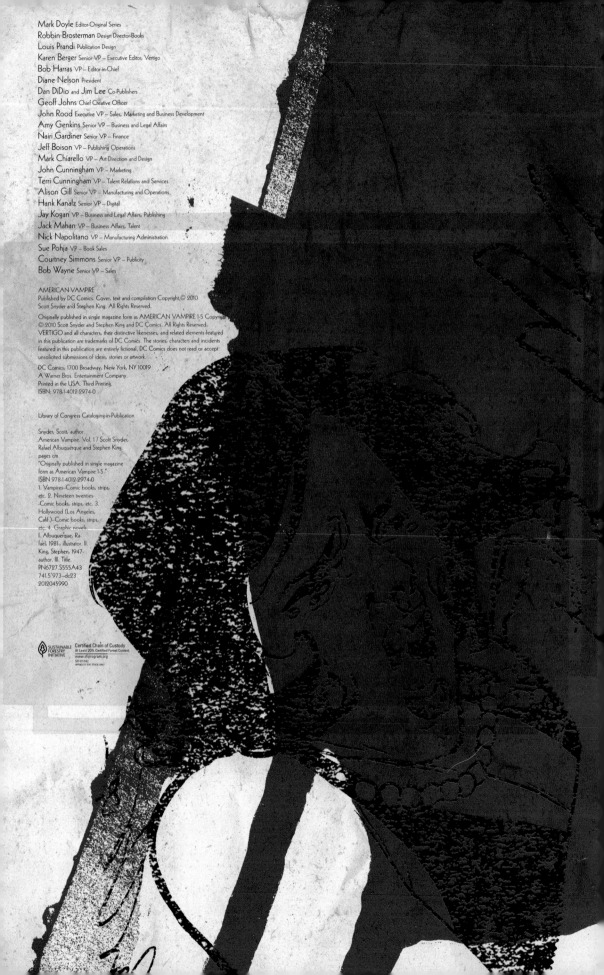

AMERICAN VAMPIRE
Published by DC Comics. Cover, text and compilation Copyright © 2010
Scott Snyder and Stephen King. All Rights Reserved.

Originally published in single magazine form as AMERICAN VAMPIRE 1-5 Copyright
© 2010 Scott Snyder and Stephen King and DC Comics. All Rights Reserved.
VERTIGO and all characters, their distinctive likenesses, and related elements featured
in this publication are trademarks of DC Comics. The stories, characters and incidents
featured in this publication are entirely fictional. DC Comics does not read or accept
unsolicited submissions of ideas, stories or artwork.

DC Comics, 1700 Broadway, New York, NY 10019
A Warner Bros. Entertainment Company.
Printed in the USA. Third Printing.
ISBN: 978-1-4012-2974-0

Library of Congress Cataloging-in-Publication

Snyder, Scott, author.
American Vampire. Vol. 1 / Scott Snyder,
Rafael Albuquerque and Stephen King.
pages cm
"Originally published in single magazine
form as American Vampire 1-5."
ISBN 978-1-4012-2974-0
1. Vampires-Comic books, strips,
etc. 2. Nineteen twenties-
-Comic books, strips, etc. 3.
Hollywood (Los Angeles,
Calif.)-Comic books, strips,
etc. 4. Graphic novels.
I. Albuquerque, Ra-
fael, 1981- illustrator. II.
King, Stephen, 1947-
author. III. Title.
PN6727.S555A43
741.5'973-dc23
2012045990

SUCK
ON
THIS

By
Stephen
King

Here's what vampires shouldn't be: pallid detectives who
drink Bloody Marys and only work at night; lovelorn southern
gentlemen; anorexic teenage girls; boy-toys with big dewy eyes.

What should they be?

Killers, honey. Stone killers who never get enough of that tasty
Type-A. Bad boys and girls. Hunters. In other words, Midnight
America. Red, white and blue, accent on the red. Those vamps got
hijacked by a lot of soft-focus romance. That's why I was so excited
when Scott Snyder—a writer I knew from his excellent book of
short stories, *Voodoo Heart*—mentioned to me in an email that he
was in talks with the folks at Vertigo about doing a vampire comic
series. His take was unique, his enthusiasm infectious.

His ambition for the continuing story of Skinner Sweet (and
his victims) was awesome: nothing more or less than to trace the
emergence of America through the immortal eyes of a new kind
of vampire, one that can walk in the sun. I saw the potential for
some terrific stories, and I also liked the resonance of the thing.
There's a subtext here that whispers powerful messages about
boundless American energy and that energy's darker side: a
grasping, stop-at-nothing hunger for money and power.

Scott wanted a blurb.

I asked him if I could write a story instead. In fact, I wanted to
light a blowtorch and burn one in, incise it like a big ole
scary tattoo.

I ended up writing the Skinner Sweet origin story, and nobody is happier about that than I am. If you like it, don't thank me; I wrote it from Scott's detailed outline, adding bells and whistles here and there but never straying too far from his narrative line. Why fuck with genius?

If you don't like it, you can blame the fact that I'm new to this kind of storytelling. (Of course, if you don't like it, why the heck are you even here???) I've been a lifelong comics reader—cut my teeth on Plastic Man and Combat Casey—but in the last fifteen years or so, the medium has grown up. I owe great thanks to Mark Doyle, who edits AMVAMP. It was Mark who eased me in, sending me scripts for most excellent comix like NORTHLANDERS and SCALPED. I learned as much from these as I could (and re-read all of my son Joe Hill's *Locke & Key* stories), then listened humbly when I was instructed on some of the new rules (thought balloons, I discovered, are now passé).

It was Mark and Scott who (with great tact) corrected my layouts when they went wrong. And this, most of all: it was the remarkable Rafael Albuquerque who brought our words and descriptions to vibrant, scary life. I can't thank him enough. As a guy who can't even draw stick figures, I am in awe. Seeing those panels grow from rough sketches to finished art has been the most rewarding thing to happen in my creative life for quite some time. I can do story, and I can do dialogue, but the spell Rafa's art casts adds a whole new dimension to those things.

In the end, though, it's all about giving back the teeth that the current "sweetie-vamp" craze has, by and large, stolen from the bloodsuckers. It's about making them *scary* again. Thanks, you guys, for letting me be a part of that. Skinner Sweet really sucks, and man, that's a good thing.

Stephen King
May, 2010

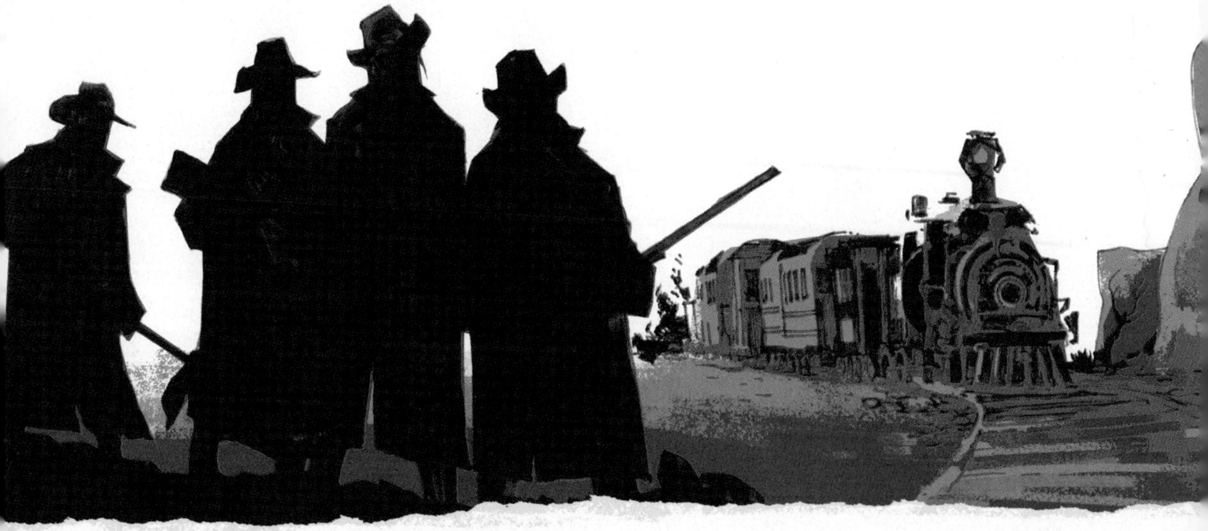

Chapter One

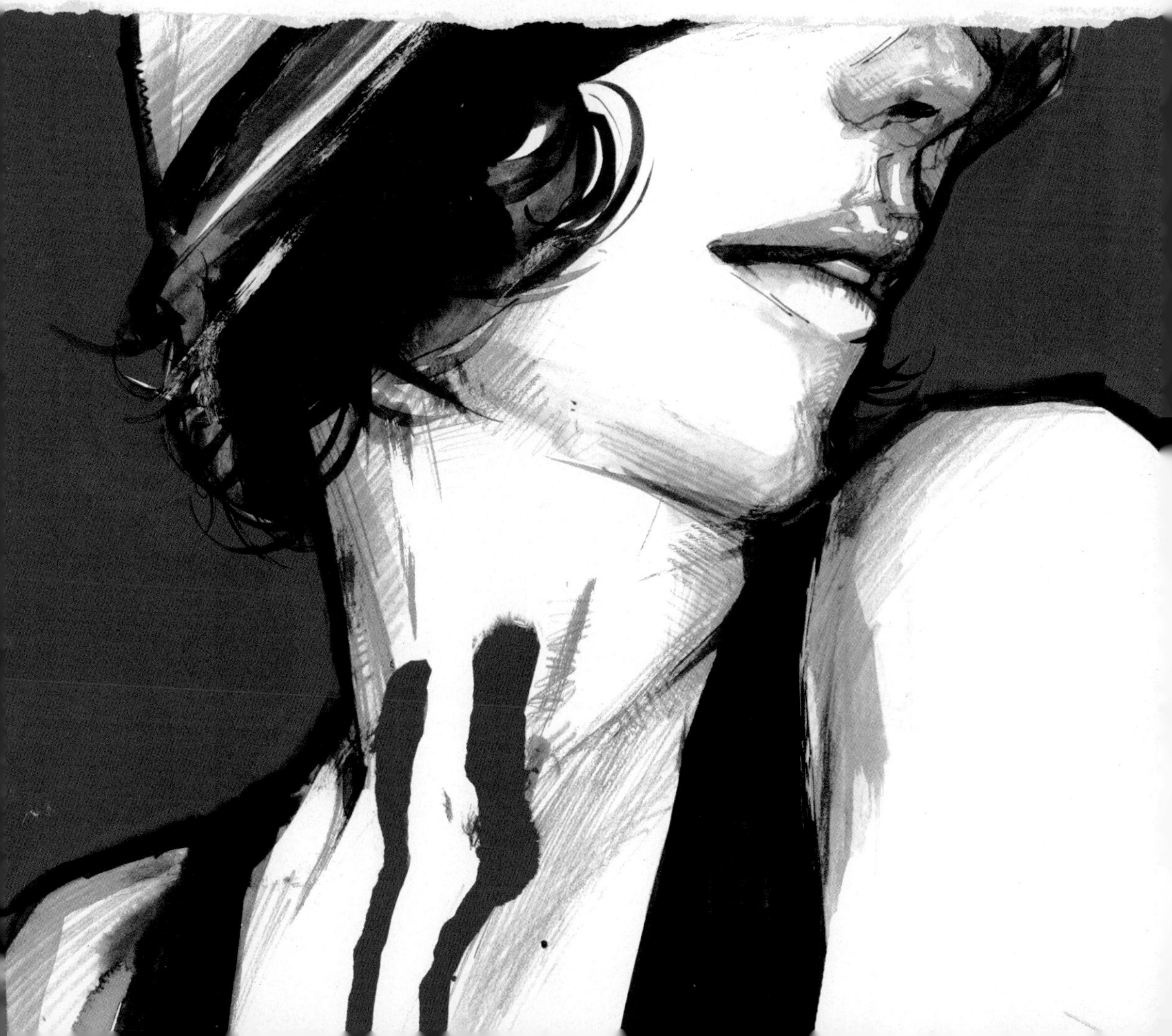

Big Break
Scott Snyder Writer

Bad Blood
Stephen King Writer

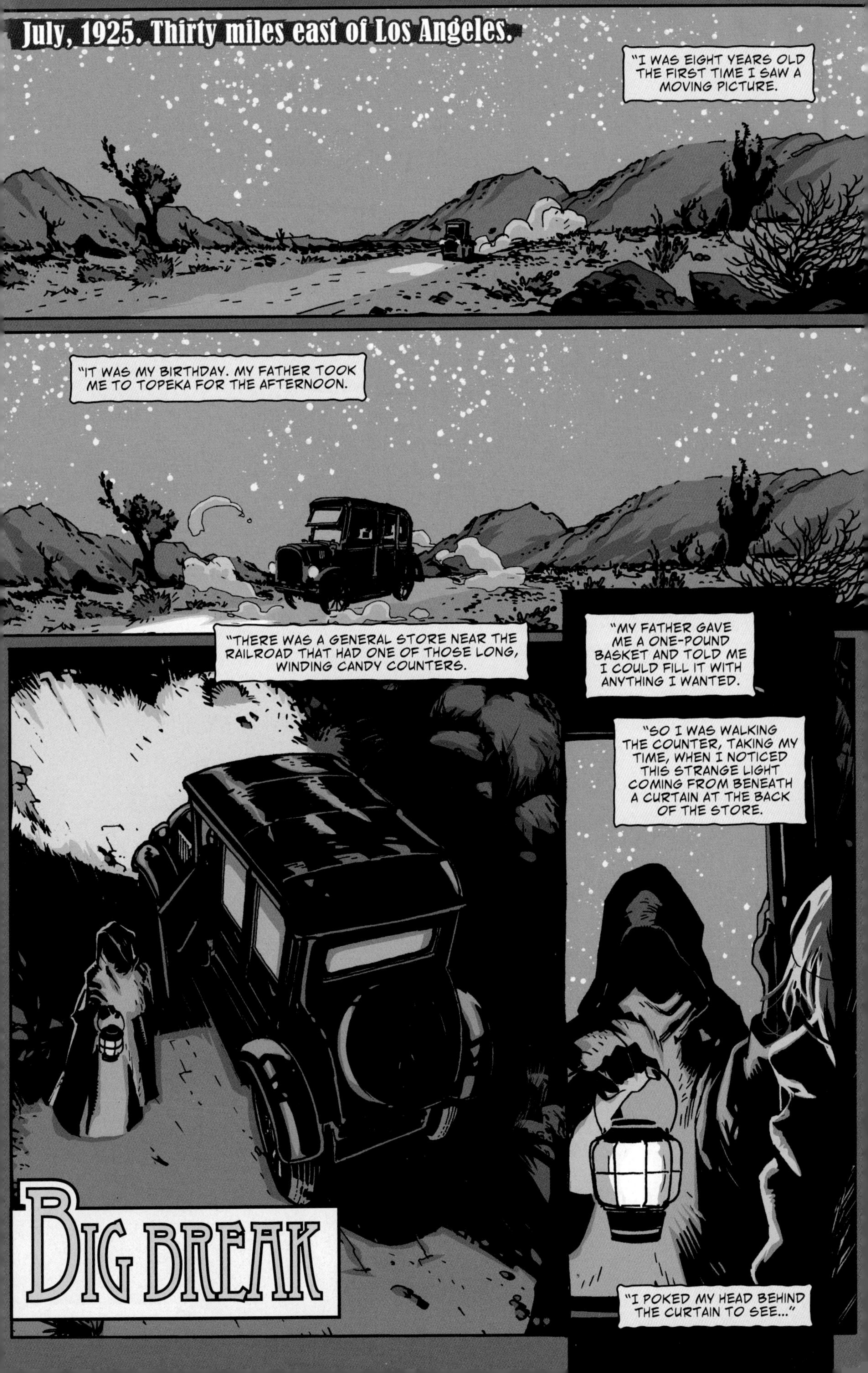
July, 1925. Thirty miles east of Los Angeles.
"I WAS EIGHT YEARS OLD THE FIRST TIME I SAW A MOVING PICTURE.
"IT WAS MY BIRTHDAY. MY FATHER TOOK ME TO TOPEKA FOR THE AFTERNOON.
"THERE WAS A GENERAL STORE NEAR THE RAILROAD THAT HAD ONE OF THOSE LONG, WINDING CANDY COUNTERS.
"MY FATHER GAVE ME A ONE-POUND BASKET AND TOLD ME I COULD FILL IT WITH ANYTHING I WANTED.
"SO I WAS WALKING THE COUNTER, TAKING MY TIME, WHEN I NOTICED THIS STRANGE LIGHT COMING FROM BENEATH A CURTAIN AT THE BACK OF THE STORE.
BIG BREAK
"I POKED MY HEAD BEHIND THE CURTAIN TO SEE..."

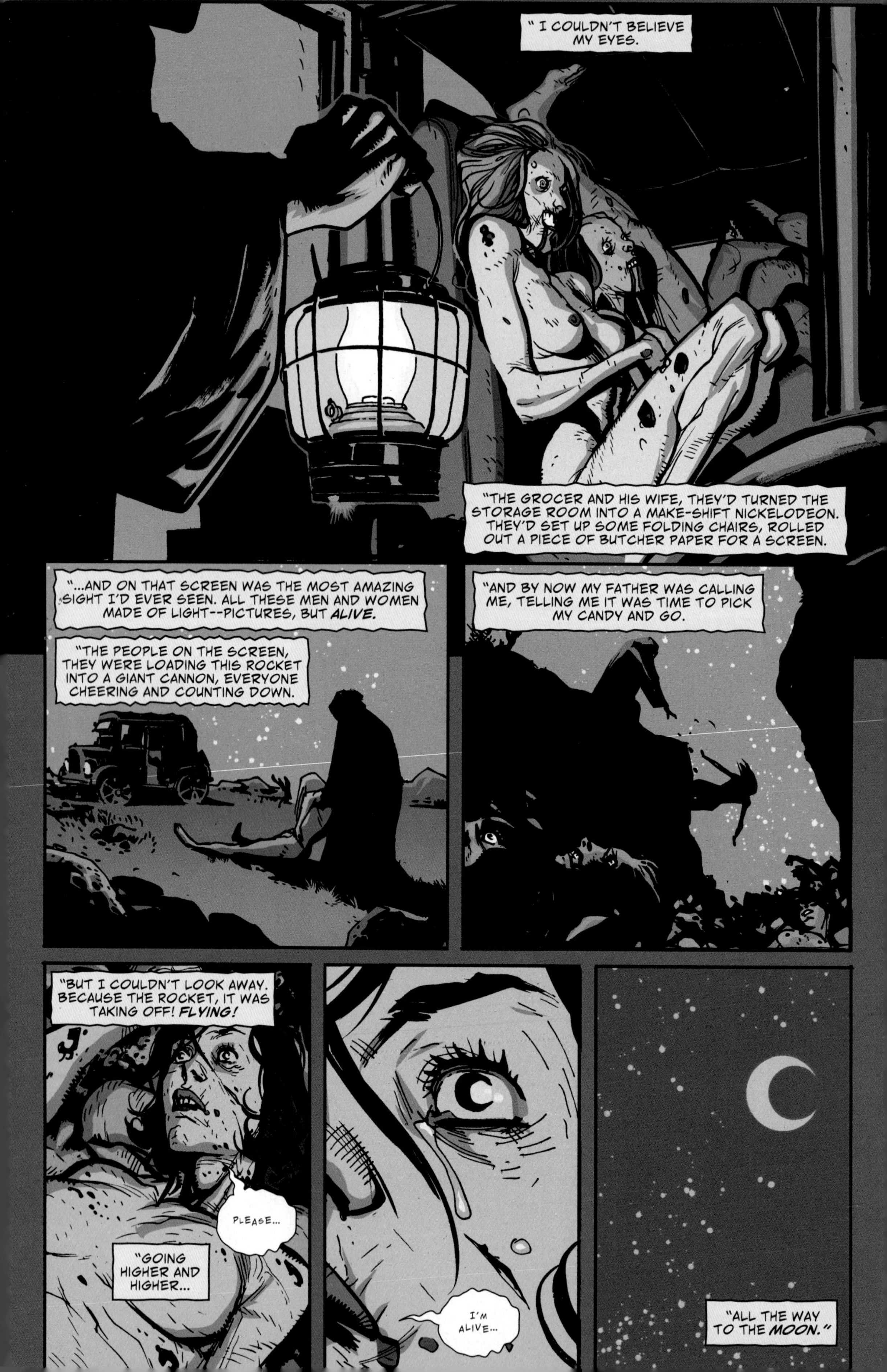
"I COULDN'T BELIEVE MY EYES.
"THE GROCER AND HIS WIFE, THEY'D TURNED THE STORAGE ROOM INTO A MAKE-SHIFT NICKELODEON. THEY'D SET UP SOME FOLDING CHAIRS, ROLLED OUT A PIECE OF BUTCHER PAPER FOR A SCREEN.
"...AND ON THAT SCREEN WAS THE MOST AMAZING SIGHT I'D EVER SEEN. ALL THESE MEN AND WOMEN MADE OF LIGHT--PICTURES, BUT *ALIVE.*
"THE PEOPLE ON THE SCREEN, THEY WERE LOADING THIS ROCKET INTO A GIANT CANNON, EVERYONE CHEERING AND COUNTING DOWN.
"AND BY NOW MY FATHER WAS CALLING ME, TELLING ME IT WAS TIME TO PICK MY CANDY AND GO.
"BUT I COULDN'T LOOK AWAY. BECAUSE THE ROCKET, IT WAS TAKING OFF! *FLYING!*
PLEASE...
"GOING HIGHER AND HIGHER...
I'M ALIVE...
"ALL THE WAY TO THE *MOON.*"

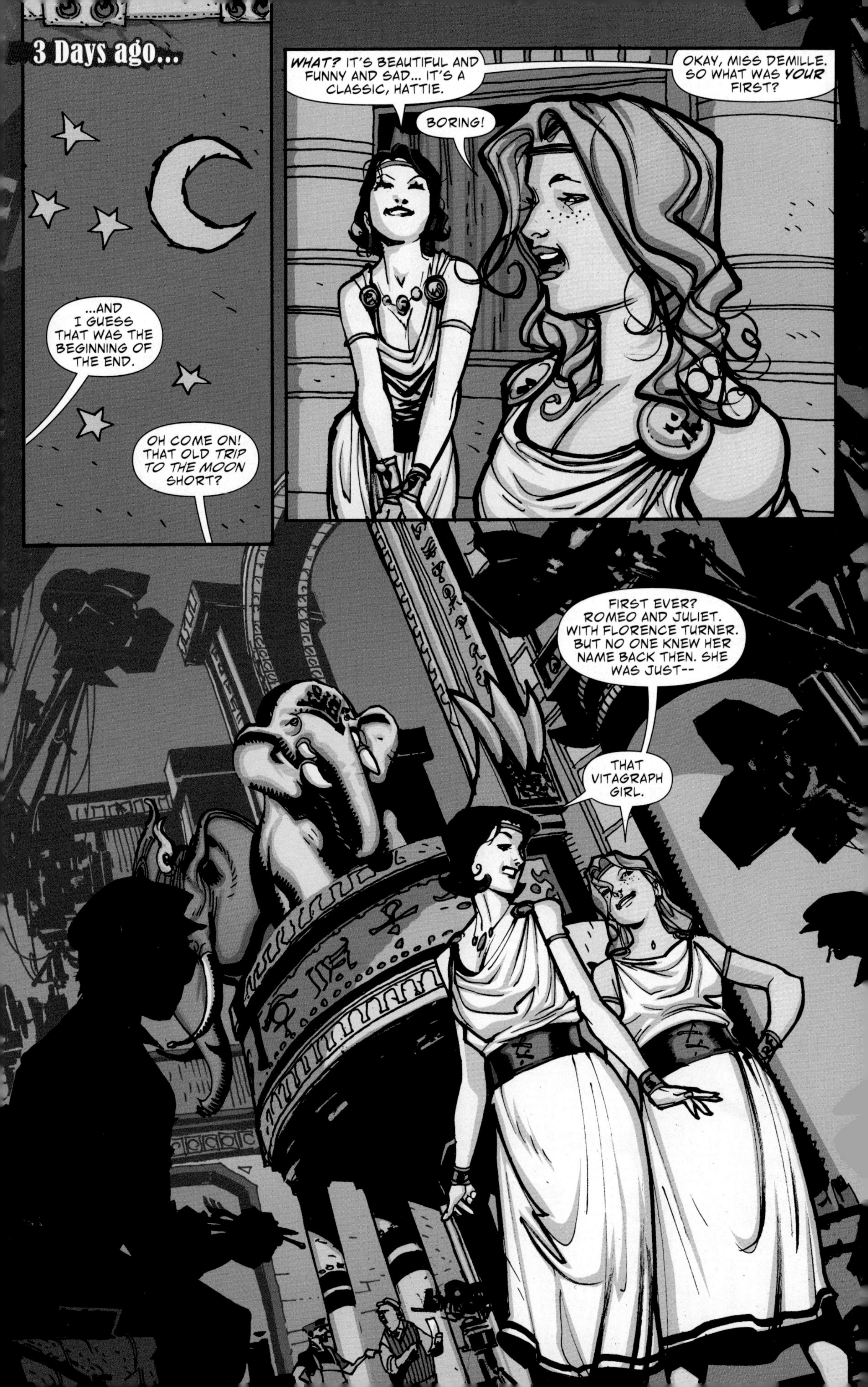
3 Days ago...
...AND I GUESS THAT WAS THE BEGINNING OF THE END.
OH COME ON! THAT OLD TRIP TO THE MOON SHORT?
WHAT? IT'S BEAUTIFUL AND FUNNY AND SAD... IT'S A CLASSIC, HATTIE.
BORING!
OKAY, MISS DEMILLE. SO WHAT WAS YOUR FIRST?
FIRST EVER? ROMEO AND JULIET. WITH FLORENCE TURNER. BUT NO ONE KNEW HER NAME BACK THEN. SHE WAS JUST--
THAT VITAGRAPH GIRL.

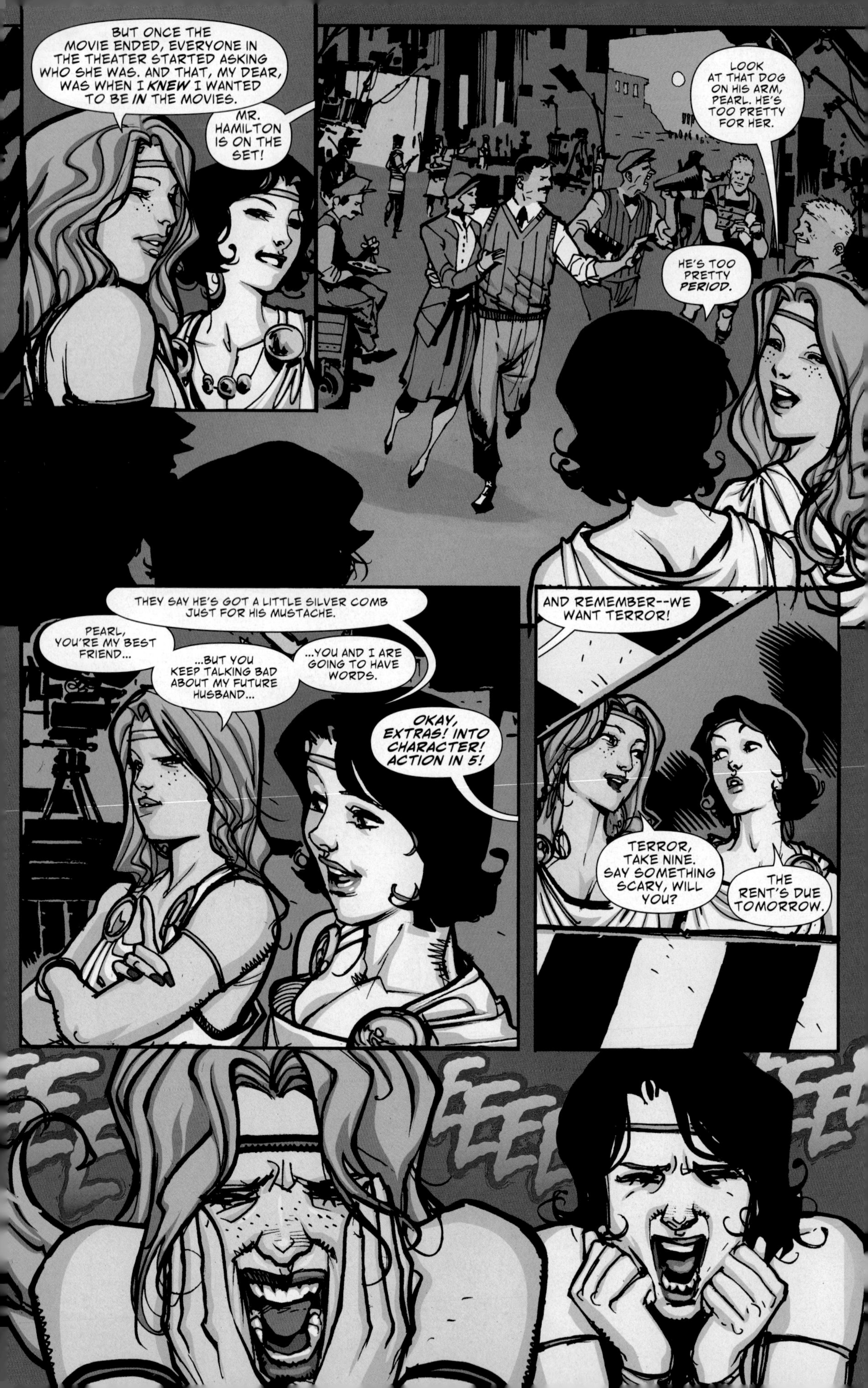

BUT ONCE THE MOVIE ENDED, EVERYONE IN THE THEATER STARTED ASKING WHO SHE WAS. AND THAT, MY DEAR, WAS WHEN I KNEW I WANTED TO BE IN THE MOVIES.
MR. HAMILTON IS ON THE SET!
LOOK AT THAT DOG ON HIS ARM, PEARL. HE'S TOO PRETTY FOR HER.
HE'S TOO PRETTY PERIOD.
THEY SAY HE'S GOT A LITTLE SILVER COMB JUST FOR HIS MUSTACHE.
PEARL, YOU'RE MY BEST FRIEND...
...BUT YOU KEEP TALKING BAD ABOUT MY FUTURE HUSBAND...
...YOU AND I ARE GOING TO HAVE WORDS.
OKAY, EXTRAS! INTO CHARACTER! ACTION IN 5!
AND REMEMBER--WE WANT TERROR!
TERROR, TAKE NINE. SAY SOMETHING SCARY, WILL YOU?
THE RENT'S DUE TOMORROW.

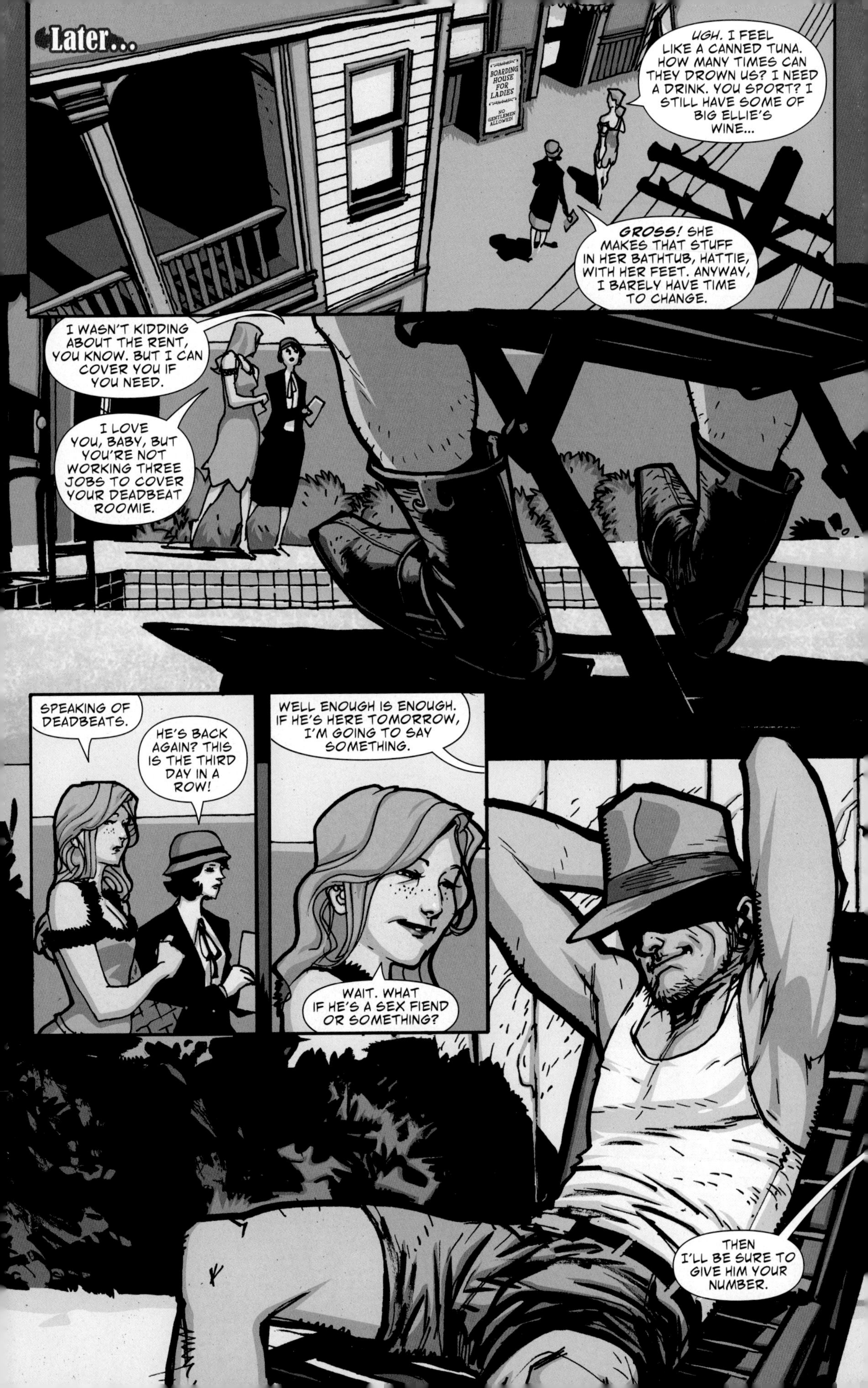
Later...
BOARDING HOUSE FOR LADIES
NO GENTLEMEN ALLOWED!
UGH. I FEEL LIKE A CANNED TUNA. HOW MANY TIMES CAN THEY DROWN US? I NEED A DRINK. YOU SPORT? I STILL HAVE SOME OF BIG ELLIE'S WINE...
GROSS! SHE MAKES THAT STUFF IN HER BATHTUB, HATTIE, WITH HER FEET. ANYWAY, I BARELY HAVE TIME TO CHANGE.
I WASN'T KIDDING ABOUT THE RENT, YOU KNOW. BUT I CAN COVER YOU IF YOU NEED.
I LOVE YOU, BABY, BUT YOU'RE NOT WORKING THREE JOBS TO COVER YOUR DEADBEAT ROOMIE.
SPEAKING OF DEADBEATS.
HE'S BACK AGAIN? THIS IS THE THIRD DAY IN A ROW!
WELL ENOUGH IS ENOUGH. IF HE'S HERE TOMORROW, I'M GOING TO SAY SOMETHING.
WAIT. WHAT IF HE'S A SEX FIEND OR SOMETHING?
THEN I'LL BE SURE TO GIVE HIM YOUR NUMBER.

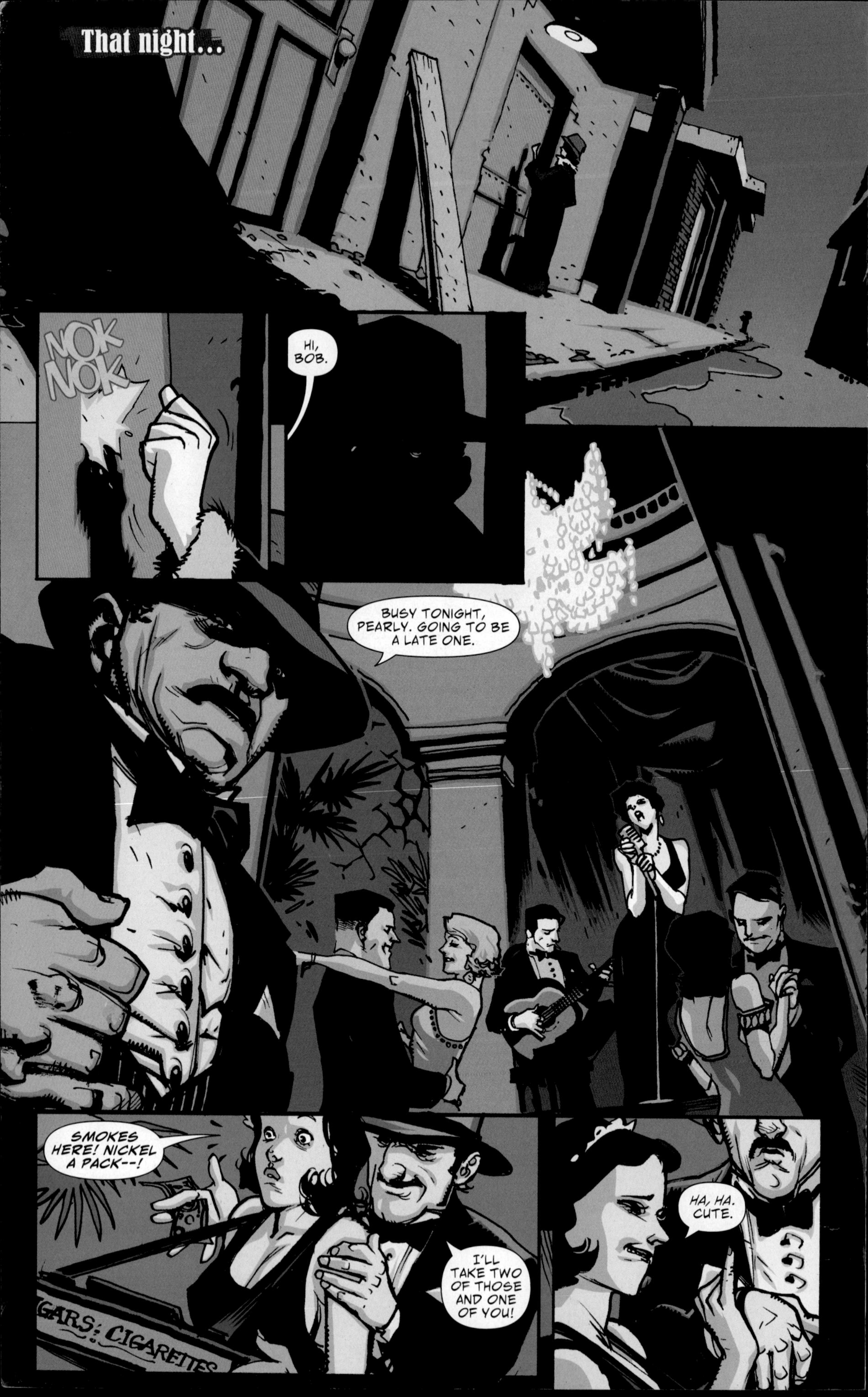
That night...
NOK NOK
HI, BOB.
BUSY TONIGHT, PEARLY. GOING TO BE A LATE ONE.
SMOKES HERE! NICKEL A PACK--!
I'LL TAKE TWO OF THOSE AND ONE OF YOU!
GARS: CIGARETTES
HA, HA. CUTE.

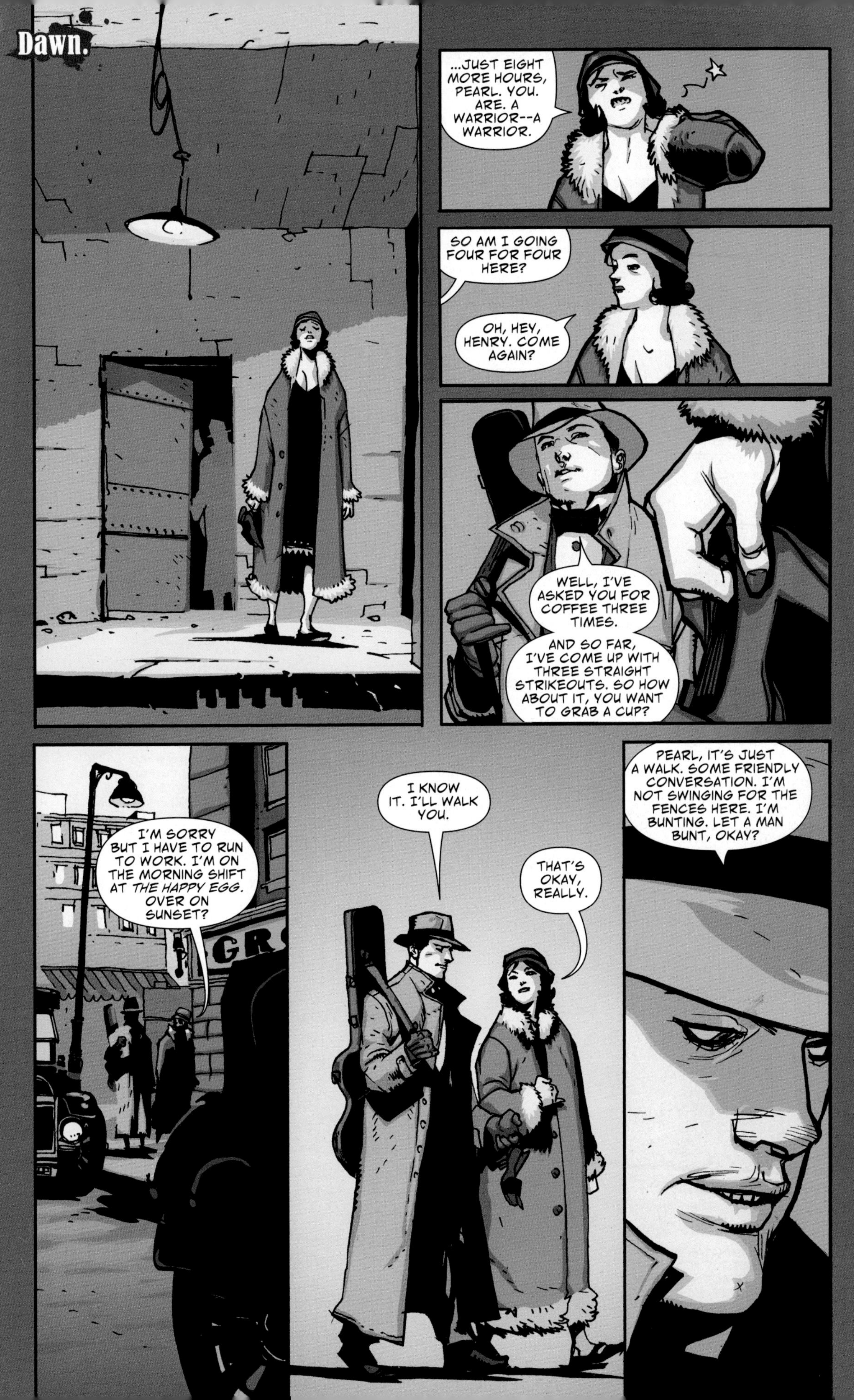
Dawn.
...JUST EIGHT MORE HOURS, PEARL. YOU. ARE. A WARRIOR--A WARRIOR.
SO AM I GOING FOUR FOR FOUR HERE?
OH, HEY, HENRY. COME AGAIN?
WELL, I'VE ASKED YOU FOR COFFEE THREE TIMES.
AND SO FAR, I'VE COME UP WITH THREE STRAIGHT STRIKEOUTS. SO HOW ABOUT IT, YOU WANT TO GRAB A CUP?
I'M SORRY BUT I HAVE TO RUN TO WORK. I'M ON THE MORNING SHIFT AT THE HAPPY EGG. OVER ON SUNSET?
I KNOW IT. I'LL WALK YOU.
THAT'S OKAY, REALLY.
PEARL, IT'S JUST A WALK. SOME FRIENDLY CONVERSATION. I'M NOT SWINGING FOR THE FENCES HERE. I'M BUNTING. LET A MAN BUNT, OKAY?

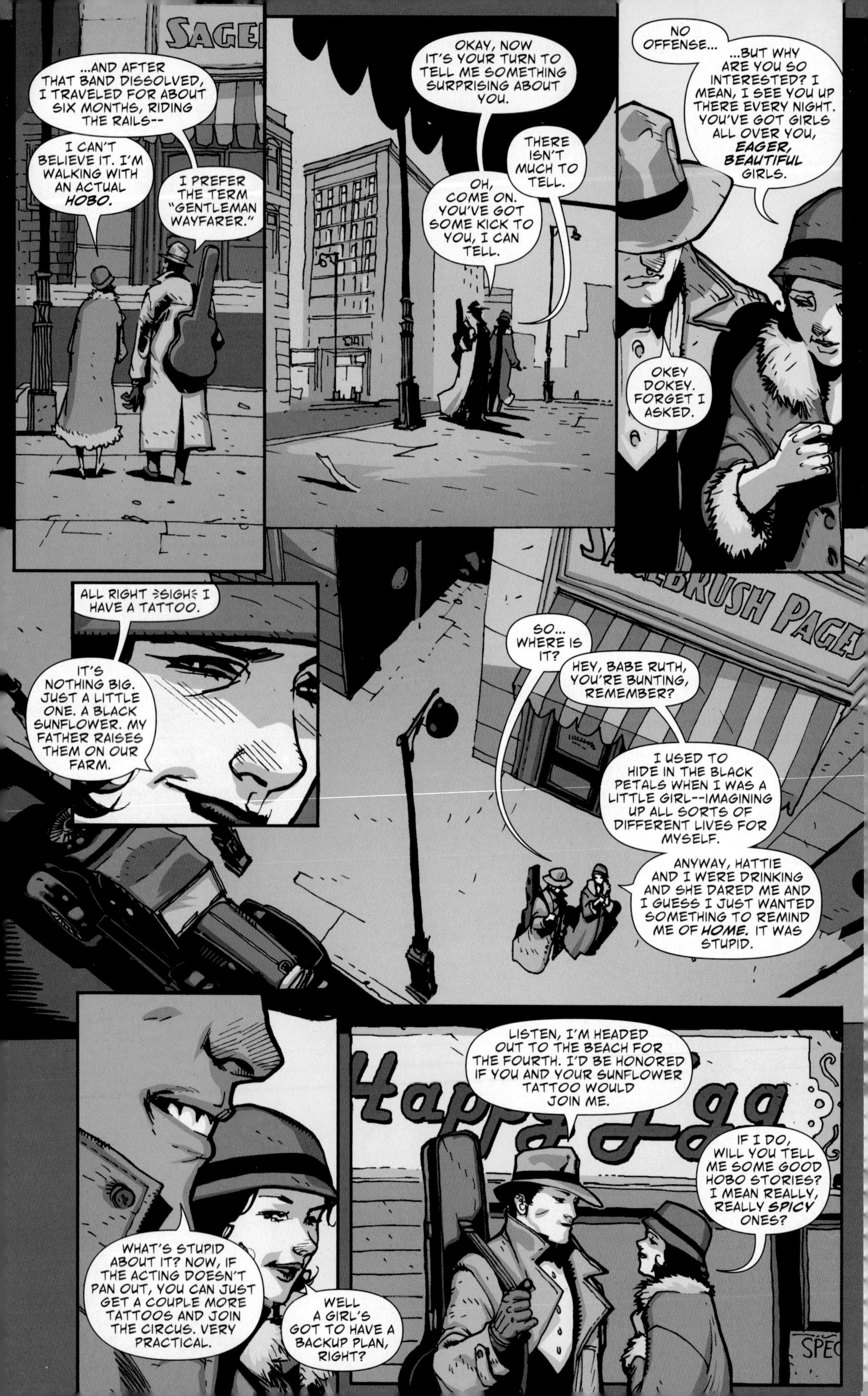
SAGEI
...AND AFTER THAT BAND DISSOLVED, I TRAVELED FOR ABOUT SIX MONTHS, RIDING THE RAILS--
I CAN'T BELIEVE IT. I'M WALKING WITH AN ACTUAL HOBO.
I PREFER THE TERM "GENTLEMAN WAYFARER."
OKAY, NOW IT'S YOUR TURN TO TELL ME SOMETHING SURPRISING ABOUT YOU.
THERE ISN'T MUCH TO TELL.
OH, COME ON. YOU'VE GOT SOME KICK TO YOU, I CAN TELL.
NO OFFENSE...
...BUT WHY ARE YOU SO INTERESTED? I MEAN, I SEE YOU UP THERE EVERY NIGHT. YOU'VE GOT GIRLS ALL OVER YOU, EAGER, BEAUTIFUL GIRLS.
OKEY DOKEY. FORGET I ASKED.
ALL RIGHT *SIGH* I HAVE A TATTOO.
IT'S NOTHING BIG. JUST A LITTLE ONE. A BLACK SUNFLOWER. MY FATHER RAISES THEM ON OUR FARM.
SAGEBRUSH PAGES
SO... WHERE IS IT?
HEY, BABE RUTH, YOU'RE BUNTING, REMEMBER?
I USED TO HIDE IN THE BLACK PETALS WHEN I WAS A LITTLE GIRL--IMAGINING UP ALL SORTS OF DIFFERENT LIVES FOR MYSELF.
ANYWAY, HATTIE AND I WERE DRINKING AND SHE DARED ME AND I GUESS I JUST WANTED SOMETHING TO REMIND ME OF HOME. IT WAS STUPID.
WHAT'S STUPID ABOUT IT? NOW, IF THE ACTING DOESN'T PAN OUT, YOU CAN JUST GET A COUPLE MORE TATTOOS AND JOIN THE CIRCUS. VERY PRACTICAL.
WELL A GIRL'S GOT TO HAVE A BACKUP PLAN, RIGHT?
LISTEN, I'M HEADED OUT TO THE BEACH FOR THE FOURTH. I'D BE HONORED IF YOU AND YOUR SUNFLOWER TATTOO WOULD JOIN ME.
IF I DO, WILL YOU TELL ME SOME GOOD HOBO STORIES? I MEAN REALLY, REALLY SPICY ONES?
SPEC

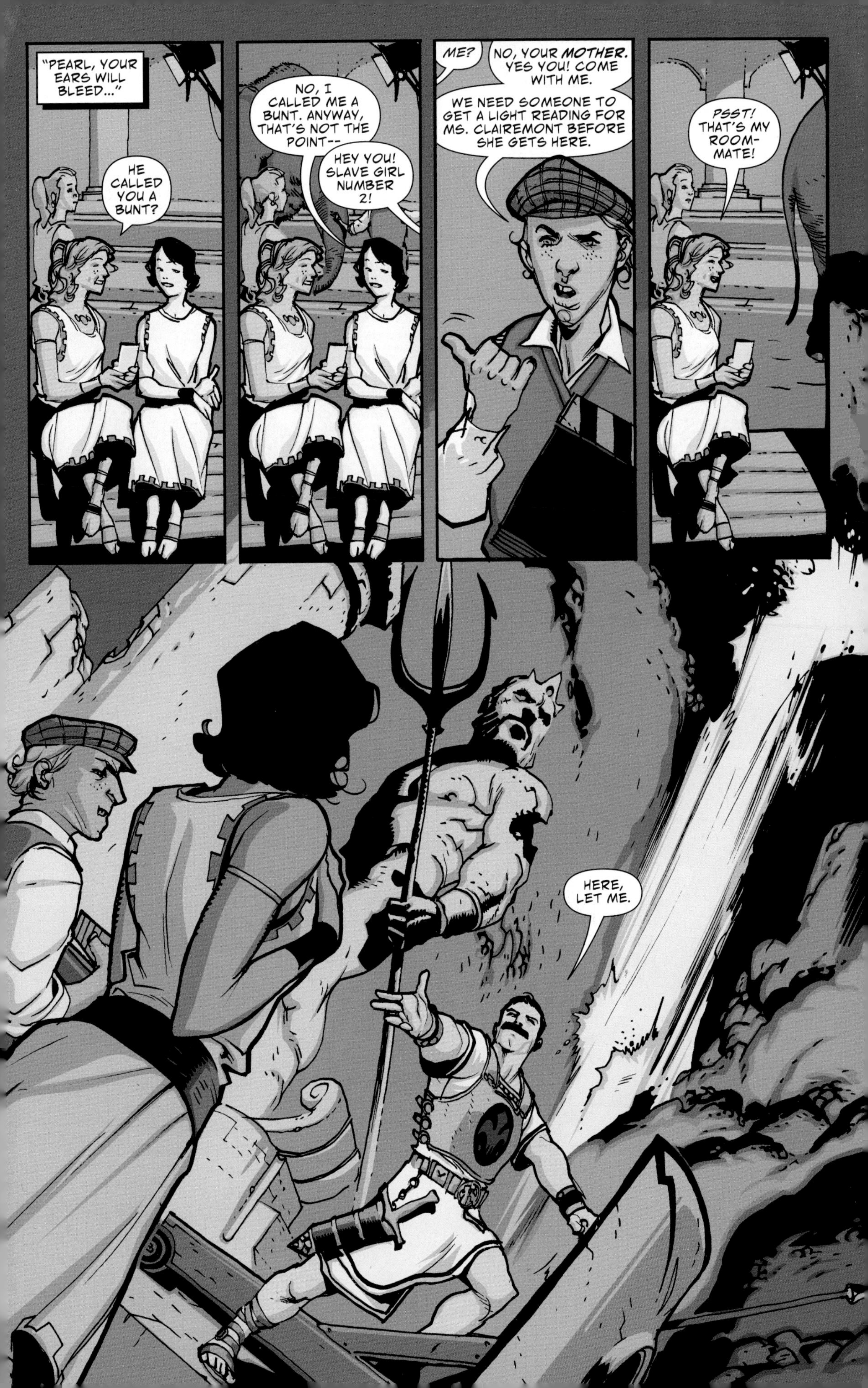
"PEARL, YOUR EARS WILL BLEED..."
HE CALLED YOU A BUNT?
NO, I CALLED ME A BUNT. ANYWAY, THAT'S NOT THE POINT--
HEY YOU! SLAVE GIRL NUMBER 2!
ME?
NO, YOUR *MOTHER*. YES YOU! COME WITH ME.
WE NEED SOMEONE TO GET A LIGHT READING FOR MS. CLAIREMONT BEFORE SHE GETS HERE.
PSST! THAT'S MY ROOM-MATE!
HERE, LET ME.

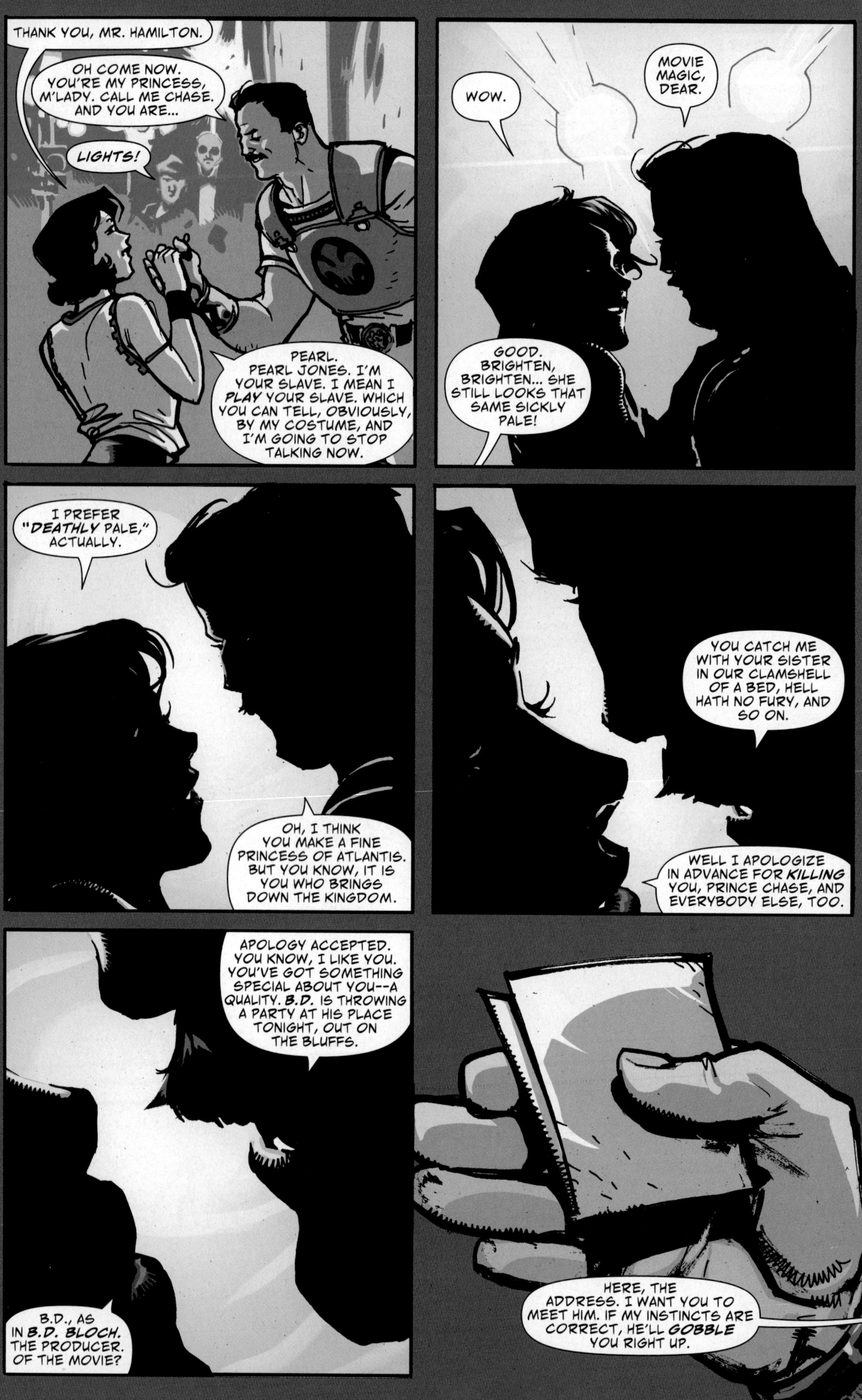
THANK YOU, MR. HAMILTON.
OH COME NOW. YOU'RE MY PRINCESS, M'LADY. CALL ME CHASE. AND YOU ARE...
LIGHTS!
PEARL. PEARL JONES. I'M YOUR SLAVE. I MEAN I PLAY YOUR SLAVE. WHICH YOU CAN TELL, OBVIOUSLY, BY MY COSTUME, AND I'M GOING TO STOP TALKING NOW.
WOW.
MOVIE MAGIC, DEAR.
GOOD. BRIGHTEN, BRIGHTEN... SHE STILL LOOKS THAT SAME SICKLY PALE!
I PREFER "DEATHLY PALE," ACTUALLY.
OH, I THINK YOU MAKE A FINE PRINCESS OF ATLANTIS. BUT YOU KNOW, IT IS YOU WHO BRINGS DOWN THE KINGDOM.
YOU CATCH ME WITH YOUR SISTER IN OUR CLAMSHELL OF A BED, HELL HATH NO FURY, AND SO ON.
WELL I APOLOGIZE IN ADVANCE FOR KILLING YOU, PRINCE CHASE, AND EVERYBODY ELSE, TOO.
APOLOGY ACCEPTED. YOU KNOW, I LIKE YOU. YOU'VE GOT SOMETHING SPECIAL ABOUT YOU--A QUALITY. B.D. IS THROWING A PARTY AT HIS PLACE TONIGHT, OUT ON THE BLUFFS.
B.D., AS IN B.D. BLOCH. THE PRODUCER. OF THE MOVIE?
HERE, THE ADDRESS. I WANT YOU TO MEET HIM. IF MY INSTINCTS ARE CORRECT, HE'LL GOBBLE YOU RIGHT UP.

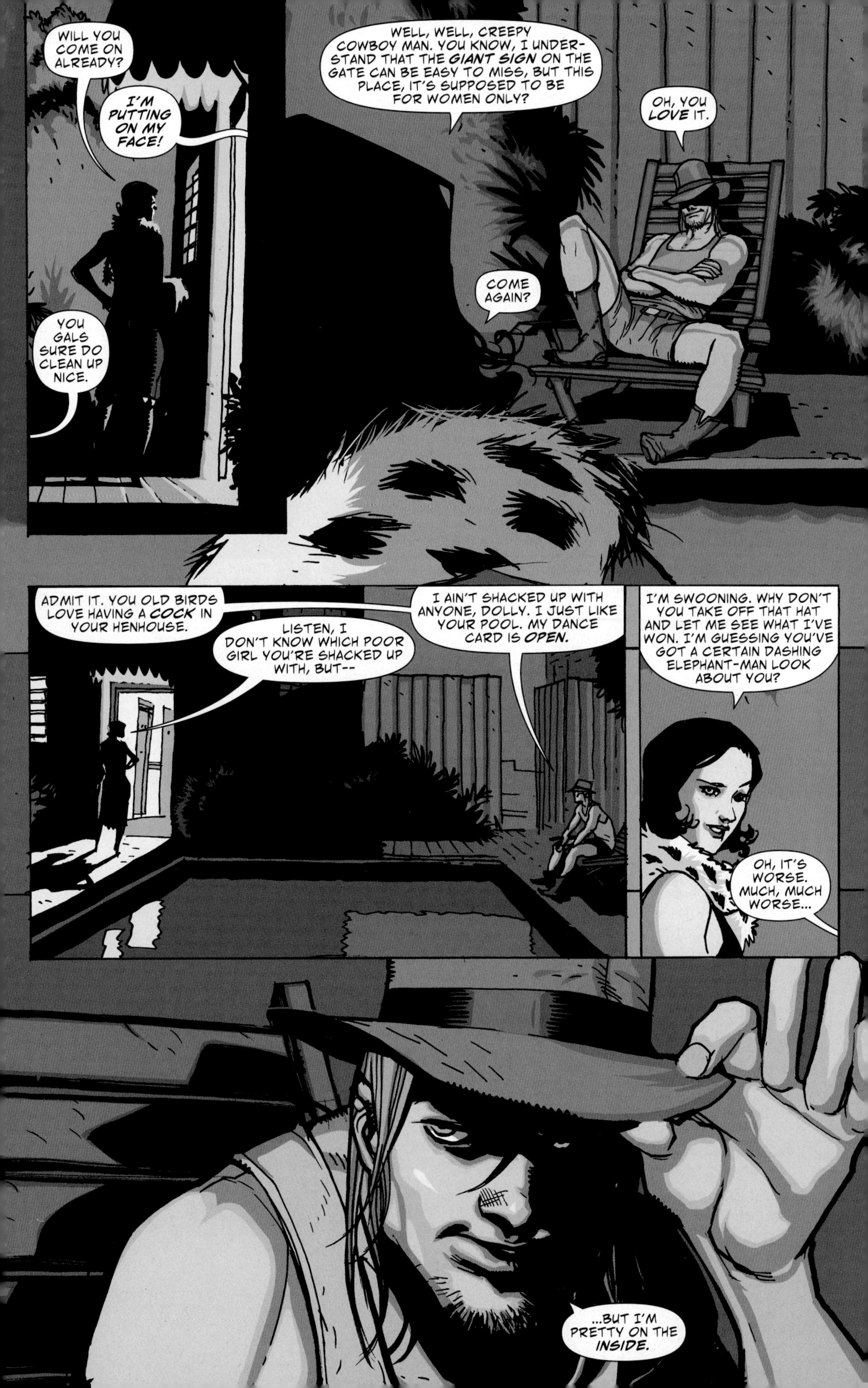
WILL YOU COME ON ALREADY?
I'M PUTTING ON MY FACE!
YOU GALS SURE DO CLEAN UP NICE.
WELL, WELL, CREEPY COWBOY MAN. YOU KNOW, I UNDERSTAND THAT THE GIANT SIGN ON THE GATE CAN BE EASY TO MISS, BUT THIS PLACE, IT'S SUPPOSED TO BE FOR WOMEN ONLY?
OH, YOU LOVE IT.
COME AGAIN?
ADMIT IT. YOU OLD BIRDS LOVE HAVING A COCK IN YOUR HENHOUSE.
LISTEN, I DON'T KNOW WHICH POOR GIRL YOU'RE SHACKED UP WITH, BUT--
I AIN'T SHACKED UP WITH ANYONE, DOLLY. I JUST LIKE YOUR POOL. MY DANCE CARD IS OPEN.
I'M SWOONING. WHY DON'T YOU TAKE OFF THAT HAT AND LET ME SEE WHAT I'VE WON. I'M GUESSING YOU'VE GOT A CERTAIN DASHING ELEPHANT-MAN LOOK ABOUT YOU?
OH, IT'S WORSE. MUCH, MUCH WORSE...
...BUT I'M PRETTY ON THE INSIDE.

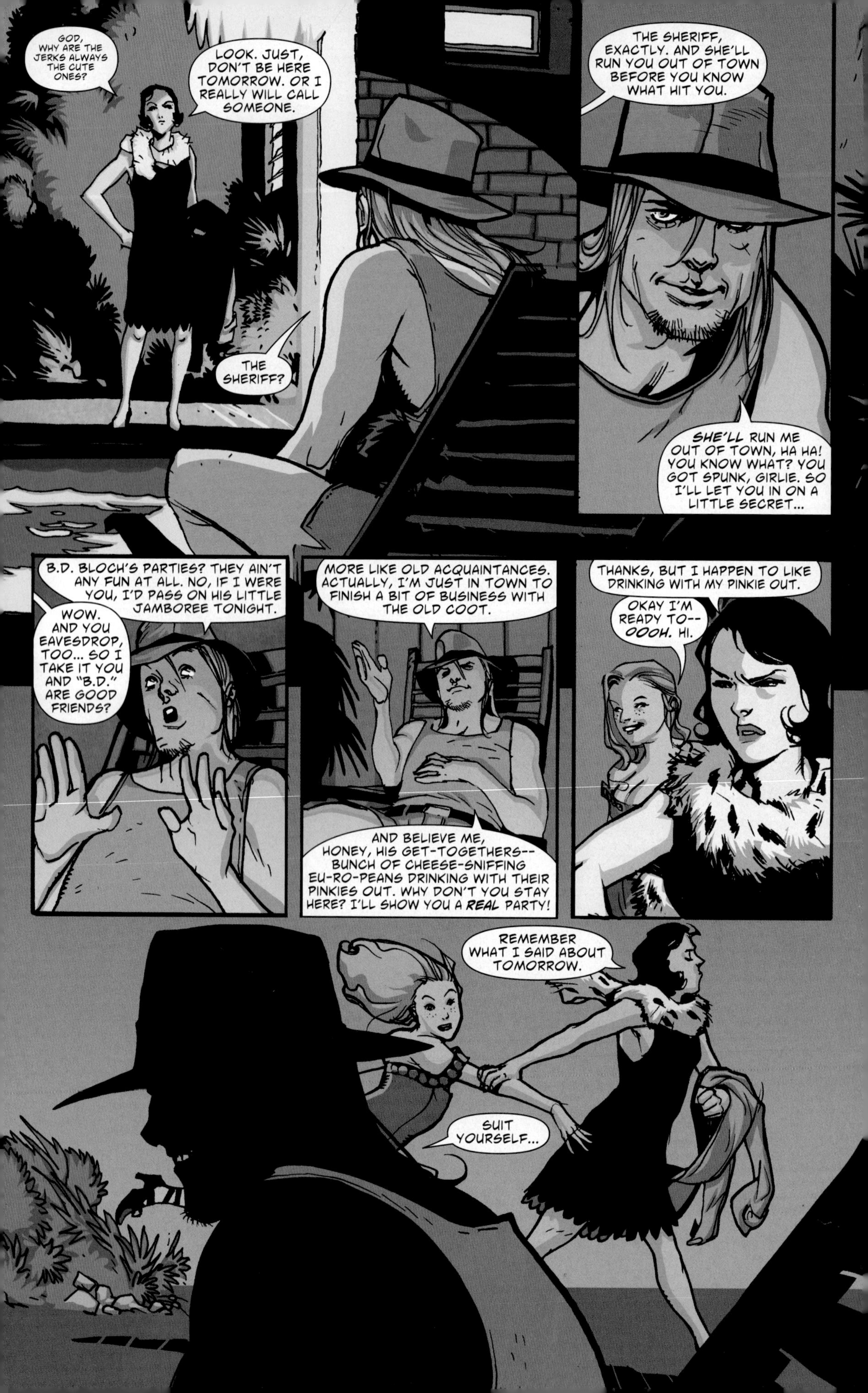
GOD, WHY ARE THE JERKS ALWAYS THE CUTE ONES?
LOOK. JUST, DON'T BE HERE TOMORROW. OR I REALLY WILL CALL SOMEONE.
THE SHERIFF?
THE SHERIFF, EXACTLY. AND SHE'LL RUN YOU OUT OF TOWN BEFORE YOU KNOW WHAT HIT YOU.
SHE'LL RUN ME OUT OF TOWN, HA HA! YOU KNOW WHAT? YOU GOT SPUNK, GIRLIE. SO I'LL LET YOU IN ON A LITTLE SECRET...
B.D. BLOCH'S PARTIES? THEY AIN'T ANY FUN AT ALL. NO, IF I WERE YOU, I'D PASS ON HIS LITTLE JAMBOREE TONIGHT.
WOW. AND YOU EAVESDROP, TOO... SO I TAKE IT YOU AND "B.D." ARE GOOD FRIENDS?
MORE LIKE OLD ACQUAINTANCES. ACTUALLY, I'M JUST IN TOWN TO FINISH A BIT OF BUSINESS WITH THE OLD COOT.
AND BELIEVE ME, HONEY, HIS GET-TOGETHERS-- BUNCH OF CHEESE-SNIFFING EU-RO-PEANS DRINKING WITH THEIR PINKIES OUT. WHY DON'T YOU STAY HERE? I'LL SHOW YOU A REAL PARTY!
THANKS, BUT I HAPPEN TO LIKE DRINKING WITH MY PINKIE OUT.
OKAY I'M READY TO-- OOOH. HI.
REMEMBER WHAT I SAID ABOUT TOMORROW.
SUIT YOURSELF...

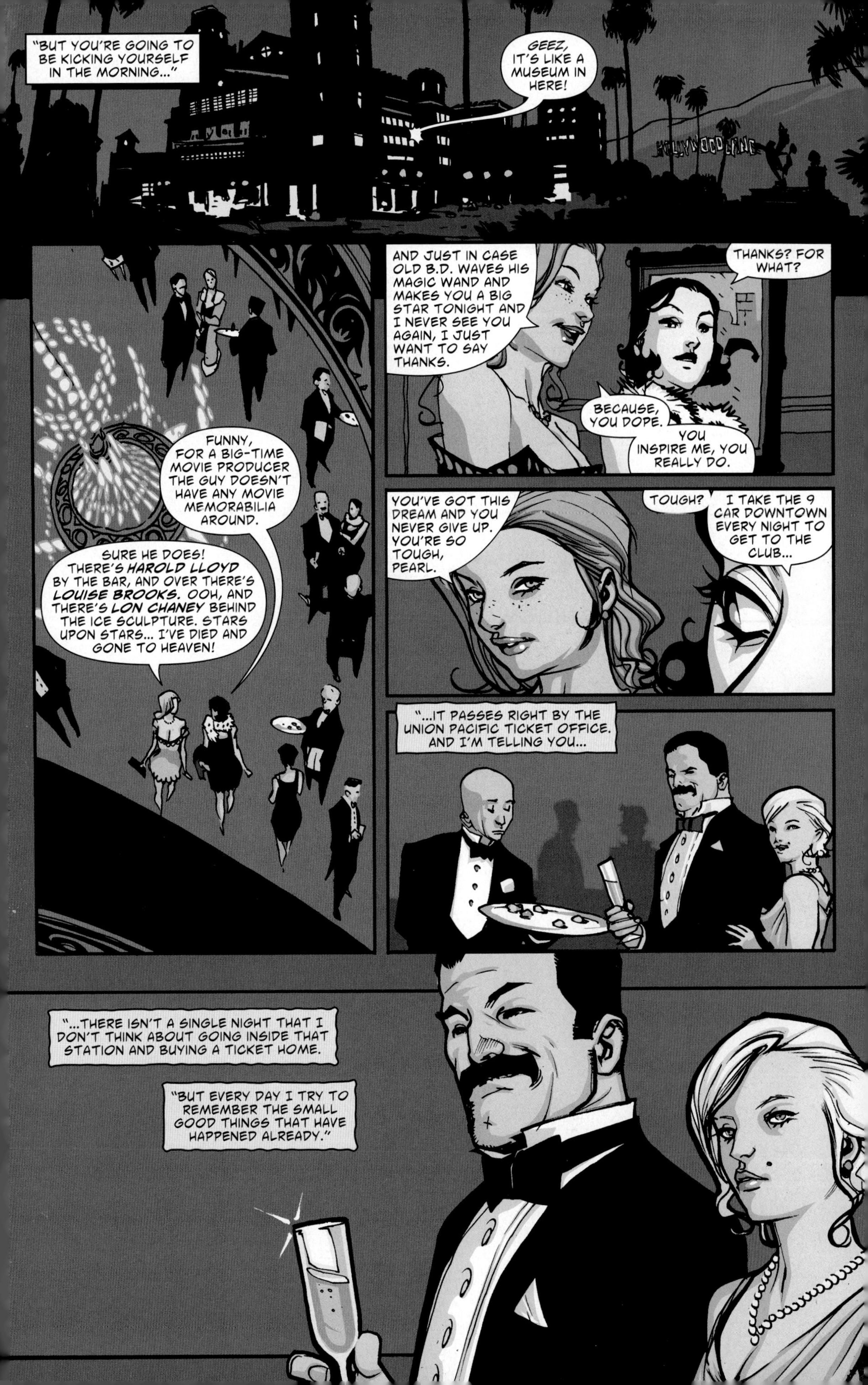
"BUT YOU'RE GOING TO BE KICKING YOURSELF IN THE MORNING..."
GEEZ, IT'S LIKE A MUSEUM IN HERE!
HOLLYWOODLAND
FUNNY, FOR A BIG-TIME MOVIE PRODUCER THE GUY DOESN'T HAVE ANY MOVIE MEMORABILIA AROUND.
SURE HE DOES! THERE'S **HAROLD LLOYD** BY THE BAR, AND OVER THERE'S **LOUISE BROOKS.** OOH, AND THERE'S **LON CHANEY** BEHIND THE ICE SCULPTURE. STARS UPON STARS... I'VE DIED AND GONE TO HEAVEN!
AND JUST IN CASE OLD B.D. WAVES HIS MAGIC WAND AND MAKES YOU A BIG STAR TONIGHT AND I NEVER SEE YOU AGAIN, I JUST WANT TO SAY THANKS.
THANKS? FOR WHAT?
BECAUSE, YOU DOPE.
YOU INSPIRE ME, YOU REALLY DO.
YOU'VE GOT THIS DREAM AND YOU NEVER GIVE UP. YOU'RE SO TOUGH, PEARL.
TOUGH?
I TAKE THE 9 CAR DOWNTOWN EVERY NIGHT TO GET TO THE CLUB...
"...IT PASSES RIGHT BY THE UNION PACIFIC TICKET OFFICE. AND I'M TELLING YOU...
"...THERE ISN'T A SINGLE NIGHT THAT I DON'T THINK ABOUT GOING INSIDE THAT STATION AND BUYING A TICKET HOME.
"BUT EVERY DAY I TRY TO REMEMBER THE SMALL GOOD THINGS THAT HAVE HAPPENED ALREADY."

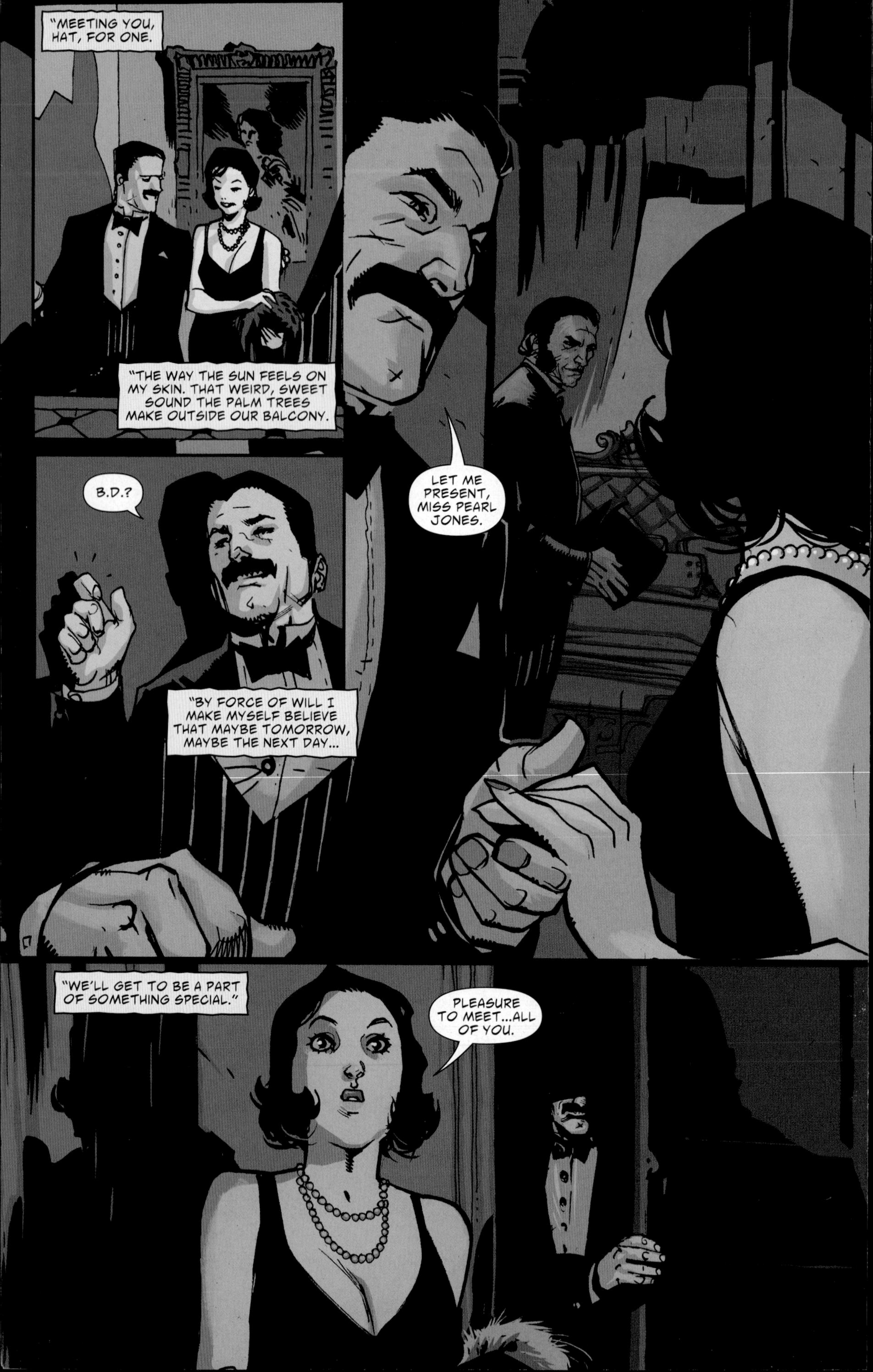
"MEETING YOU, HAT, FOR ONE.
"THE WAY THE SUN FEELS ON MY SKIN. THAT WEIRD, SWEET SOUND THE PALM TREES MAKE OUTSIDE OUR BALCONY.
B.D.?
"BY FORCE OF WILL I MAKE MYSELF BELIEVE THAT MAYBE TOMORROW, MAYBE THE NEXT DAY...
LET ME PRESENT, MISS PEARL JONES.
"WE'LL GET TO BE A PART OF SOMETHING SPECIAL."
PLEASURE TO MEET...ALL OF YOU.

I JUST WANT TO SAY WHAT AN HONOR IT IS TO MEET YOU, MR. BLOCH.

I'VE BEEN A FAN OF YOUR FILMS FOR YEARS, EVER SINCE I WAS A LITTLE GIRL.

FUNNY, I HAVE STOPPED PAYING MUCH ATTENTION TO THEM MYSELF.

OH, THAT CAN'T BE--

TRUE? IT IS, MY GIRL. BUT IMPOSSIBLE TO IGNORE IS ALL THIS NOISE ABOUT THE SO-CALLED "TALKIES." HAVE YOU HEARD OF THESE?

FILMS WITH SYNCHRONIZED SOUND?

WHAT'S GOING ON?

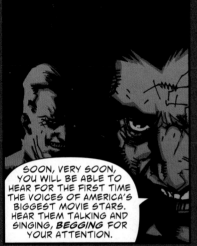

SOON, VERY SOON, YOU WILL BE ABLE TO HEAR FOR THE FIRST TIME THE VOICES OF AMERICA'S BIGGEST MOVIE STARS. HEAR THEM TALKING AND SINGING, *BEGGING* FOR YOUR ATTENTION.

AND I WILL MAKE THESE FILMS FOR YOU, MISS PEARL... BUT, YOU SEE, THE BITTER IRONY OF THE SITUATION...

PLEASE... PLEASE DON'T...

...IS THAT I MYSELF DON'T WANT TO HEAR *ANYTHING* YOU HAVE TO SAY.

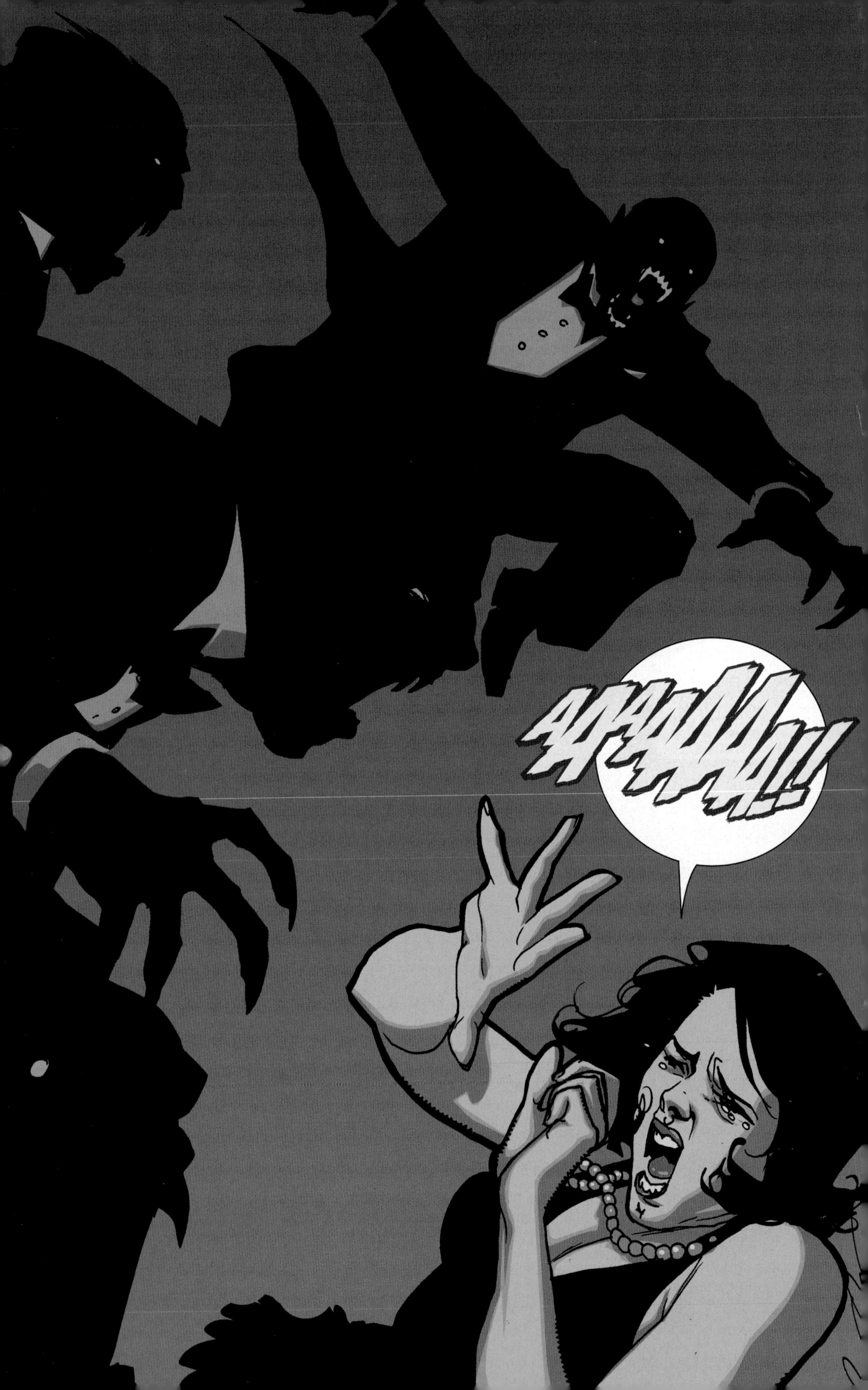
AAAAAAH!!

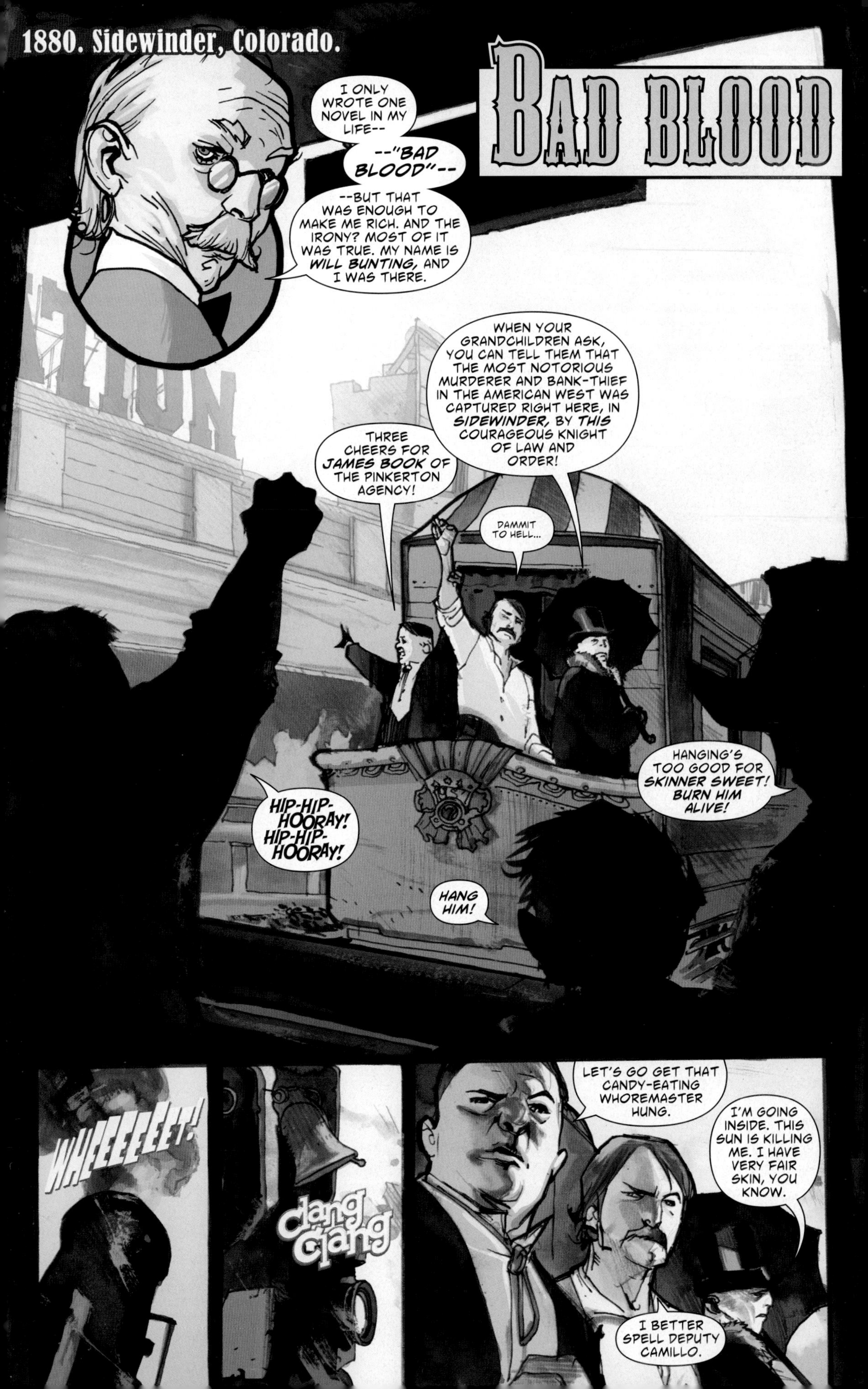
1880. Sidewinder, Colorado.
BAD BLOOD
I ONLY WROTE ONE NOVEL IN MY LIFE--
--"BAD BLOOD"--
--BUT THAT WAS ENOUGH TO MAKE ME RICH. AND THE IRONY? MOST OF IT WAS TRUE. MY NAME IS WILL BUNTING, AND I WAS THERE.
WHEN YOUR GRANDCHILDREN ASK, YOU CAN TELL THEM THAT THE MOST NOTORIOUS MURDERER AND BANK-THIEF IN THE AMERICAN WEST WAS CAPTURED RIGHT HERE, IN SIDEWINDER, BY THIS COURAGEOUS KNIGHT OF LAW AND ORDER!
THREE CHEERS FOR JAMES BOOK OF THE PINKERTON AGENCY!
DAMMIT TO HELL...
HIP-HIP-HOORAY! HIP-HIP-HOORAY!
HANGING'S TOO GOOD FOR SKINNER SWEET! BURN HIM ALIVE!
HANG HIM!
WHEEEEEEET!
CLANG CLANG
LET'S GO GET THAT CANDY-EATING WHOREMASTER HUNG.
I'M GOING INSIDE. THIS SUN IS KILLING ME. I HAVE VERY FAIR SKIN, YOU KNOW.
I BETTER SPELL DEPUTY CAMILLO.

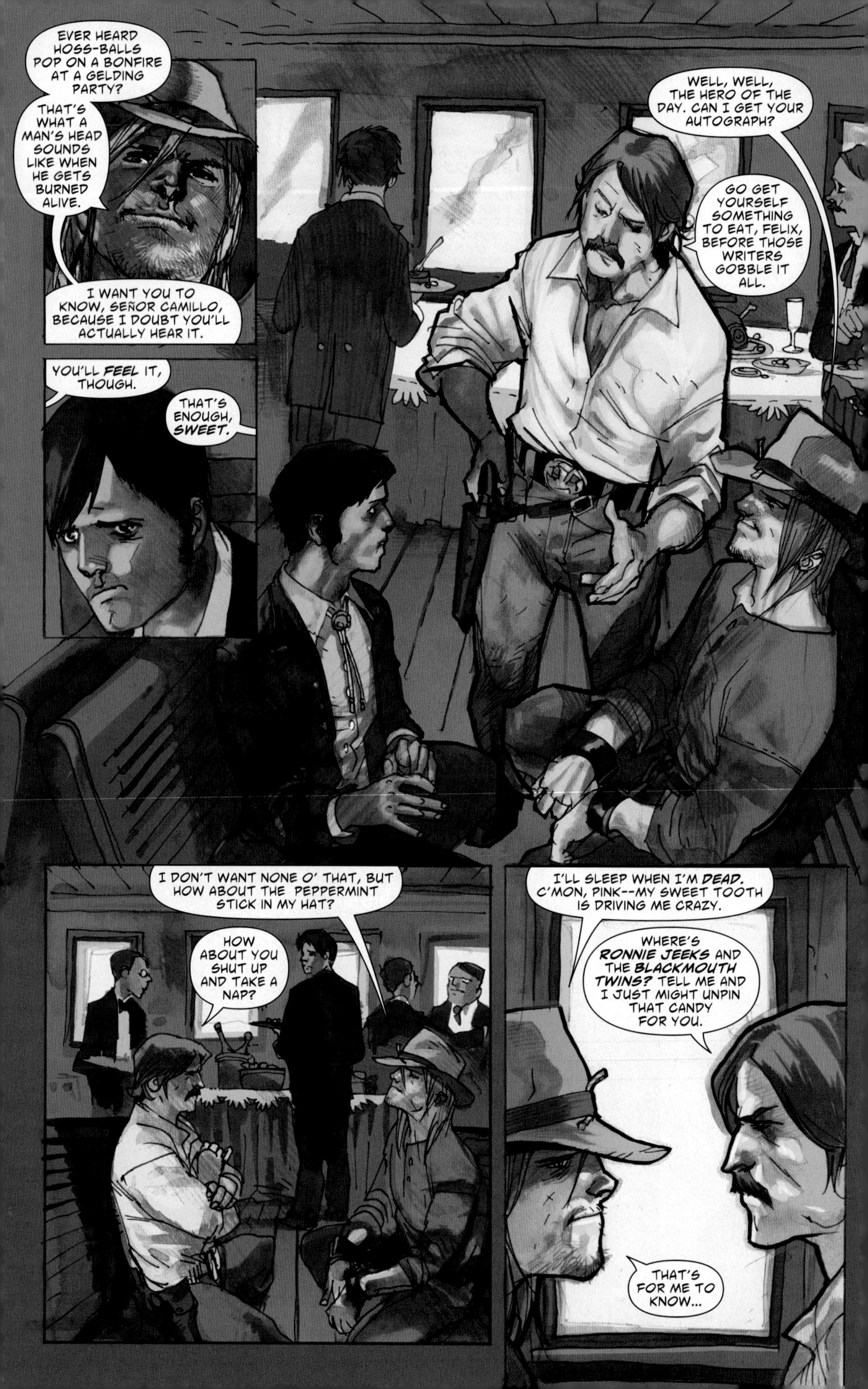
EVER HEARD HOSS-BALLS POP ON A BONFIRE AT A GELDING PARTY?
THAT'S WHAT A MAN'S HEAD SOUNDS LIKE WHEN HE GETS BURNED ALIVE.
I WANT YOU TO KNOW, SEÑOR CAMILLO, BECAUSE I DOUBT YOU'LL ACTUALLY HEAR IT.
YOU'LL FEEL IT, THOUGH.
THAT'S ENOUGH, SWEET.
WELL, WELL, THE HERO OF THE DAY. CAN I GET YOUR AUTOGRAPH?
GO GET YOURSELF SOMETHING TO EAT, FELIX, BEFORE THOSE WRITERS GOBBLE IT ALL.
I DON'T WANT NONE O' THAT, BUT HOW ABOUT THE PEPPERMINT STICK IN MY HAT?
HOW ABOUT YOU SHUT UP AND TAKE A NAP?
I'LL SLEEP WHEN I'M DEAD. C'MON, PINK--MY SWEET TOOTH IS DRIVING ME CRAZY.
WHERE'S RONNIE JEEKS AND THE BLACKMOUTH TWINS? TELL ME AND I JUST MIGHT UNPIN THAT CANDY FOR YOU.
THAT'S FOR ME TO KNOW...

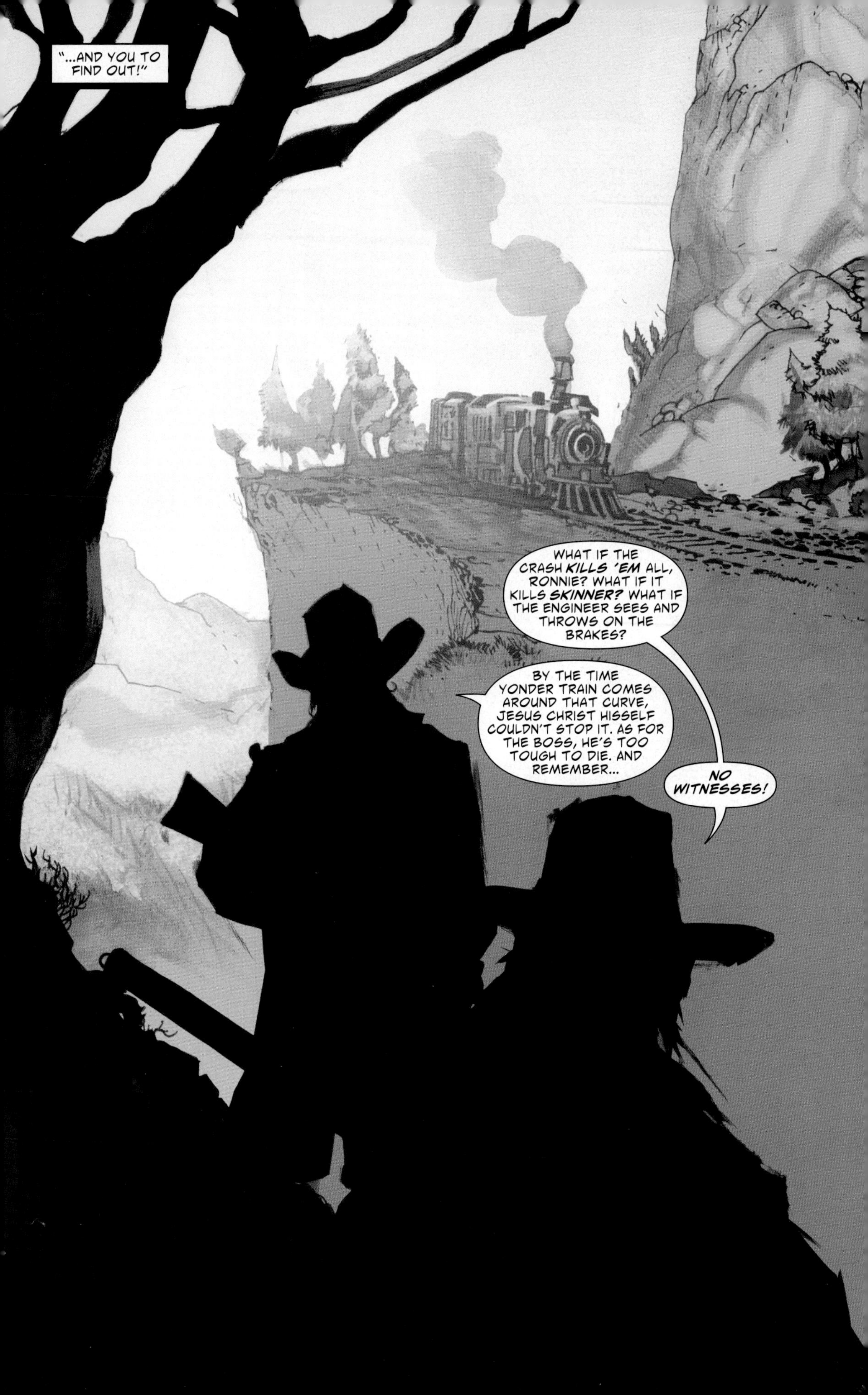
"...AND YOU TO FIND OUT!"
WHAT IF THE CRASH KILLS 'EM ALL, RONNIE? WHAT IF IT KILLS SKINNER? WHAT IF THE ENGINEER SEES AND THROWS ON THE BRAKES?
BY THE TIME YONDER TRAIN COMES AROUND THAT CURVE, JESUS CHRIST HISSELF COULDN'T STOP IT. AS FOR THE BOSS, HE'S TOO TOUGH TO DIE. AND REMEMBER...
NO WITNESSES!

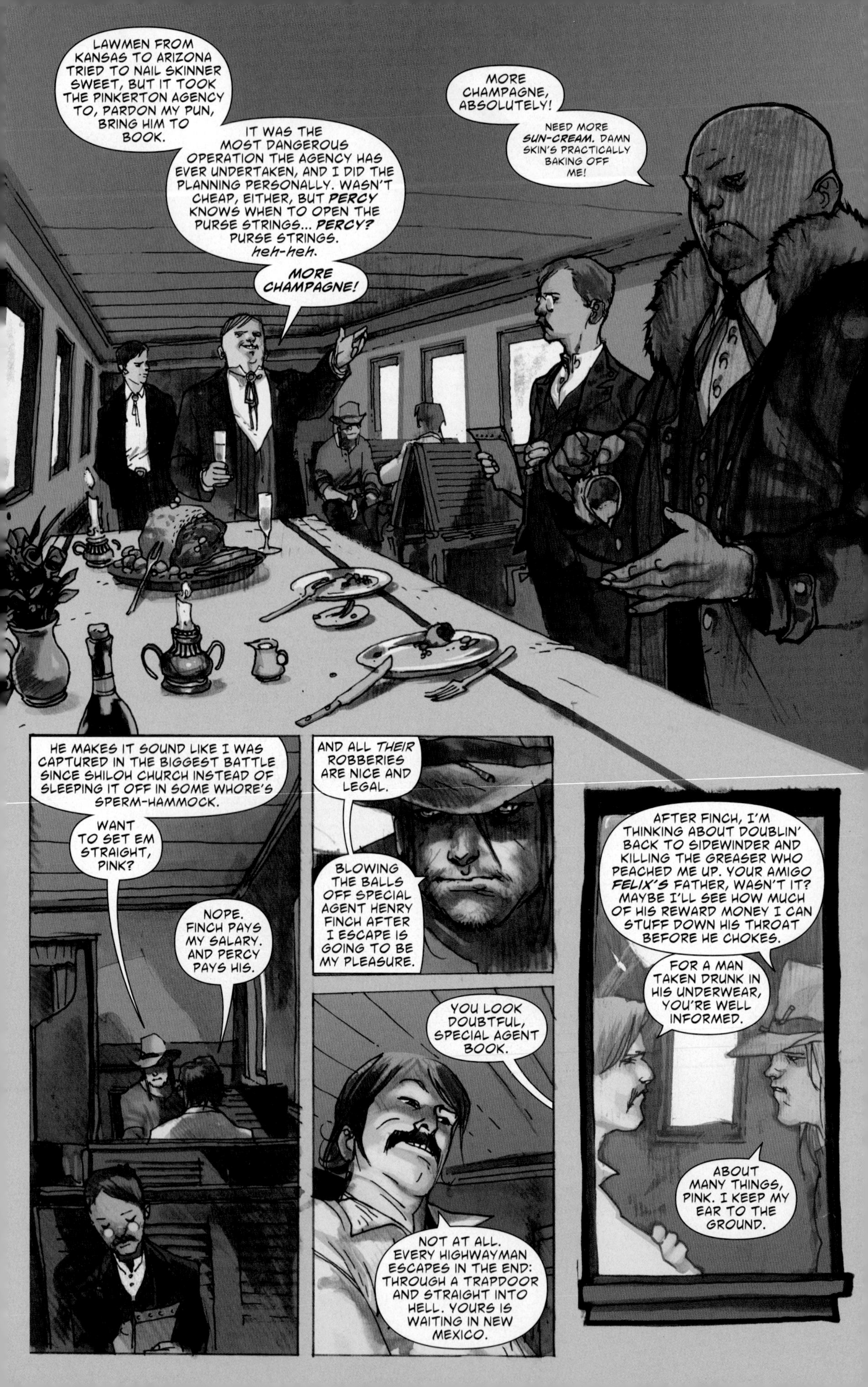

LAWMEN FROM KANSAS TO ARIZONA TRIED TO NAIL SKINNER SWEET, BUT IT TOOK THE PINKERTON AGENCY TO, PARDON MY PUN, BRING HIM TO BOOK.
IT WAS THE MOST DANGEROUS OPERATION THE AGENCY HAS EVER UNDERTAKEN, AND I DID THE PLANNING PERSONALLY. WASN'T CHEAP, EITHER, BUT PERCY KNOWS WHEN TO OPEN THE PURSE STRINGS... PERCY? PURSE STRINGS. heh-heh.
MORE CHAMPAGNE!
MORE CHAMPAGNE, ABSOLUTELY!
NEED MORE SUN-CREAM. DAMN SKIN'S PRACTICALLY BAKING OFF ME!
HE MAKES IT SOUND LIKE I WAS CAPTURED IN THE BIGGEST BATTLE SINCE SHILOH CHURCH INSTEAD OF SLEEPING IT OFF IN SOME WHORE'S SPERM-HAMMOCK.
WANT TO SET EM STRAIGHT, PINK?
NOPE. FINCH PAYS MY SALARY. AND PERCY PAYS HIS.
AND ALL THEIR ROBBERIES ARE NICE AND LEGAL.
BLOWING THE BALLS OFF SPECIAL AGENT HENRY FINCH AFTER I ESCAPE IS GOING TO BE MY PLEASURE.
YOU LOOK DOUBTFUL, SPECIAL AGENT BOOK.
NOT AT ALL. EVERY HIGHWAYMAN ESCAPES IN THE END: THROUGH A TRAPDOOR AND STRAIGHT INTO HELL. YOURS IS WAITING IN NEW MEXICO.
AFTER FINCH, I'M THINKING ABOUT DOUBLIN' BACK TO SIDEWINDER AND KILLING THE GREASER WHO PEACHED ME UP. YOUR AMIGO FELIX'S FATHER, WASN'T IT? MAYBE I'LL SEE HOW MUCH OF HIS REWARD MONEY I CAN STUFF DOWN HIS THROAT BEFORE HE CHOKES.
FOR A MAN TAKEN DRUNK IN HIS UNDERWEAR, YOU'RE WELL INFORMED.
ABOUT MANY THINGS, PINK. I KEEP MY EAR TO THE GROUND.

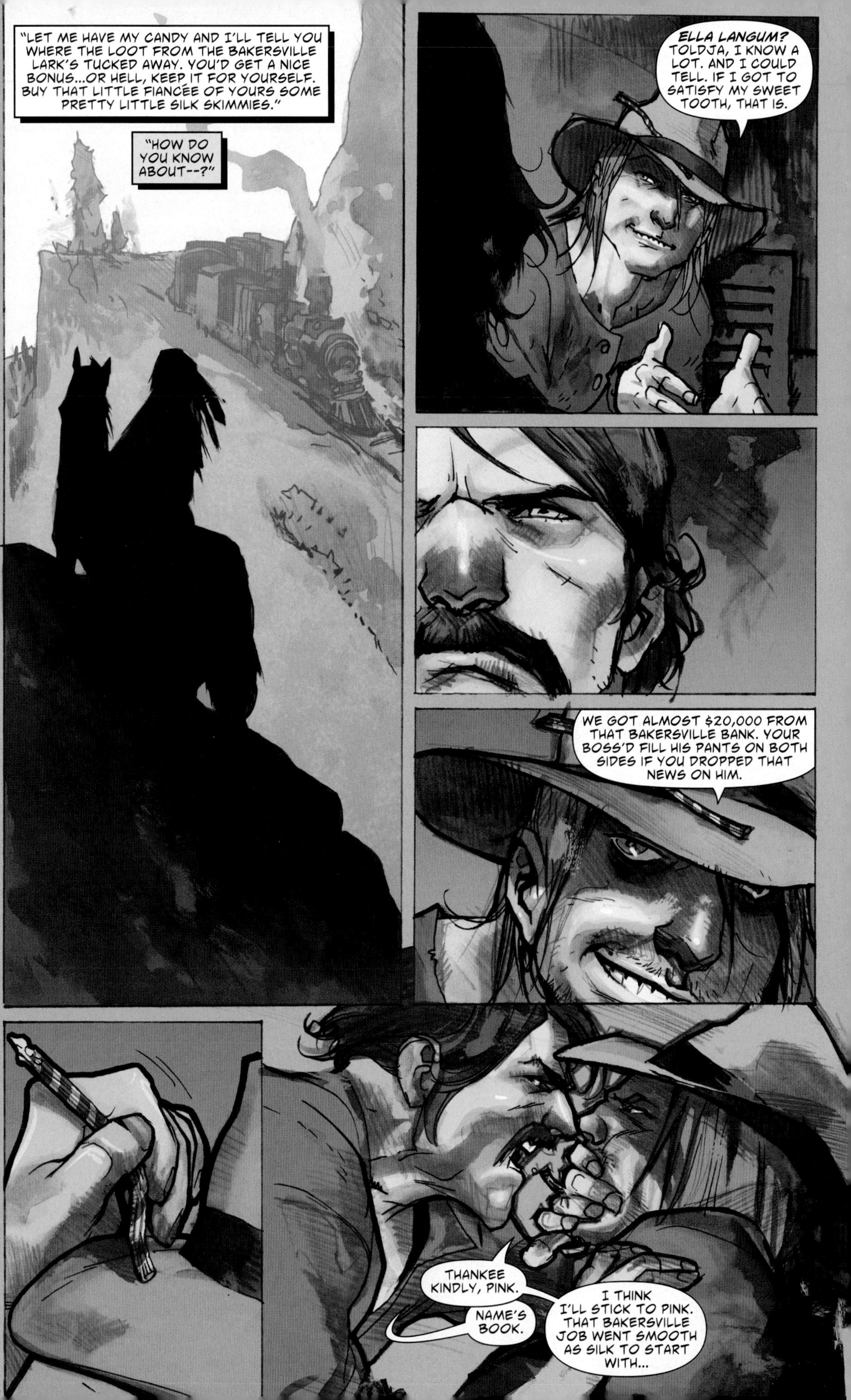
"LET ME HAVE MY CANDY AND I'LL TELL YOU WHERE THE LOOT FROM THE BAKERSVILLE LARK'S TUCKED AWAY. YOU'D GET A NICE BONUS...OR HELL, KEEP IT FOR YOURSELF. BUY THAT LITTLE FIANCÉE OF YOURS SOME PRETTY LITTLE SILK SKIMMIES."
"HOW DO YOU KNOW ABOUT--?"
ELLA LANGUM? TOLDJA, I KNOW A LOT. AND I COULD TELL. IF I GOT TO SATISFY MY SWEET TOOTH, THAT IS.
WE GOT ALMOST $20,000 FROM THAT BAKERSVILLE BANK. YOUR BOSS'D FILL HIS PANTS ON BOTH SIDES IF YOU DROPPED THAT NEWS ON HIM.
THANKEE KINDLY, PINK.
NAME'S BOOK.
I THINK I'LL STICK TO PINK. THAT BAKERSVILLE JOB WENT SMOOTH AS SILK TO START WITH...

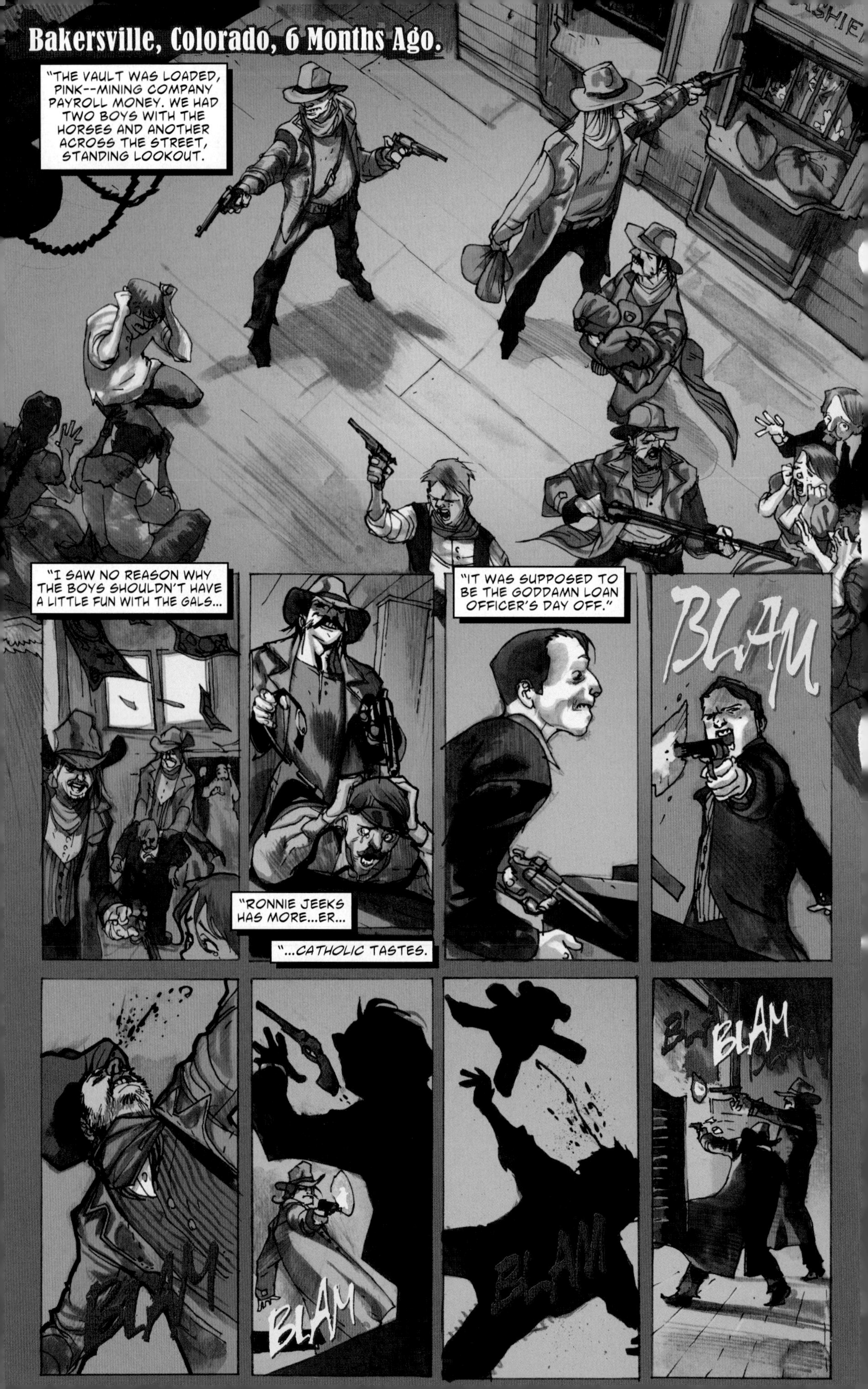
Bakersville, Colorado, 6 Months Ago.
"THE VAULT WAS LOADED, PINK--MINING COMPANY PAYROLL MONEY. WE HAD TWO BOYS WITH THE HORSES AND ANOTHER ACROSS THE STREET, STANDING LOOKOUT.
"I SAW NO REASON WHY THE BOYS SHOULDN'T HAVE A LITTLE FUN WITH THE GALS...
"RONNIE JEEKS HAS MORE...ER...
"...CATHOLIC TASTES.
"IT WAS SUPPOSED TO BE THE GODDAMN LOAN OFFICER'S DAY OFF."
BLAM
?
BLAM
BLAM
BLAM
BLAM

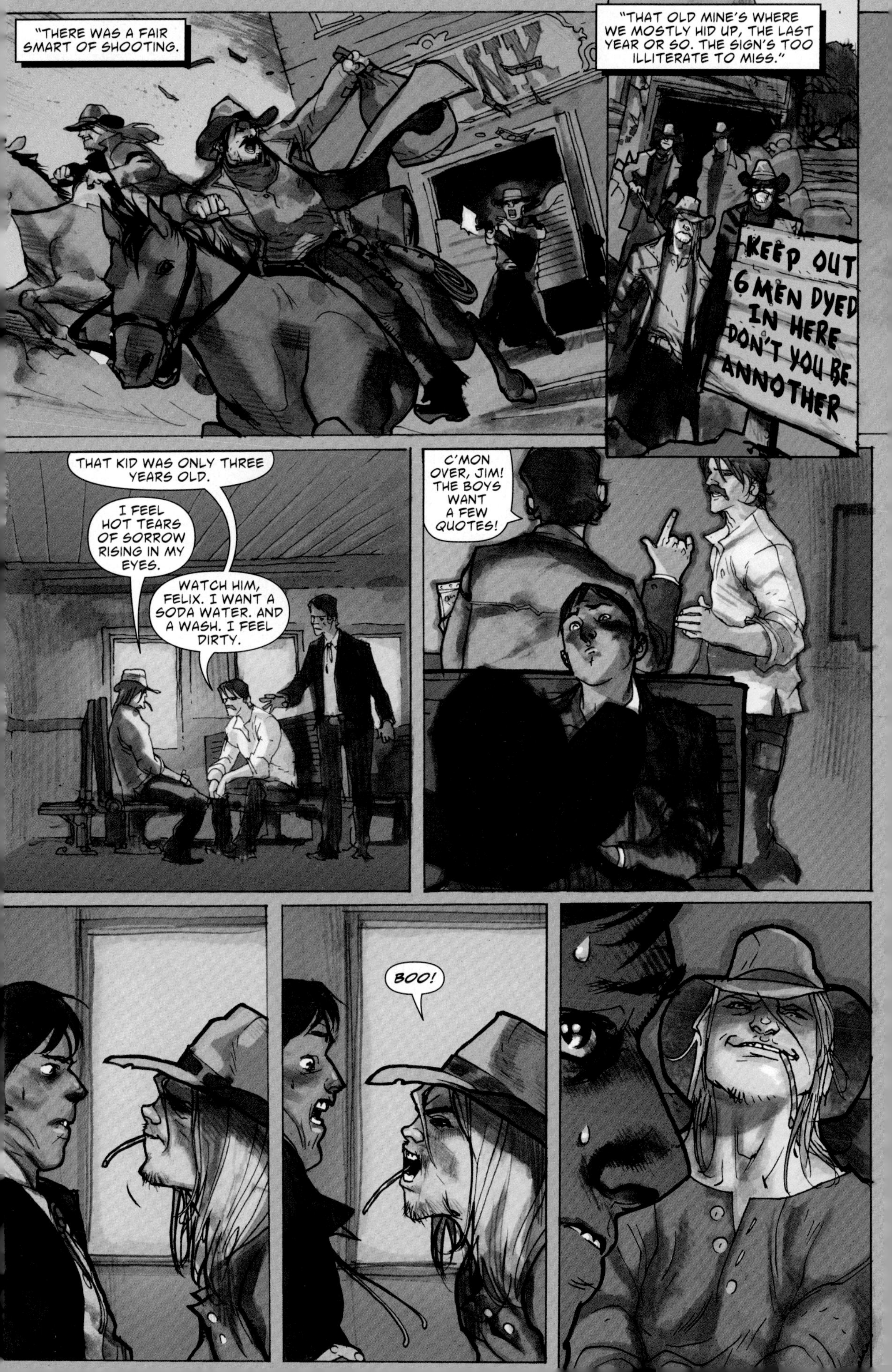
"THERE WAS A FAIR SMART OF SHOOTING.
"THAT OLD MINE'S WHERE WE MOSTLY HID UP, THE LAST YEAR OR SO. THE SIGN'S TOO ILLITERATE TO MISS."
KEEP OUT 6 MEN DYED IN HERE DON'T YOU BE ANNOTHER
THAT KID WAS ONLY THREE YEARS OLD.
I FEEL HOT TEARS OF SORROW RISING IN MY EYES.
WATCH HIM, FELIX. I WANT A SODA WATER. AND A WASH. I FEEL DIRTY.
C'MON OVER, JIM! THE BOYS WANT A FEW QUOTES!
BOO!

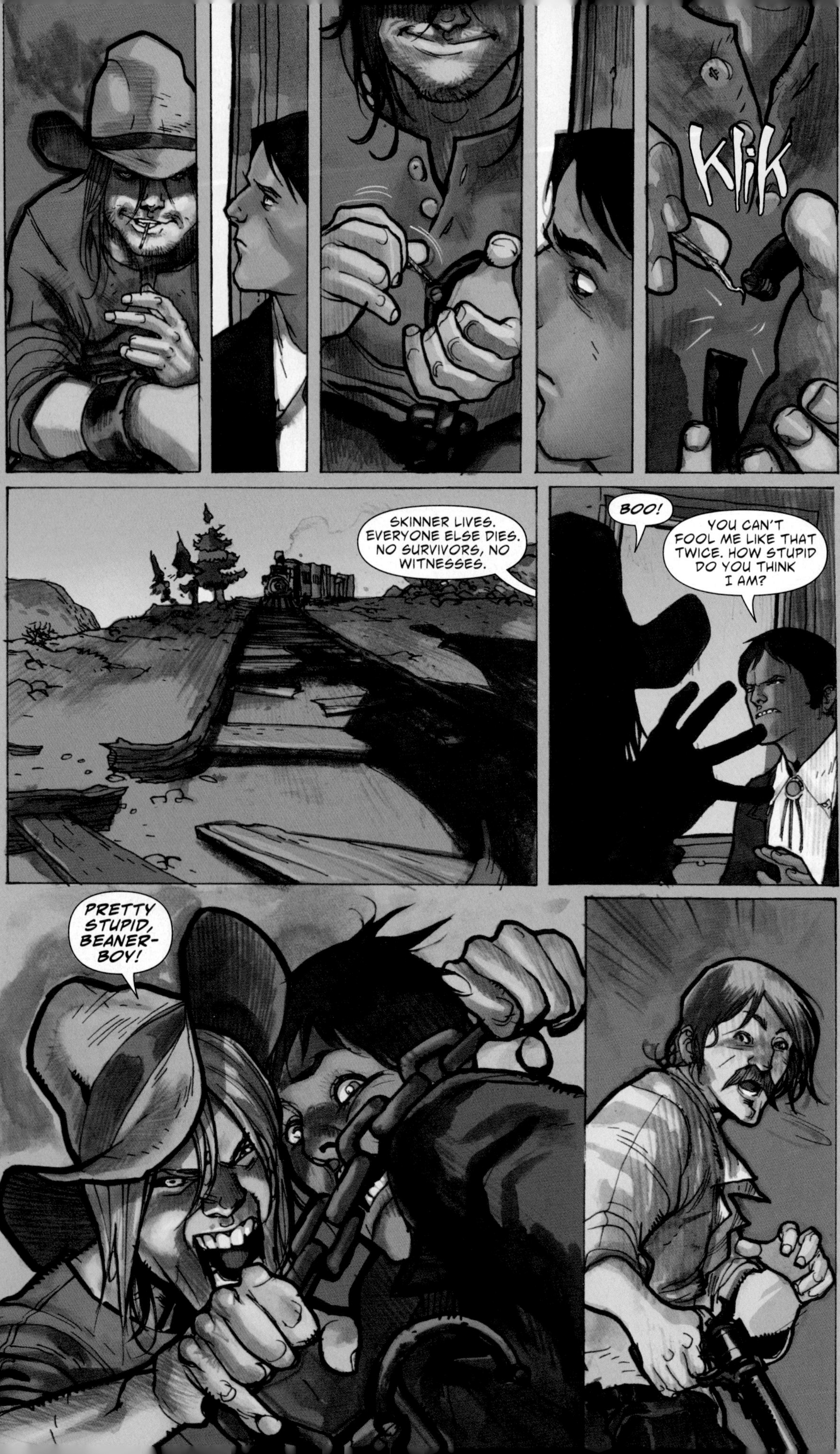
KLIK
SKINNER LIVES. EVERYONE ELSE DIES. NO SURVIVORS, NO WITNESSES.
BOO!
YOU CAN'T FOOL ME LIKE THAT TWICE. HOW STUPID DO YOU THINK I AM?
PRETTY STUPID, BEANER-BOY!

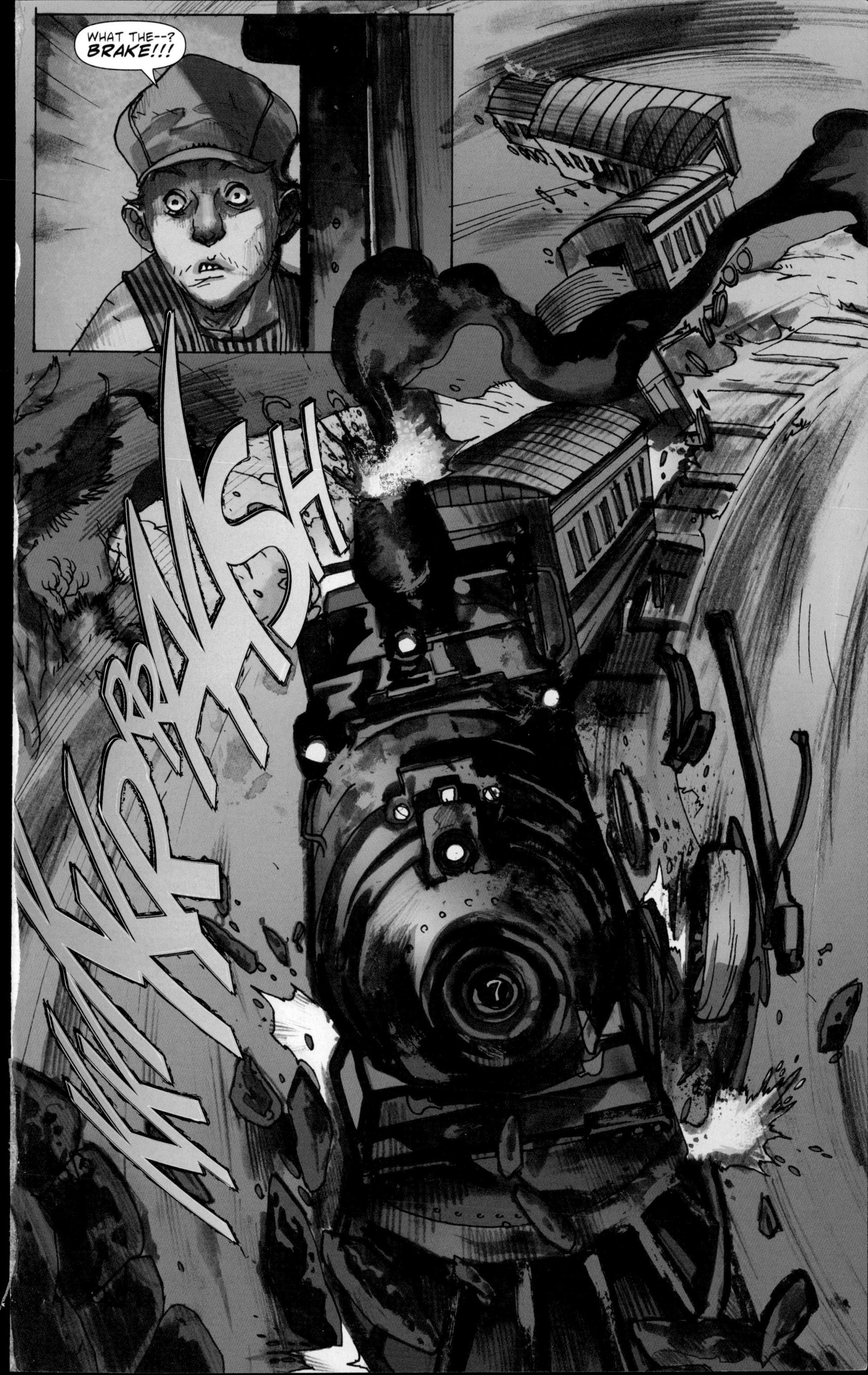

WHAT THE--? BRAKE!!!
WHHRRASH

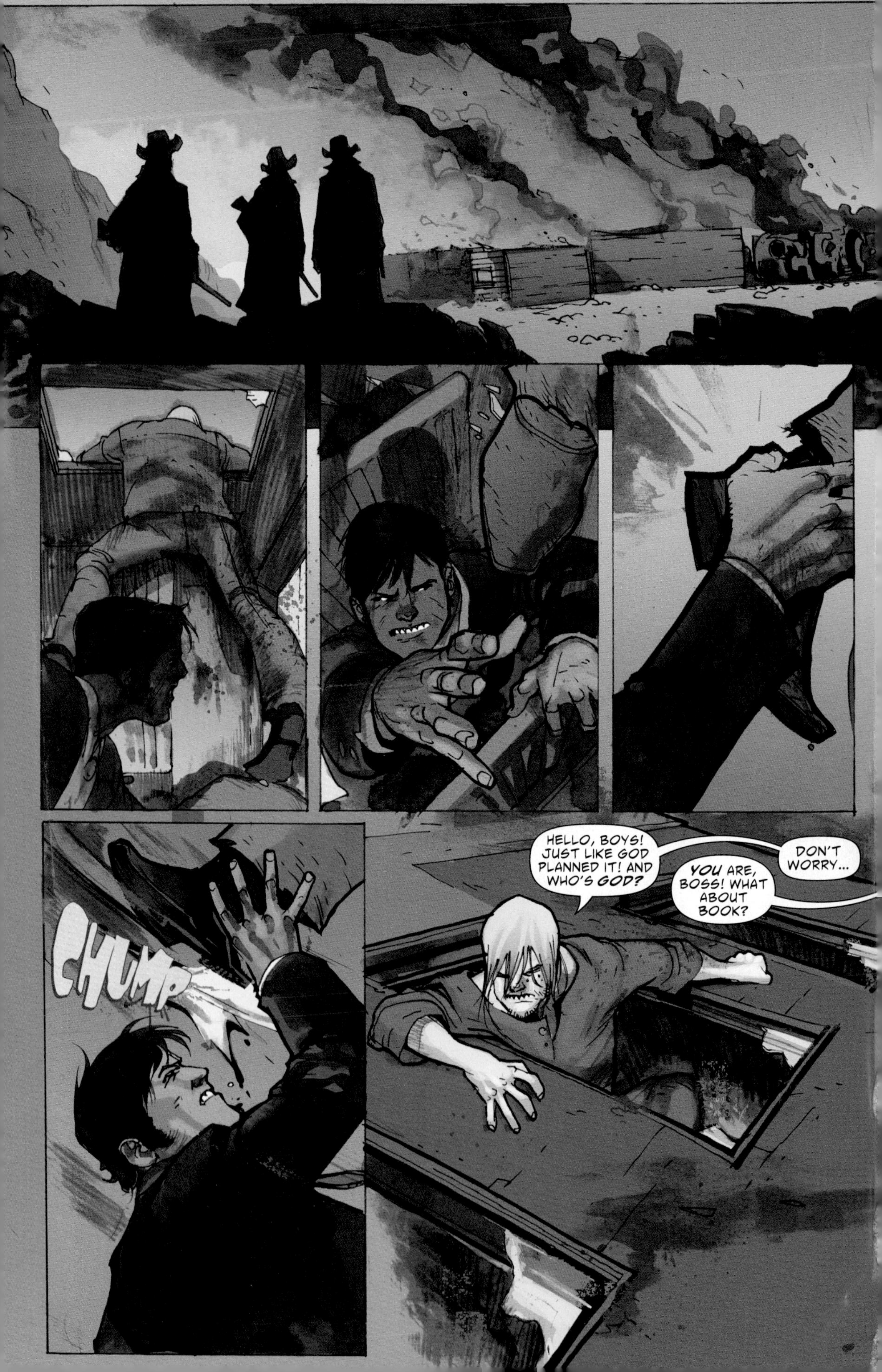
CHUMP
HELLO, BOYS! JUST LIKE GOD PLANNED IT! AND WHO'S GOD?
DON'T WORRY...
YOU ARE, BOSS! WHAT ABOUT BOOK?

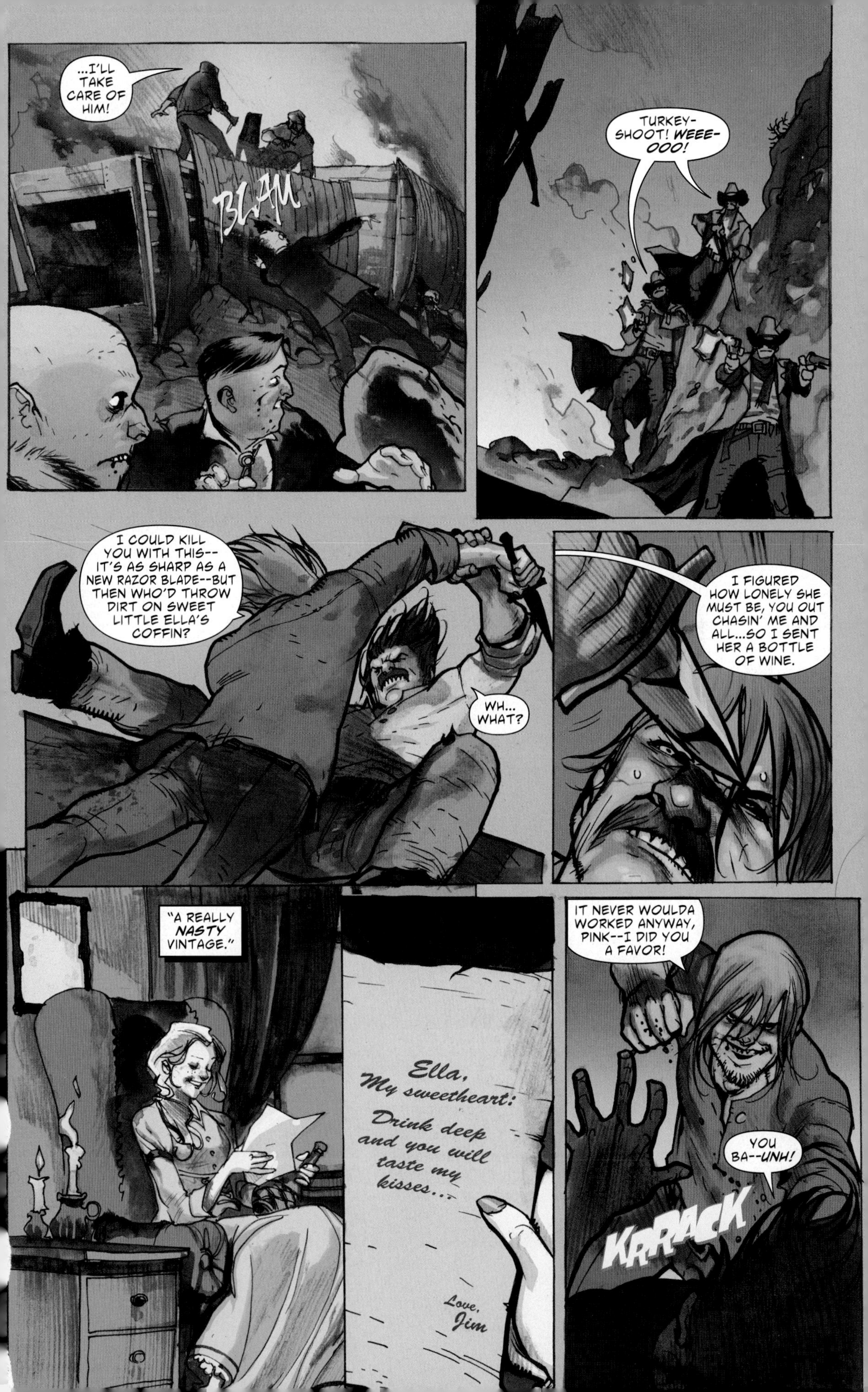
...I'LL TAKE CARE OF HIM!
BLAM
TURKEY-SHOOT! WEEE-OOO!
I COULD KILL YOU WITH THIS--IT'S AS SHARP AS A NEW RAZOR BLADE--BUT THEN WHO'D THROW DIRT ON SWEET LITTLE ELLA'S COFFIN?
WH... WHAT?
I FIGURED HOW LONELY SHE MUST BE, YOU OUT CHASIN' ME AND ALL...SO I SENT HER A BOTTLE OF WINE.
"A REALLY NASTY VINTAGE."
Ella, My sweetheart: Drink deep and you will taste my kisses...
Love, Jim
IT NEVER WOULDA WORKED ANYWAY, PINK--I DID YOU A FAVOR!
YOU BA--UNH!
KRRACK

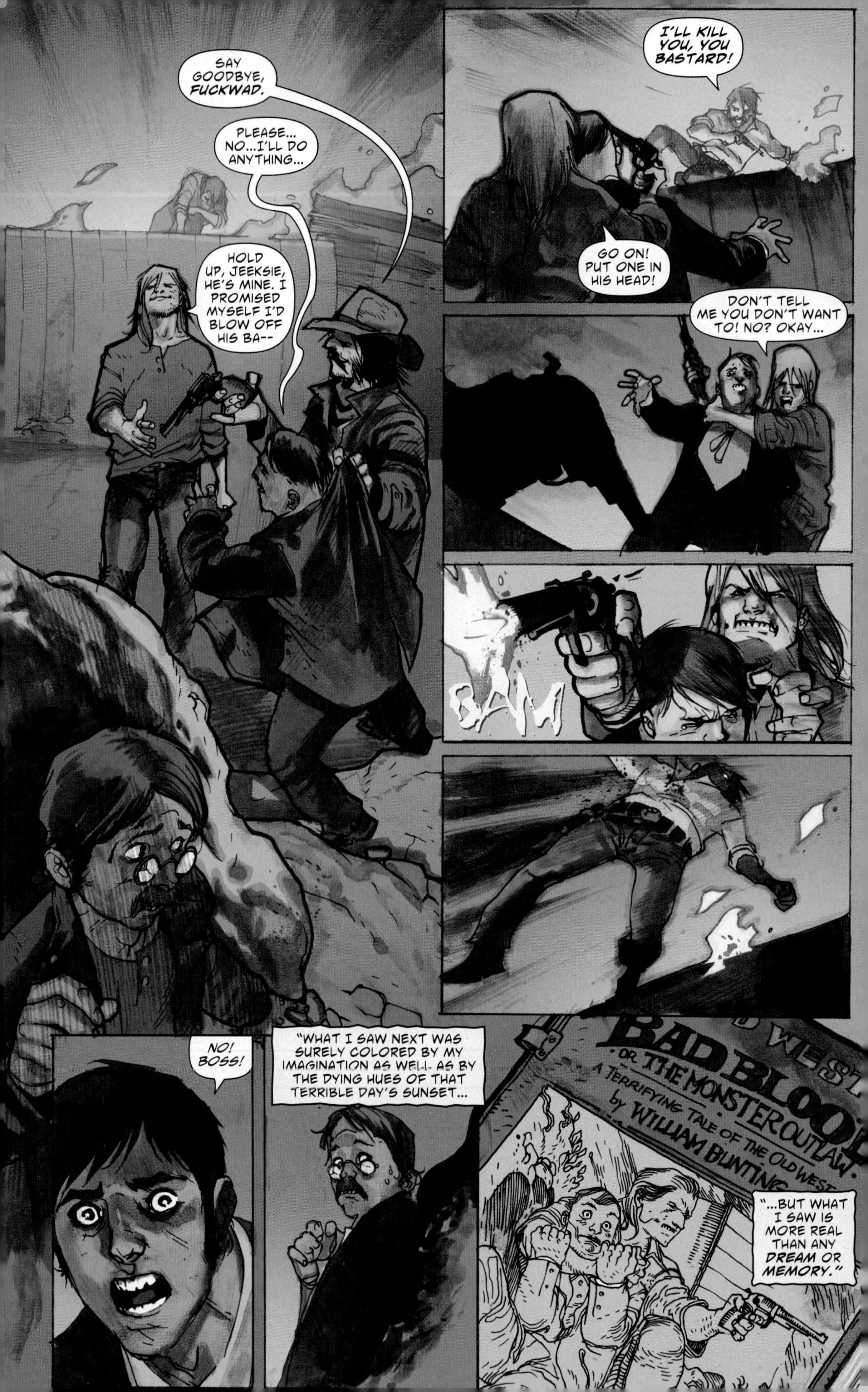
SAY GOODBYE, FUCKWAD.
PLEASE... NO...I'LL DO ANYTHING...
HOLD UP, JEEKSIE, HE'S MINE. I PROMISED MYSELF I'D BLOW OFF HIS BA--
I'LL KILL YOU, YOU BASTARD!
GO ON! PUT ONE IN HIS HEAD!
DON'T TELL ME YOU DON'T WANT TO! NO? OKAY...
BAM
NO! BOSS!
"WHAT I SAW NEXT WAS SURELY COLORED BY MY IMAGINATION AS WELL AS BY THE DYING HUES OF THAT TERRIBLE DAY'S SUNSET...
BAD BLOOD
OR THE MONSTER OUTLAW
A TERRIFYING TALE OF THE OLD WEST
by WILLIAM BUNTING
"...BUT WHAT I SAW IS MORE REAL THAN ANY DREAM OR MEMORY."

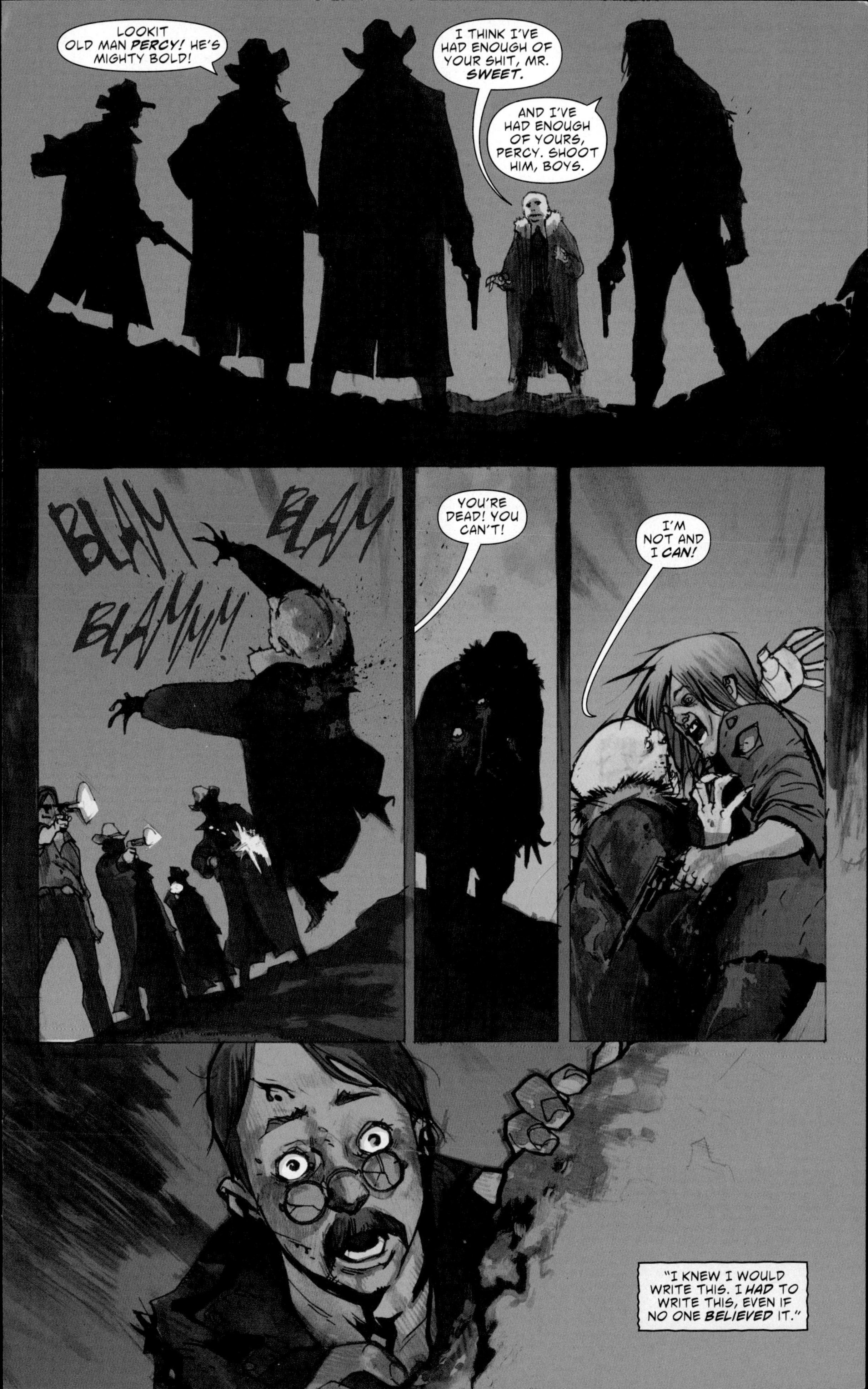
LOOKIT OLD MAN PERCY! HE'S MIGHTY BOLD!
I THINK I'VE HAD ENOUGH OF YOUR SHIT, MR. SWEET.
AND I'VE HAD ENOUGH OF YOURS, PERCY. SHOOT HIM, BOYS.
BLAM BLAM
BLAMMM
YOU'RE DEAD! YOU CAN'T!
I'M NOT AND I CAN!
"I KNEW I WOULD WRITE THIS. I HAD TO WRITE THIS, EVEN IF NO ONE BELIEVED IT."

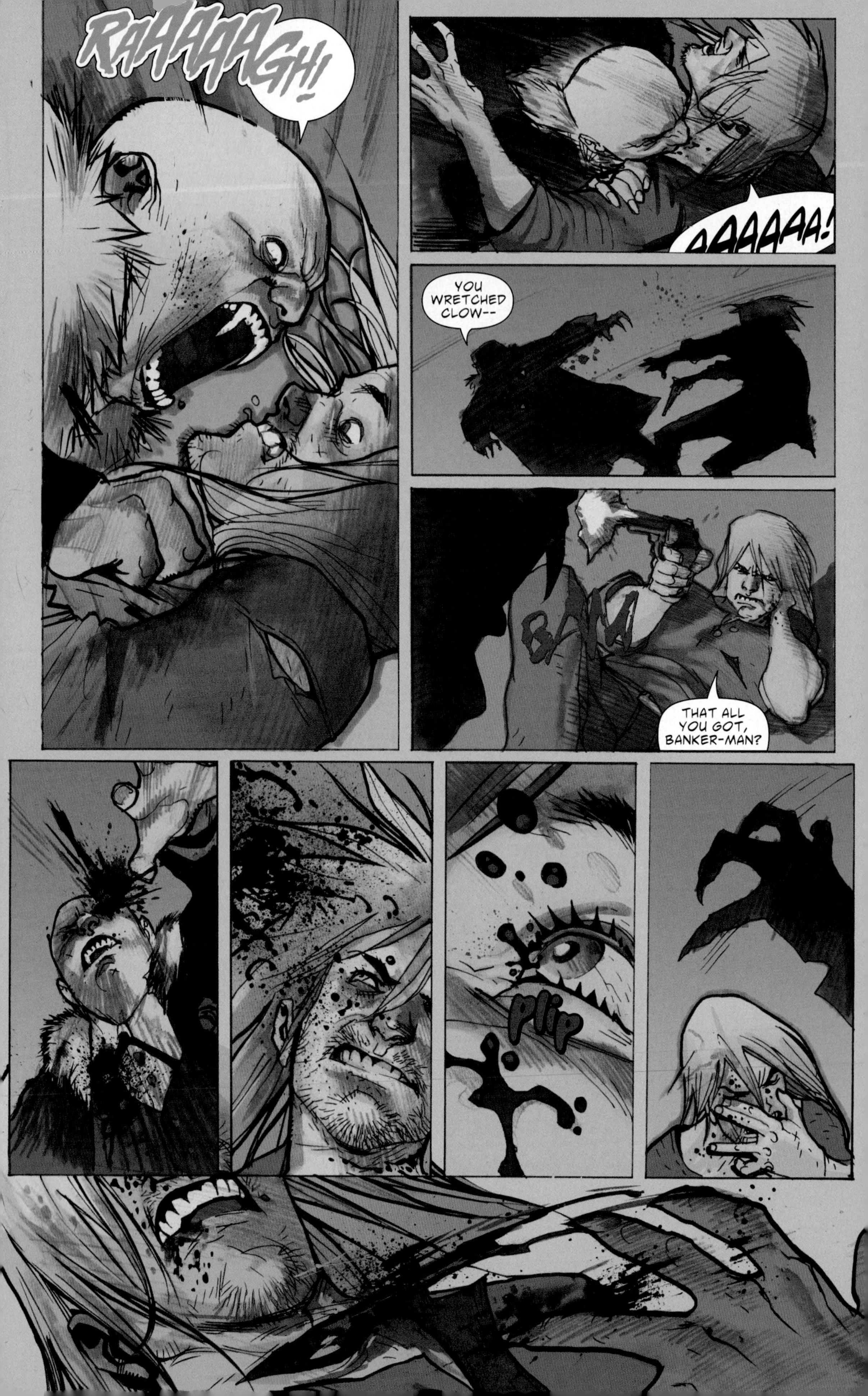
RAAAAAAGH!
AAAAAA!
YOU WRETCHED CLOW--
BAM
THAT ALL YOU GOT, BANKER-MAN?
plip

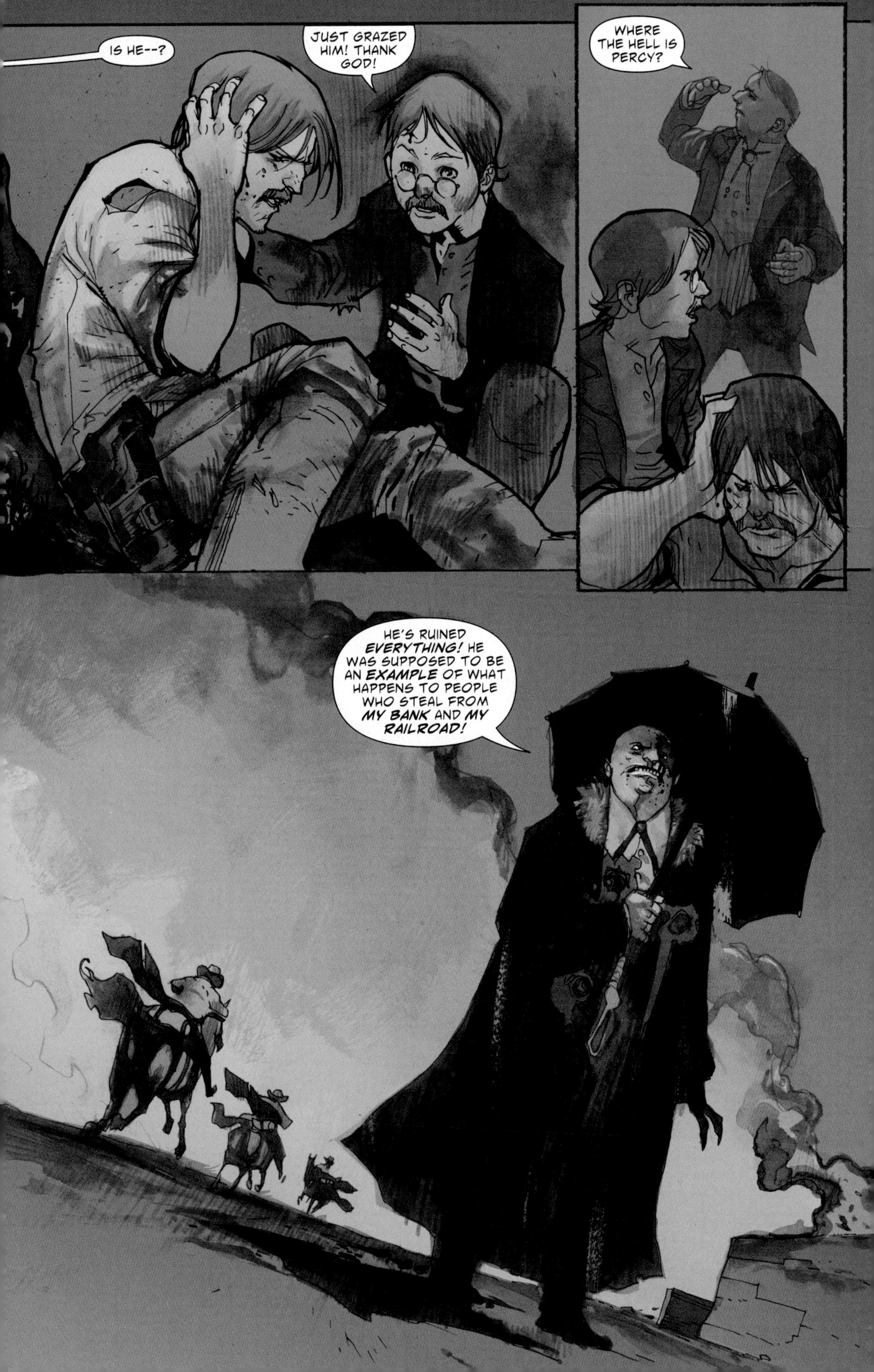
IS HE--?
JUST GRAZED HIM! THANK GOD!
WHERE THE HELL IS PERCY?
HE'S RUINED *EVERYTHING!* HE WAS SUPPOSED TO BE AN *EXAMPLE* OF WHAT HAPPENS TO PEOPLE WHO STEAL FROM *MY BANK* AND *MY RAILROAD!*

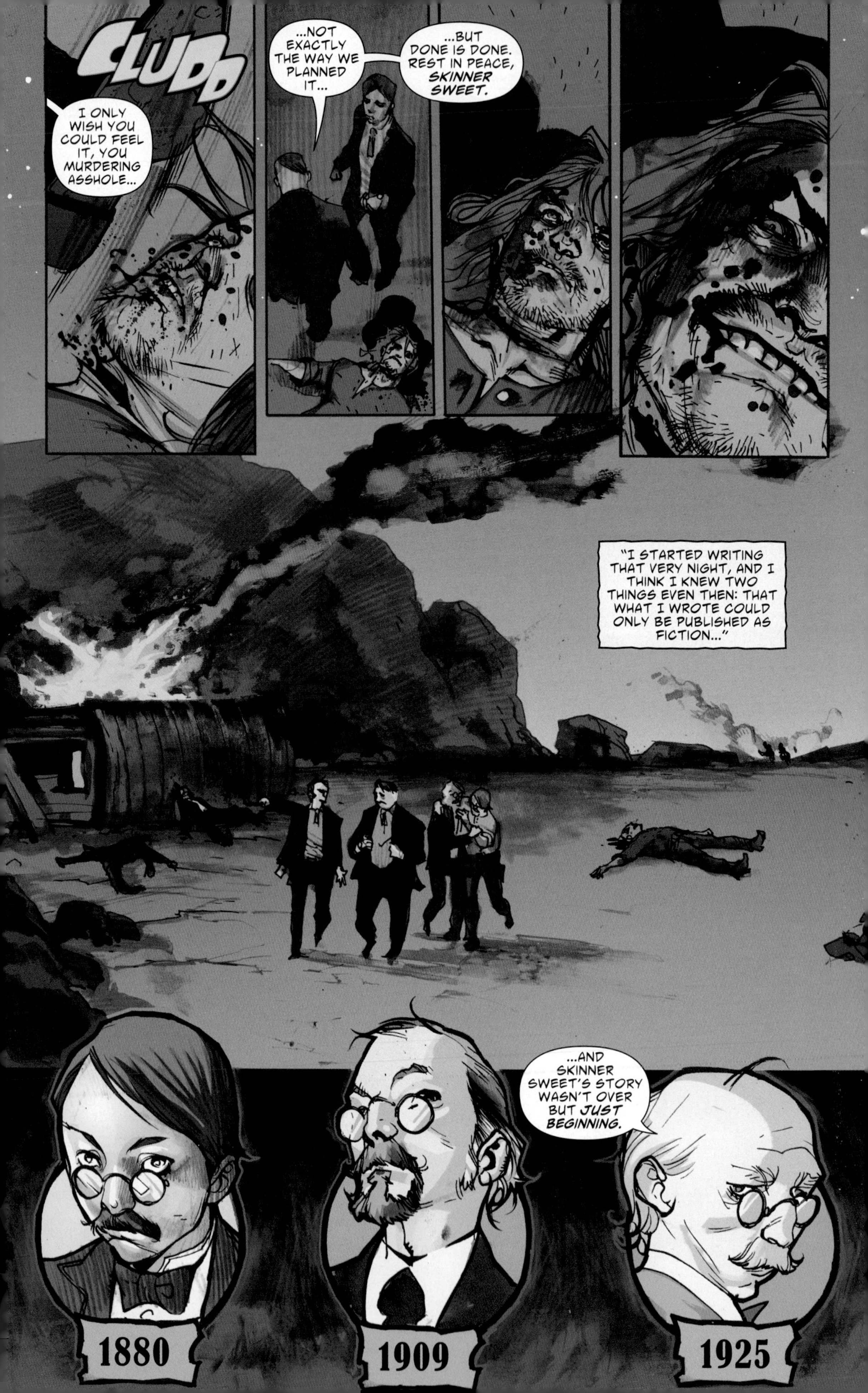
CLUDD
I ONLY WISH YOU COULD FEEL IT, YOU MURDERING ASSHOLE...
...NOT EXACTLY THE WAY WE PLANNED IT...
...BUT DONE IS DONE. REST IN PEACE, SKINNER SWEET.
"I STARTED WRITING THAT VERY NIGHT, AND I THINK I KNEW TWO THINGS EVEN THEN: THAT WHAT I WROTE COULD ONLY BE PUBLISHED AS FICTION..."
...AND SKINNER SWEET'S STORY WASN'T OVER BUT JUST BEGINNING.
1880
1909
1925

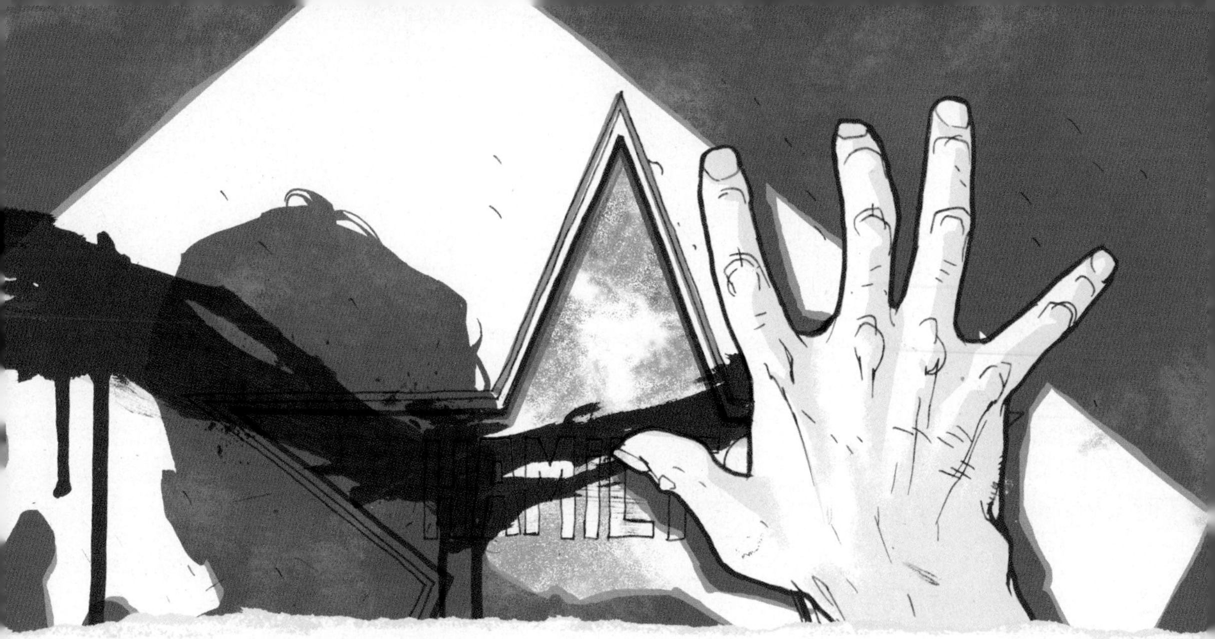

Chapter Two

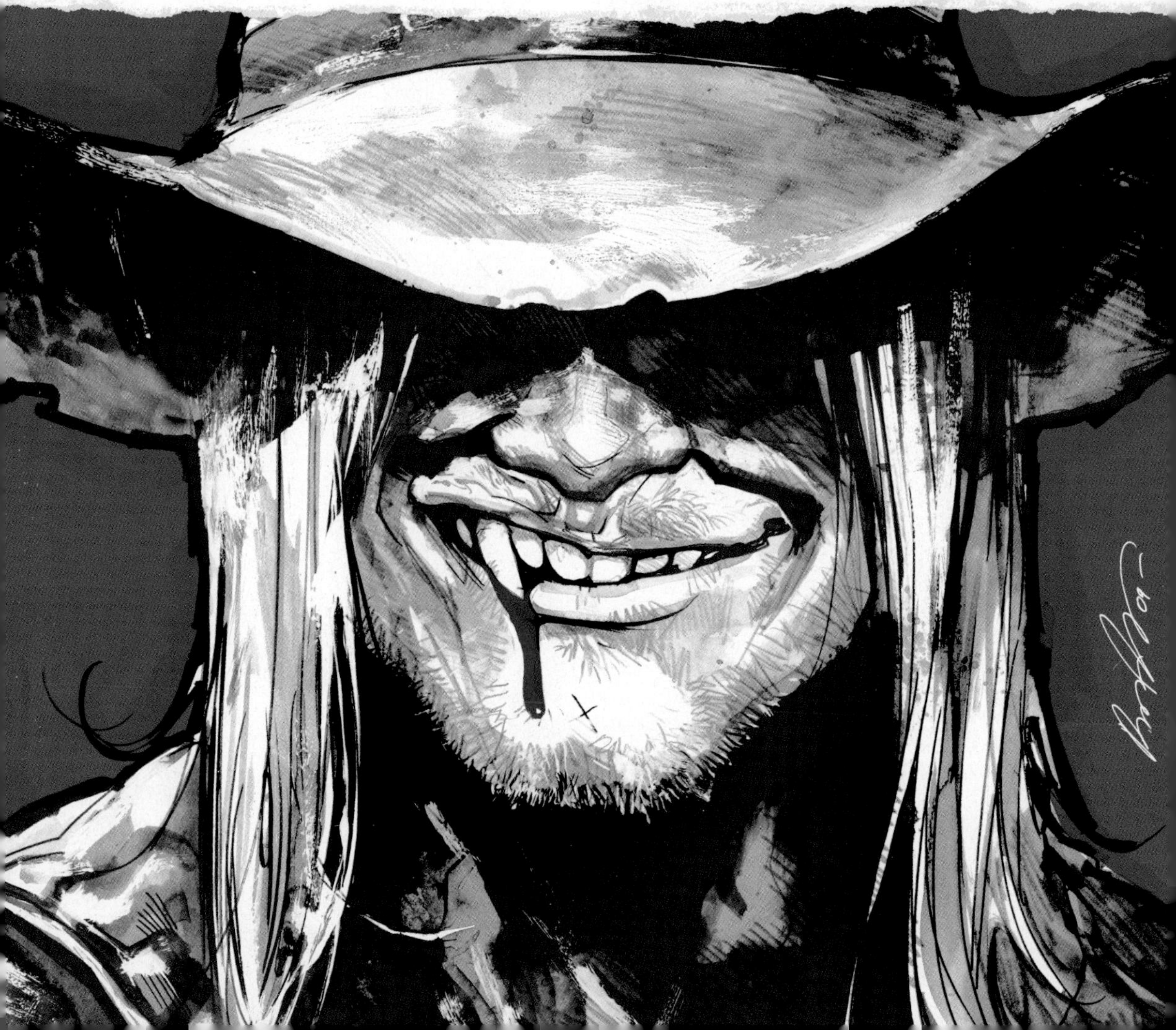

Morning Star
Scott Snyder Writer

❦

Deep Water
Stephen King Writer

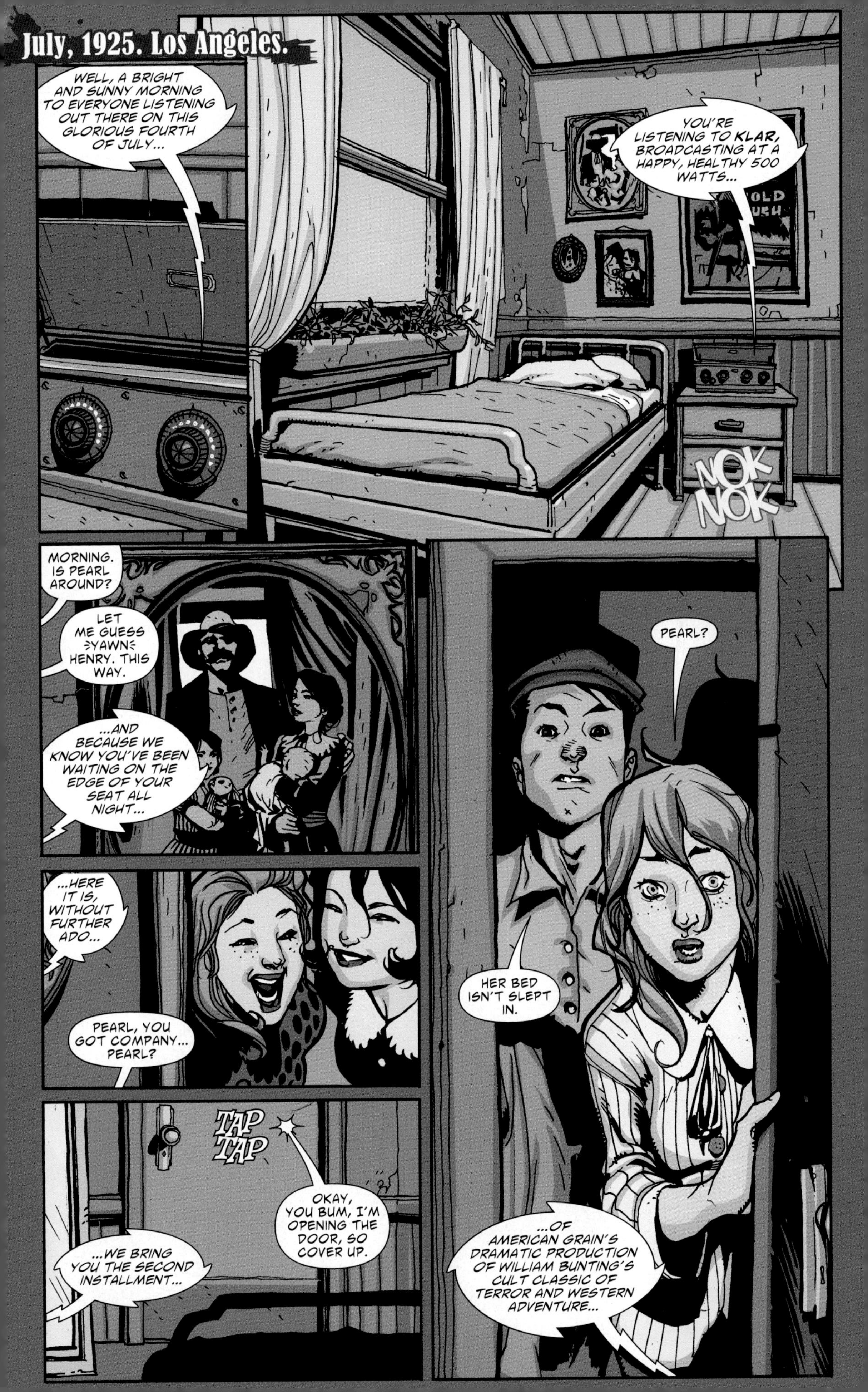
July, 1925. Los Angeles.
WELL, A BRIGHT AND SUNNY MORNING TO EVERYONE LISTENING OUT THERE ON THIS GLORIOUS FOURTH OF JULY...
YOU'RE LISTENING TO KLAR, BROADCASTING AT A HAPPY, HEALTHY 500 WATTS...
NOK NOK
MORNING. IS PEARL AROUND?
LET ME GUESS =YAWN= HENRY. THIS WAY.
...AND BECAUSE WE KNOW YOU'VE BEEN WAITING ON THE EDGE OF YOUR SEAT ALL NIGHT...
...HERE IT IS, WITHOUT FURTHER ADO...
PEARL, YOU GOT COMPANY... PEARL?
TAP TAP
OKAY, YOU BUM, I'M OPENING THE DOOR, SO COVER UP.
...WE BRING YOU THE SECOND INSTALLMENT...
PEARL?
HER BED ISN'T SLEPT IN.
...OF AMERICAN GRAIN'S DRAMATIC PRODUCTION OF WILLIAM BUNTING'S CULT CLASSIC OF TERROR AND WESTERN ADVENTURE...

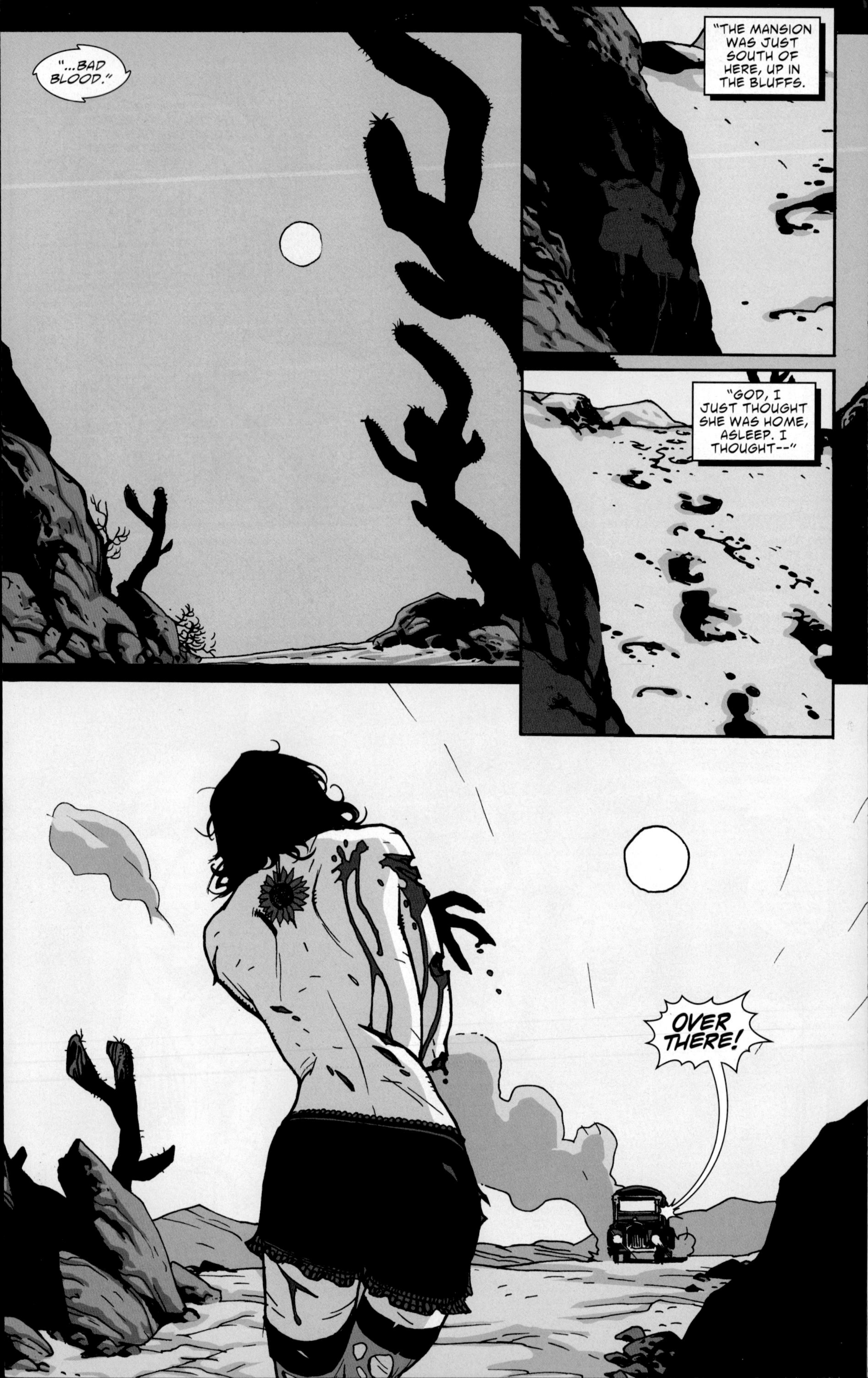
"...BAD BLOOD."
"THE MANSION WAS JUST SOUTH OF HERE, UP IN THE BLUFFS.
"GOD, I JUST THOUGHT SHE WAS HOME, ASLEEP. I THOUGHT--"
OVER THERE!

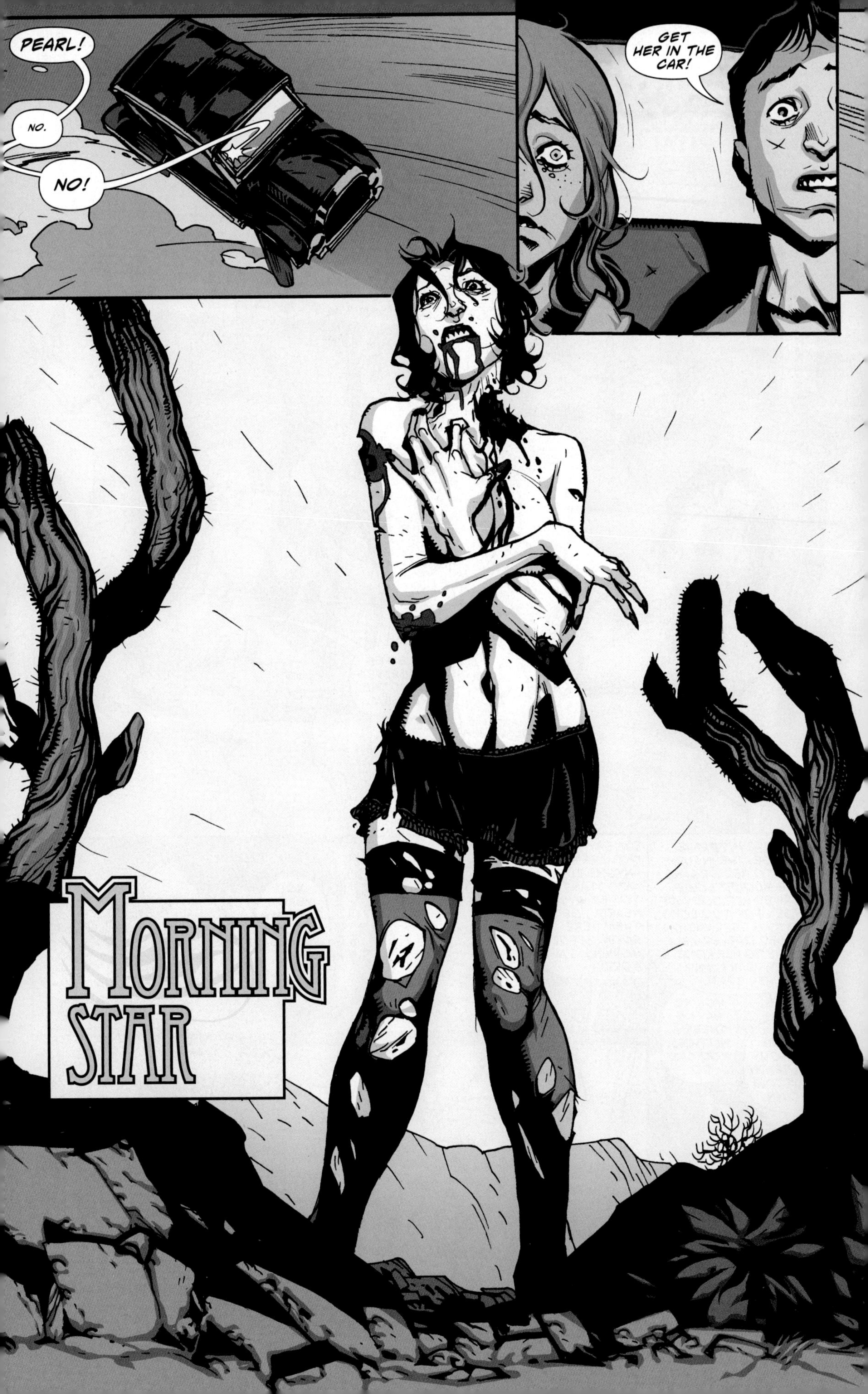
PEARL!
NO.
NO!
GET HER IN THE CAR!
MORNING STAR

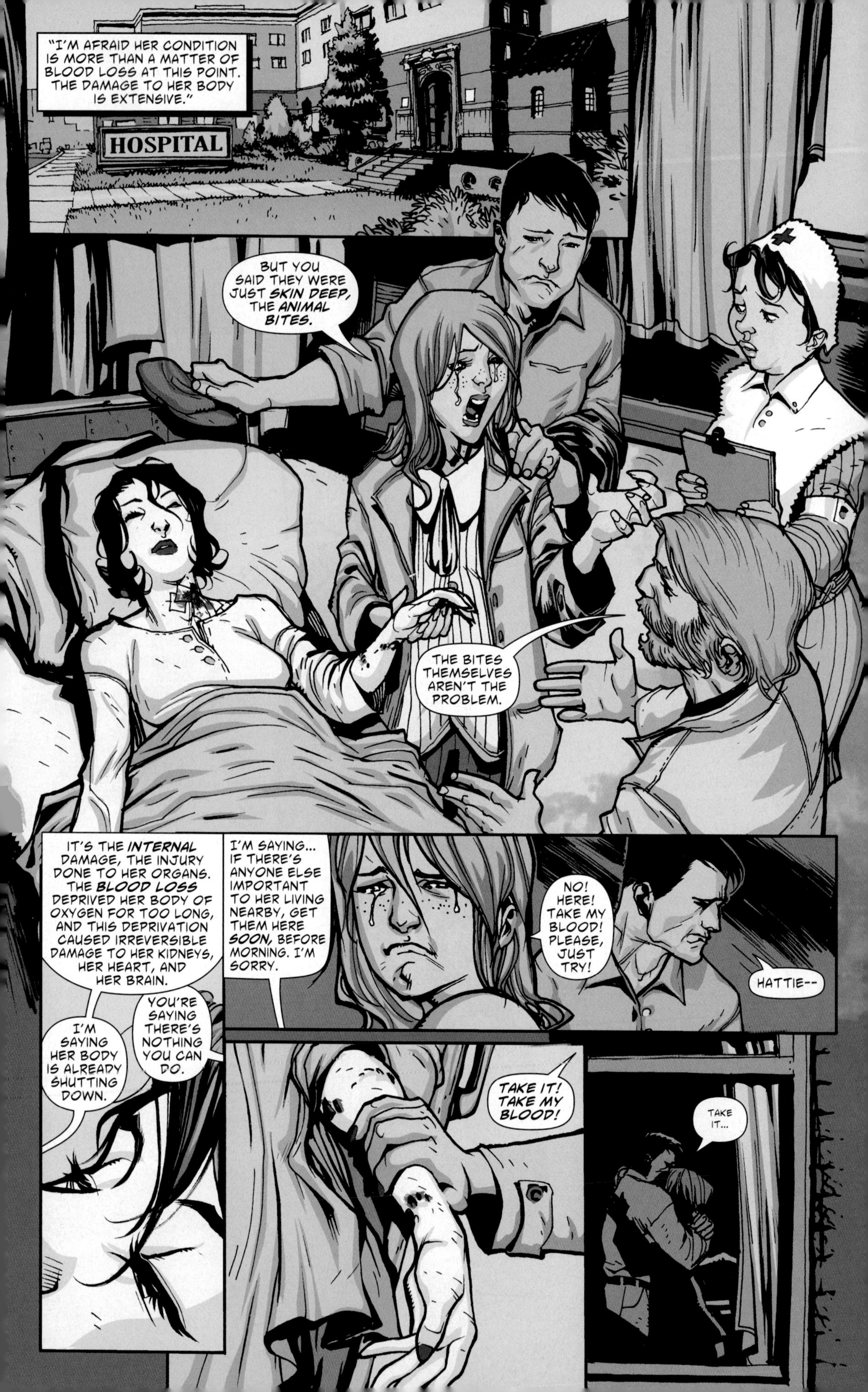
"I'M AFRAID HER CONDITION IS MORE THAN A MATTER OF BLOOD LOSS AT THIS POINT. THE DAMAGE TO HER BODY IS EXTENSIVE."
HOSPITAL
BUT YOU SAID THEY WERE JUST SKIN DEEP, THE ANIMAL BITES.
THE BITES THEMSELVES AREN'T THE PROBLEM.
IT'S THE INTERNAL DAMAGE, THE INJURY DONE TO HER ORGANS. THE BLOOD LOSS DEPRIVED HER BODY OF OXYGEN FOR TOO LONG, AND THIS DEPRIVATION CAUSED IRREVERSIBLE DAMAGE TO HER KIDNEYS, HER HEART, AND HER BRAIN.
YOU'RE SAYING THERE'S NOTHING YOU CAN DO.
I'M SAYING HER BODY IS ALREADY SHUTTING DOWN.
I'M SAYING... IF THERE'S ANYONE ELSE IMPORTANT TO HER LIVING NEARBY, GET THEM HERE SOON, BEFORE MORNING. I'M SORRY.
NO! HERE! TAKE MY BLOOD! PLEASE, JUST TRY!
HATTIE--
TAKE IT! TAKE MY BLOOD!
TAKE IT...

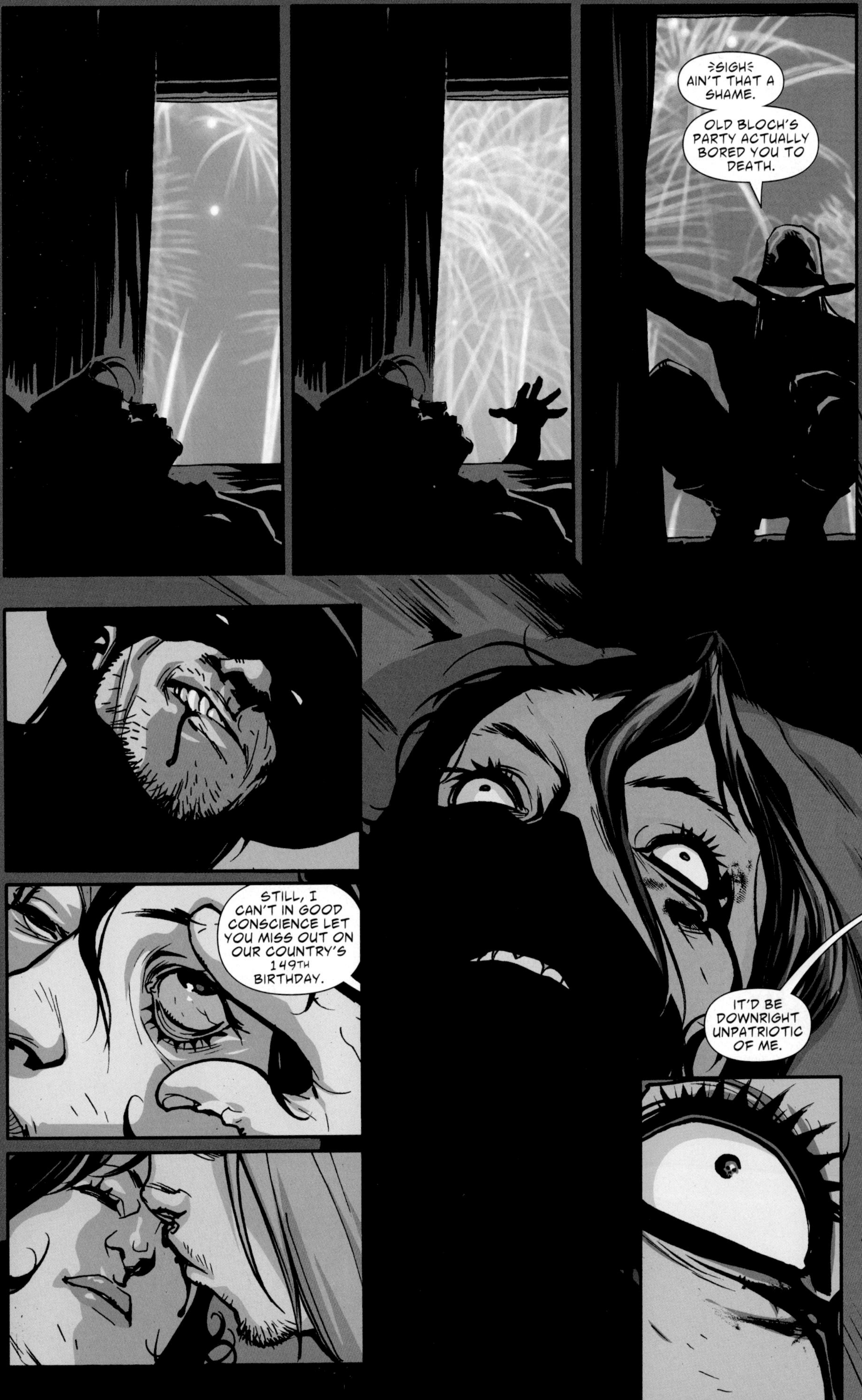

≥SIGH≤ AIN'T THAT A SHAME.
OLD BLOCH'S PARTY ACTUALLY BORED YOU TO DEATH.
STILL, I CAN'T IN GOOD CONSCIENCE LET YOU MISS OUT ON OUR COUNTRY'S 149TH BIRTHDAY.
IT'D BE DOWNRIGHT UNPATRIOTIC OF ME.

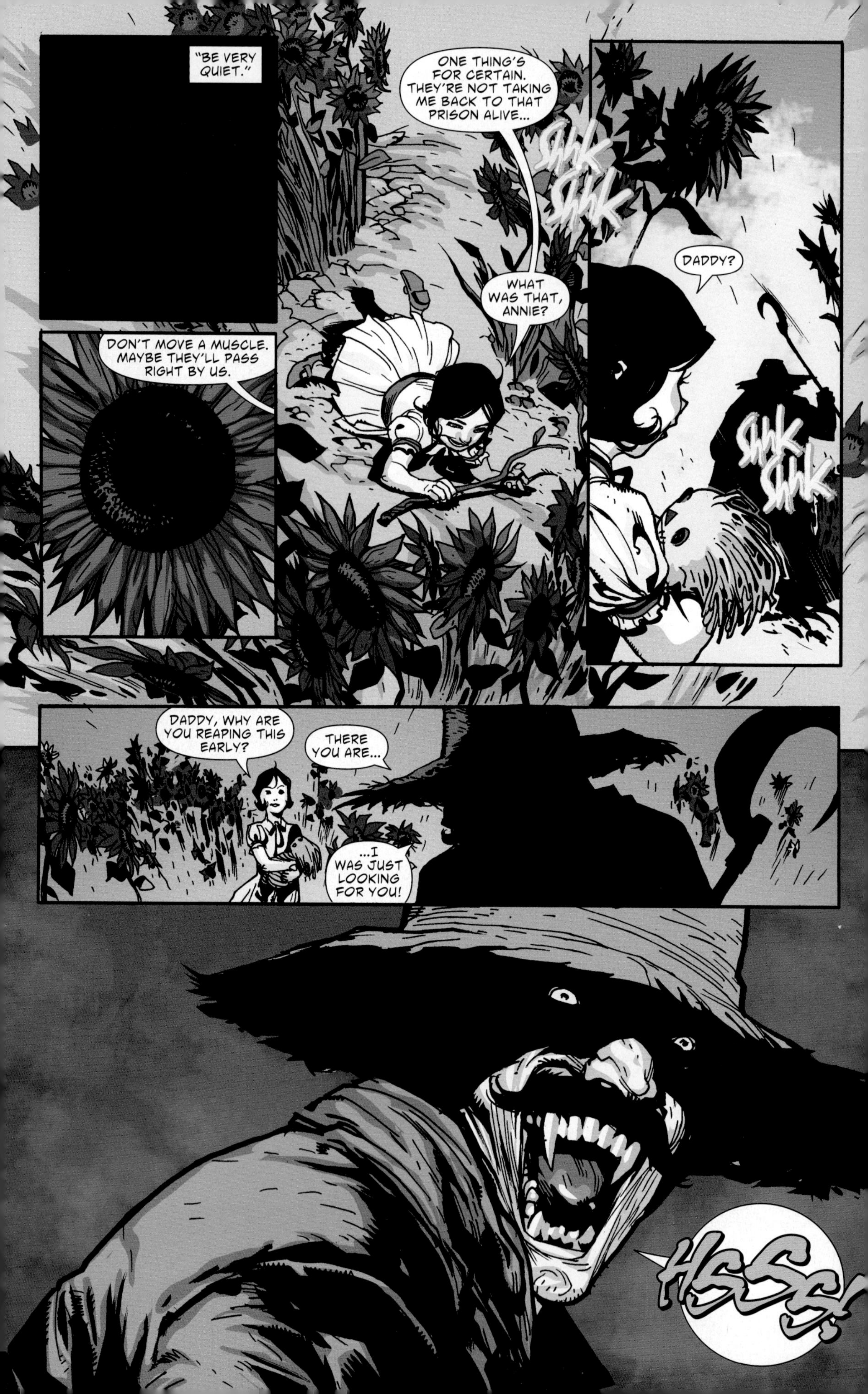
"BE VERY QUIET."
ONE THING'S FOR CERTAIN. THEY'RE NOT TAKING ME BACK TO THAT PRISON ALIVE...
WHAT WAS THAT, ANNIE?
DON'T MOVE A MUSCLE. MAYBE THEY'LL PASS RIGHT BY US.
SHHK SHHK
DADDY?
SHHK SHHK
DADDY, WHY ARE YOU REAPING THIS EARLY?
THERE YOU ARE...
...I WAS JUST LOOKING FOR YOU!
HSSS!

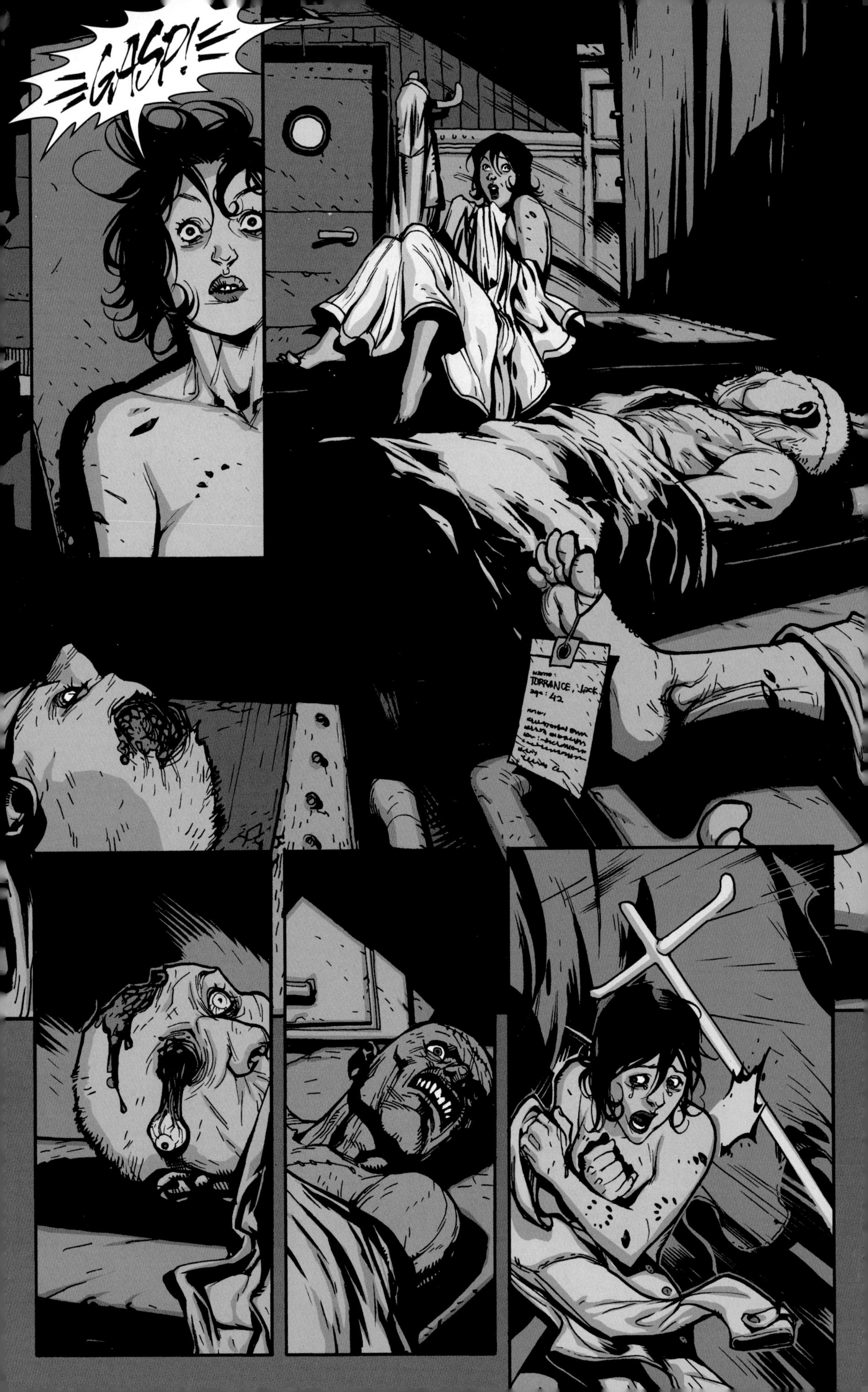
GASP!
name:
TORRANCE, Jack
age: 42

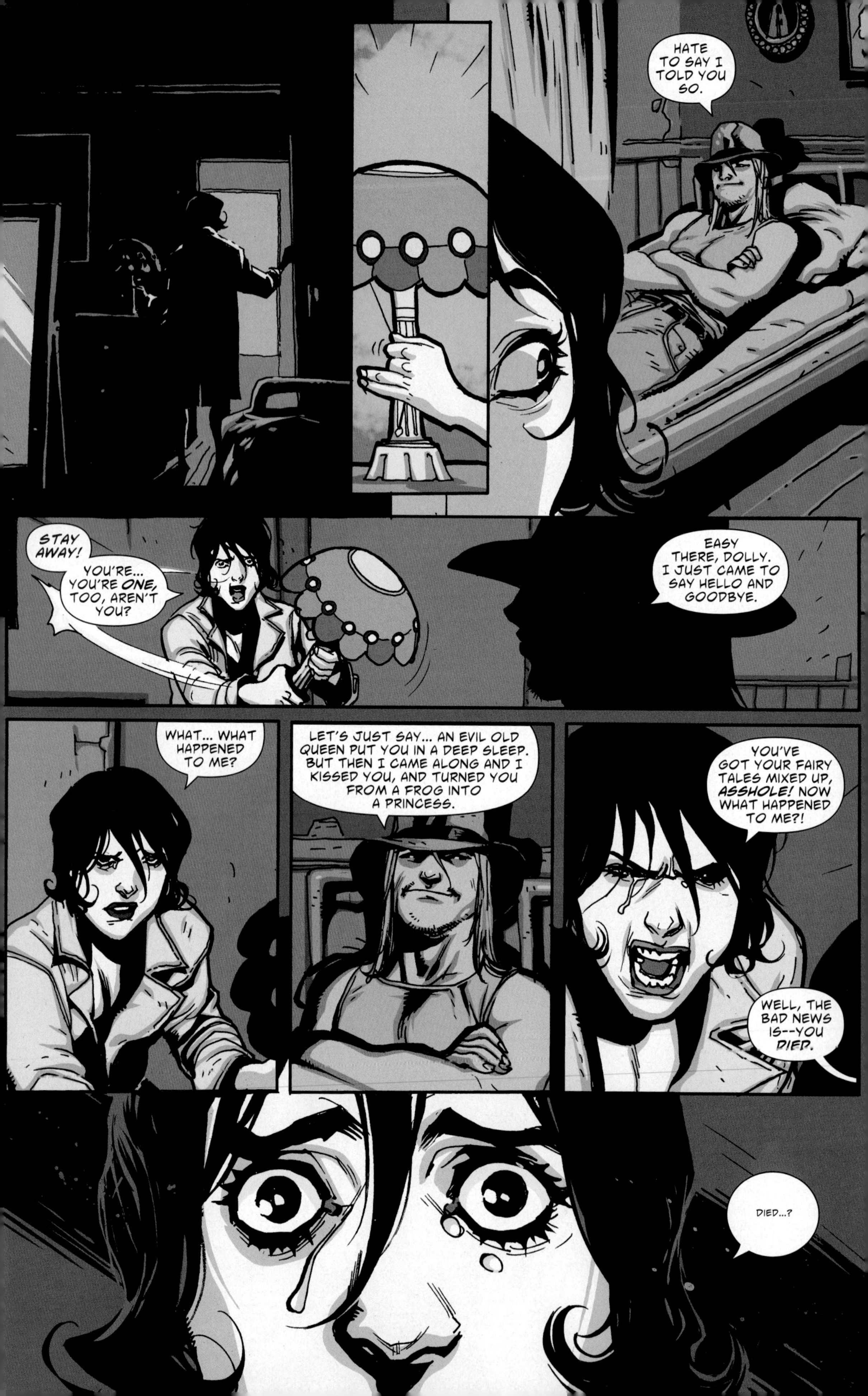
HATE TO SAY I TOLD YOU SO.
STAY AWAY!
YOU'RE... YOU'RE ONE, TOO, AREN'T YOU?
EASY THERE, DOLLY. I JUST CAME TO SAY HELLO AND GOODBYE.
WHAT... WHAT HAPPENED TO ME?
LET'S JUST SAY... AN EVIL OLD QUEEN PUT YOU IN A DEEP SLEEP. BUT THEN I CAME ALONG AND I KISSED YOU, AND TURNED YOU FROM A FROG INTO A PRINCESS.
YOU'VE GOT YOUR FAIRY TALES MIXED UP, ASSHOLE! NOW WHAT HAPPENED TO ME?!
WELL, THE BAD NEWS IS--YOU DIED.
DIED...?

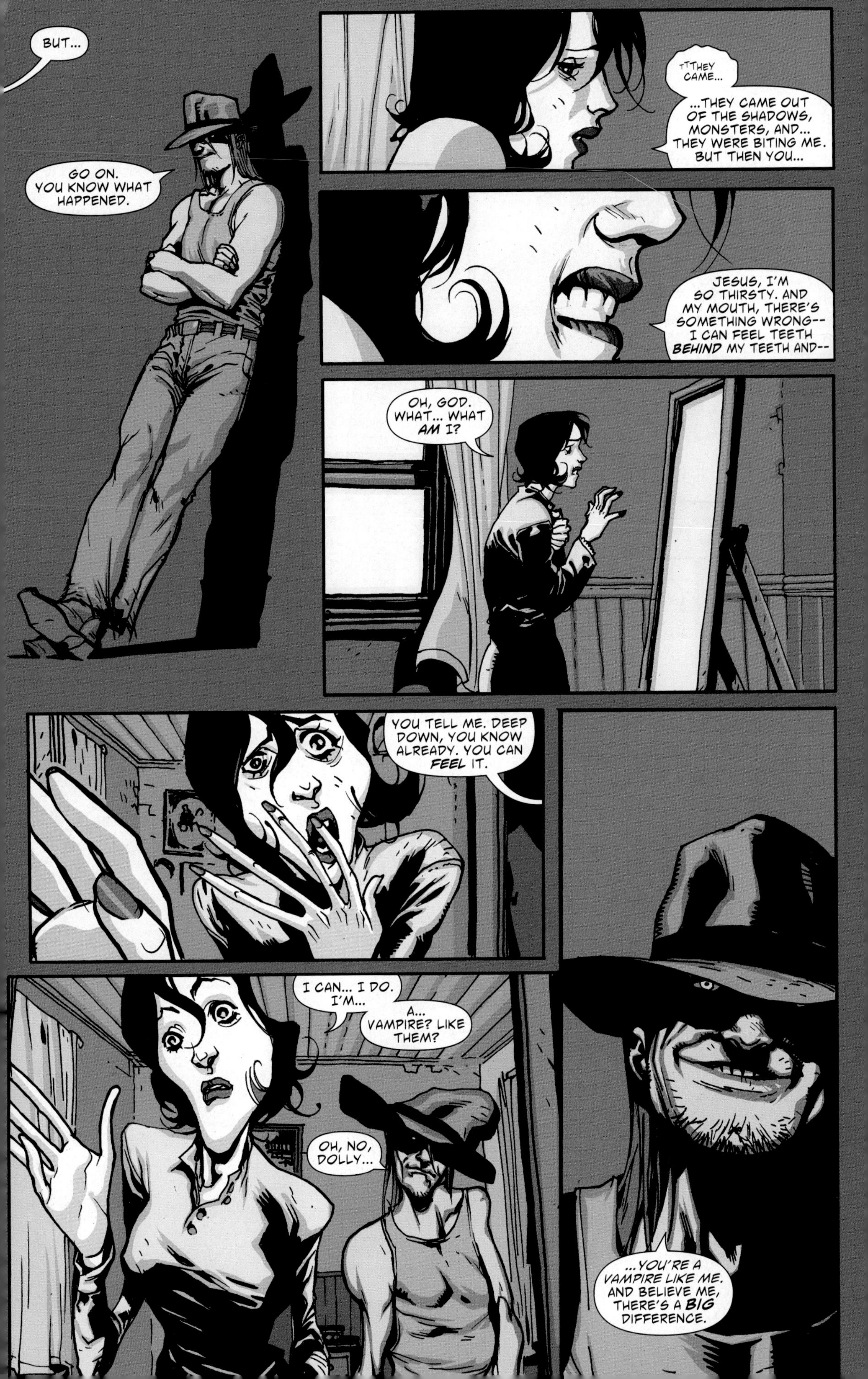
BUT...
TTTHEY CAME...
...THEY CAME OUT OF THE SHADOWS, MONSTERS, AND... THEY WERE BITING ME. BUT THEN YOU...
GO ON. YOU KNOW WHAT HAPPENED.
JESUS, I'M SO THIRSTY. AND MY MOUTH, THERE'S SOMETHING WRONG-- I CAN FEEL TEETH *BEHIND* MY TEETH AND--
OH, GOD. WHAT... WHAT *AM* I?
YOU TELL ME. DEEP DOWN, YOU KNOW ALREADY. YOU CAN *FEEL* IT.
I CAN... I DO. I'M...
A... VAMPIRE? LIKE THEM?
OH, NO, DOLLY...
...YOU'RE A VAMPIRE LIKE ME. AND BELIEVE ME, THERE'S A *BIG* DIFFERENCE.

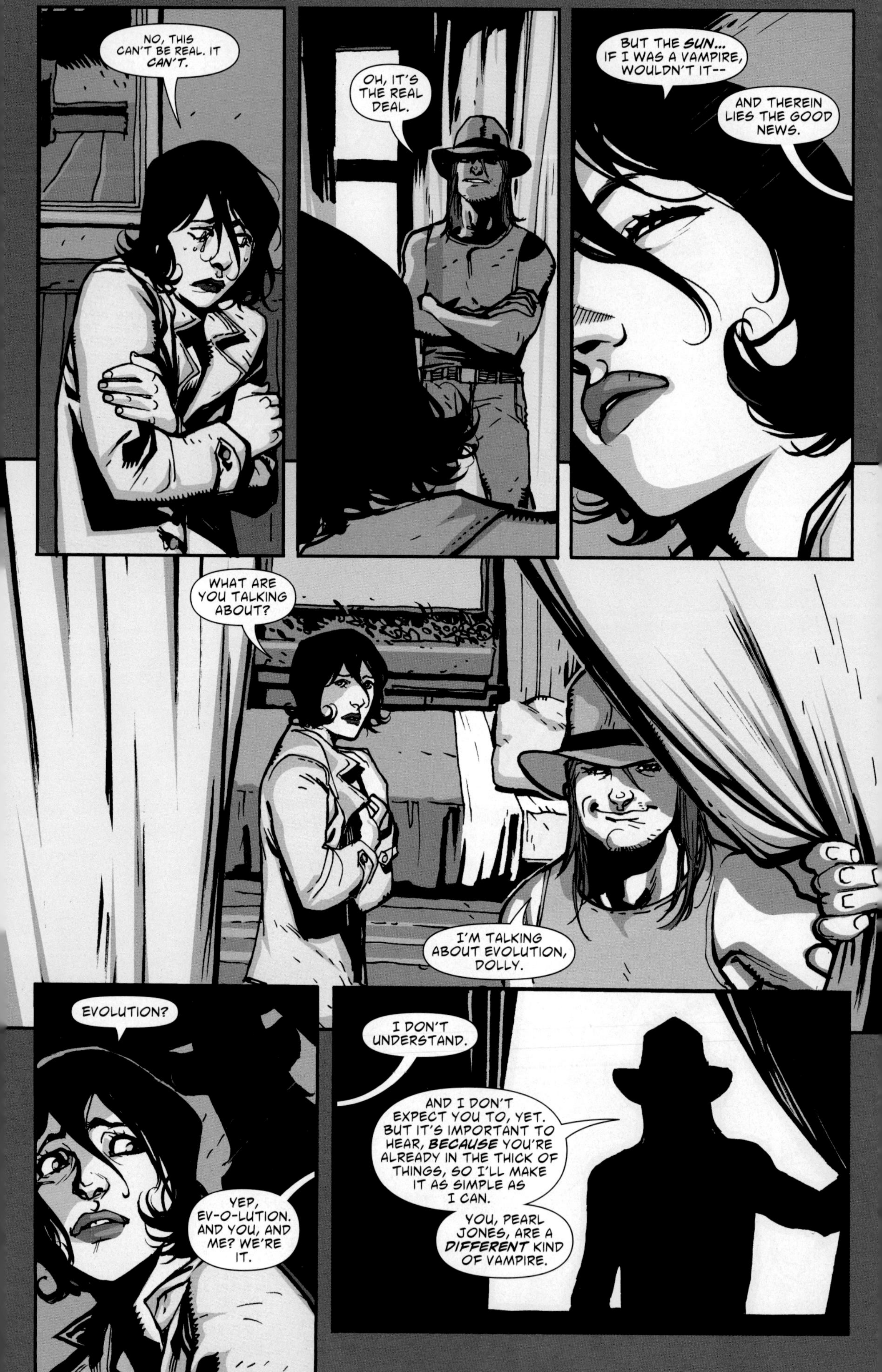
NO, THIS CAN'T BE REAL. IT *CAN'T*.
OH, IT'S THE REAL DEAL.
BUT THE *SUN*... IF I WAS A VAMPIRE, WOULDN'T IT--
AND THEREIN LIES THE GOOD NEWS.
WHAT ARE YOU TALKING ABOUT?
I'M TALKING ABOUT EVOLUTION, DOLLY.
EVOLUTION?
YEP, EV-O-LUTION. AND YOU, AND ME? WE'RE IT.
I DON'T UNDERSTAND.
AND I DON'T EXPECT YOU TO, YET. BUT IT'S IMPORTANT TO HEAR, *BECAUSE* YOU'RE ALREADY IN THE THICK OF THINGS, SO I'LL MAKE IT AS SIMPLE AS I CAN.
YOU, PEARL JONES, ARE A *DIFFERENT* KIND OF VAMPIRE.

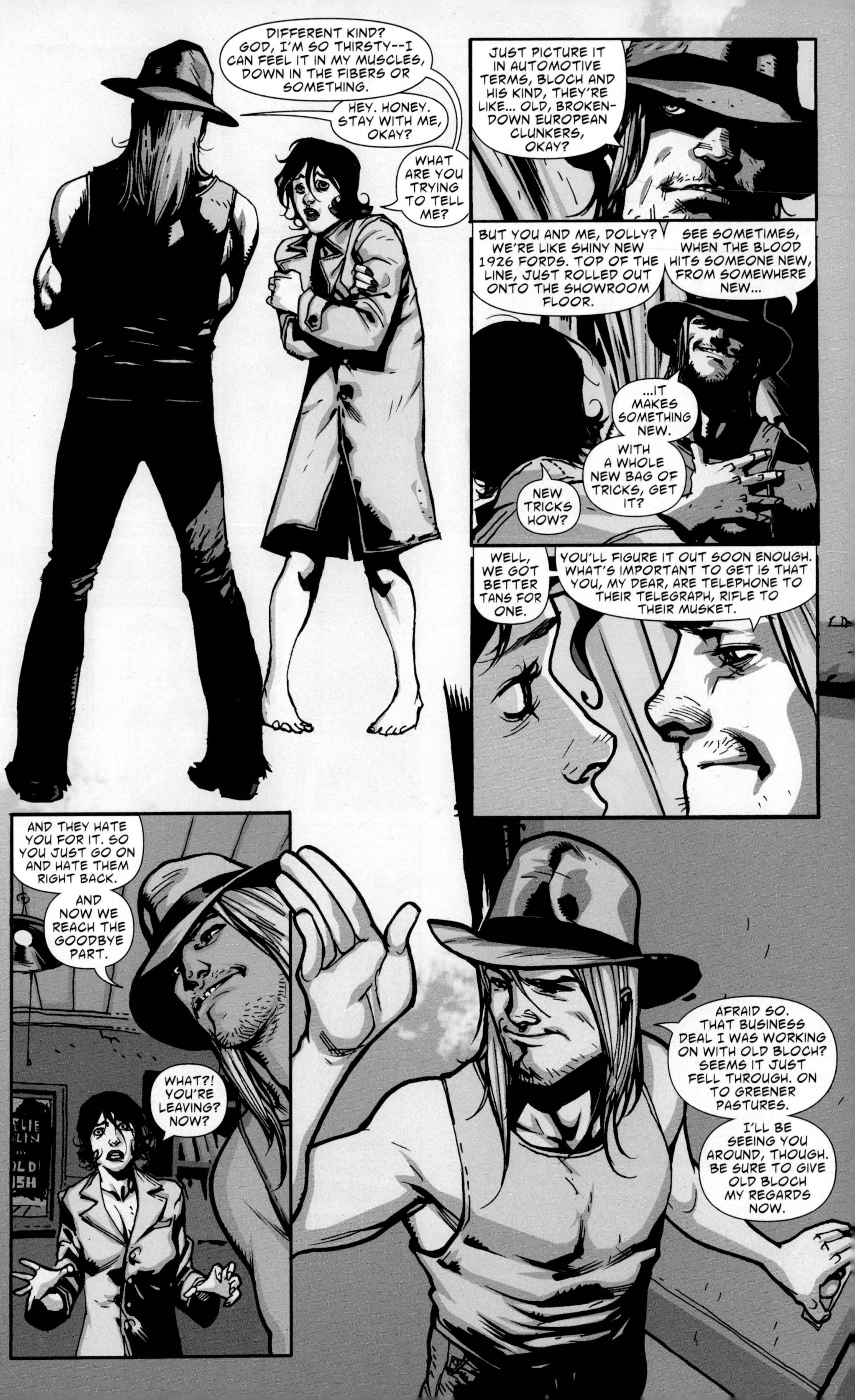
DIFFERENT KIND? GOD, I'M SO THIRSTY--I CAN FEEL IT IN MY MUSCLES, DOWN IN THE FIBERS OR SOMETHING.
HEY. HONEY. STAY WITH ME, OKAY?
WHAT ARE YOU TRYING TO TELL ME?
JUST PICTURE IT IN AUTOMOTIVE TERMS, BLOCH AND HIS KIND, THEY'RE LIKE... OLD, BROKEN-DOWN EUROPEAN CLUNKERS, OKAY?
BUT YOU AND ME, DOLLY? WE'RE LIKE SHINY NEW 1926 FORDS. TOP OF THE LINE, JUST ROLLED OUT ONTO THE SHOWROOM FLOOR.
SEE SOMETIMES, WHEN THE BLOOD HITS SOMEONE NEW, FROM SOMEWHERE NEW...
...IT MAKES SOMETHING NEW.
WITH A WHOLE NEW BAG OF TRICKS, GET IT?
NEW TRICKS HOW?
WELL, WE GOT BETTER TANS FOR ONE.
YOU'LL FIGURE IT OUT SOON ENOUGH. WHAT'S IMPORTANT TO GET IS THAT YOU, MY DEAR, ARE TELEPHONE TO THEIR TELEGRAPH, RIFLE TO THEIR MUSKET.
AND THEY HATE YOU FOR IT. SO YOU JUST GO ON AND HATE THEM RIGHT BACK.
AND NOW WE REACH THE GOODBYE PART.
WHAT?! YOU'RE LEAVING? NOW?
AFRAID SO. THAT BUSINESS DEAL I WAS WORKING ON WITH OLD BLOCH? SEEMS IT JUST FELL THROUGH. ON TO GREENER PASTURES.
I'LL BE SEEING YOU AROUND, THOUGH. BE SURE TO GIVE OLD BLOCH MY REGARDS NOW.

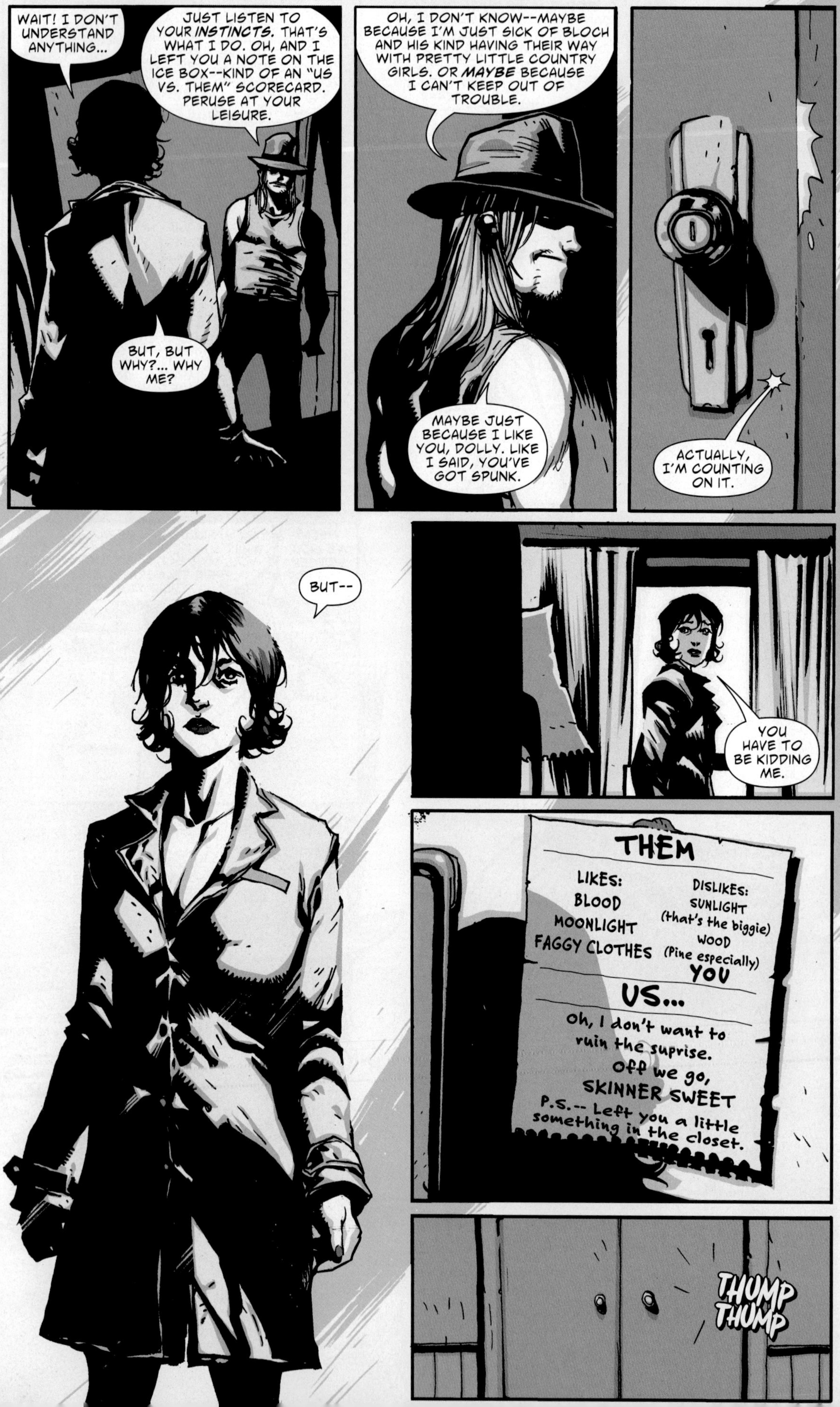
WAIT! I DON'T UNDERSTAND ANYTHING...
JUST LISTEN TO YOUR INSTINCTS. THAT'S WHAT I DO. OH, AND I LEFT YOU A NOTE ON THE ICE BOX--KIND OF AN "US VS. THEM" SCORECARD. PERUSE AT YOUR LEISURE.
BUT, BUT WHY?... WHY ME?
OH, I DON'T KNOW--MAYBE BECAUSE I'M JUST SICK OF BLOCH AND HIS KIND HAVING THEIR WAY WITH PRETTY LITTLE COUNTRY GIRLS. OR MAYBE BECAUSE I CAN'T KEEP OUT OF TROUBLE.
MAYBE JUST BECAUSE I LIKE YOU, DOLLY. LIKE I SAID, YOU'VE GOT SPUNK.
ACTUALLY, I'M COUNTING ON IT.
BUT--
YOU HAVE TO BE KIDDING ME.
THEM
LIKES:
BLOOD
MOONLIGHT
FAGGY CLOTHES
DISLIKES:
SUNLIGHT
(that's the biggie)
WOOD
(Pine especially)
YOU
US...
Oh, I don't want to ruin the suprise.
Off we go,
SKINNER SWEET
P.S.-- Left you a little something in the closet.
THUMP THUMP

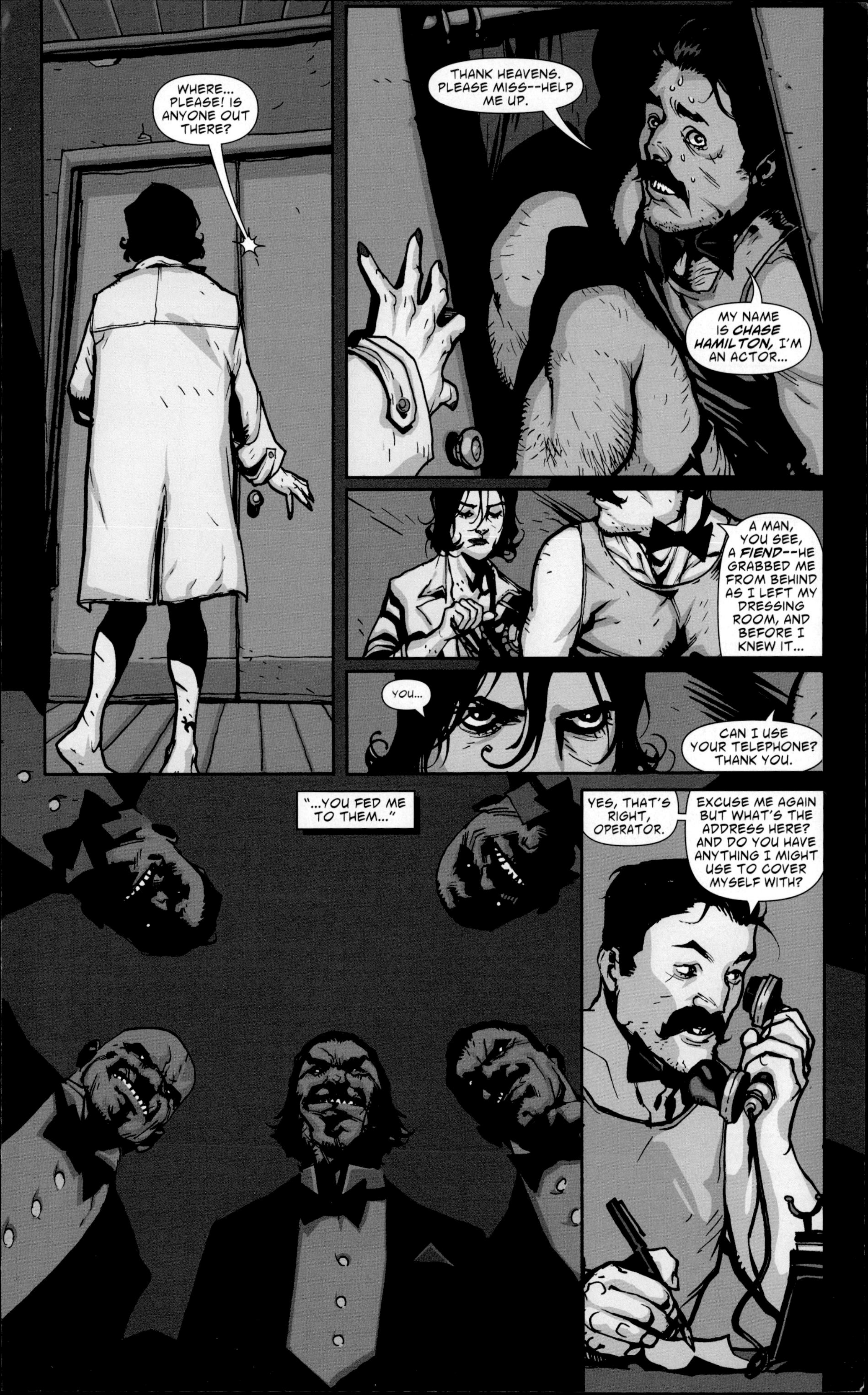
WHERE... PLEASE! IS ANYONE OUT THERE?
THANK HEAVENS. PLEASE MISS--HELP ME UP.
MY NAME IS **CHASE HAMILTON,** I'M AN ACTOR...
A MAN, YOU SEE, A **FIEND**--HE GRABBED ME FROM BEHIND AS I LEFT MY DRESSING ROOM, AND BEFORE I KNEW IT...
YOU...
CAN I USE YOUR TELEPHONE? THANK YOU.
"...YOU FED ME TO THEM..."
YES, THAT'S RIGHT, OPERATOR.
EXCUSE ME AGAIN BUT WHAT'S THE ADDRESS HERE? AND DO YOU HAVE ANYTHING I MIGHT USE TO COVER MYSELF WITH?

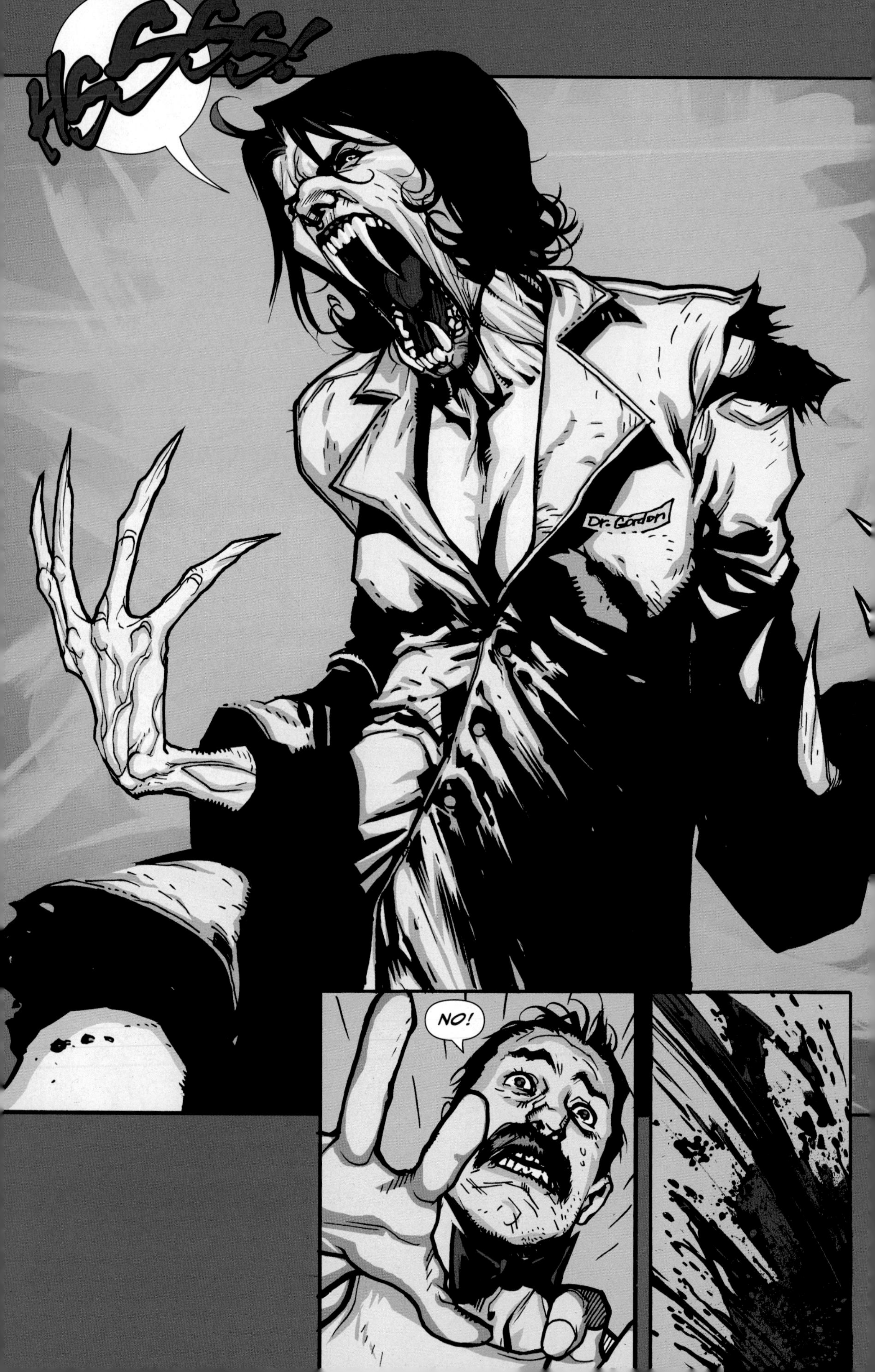
HSSSS!
Dr. Gordon
NO!

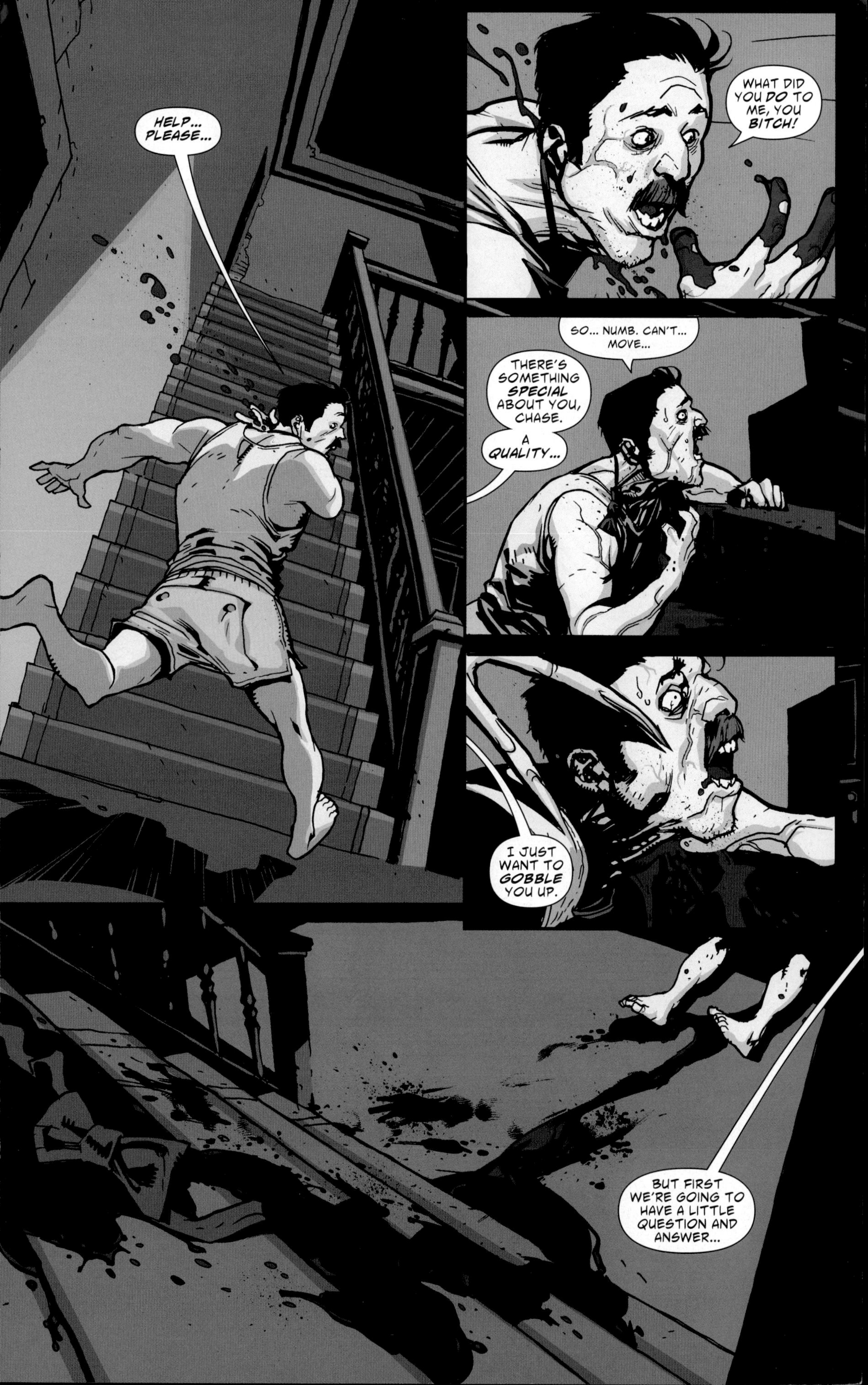
HELP... PLEASE...
WHAT DID YOU DO TO ME, YOU BITCH!
SO... NUMB. CAN'T... MOVE...
THERE'S SOMETHING SPECIAL ABOUT YOU, CHASE.
A QUALITY...
I JUST WANT TO GOBBLE YOU UP.
BUT FIRST WE'RE GOING TO HAVE A LITTLE QUESTION AND ANSWER...

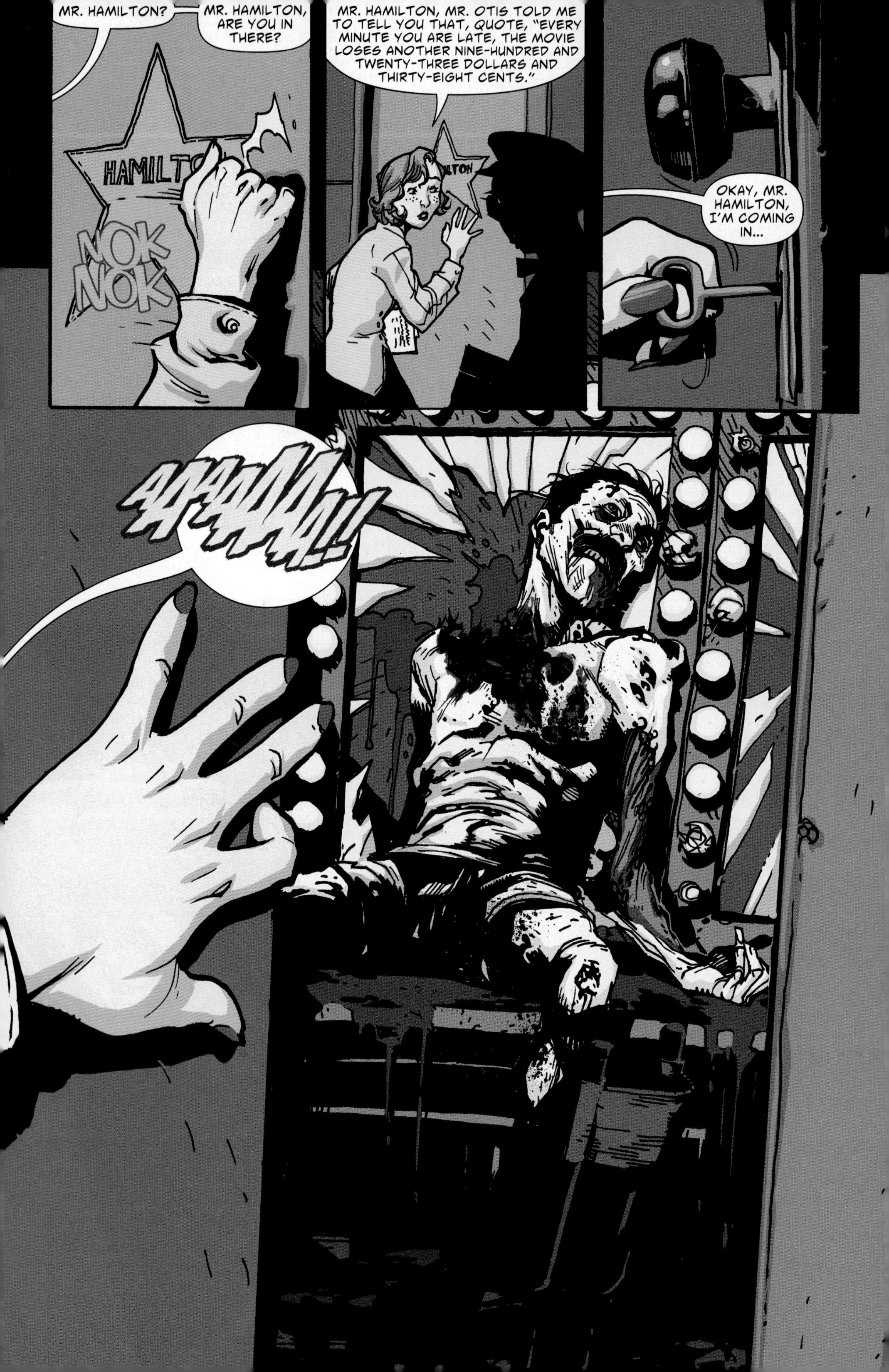
MR. HAMILTON?
MR. HAMILTON, ARE YOU IN THERE?
HAMILTON
NOK NOK
MR. HAMILTON, MR. OTIS TOLD ME TO TELL YOU THAT, QUOTE, "EVERY MINUTE YOU ARE LATE, THE MOVIE LOSES ANOTHER NINE-HUNDRED AND TWENTY-THREE DOLLARS AND THIRTY-EIGHT CENTS."
OKAY, MR. HAMILTON, I'M COMING IN...
AAAAAAH!!

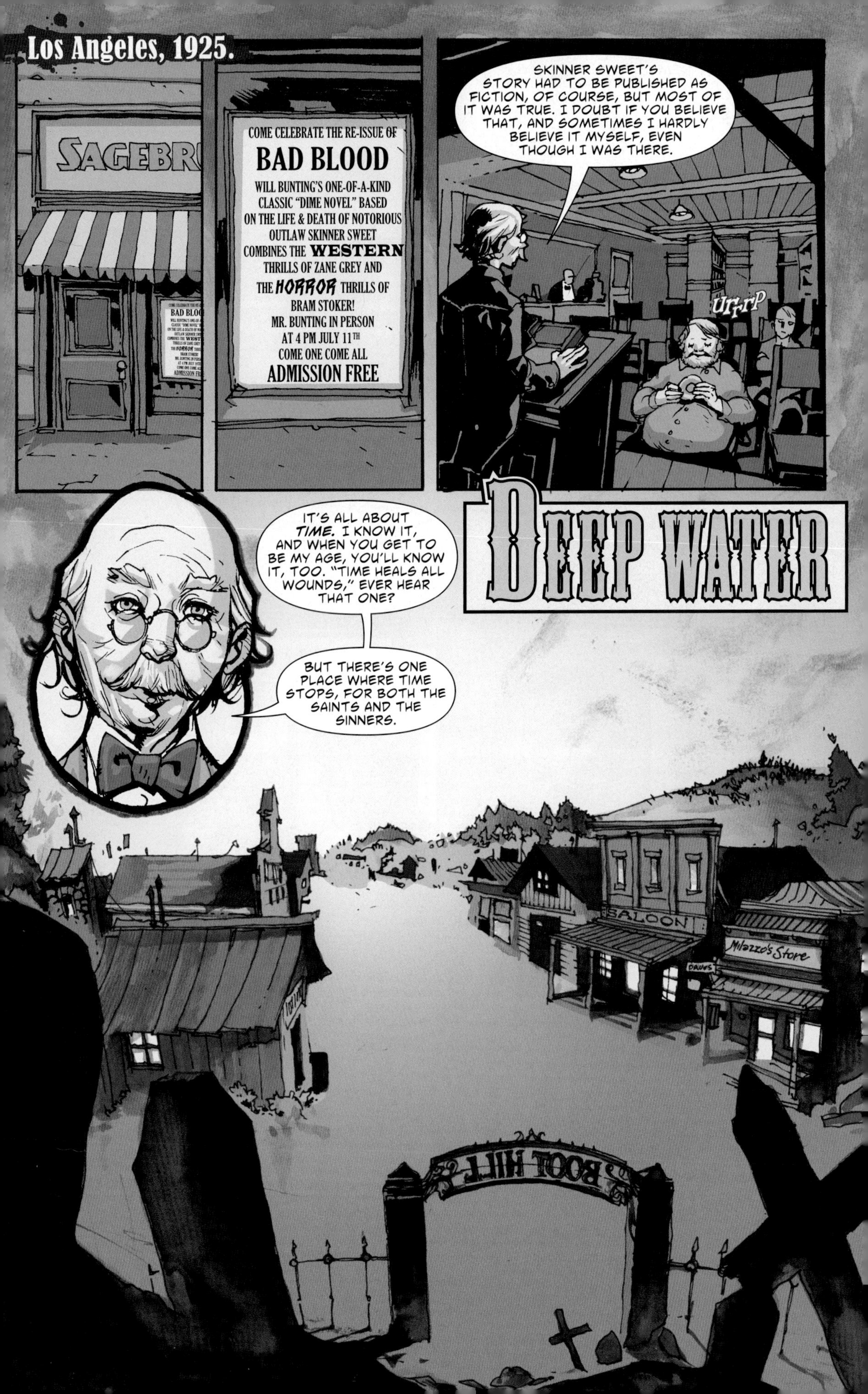

Los Angeles, 1925.
SAGEBRU
COME CELEBRATE THE RE-ISSUE OF BAD BLOOD WILL BUNTING'S ONE-OF-A-KIND CLASSIC "DIME NOVEL" BASED ON THE LIFE & DEATH OF NOTORIOUS OUTLAW SKINNER SWEET COMBINES THE WESTERN THRILLS OF ZANE GREY AND THE HORROR THRILLS OF BRAM STOKER! MR. BUNTING IN PERSON AT 4 PM JULY 11TH COME ONE COME ALL ADMISSION FREE
SKINNER SWEET'S STORY HAD TO BE PUBLISHED AS FICTION, OF COURSE, BUT MOST OF IT WAS TRUE. I DOUBT IF YOU BELIEVE THAT, AND SOMETIMES I HARDLY BELIEVE IT MYSELF, EVEN THOUGH I WAS THERE.
URrrP
DEEP WATER
IT'S ALL ABOUT TIME. I KNOW IT, AND WHEN YOU GET TO BE MY AGE, YOU'LL KNOW IT, TOO. "TIME HEALS ALL WOUNDS," EVER HEAR THAT ONE?
BUT THERE'S ONE PLACE WHERE TIME STOPS, FOR BOTH THE SAINTS AND THE SINNERS.
SALOON
Milazzo's Store
BOOT HILL

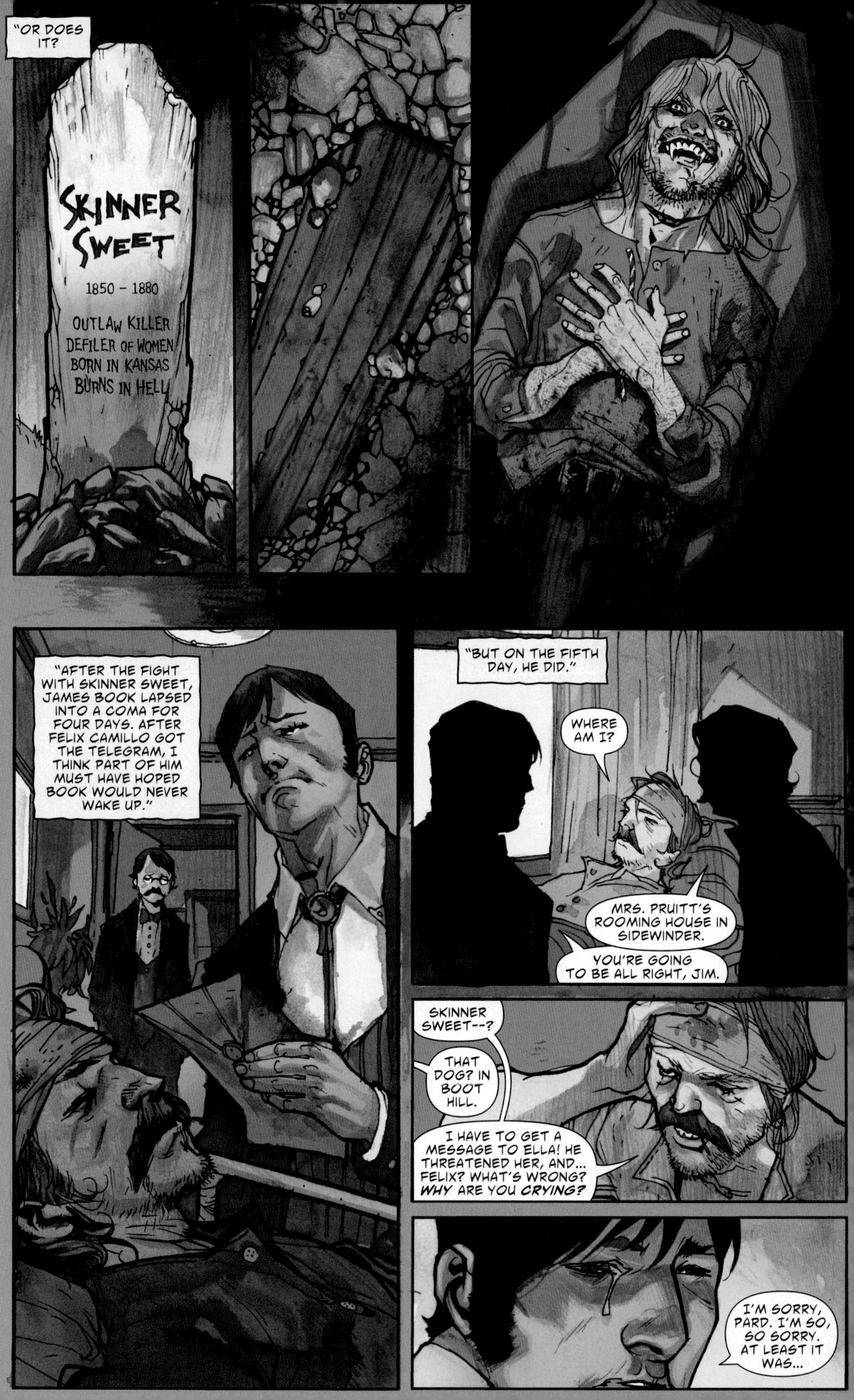
"OR DOES IT?
SKINNER SWEET
1850 – 1880
OUTLAW KILLER
DEFILER OF WOMEN
BORN IN KANSAS
BURNS IN HELL
"AFTER THE FIGHT WITH SKINNER SWEET, JAMES BOOK LAPSED INTO A COMA FOR FOUR DAYS. AFTER FELIX CAMILLO GOT THE TELEGRAM, I THINK PART OF HIM MUST HAVE HOPED BOOK WOULD NEVER WAKE UP."
"BUT ON THE FIFTH DAY, HE DID."
WHERE AM I?
MRS. PRUITT'S ROOMING HOUSE IN SIDEWINDER.
YOU'RE GOING TO BE ALL RIGHT, JIM.
SKINNER SWEET--?
THAT DOG? IN BOOT HILL.
I HAVE TO GET A MESSAGE TO ELLA! HE THREATENED HER, AND... FELIX? WHAT'S WRONG? *WHY* ARE YOU *CRYING*?
I'M SORRY, PARD. I'M SO, SO SORRY. AT LEAST IT WAS...

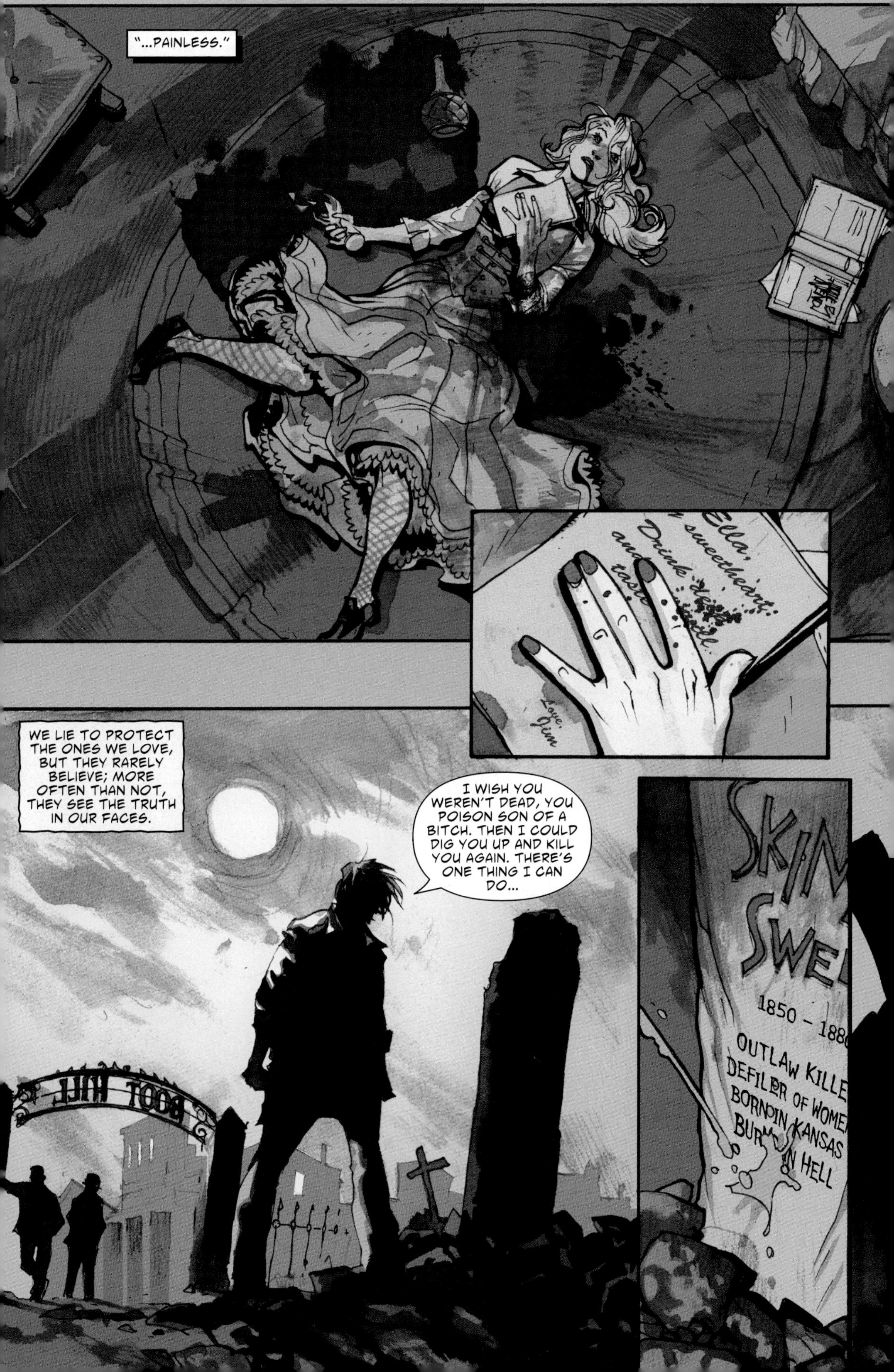
"...PAINLESS."
Love, Jim
WE LIE TO PROTECT THE ONES WE LOVE, BUT THEY RARELY BELIEVE; MORE OFTEN THAN NOT, THEY SEE THE TRUTH IN OUR FACES.
I WISH YOU WEREN'T DEAD, YOU POISON SON OF A BITCH. THEN I COULD DIG YOU UP AND KILL YOU AGAIN. THERE'S ONE THING I CAN DO...
DEFILER OF WOMEN
BORN IN KANSAS
HELL

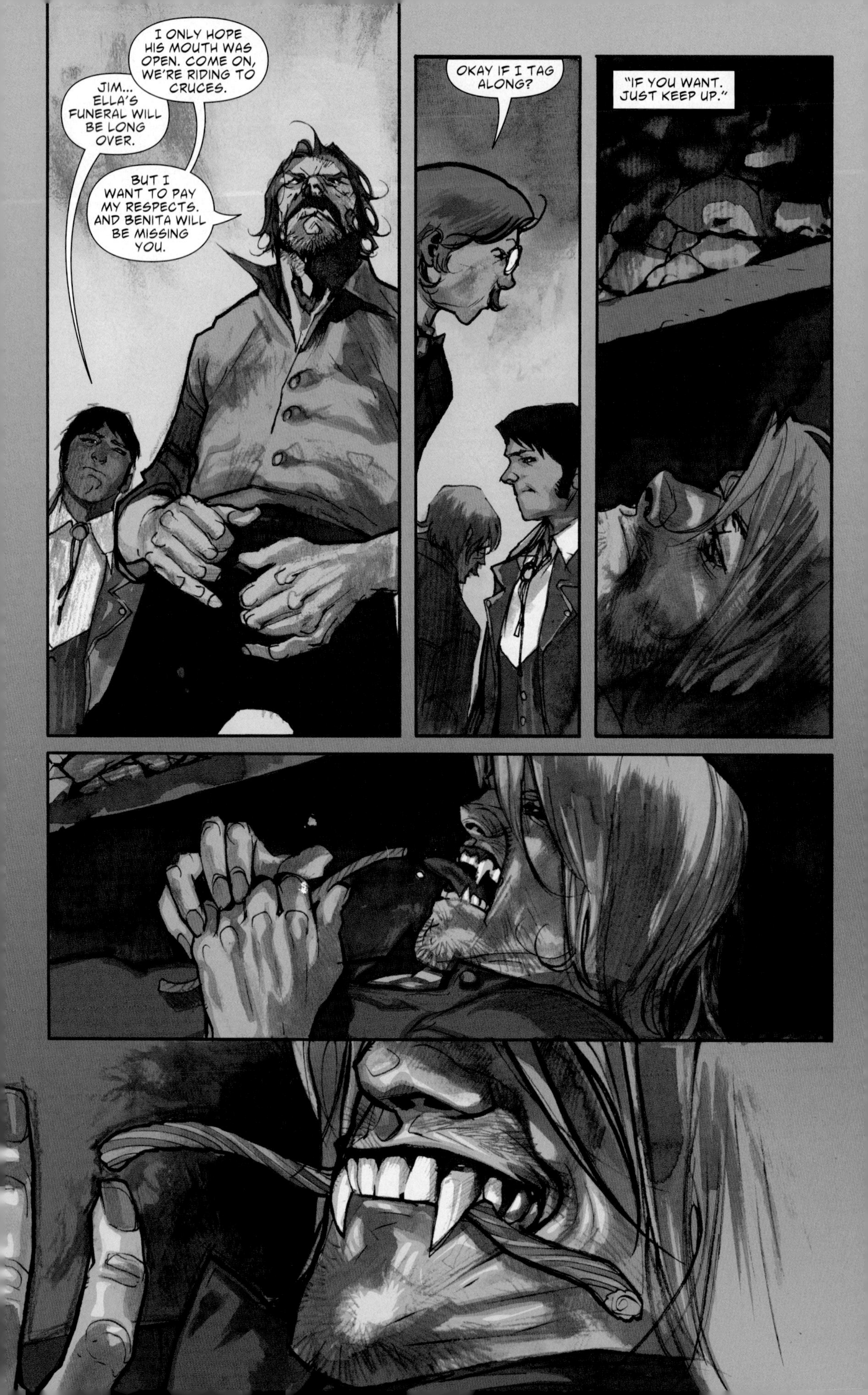

JIM... ELLA'S FUNERAL WILL BE LONG OVER.
I ONLY HOPE HIS MOUTH WAS OPEN. COME ON, WE'RE RIDING TO CRUCES.
BUT I WANT TO PAY MY RESPECTS. AND BENITA WILL BE MISSING YOU.
OKAY IF I TAG ALONG?
"IF YOU WANT. JUST KEEP UP."

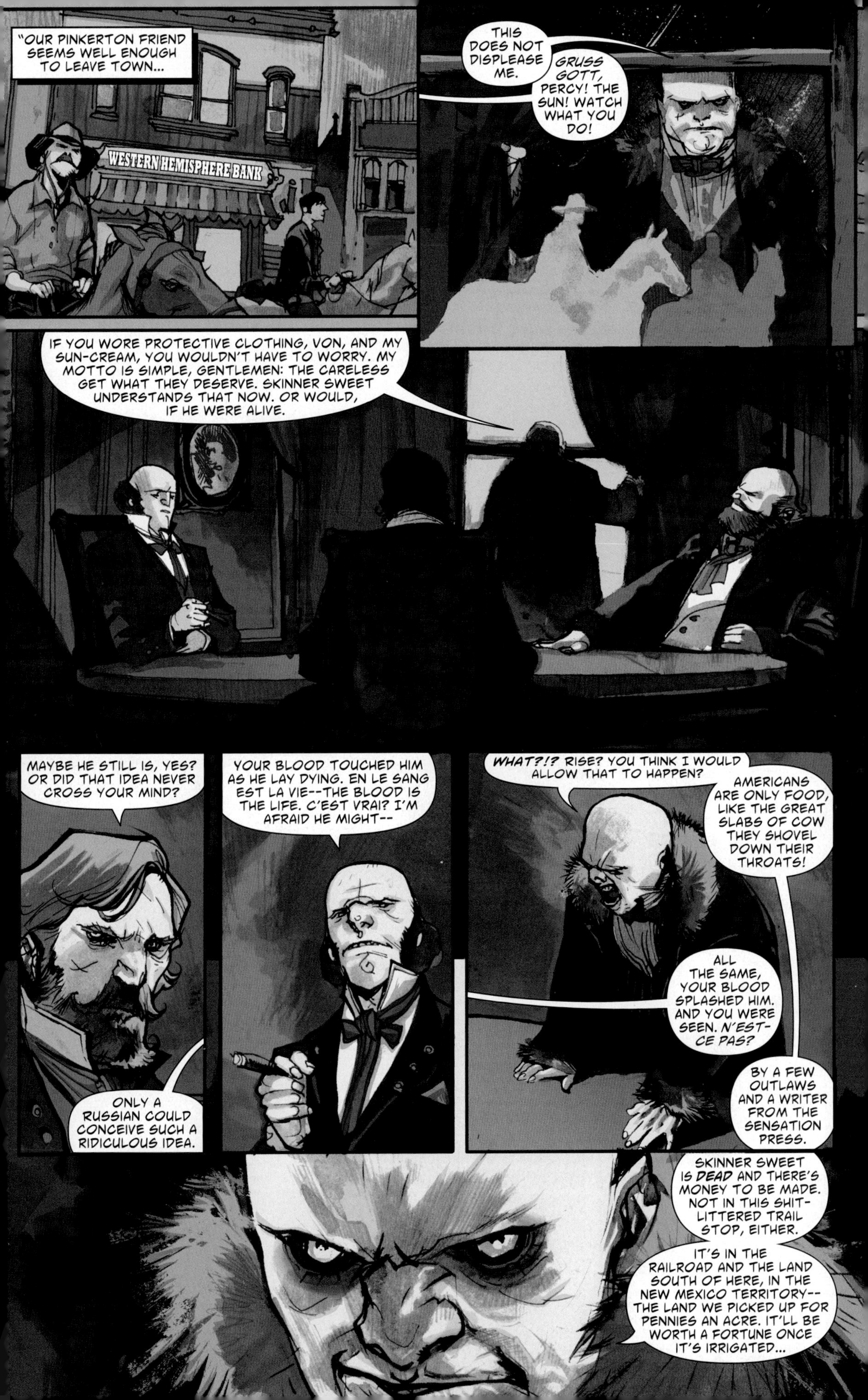

"OUR PINKERTON FRIEND SEEMS WELL ENOUGH TO LEAVE TOWN...
WESTERN HEMISPHERE BANK
THIS DOES NOT DISPLEASE ME.
GRUSS GOTT, PERCY! THE SUN! WATCH WHAT YOU DO!
IF YOU WORE PROTECTIVE CLOTHING, VON, AND MY SUN-CREAM, YOU WOULDN'T HAVE TO WORRY. MY MOTTO IS SIMPLE, GENTLEMEN: THE CARELESS GET WHAT THEY DESERVE. SKINNER SWEET UNDERSTANDS THAT NOW. OR WOULD, IF HE WERE ALIVE.
MAYBE HE STILL IS, YES? OR DID THAT IDEA NEVER CROSS YOUR MIND?
ONLY A RUSSIAN COULD CONCEIVE SUCH A RIDICULOUS IDEA.
YOUR BLOOD TOUCHED HIM AS HE LAY DYING. EN LE SANG EST LA VIE--THE BLOOD IS THE LIFE. C'EST VRAI? I'M AFRAID HE MIGHT--
WHAT?!? RISE? YOU THINK I WOULD ALLOW THAT TO HAPPEN?
AMERICANS ARE ONLY FOOD, LIKE THE GREAT SLABS OF COW THEY SHOVEL DOWN THEIR THROATS!
ALL THE SAME, YOUR BLOOD SPLASHED HIM. AND YOU WERE SEEN. *N'EST-CE PAS?*
BY A FEW OUTLAWS AND A WRITER FROM THE SENSATION PRESS.
SKINNER SWEET IS *DEAD* AND THERE'S MONEY TO BE MADE. NOT IN THIS SHIT-LITTERED TRAIL STOP, EITHER.
IT'S IN THE RAILROAD AND THE LAND SOUTH OF HERE, IN THE NEW MEXICO TERRITORY--THE LAND WE PICKED UP FOR PENNIES AN ACRE. IT'LL BE WORTH A FORTUNE ONCE IT'S IRRIGATED...

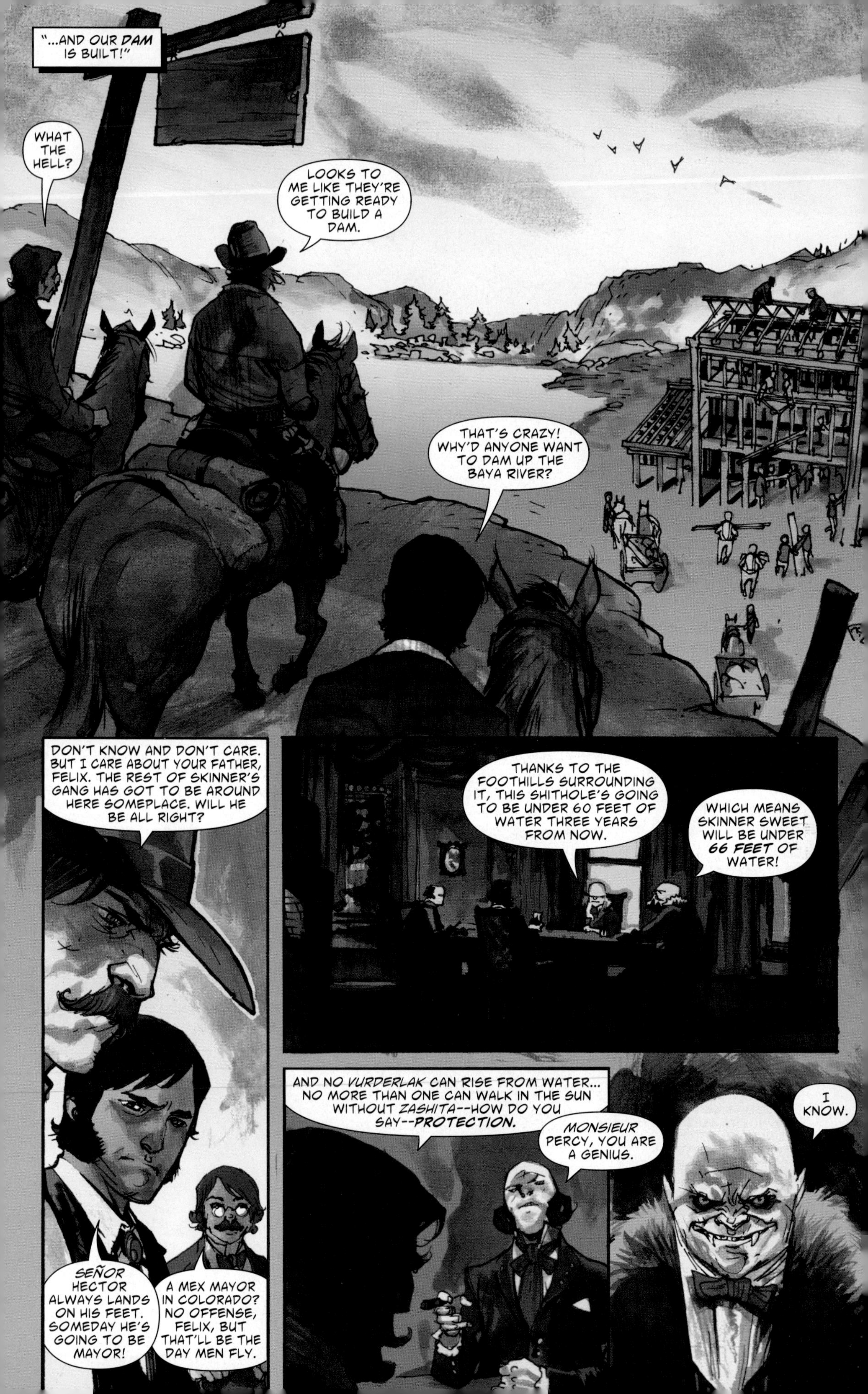
"...AND OUR *DAM* IS BUILT!"
WHAT THE HELL?
LOOKS TO ME LIKE THEY'RE GETTING READY TO BUILD A DAM.
THAT'S CRAZY! WHY'D ANYONE WANT TO DAM UP THE BAYA RIVER?
DON'T KNOW AND DON'T CARE. BUT I CARE ABOUT YOUR FATHER, FELIX. THE REST OF SKINNER'S GANG HAS GOT TO BE AROUND HERE SOMEPLACE. WILL HE BE ALL RIGHT?
SEÑOR HECTOR ALWAYS LANDS ON HIS FEET. SOMEDAY HE'S GOING TO BE MAYOR!
A MEX MAYOR IN COLORADO? NO OFFENSE, FELIX, BUT THAT'LL BE THE DAY MEN FLY.
THANKS TO THE FOOTHILLS SURROUNDING IT, THIS SHITHOLE'S GOING TO BE UNDER 60 FEET OF WATER THREE YEARS FROM NOW.
WHICH MEANS SKINNER SWEET WILL BE UNDER **66 FEET** OF WATER!
AND NO *VURDERLAK* CAN RISE FROM WATER... NO MORE THAN ONE CAN WALK IN THE SUN WITHOUT *ZASHITA*--HOW DO YOU SAY--***PROTECTION.***
MONSIEUR PERCY, YOU ARE A GENIUS.
I KNOW.

TWO DAYS LATER WE WERE IN THE NORTHEAST PART OF THE NEW MEXICO TERRITORY.

A LITTLE TOWN CALLED CRUCES...

"...WITH A GRAVEYARD A LOT NICER THAN SIDEWINDER'S BOOT HILL. BUT A GRAVEYARD IS STILL A *GRAVEYARD*."

ELLA LANGUM

~OVED DAUGHTER

MAY 19, 1855
JULY 19, 1880

~ELY MISSED
~ILL RESURRECT

HE GOING TO BE ALL RIGHT?

IS HE A MAN? SI.

COME ON, AMIGO. LET'S RIDE.

OKAY IF I TAG ALONG?

JUST KEEP UP.

WHERE ARE WE HEADED?

IT TURNED OUT TO BE ARIZONA THAT TIME...BUT THE PLACE WE WERE REALLY HEADED FOR WAS THE 20TH CENTURY. A MAN WITH A BROKEN HEART THINKS DISTANCE WILL CURE HIM, BUT HE'S WRONG.

TIME IS THE ONLY CONSTANT. FOR THE LIVING IT NEVER STOPS...

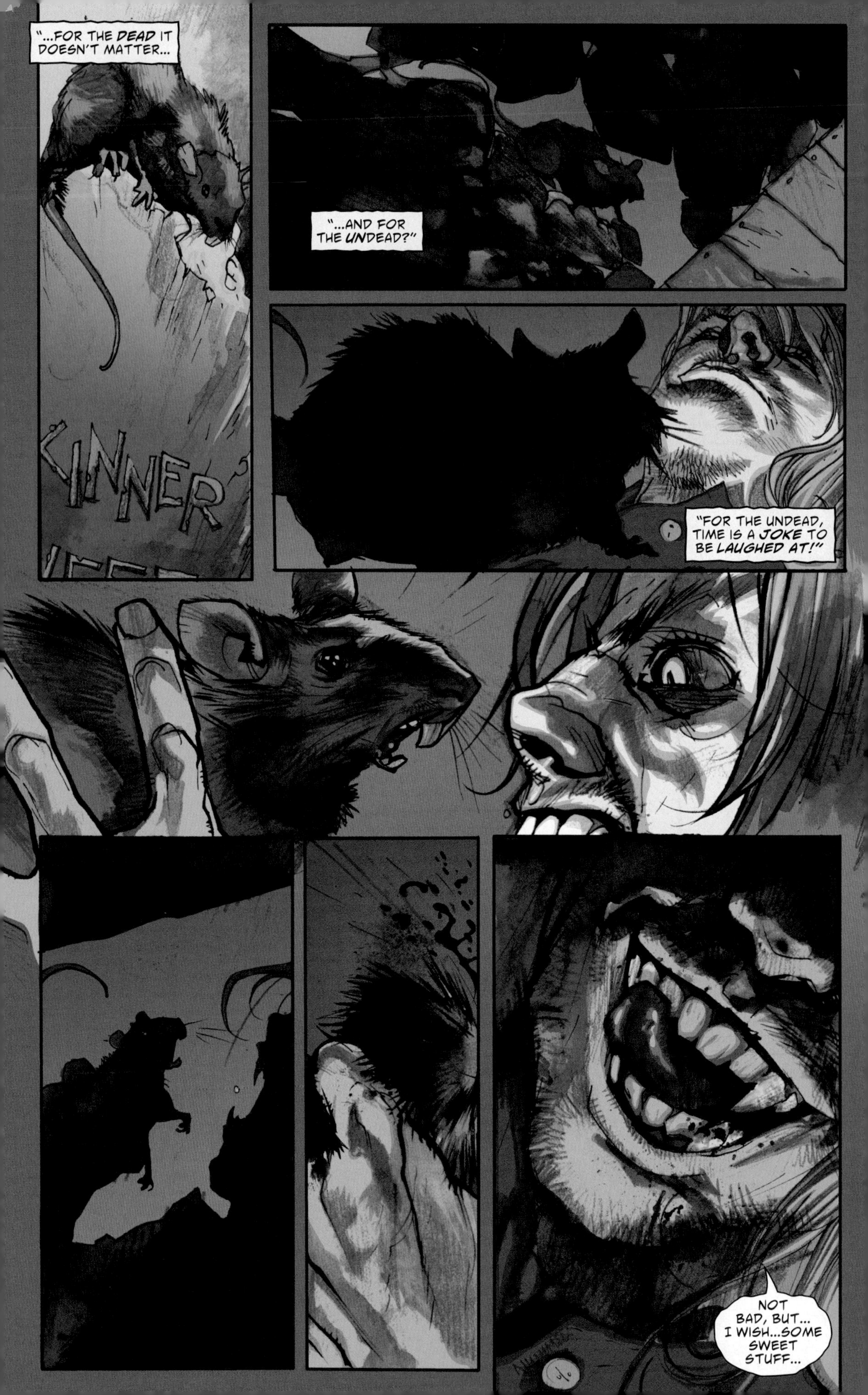
"...FOR THE DEAD IT DOESN'T MATTER...
"...AND FOR THE UNDEAD?"
"FOR THE UNDEAD, TIME IS A JOKE TO BE LAUGHED AT!"
NOT BAD, BUT... I WISH...SOME SWEET STUFF...

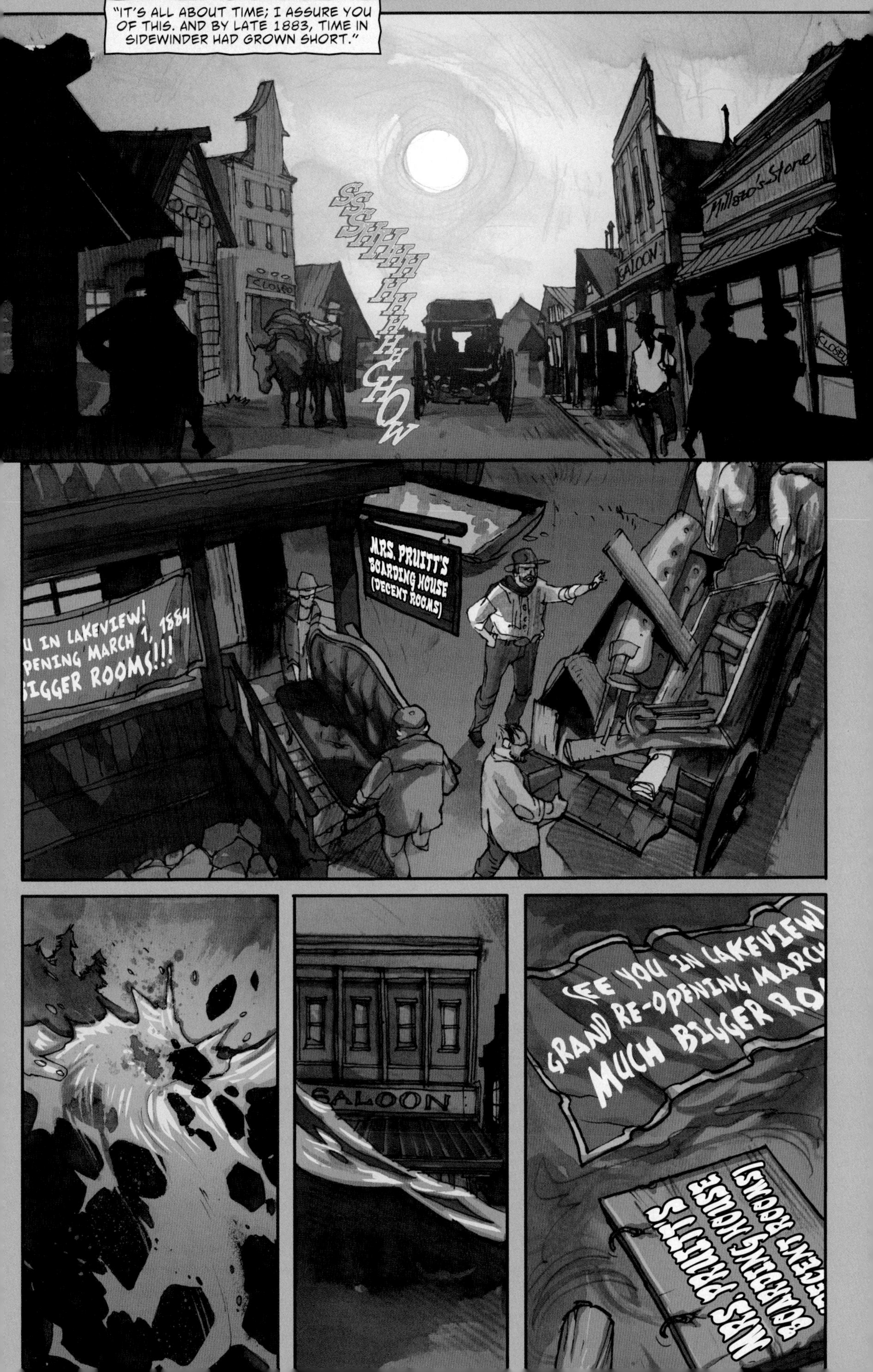
"IT'S ALL ABOUT TIME; I ASSURE YOU OF THIS. AND BY LATE 1883, TIME IN SIDEWINDER HAD GROWN SHORT."
SSSHHHHHHHCHOW
CLOSED
SALOON
CLOSED
MRS. PRUITT'S BOARDING HOUSE (DECENT ROOMS)
U IN LAKEVIEW! PENING MARCH 1, 1884 BIGGER ROOMS!!!
SALOON
SEE YOU IN LAKEVIEW! GRAND RE-OPENING MARCH MUCH BIGGER RO

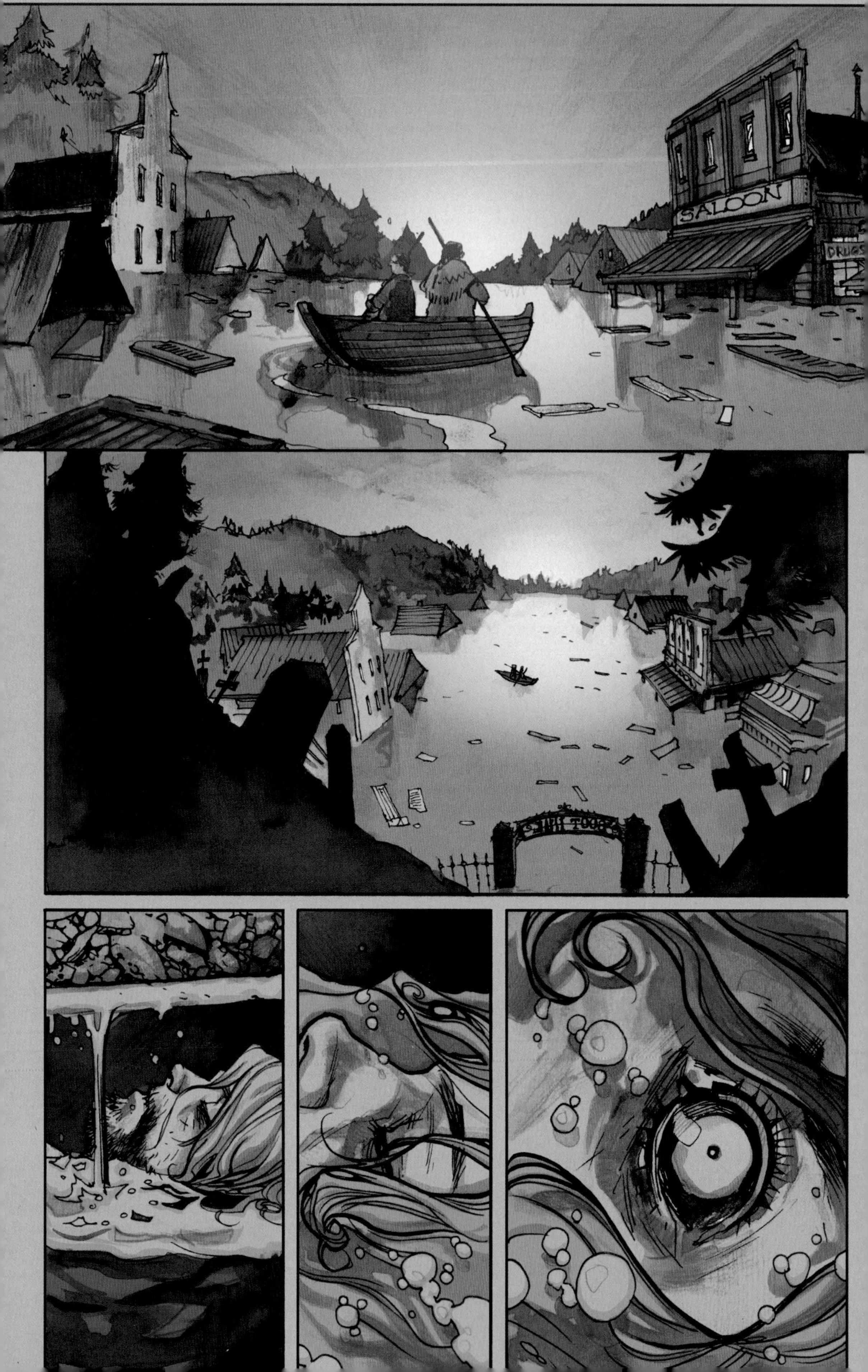
SALOON
DRUGS

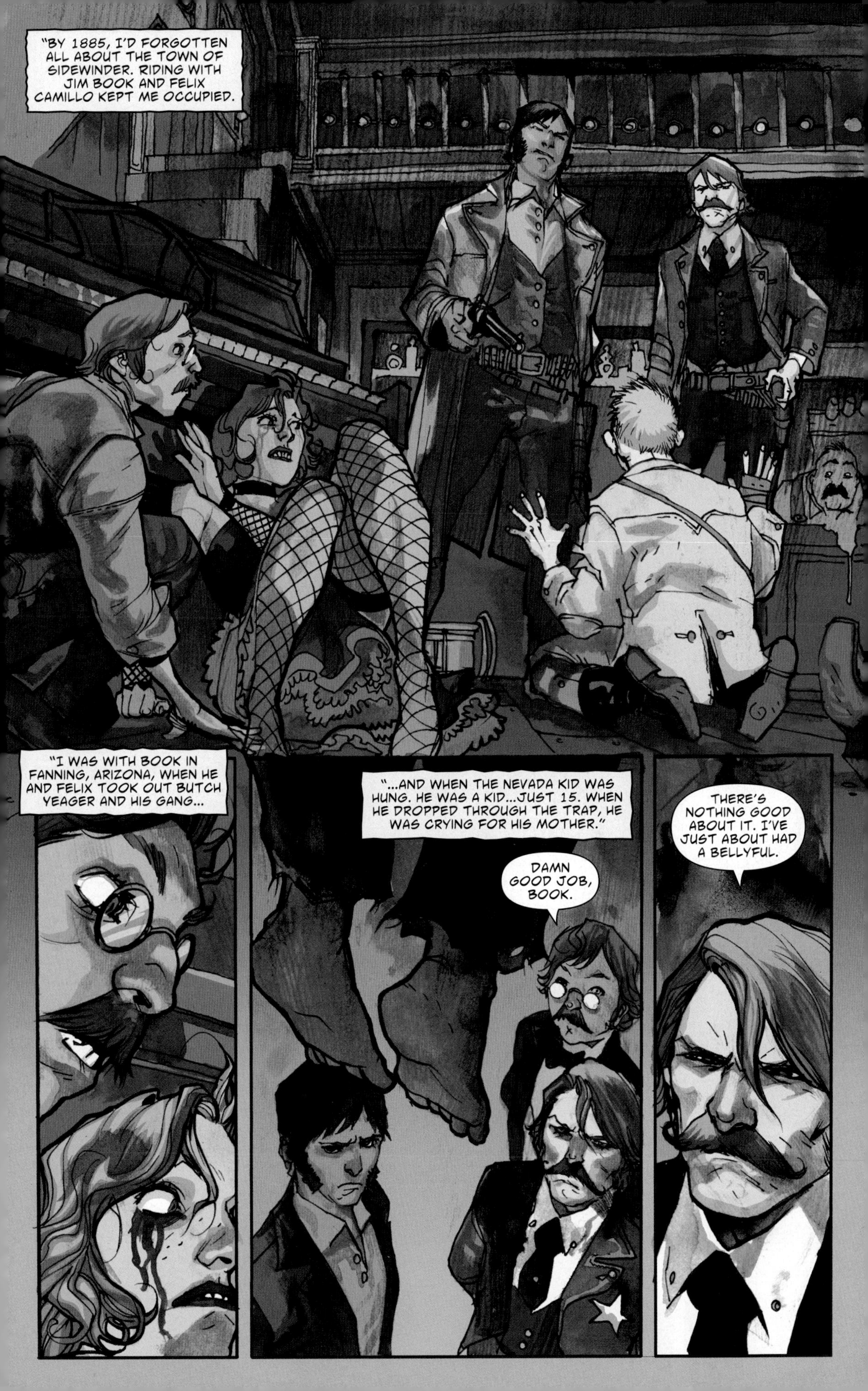
"BY 1885, I'D FORGOTTEN ALL ABOUT THE TOWN OF SIDEWINDER. RIDING WITH JIM BOOK AND FELIX CAMILLO KEPT ME OCCUPIED.
"I WAS WITH BOOK IN FANNING, ARIZONA, WHEN HE AND FELIX TOOK OUT BUTCH YEAGER AND HIS GANG...
"...AND WHEN THE NEVADA KID WAS HUNG. HE WAS A KID...JUST 15. WHEN HE DROPPED THROUGH THE TRAP, HE WAS CRYING FOR HIS MOTHER."
DAMN GOOD JOB, BOOK.
THERE'S NOTHING GOOD ABOUT IT. I'VE JUST ABOUT HAD A BELLYFUL.

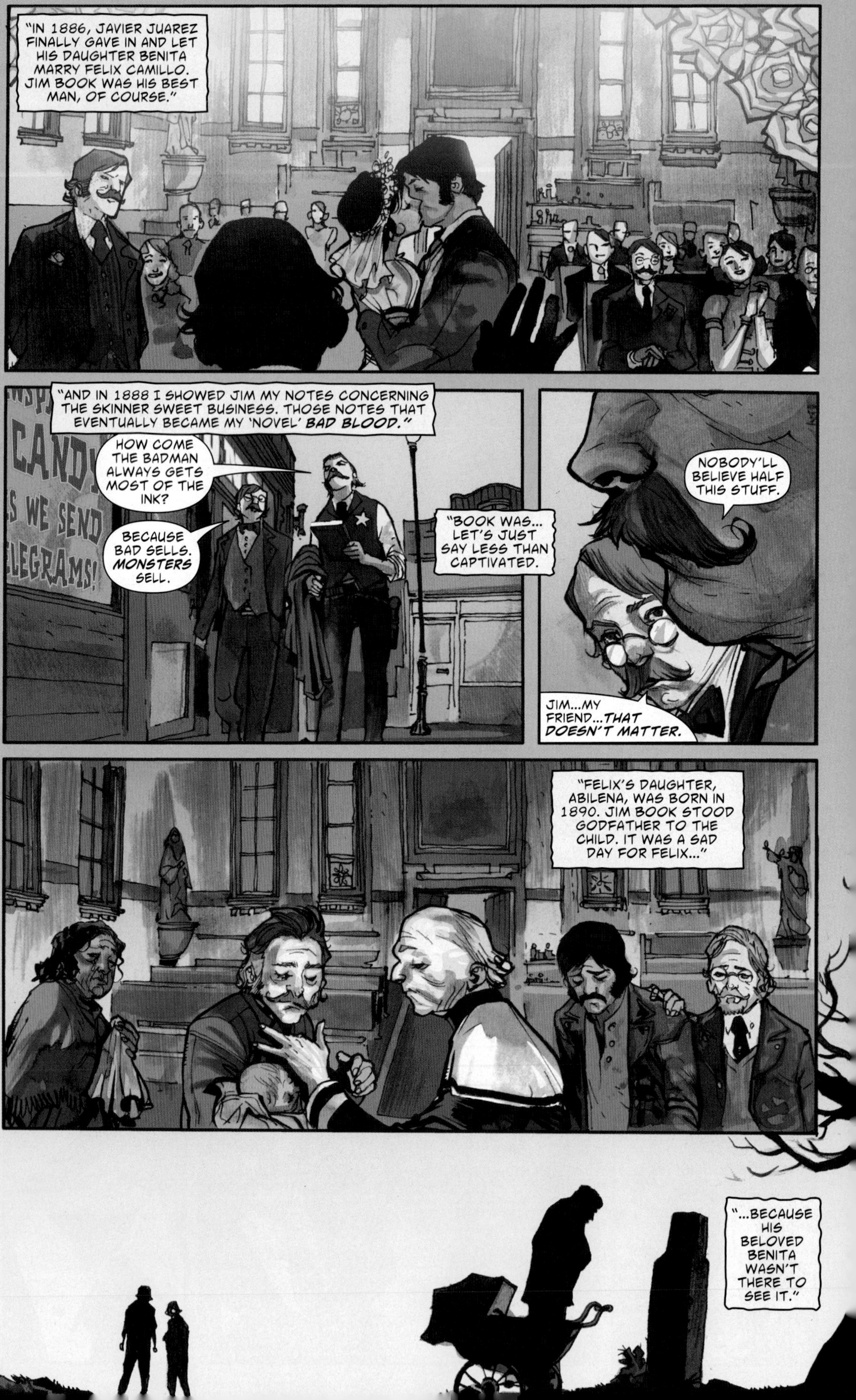
"IN 1886, JAVIER JUAREZ FINALLY GAVE IN AND LET HIS DAUGHTER BENITA MARRY FELIX CAMILLO. JIM BOOK WAS HIS BEST MAN, OF COURSE."
"AND IN 1888 I SHOWED JIM MY NOTES CONCERNING THE SKINNER SWEET BUSINESS. THOSE NOTES THAT EVENTUALLY BECAME MY 'NOVEL' *BAD BLOOD.*"
CANDY
S WE SEND
LEGRAMS!
HOW COME THE BADMAN ALWAYS GETS MOST OF THE INK?
BECAUSE BAD SELLS. *MONSTERS* SELL.
"BOOK WAS... LET'S JUST SAY LESS THAN CAPTIVATED.
NOBODY'LL BELIEVE HALF THIS STUFF.
JIM...MY FRIEND...*THAT DOESN'T MATTER.*
"FELIX'S DAUGHTER, ABILENA, WAS BORN IN 1890. JIM BOOK STOOD GODFATHER TO THE CHILD. IT WAS A SAD DAY FOR FELIX..."
"...BECAUSE HIS BELOVED BENITA WASN'T THERE TO SEE IT."

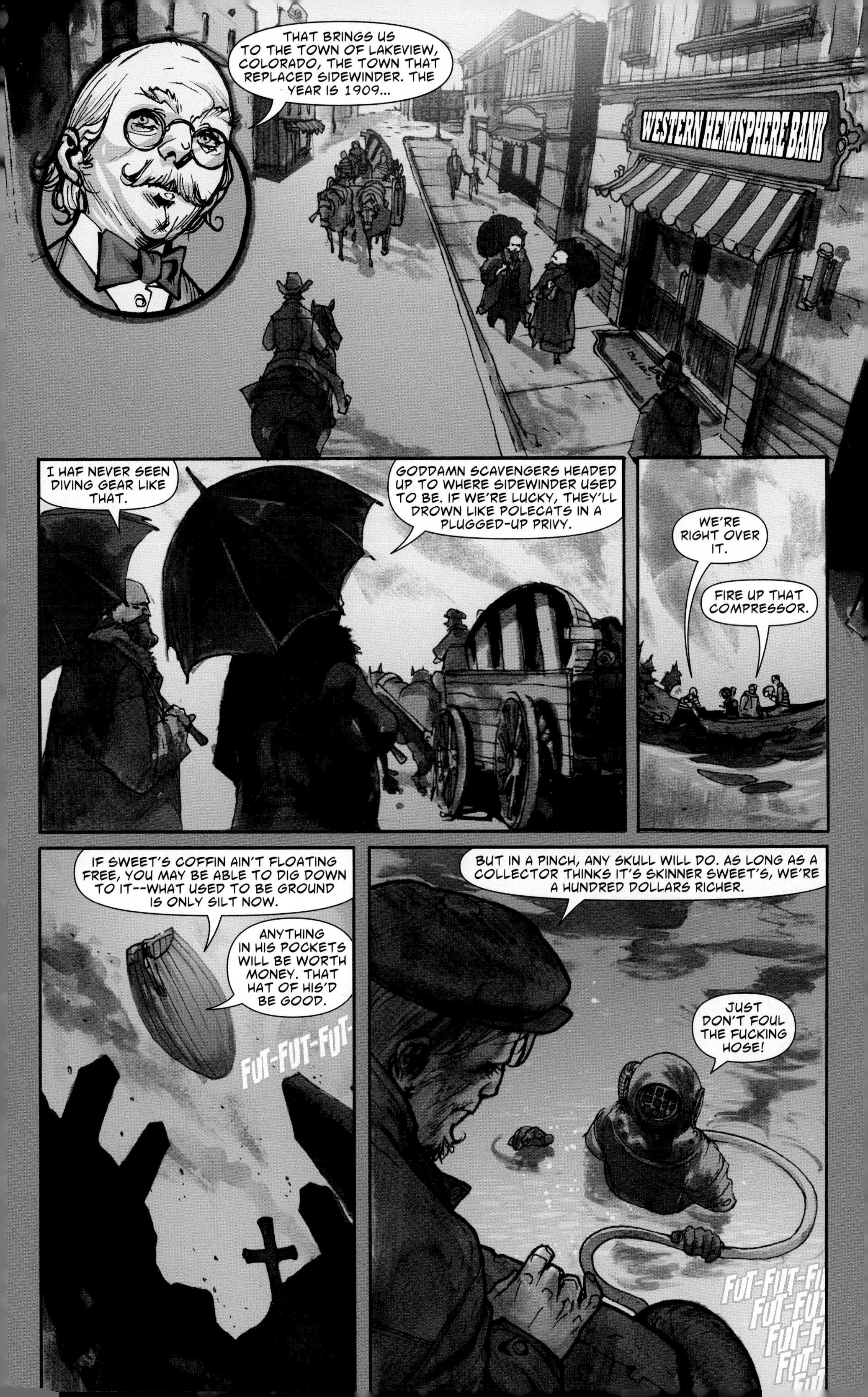
THAT BRINGS US TO THE TOWN OF LAKEVIEW, COLORADO, THE TOWN THAT REPLACED SIDEWINDER. THE YEAR IS 1909...
WESTERN HEMISPHERE BANK
I HAF NEVER SEEN DIVING GEAR LIKE THAT.
GODDAMN SCAVENGERS HEADED UP TO WHERE SIDEWINDER USED TO BE. IF WE'RE LUCKY, THEY'LL DROWN LIKE POLECATS IN A PLUGGED-UP PRIVY.
WE'RE RIGHT OVER IT.
FIRE UP THAT COMPRESSOR.
IF SWEET'S COFFIN AIN'T FLOATING FREE, YOU MAY BE ABLE TO DIG DOWN TO IT--WHAT USED TO BE GROUND IS ONLY SILT NOW.
ANYTHING IN HIS POCKETS WILL BE WORTH MONEY. THAT HAT OF HIS'D BE GOOD.
FUT-FUT-FUT-
BUT IN A PINCH, ANY SKULL WILL DO. AS LONG AS A COLLECTOR THINKS IT'S SKINNER SWEET'S, WE'RE A HUNDRED DOLLARS RICHER.
JUST DON'T FOUL THE FUCKING HOSE!
FUT-FUT-FU
FUT-FU
FUT-F
FUT-

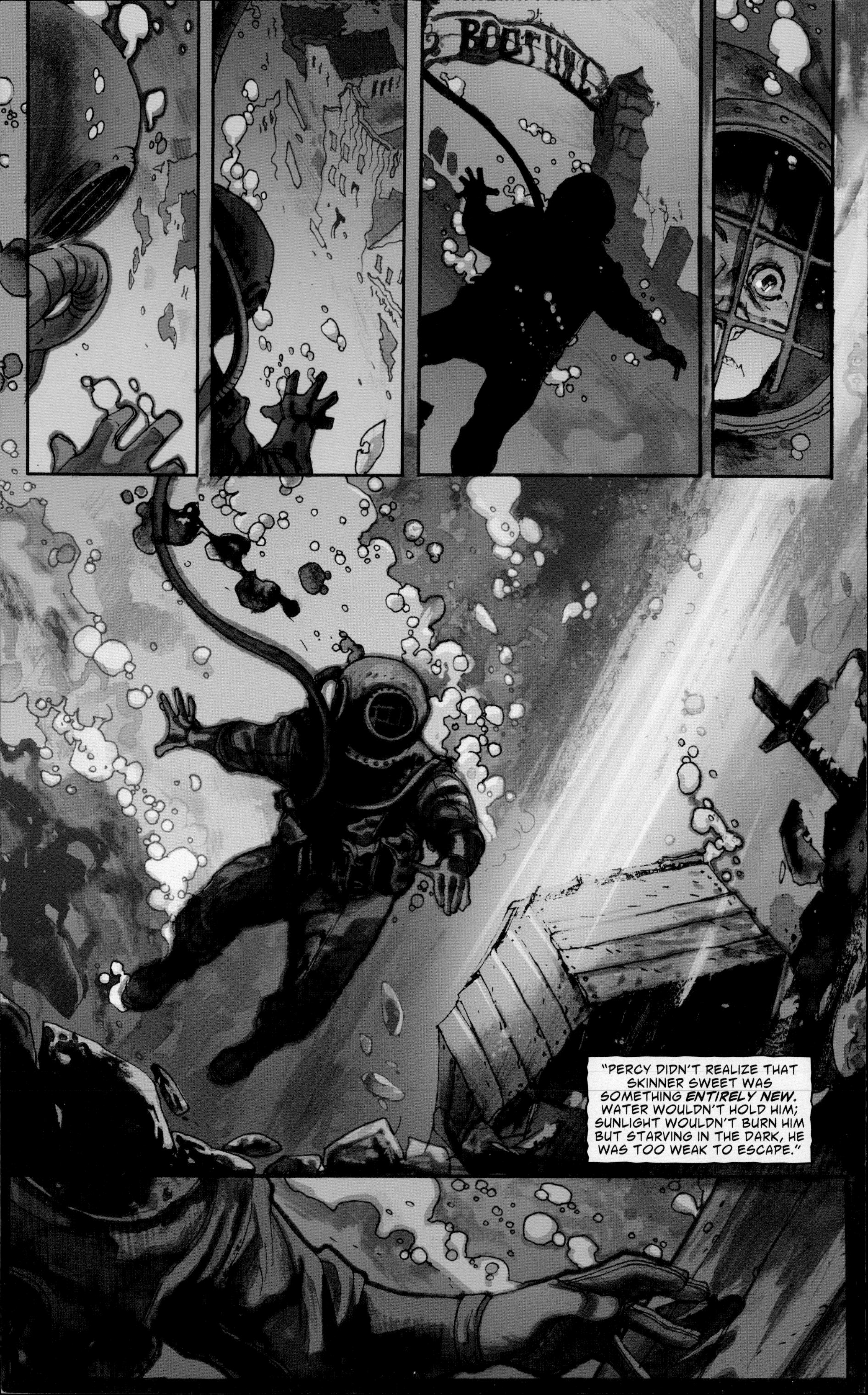
BOOT HILL
"PERCY DIDN'T REALIZE THAT SKINNER SWEET WAS SOMETHING **ENTIRELY NEW.** WATER WOULDN'T HOLD HIM; SUNLIGHT WOULDN'T BURN HIM BUT STARVING IN THE DARK, HE WAS TOO WEAK TO ESCAPE."

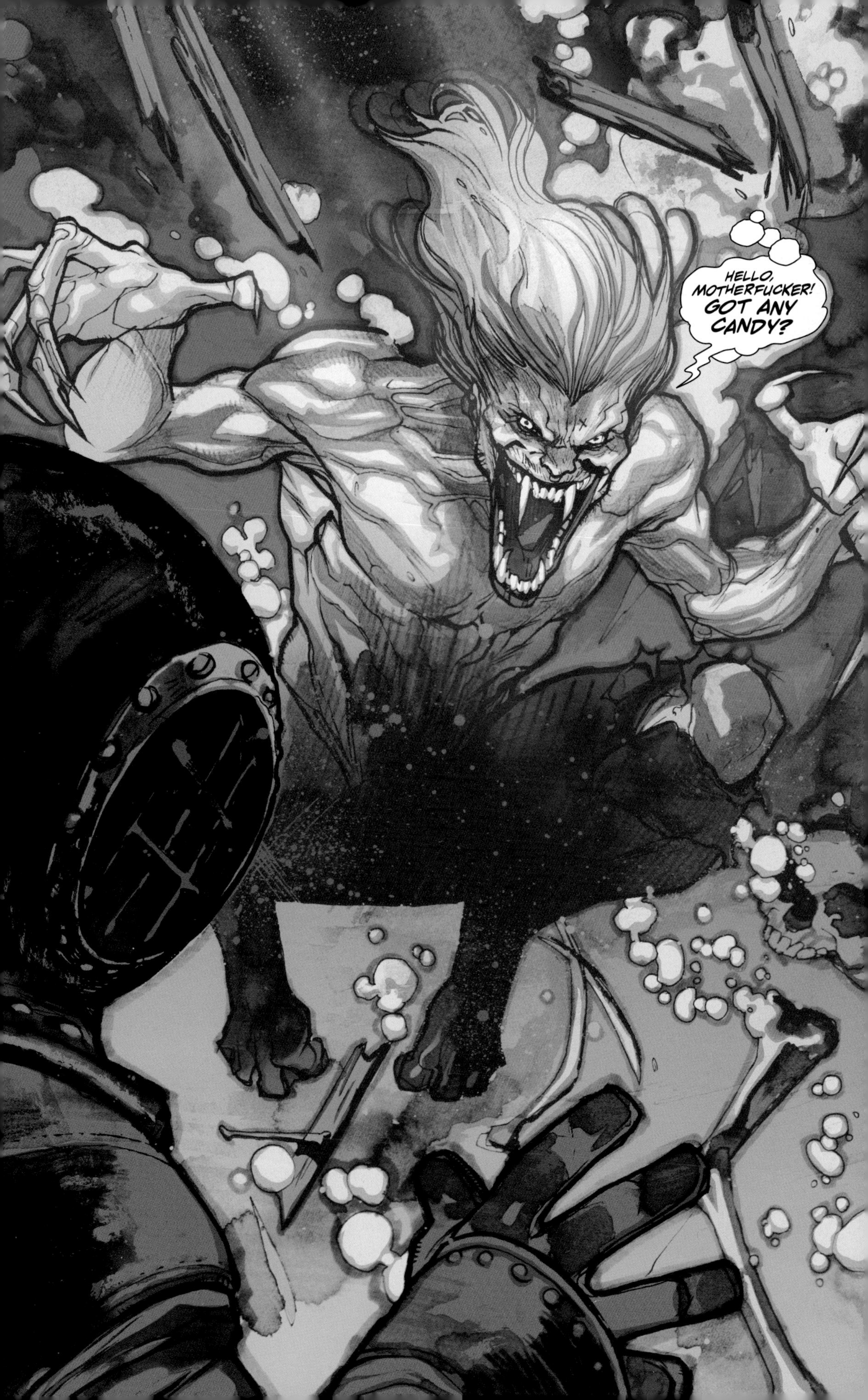
HELLO, MOTHERFUCKER! GOT ANY CANDY?

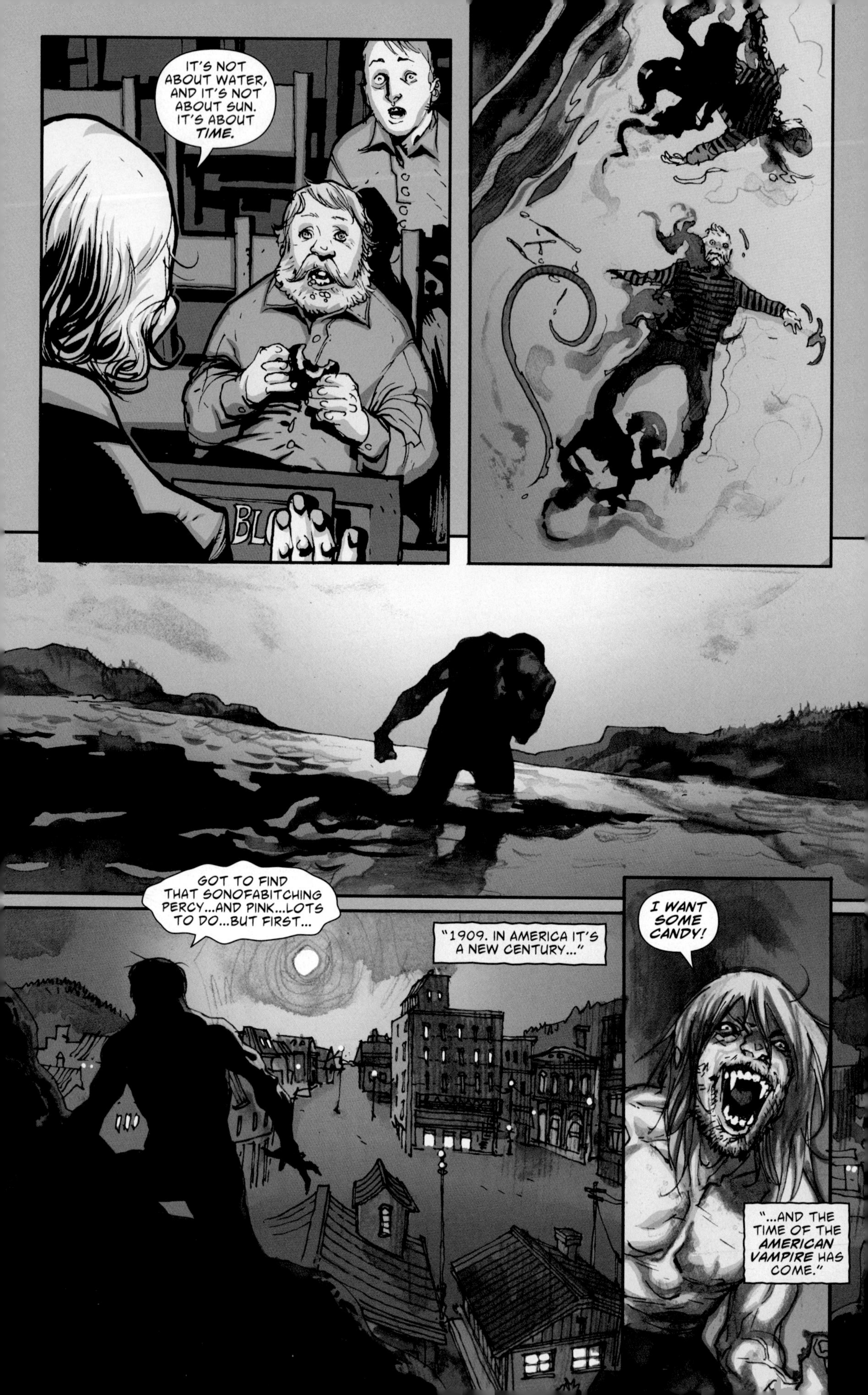
IT'S NOT ABOUT WATER, AND IT'S NOT ABOUT SUN. IT'S ABOUT *TIME.*
BL
GOT TO FIND THAT SONOFABITCHING PERCY...AND PINK...LOTS TO DO...BUT FIRST...
"1909. IN AMERICA IT'S A NEW CENTURY..."
I WANT SOME CANDY!
"...AND THE TIME OF THE *AMERICAN VAMPIRE* HAS COME."

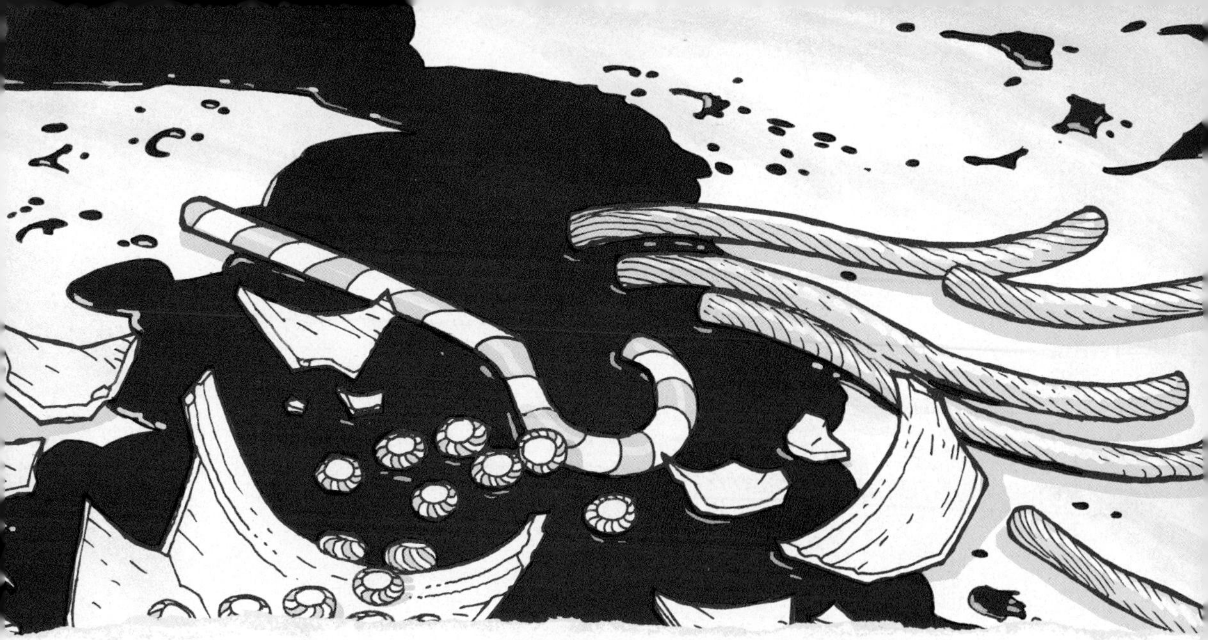

Chapter Three

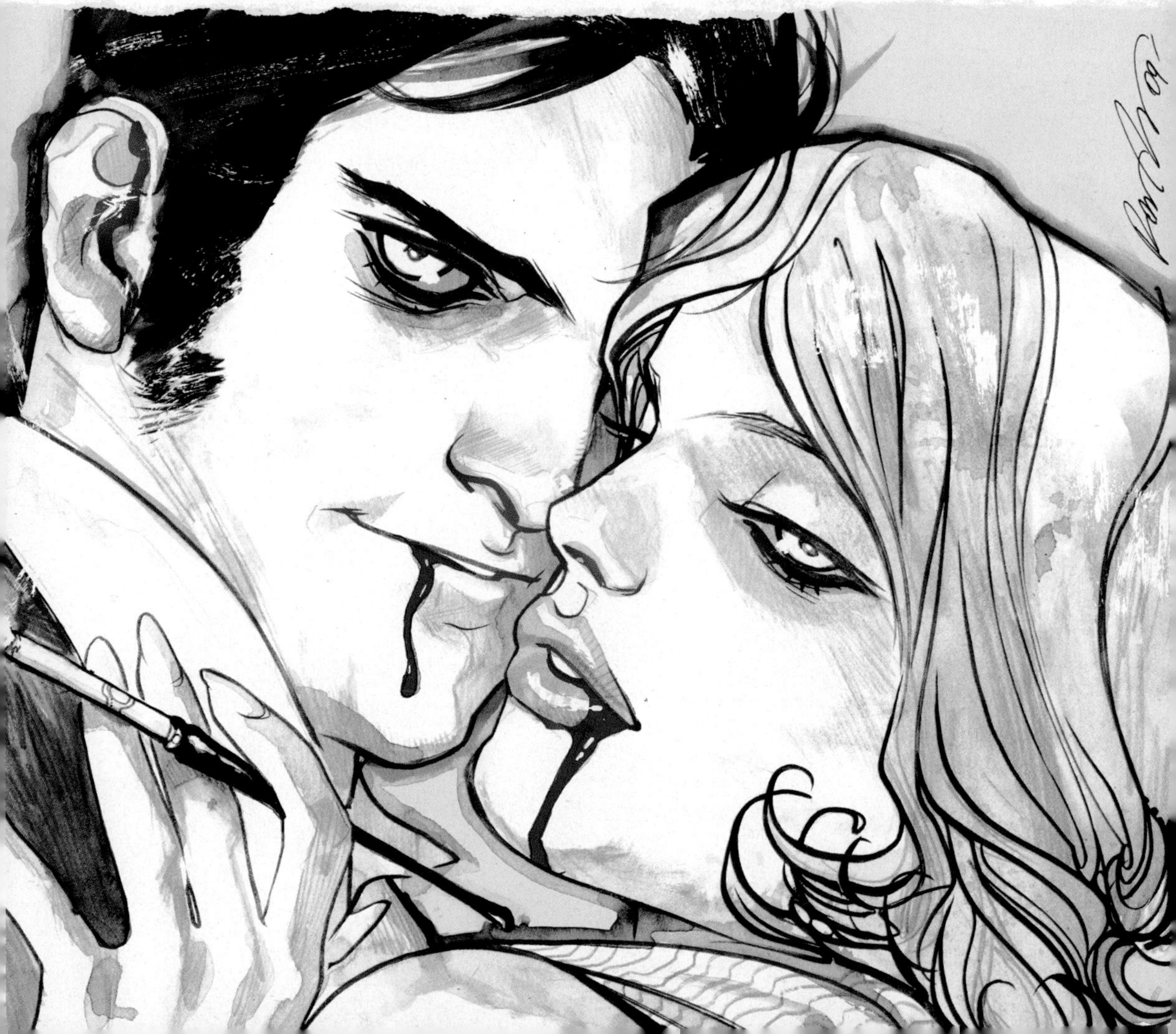

Rough Cut
Scott Snyder <small>Writer</small>

Blood Vengeance
Stephen King <small>Writer</small>

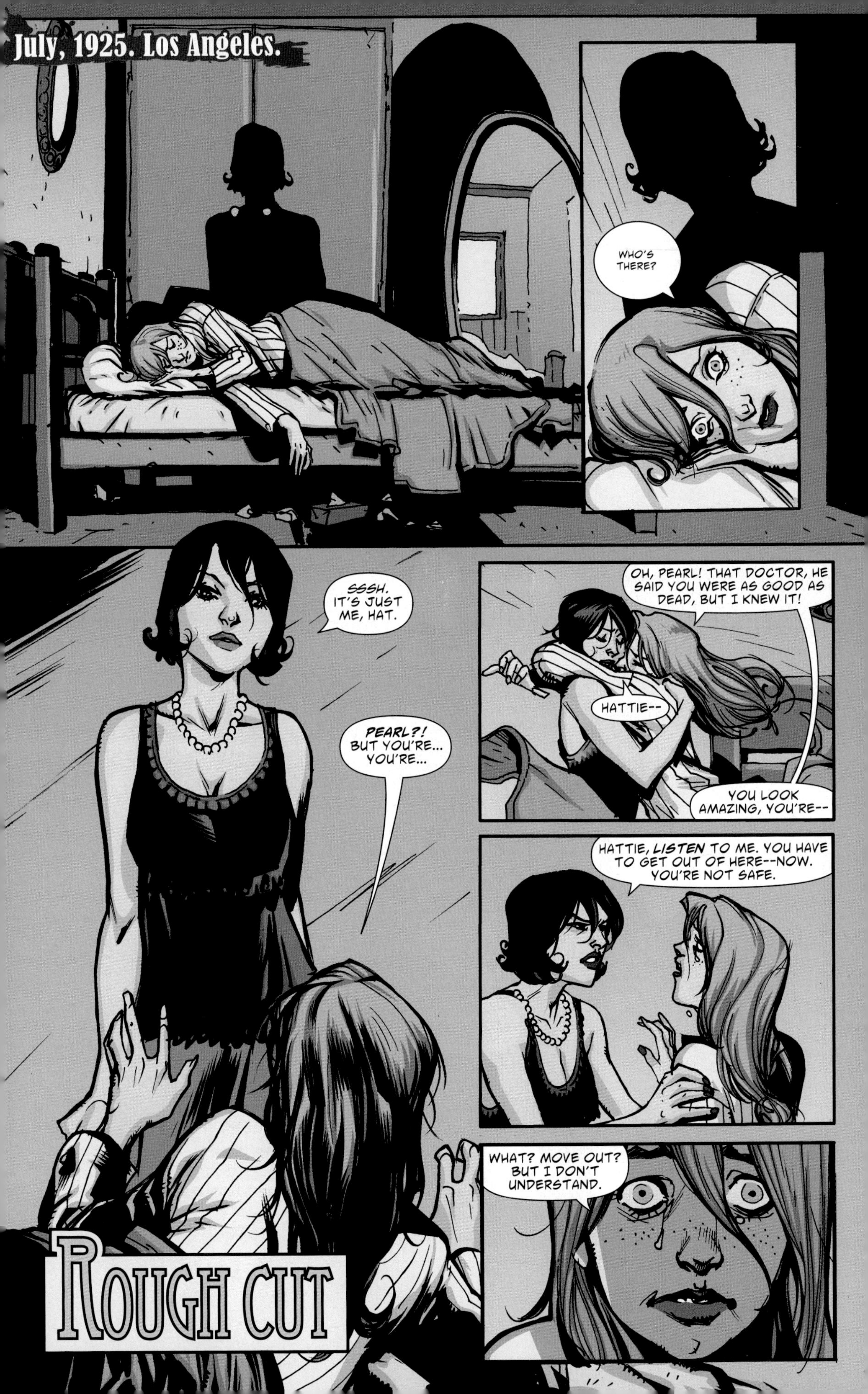
July, 1925. Los Angeles.
WHO'S THERE?
SSSH. IT'S JUST ME, HAT.
PEARL?! BUT YOU'RE... YOU'RE...
ROUGH CUT
OH, PEARL! THAT DOCTOR, HE SAID YOU WERE AS GOOD AS DEAD, BUT I KNEW IT!
HATTIE--
YOU LOOK AMAZING, YOU'RE--
HATTIE, LISTEN TO ME. YOU HAVE TO GET OUT OF HERE--NOW. YOU'RE NOT SAFE.
WHAT? MOVE OUT? BUT I DON'T UNDERSTAND.

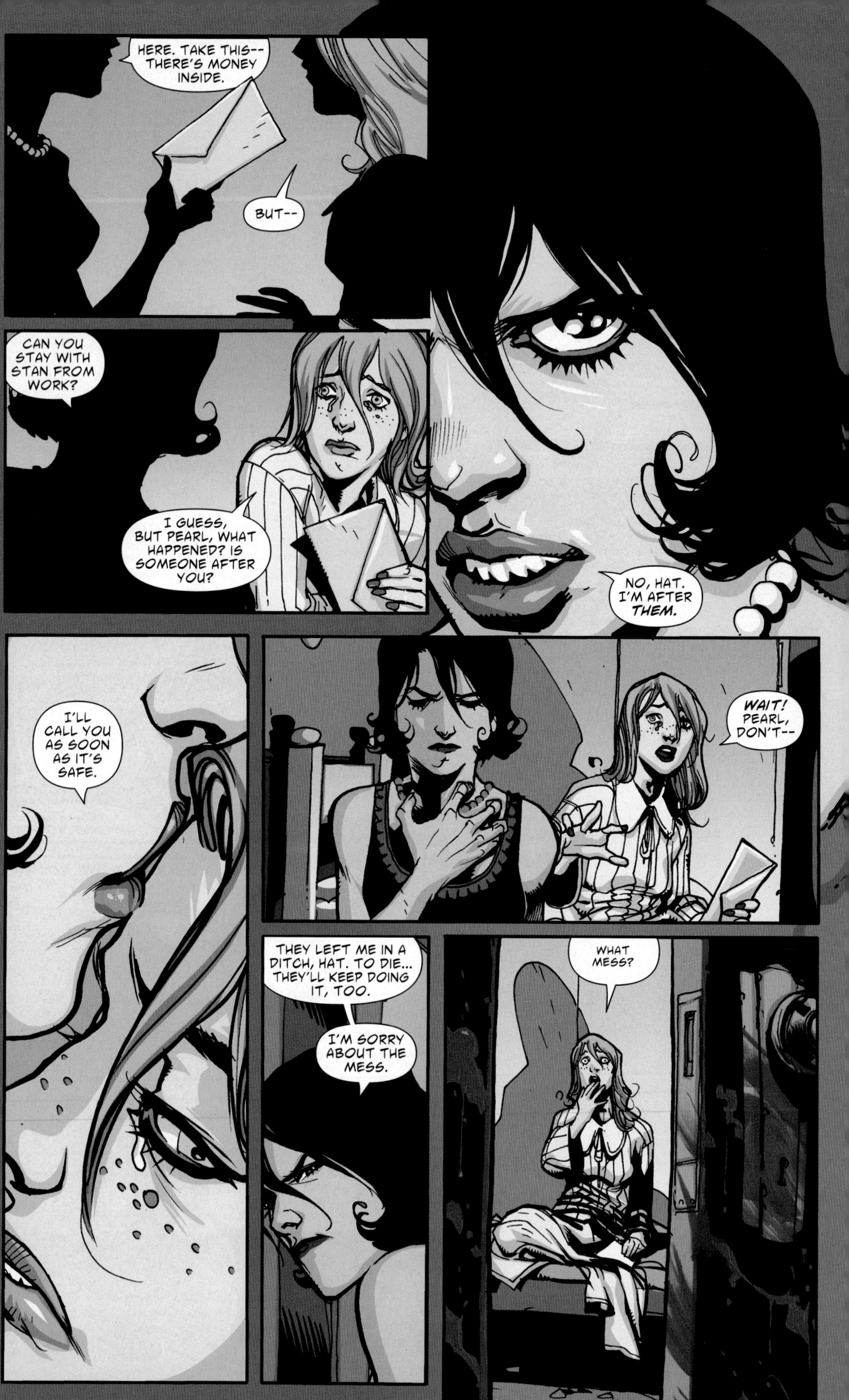
HERE. TAKE THIS-- THERE'S MONEY INSIDE.
BUT--
CAN YOU STAY WITH STAN FROM WORK?
I GUESS, BUT PEARL, WHAT HAPPENED? IS SOMEONE AFTER YOU?
NO, HAT. I'M AFTER *THEM.*
I'LL CALL YOU AS SOON AS IT'S SAFE.
WAIT! PEARL, DON'T--
THEY LEFT ME IN A DITCH, HAT. TO DIE... THEY'LL KEEP DOING IT, TOO.
I'M SORRY ABOUT THE MESS.
WHAT MESS?

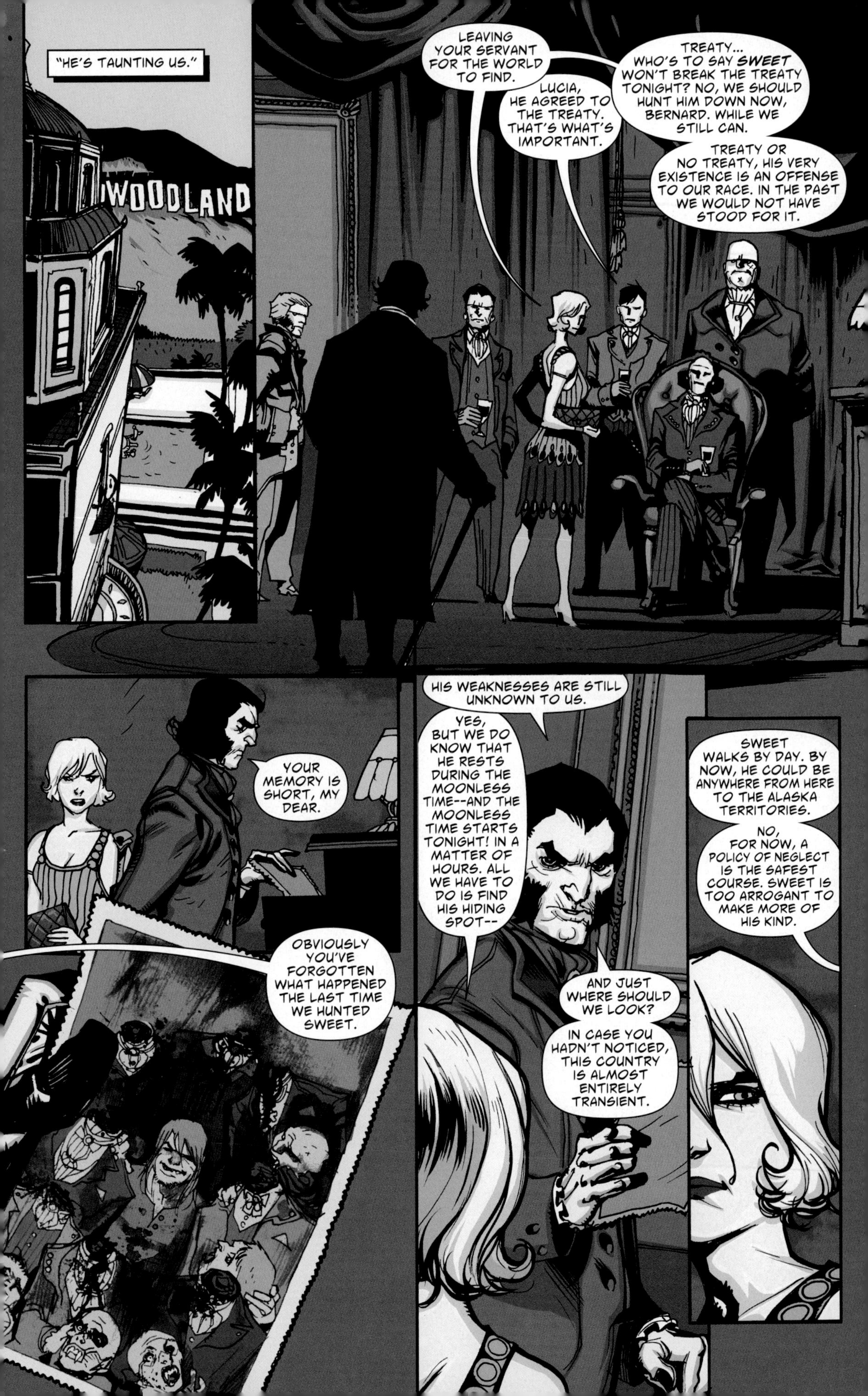
"HE'S TAUNTING US."
WOODLAND
LEAVING YOUR SERVANT FOR THE WORLD TO FIND.
LUCIA, HE AGREED TO THE TREATY. THAT'S WHAT'S IMPORTANT.
TREATY... WHO'S TO SAY SWEET WON'T BREAK THE TREATY TONIGHT? NO, WE SHOULD HUNT HIM DOWN NOW, BERNARD. WHILE WE STILL CAN.
TREATY OR NO TREATY, HIS VERY EXISTENCE IS AN OFFENSE TO OUR RACE. IN THE PAST WE WOULD NOT HAVE STOOD FOR IT.
YOUR MEMORY IS SHORT, MY DEAR.
OBVIOUSLY YOU'VE FORGOTTEN WHAT HAPPENED THE LAST TIME WE HUNTED SWEET.
HIS WEAKNESSES ARE STILL UNKNOWN TO US.
YES, BUT WE DO KNOW THAT HE RESTS DURING THE MOONLESS TIME--AND THE MOONLESS TIME STARTS TONIGHT! IN A MATTER OF HOURS. ALL WE HAVE TO DO IS FIND HIS HIDING SPOT--
AND JUST WHERE SHOULD WE LOOK?
IN CASE YOU HADN'T NOTICED, THIS COUNTRY IS ALMOST ENTIRELY TRANSIENT.
SWEET WALKS BY DAY. BY NOW, HE COULD BE ANYWHERE FROM HERE TO THE ALASKA TERRITORIES.
NO, FOR NOW, A POLICY OF NEGLECT IS THE SAFEST COURSE. SWEET IS TOO ARROGANT TO MAKE MORE OF HIS KIND.

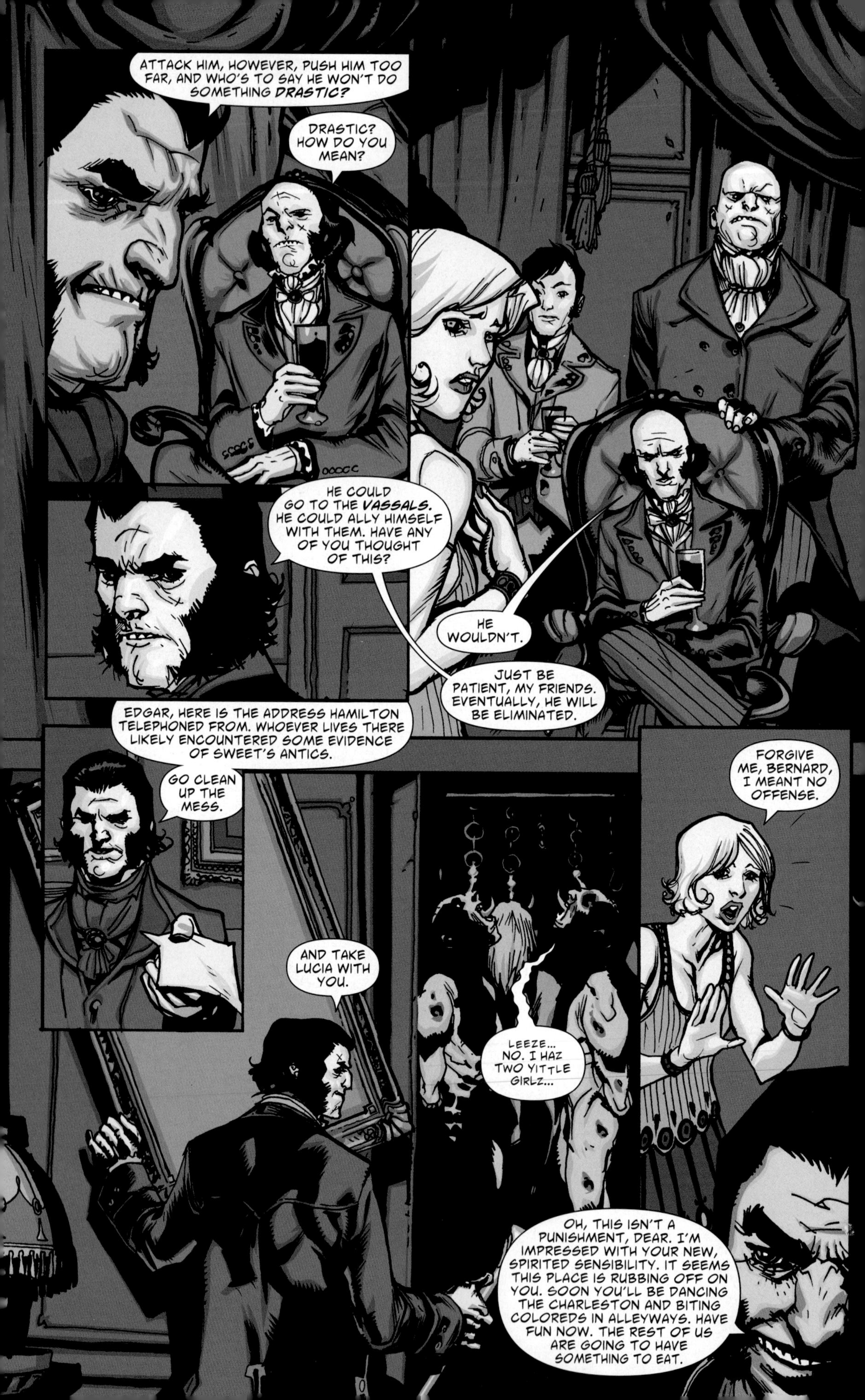
ATTACK HIM, HOWEVER, PUSH HIM TOO FAR, AND WHO'S TO SAY HE WON'T DO SOMETHING DRASTIC?
DRASTIC? HOW DO YOU MEAN?
HE COULD GO TO THE VASSALS. HE COULD ALLY HIMSELF WITH THEM. HAVE ANY OF YOU THOUGHT OF THIS?
HE WOULDN'T.
JUST BE PATIENT, MY FRIENDS. EVENTUALLY, HE WILL BE ELIMINATED.
EDGAR, HERE IS THE ADDRESS HAMILTON TELEPHONED FROM. WHOEVER LIVES THERE LIKELY ENCOUNTERED SOME EVIDENCE OF SWEET'S ANTICS.
GO CLEAN UP THE MESS.
AND TAKE LUCIA WITH YOU.
LEEZE... NO. I HAZ TWO YITTLE GIRLZ...
FORGIVE ME, BERNARD, I MEANT NO OFFENSE.
OH, THIS ISN'T A PUNISHMENT, DEAR. I'M IMPRESSED WITH YOUR NEW, SPIRITED SENSIBILITY. IT SEEMS THIS PLACE IS RUBBING OFF ON YOU. SOON YOU'LL BE DANCING THE CHARLESTON AND BITING COLOREDS IN ALLEYWAYS. HAVE FUN NOW. THE REST OF US ARE GOING TO HAVE SOMETHING TO EAT.

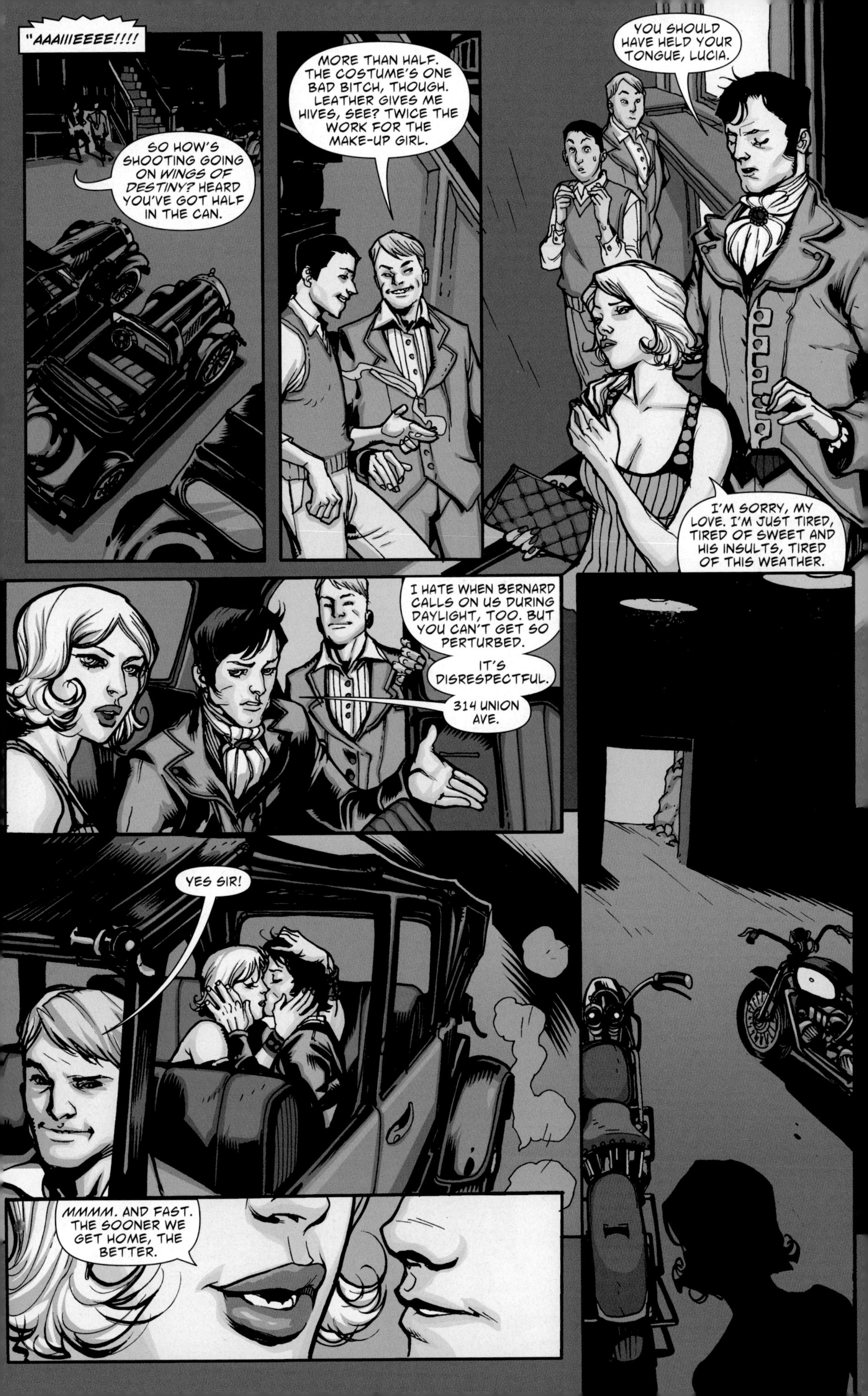
"AAAIIIEEEE!!!!
SO HOW'S SHOOTING GOING ON *WINGS OF DESTINY*? HEARD YOU'VE GOT HALF IN THE CAN.
MORE THAN HALF. THE COSTUME'S ONE BAD BITCH, THOUGH. LEATHER GIVES ME HIVES, SEE? TWICE THE WORK FOR THE MAKE-UP GIRL.
YOU SHOULD HAVE HELD YOUR TONGUE, LUCIA.
I'M SORRY, MY LOVE. I'M JUST TIRED, TIRED OF SWEET AND HIS INSULTS, TIRED OF THIS WEATHER.
I HATE WHEN BERNARD CALLS ON US DURING DAYLIGHT, TOO. BUT YOU CAN'T GET SO PERTURBED.
IT'S DISRESPECTFUL.
314 UNION AVE.
YES SIR!
MMMM. AND FAST. THE SOONER WE GET HOME, THE BETTER.

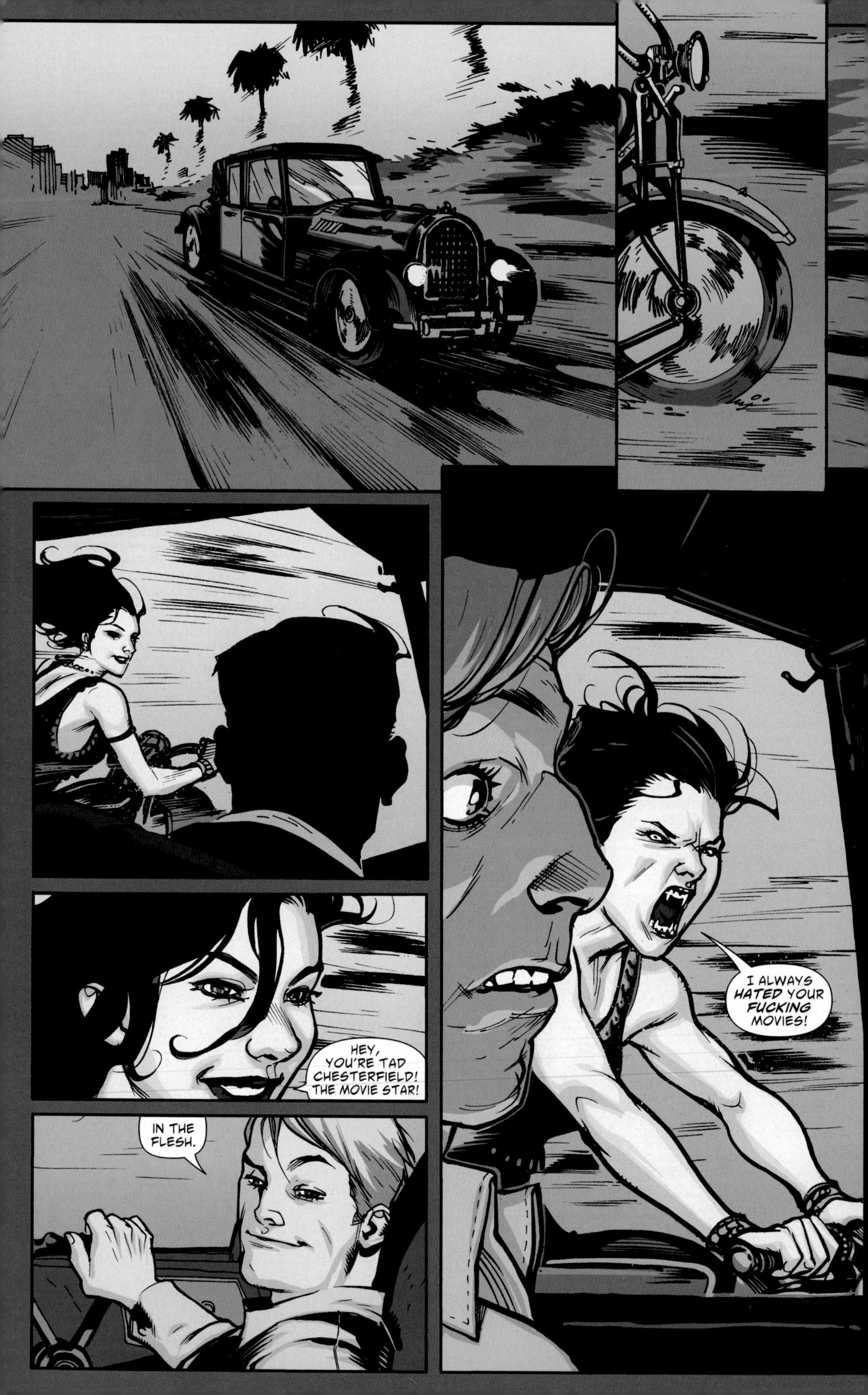
HEY, YOU'RE TAD CHESTERFIELD! THE MOVIE STAR!
IN THE FLESH.
I ALWAYS HATED YOUR FUCKING MOVIES!

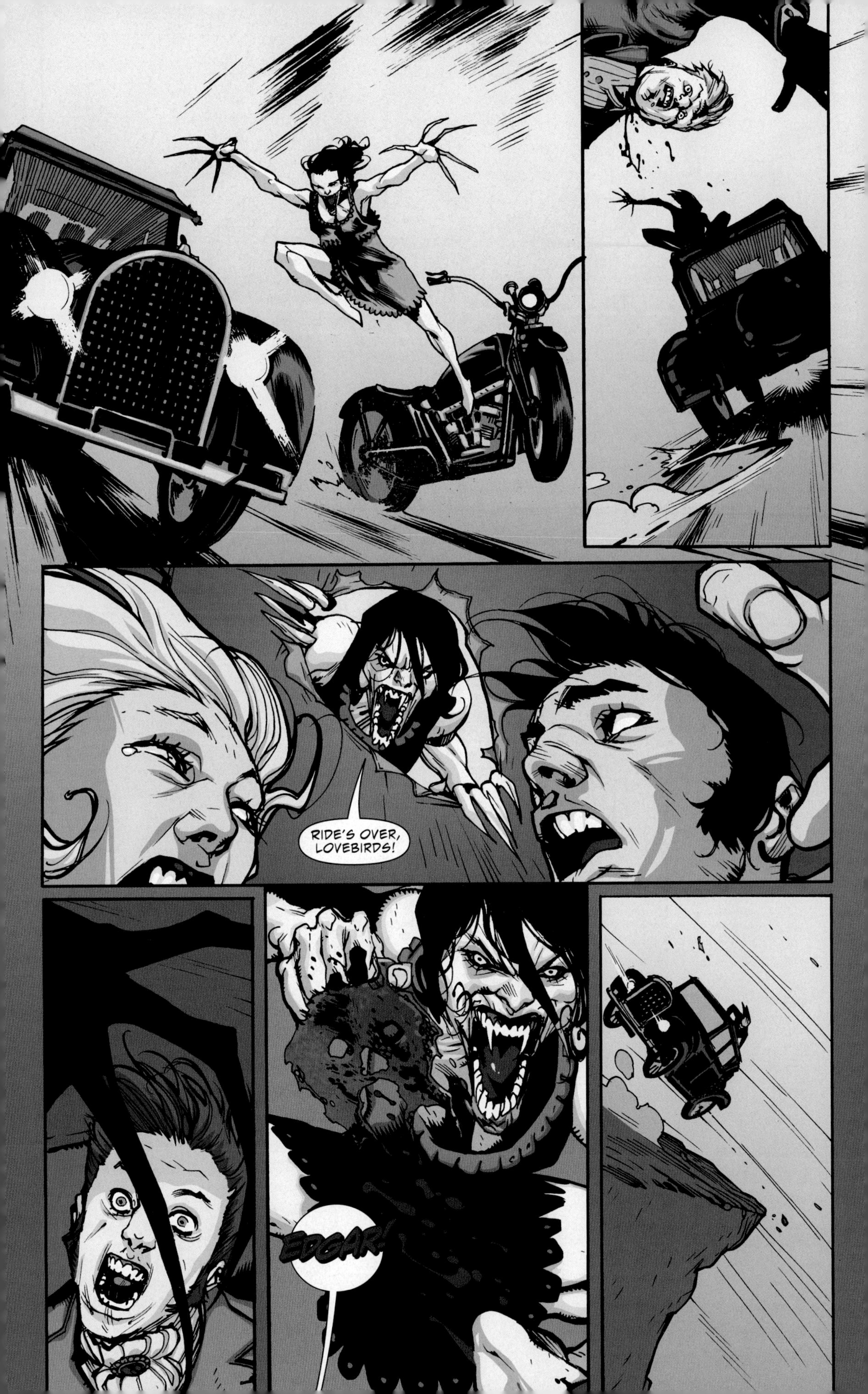
RIDE'S OVER, LOVEBIRDS!
EDGAR!

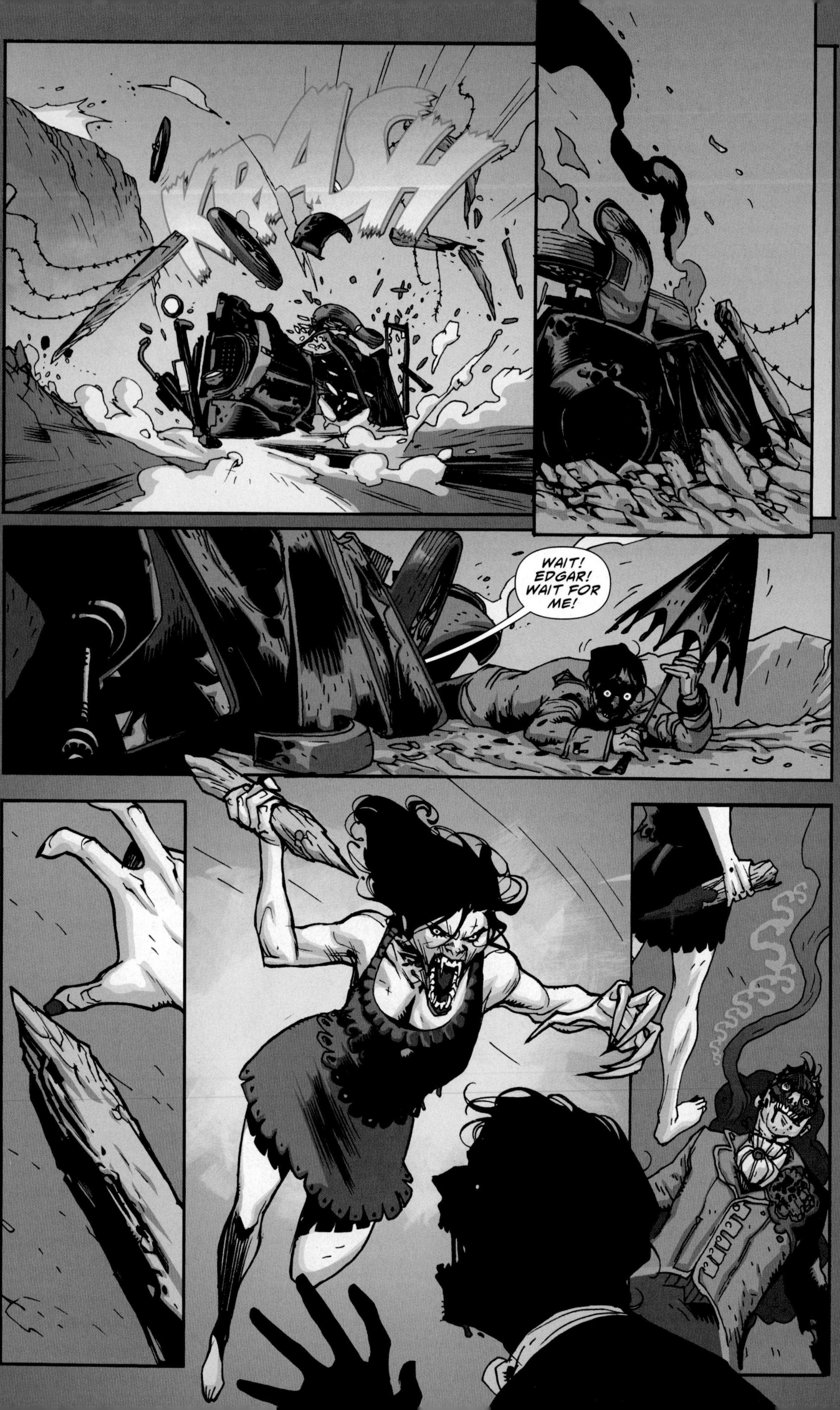
KRASH
WAIT! EDGAR! WAIT FOR ME!

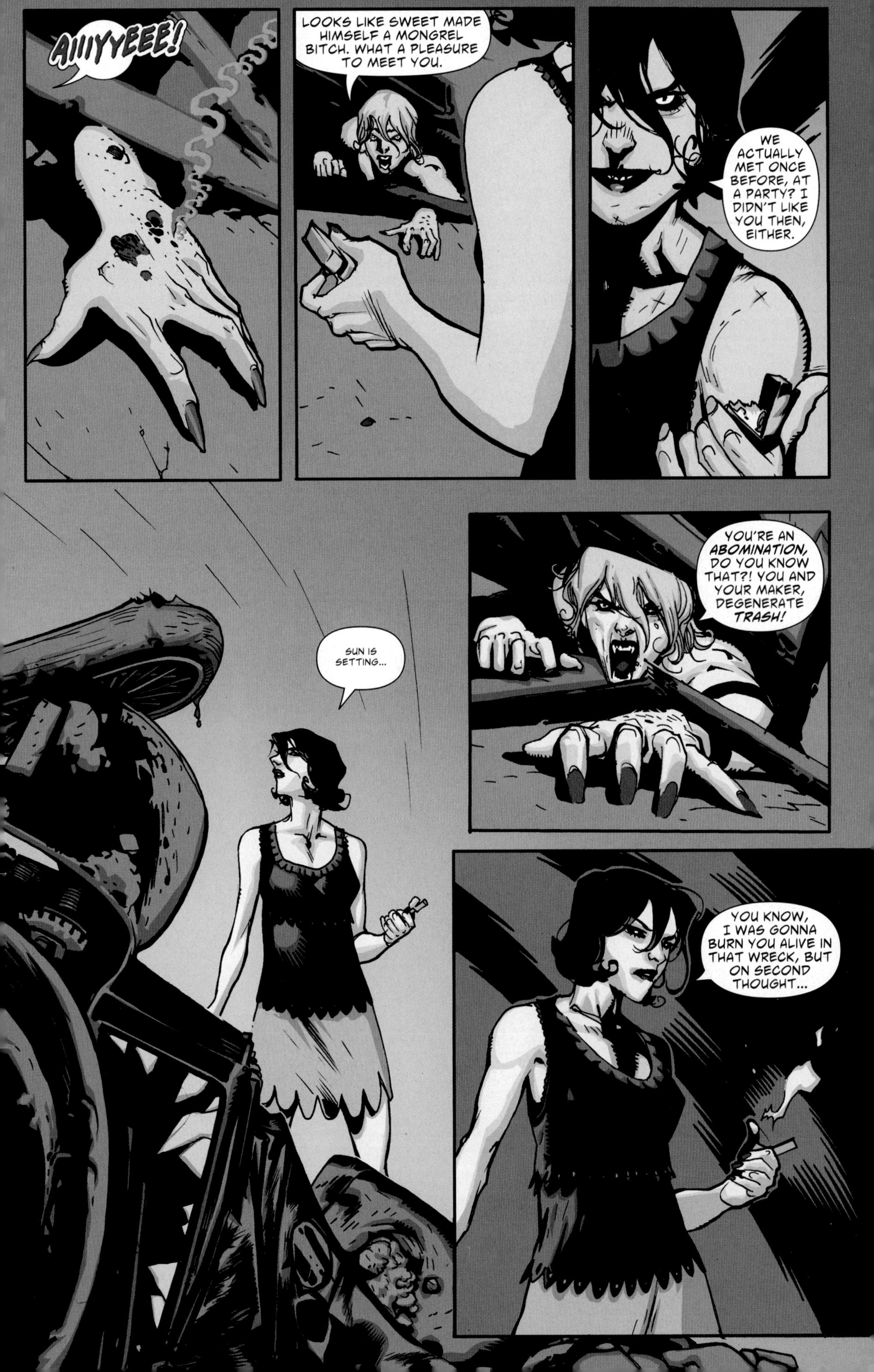
AIIIYYEEE!
LOOKS LIKE SWEET MADE HIMSELF A MONGREL BITCH. WHAT A PLEASURE TO MEET YOU.
WE ACTUALLY MET ONCE BEFORE, AT A PARTY? I DIDN'T LIKE YOU THEN, EITHER.
YOU'RE AN ABOMINATION, DO YOU KNOW THAT?! YOU AND YOUR MAKER, DEGENERATE TRASH!
SUN IS SETTING...
YOU KNOW, I WAS GONNA BURN YOU ALIVE IN THAT WRECK, BUT ON SECOND THOUGHT...

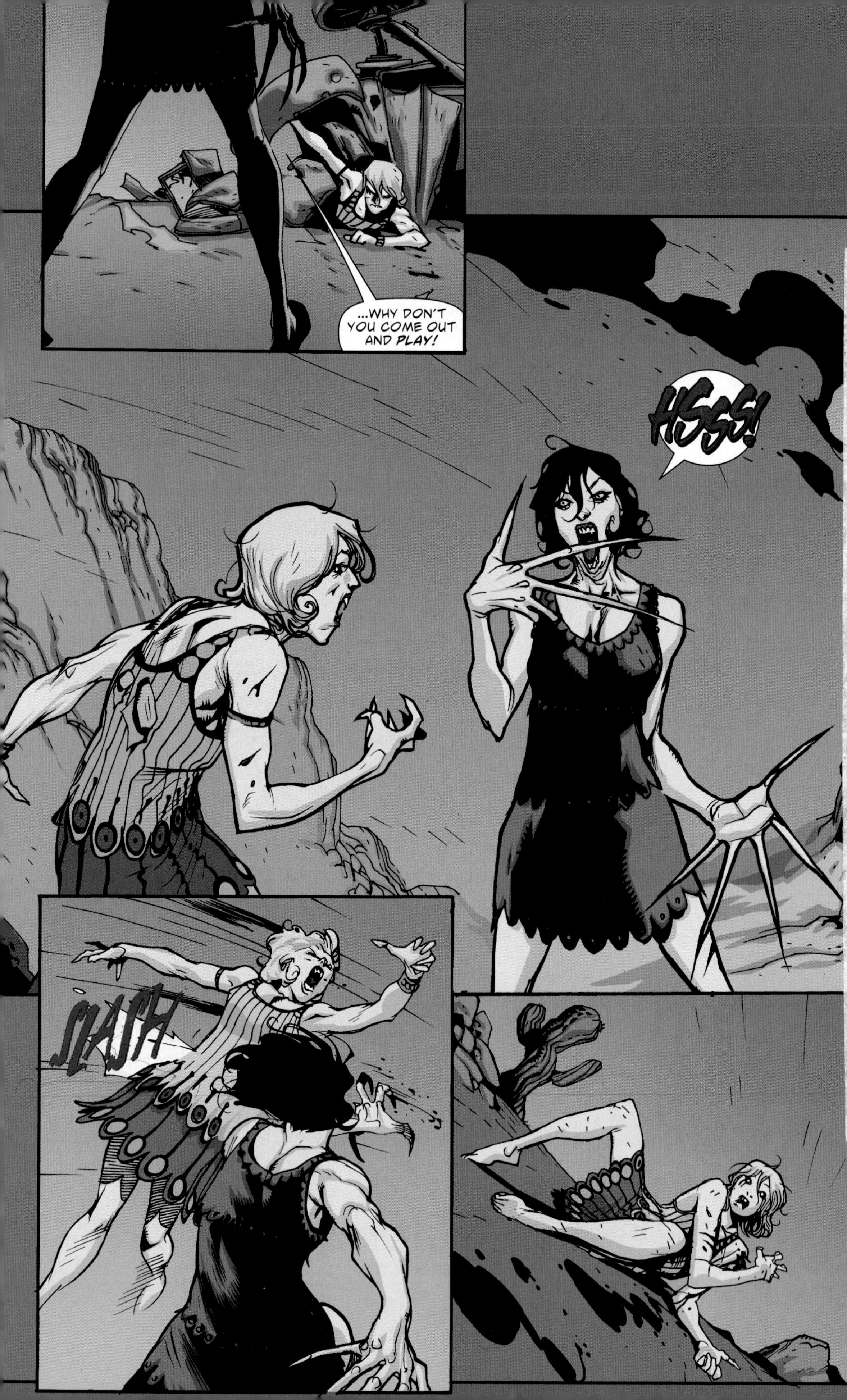
...WHY DON'T YOU COME OUT AND PLAY!
HSSS!
SLASH

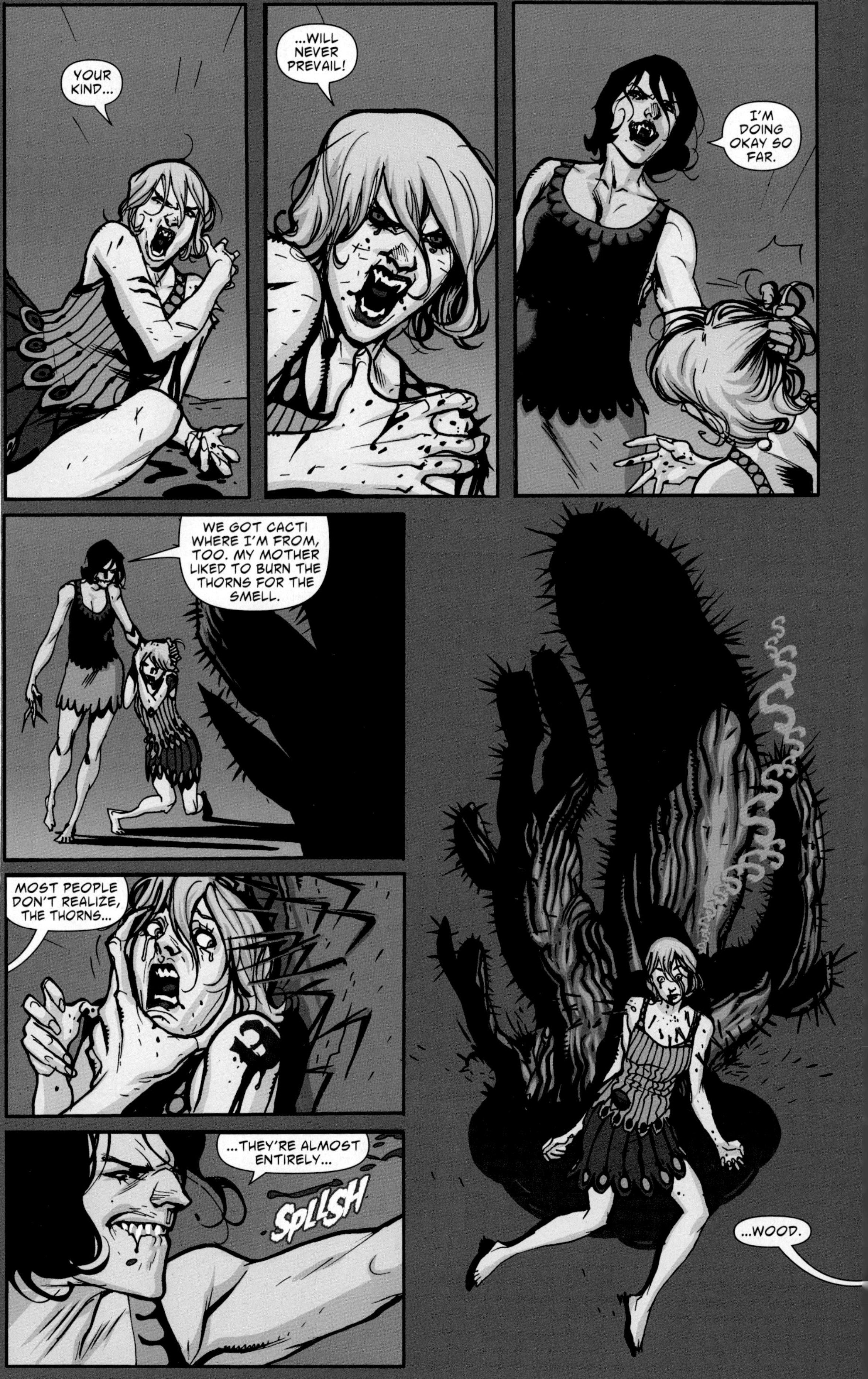
YOUR KIND...
...WILL NEVER PREVAIL!
I'M DOING OKAY SO FAR.
WE GOT CACTI WHERE I'M FROM, TOO. MY MOTHER LIKED TO BURN THE THORNS FOR THE SMELL.
MOST PEOPLE DON'T REALIZE, THE THORNS...
...THEY'RE ALMOST ENTIRELY...
SPLLSH
...WOOD.

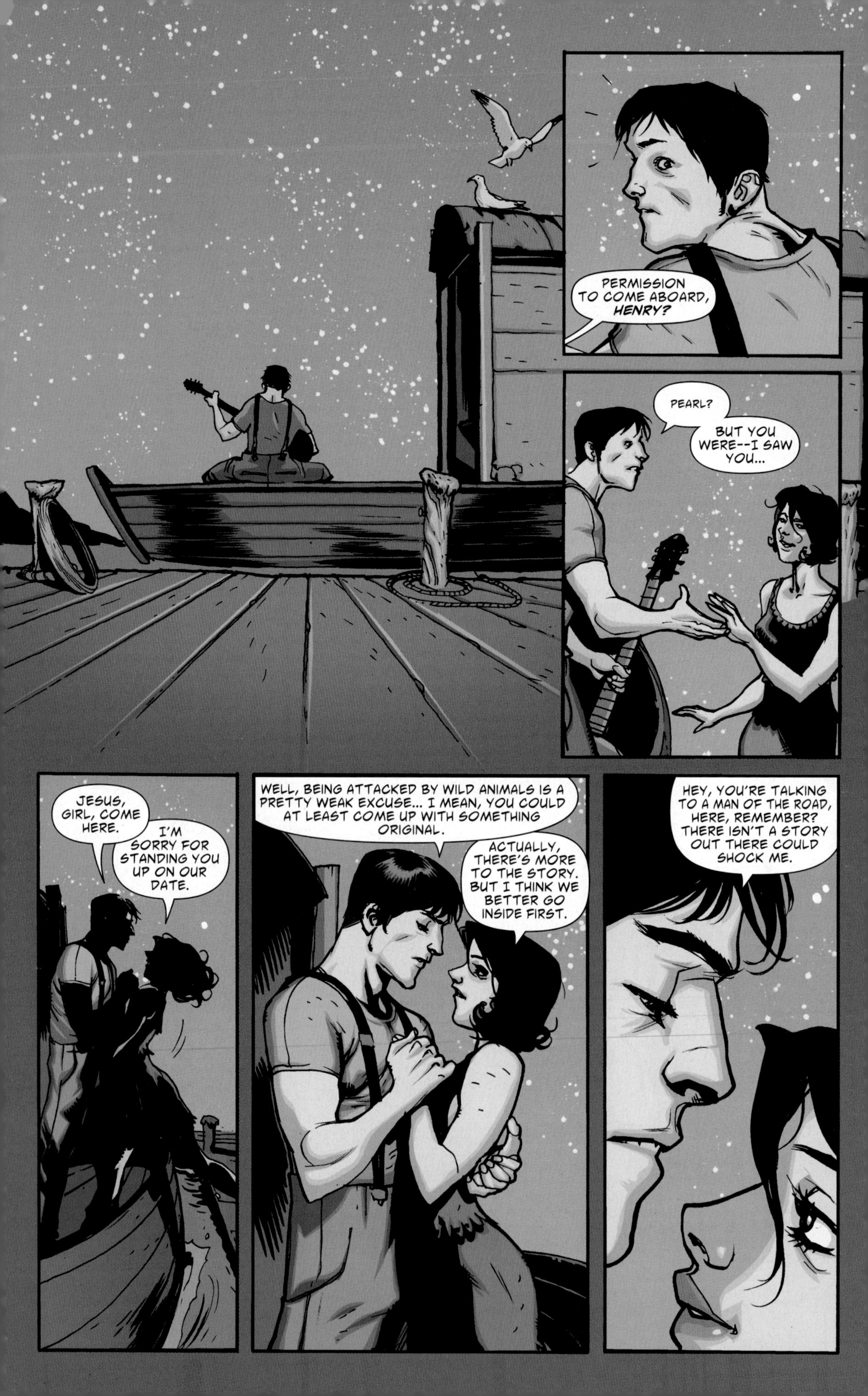
PERMISSION TO COME ABOARD, HENRY?
PEARL?
BUT YOU WERE--I SAW YOU...
JESUS, GIRL, COME HERE.
I'M SORRY FOR STANDING YOU UP ON OUR DATE.
WELL, BEING ATTACKED BY WILD ANIMALS IS A PRETTY WEAK EXCUSE... I MEAN, YOU COULD AT LEAST COME UP WITH SOMETHING ORIGINAL.
ACTUALLY, THERE'S MORE TO THE STORY. BUT I THINK WE BETTER GO INSIDE FIRST.
HEY, YOU'RE TALKING TO A MAN OF THE ROAD, HERE, REMEMBER? THERE ISN'T A STORY OUT THERE COULD SHOCK ME.

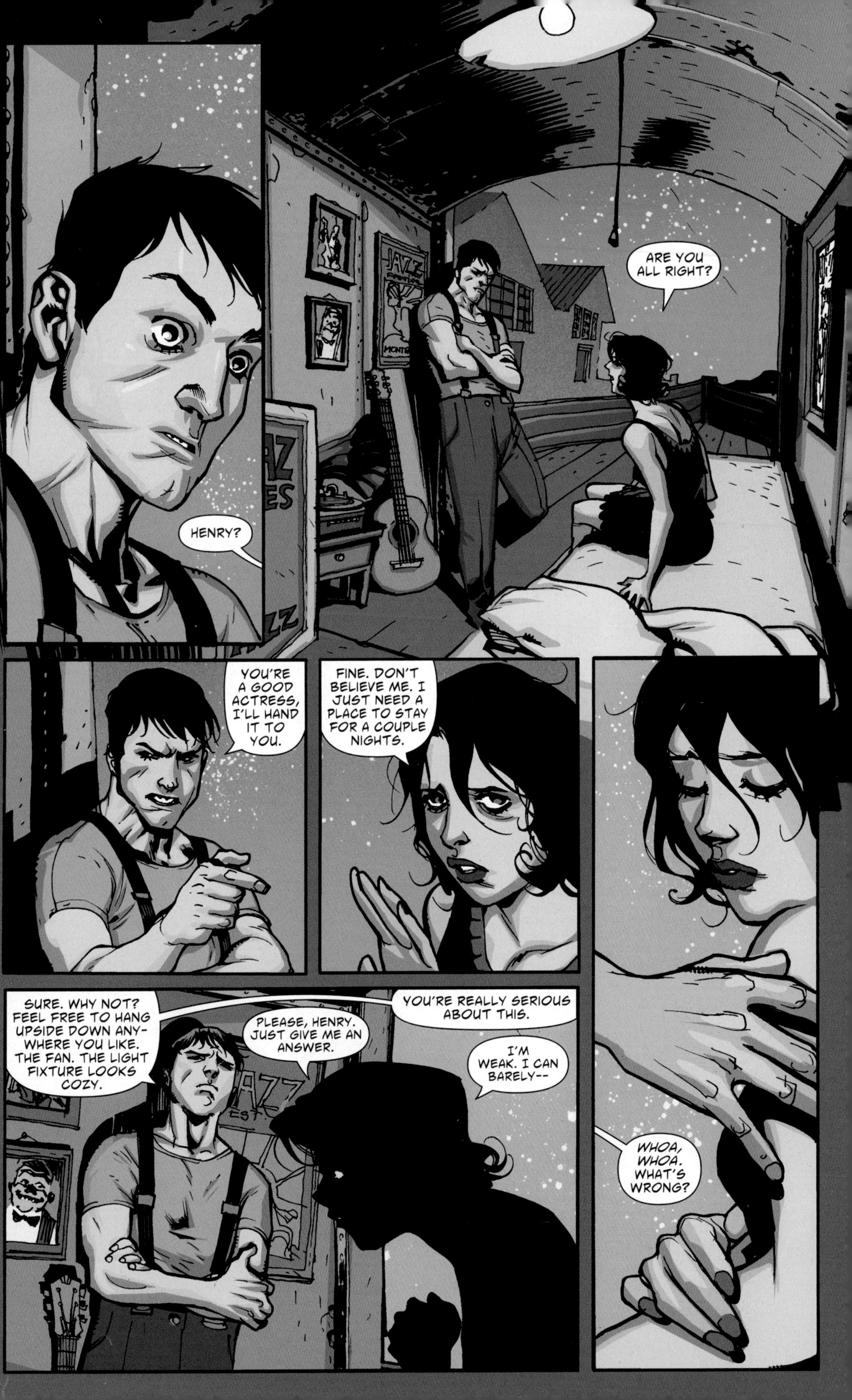
HENRY?
ARE YOU ALL RIGHT?
YOU'RE A GOOD ACTRESS, I'LL HAND IT TO YOU.
FINE. DON'T BELIEVE ME. I JUST NEED A PLACE TO STAY FOR A COUPLE NIGHTS.
SURE. WHY NOT? FEEL FREE TO HANG UPSIDE DOWN ANY-WHERE YOU LIKE. THE FAN. THE LIGHT FIXTURE LOOKS COZY.
PLEASE, HENRY. JUST GIVE ME AN ANSWER.
YOU'RE REALLY SERIOUS ABOUT THIS.
I'M WEAK. I CAN BARELY--
WHOA, WHOA. WHAT'S WRONG?

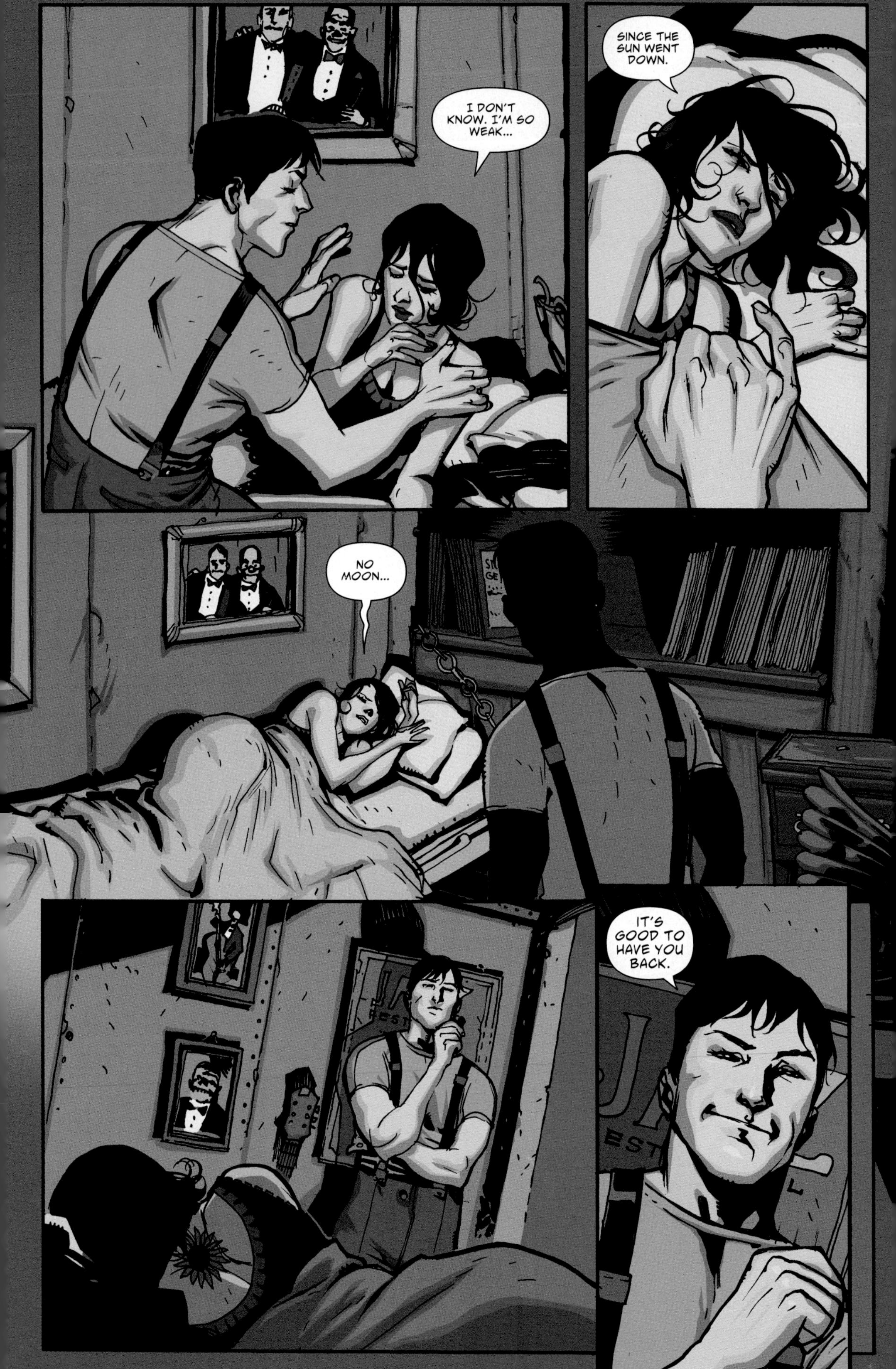
I DON'T KNOW. I'M SO WEAK...
SINCE THE SUN WENT DOWN.
NO MOON...
IT'S GOOD TO HAVE YOU BACK.

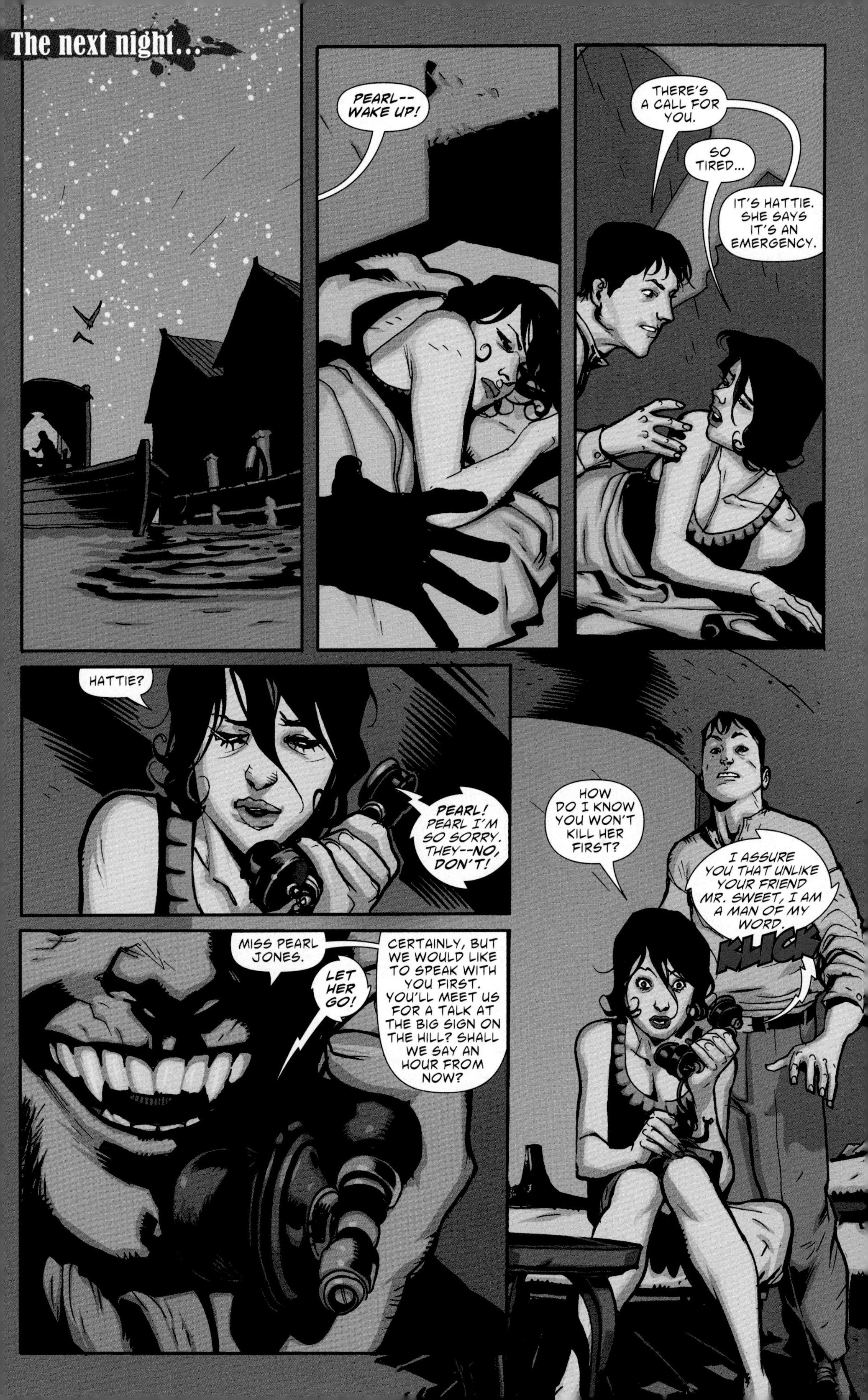
The next night...
PEARL--
WAKE UP!
THERE'S A CALL FOR YOU.
SO TIRED...
IT'S HATTIE. SHE SAYS IT'S AN EMERGENCY.
HATTIE?
PEARL! PEARL I'M SO SORRY. THEY--NO, DON'T!
MISS PEARL JONES.
LET HER GO!
CERTAINLY, BUT WE WOULD LIKE TO SPEAK WITH YOU FIRST. YOU'LL MEET US FOR A TALK AT THE BIG SIGN ON THE HILL? SHALL WE SAY AN HOUR FROM NOW?
HOW DO I KNOW YOU WON'T KILL HER FIRST?
I ASSURE YOU THAT UNLIKE YOUR FRIEND MR. SWEET, I AM A MAN OF MY WORD.
KLICK

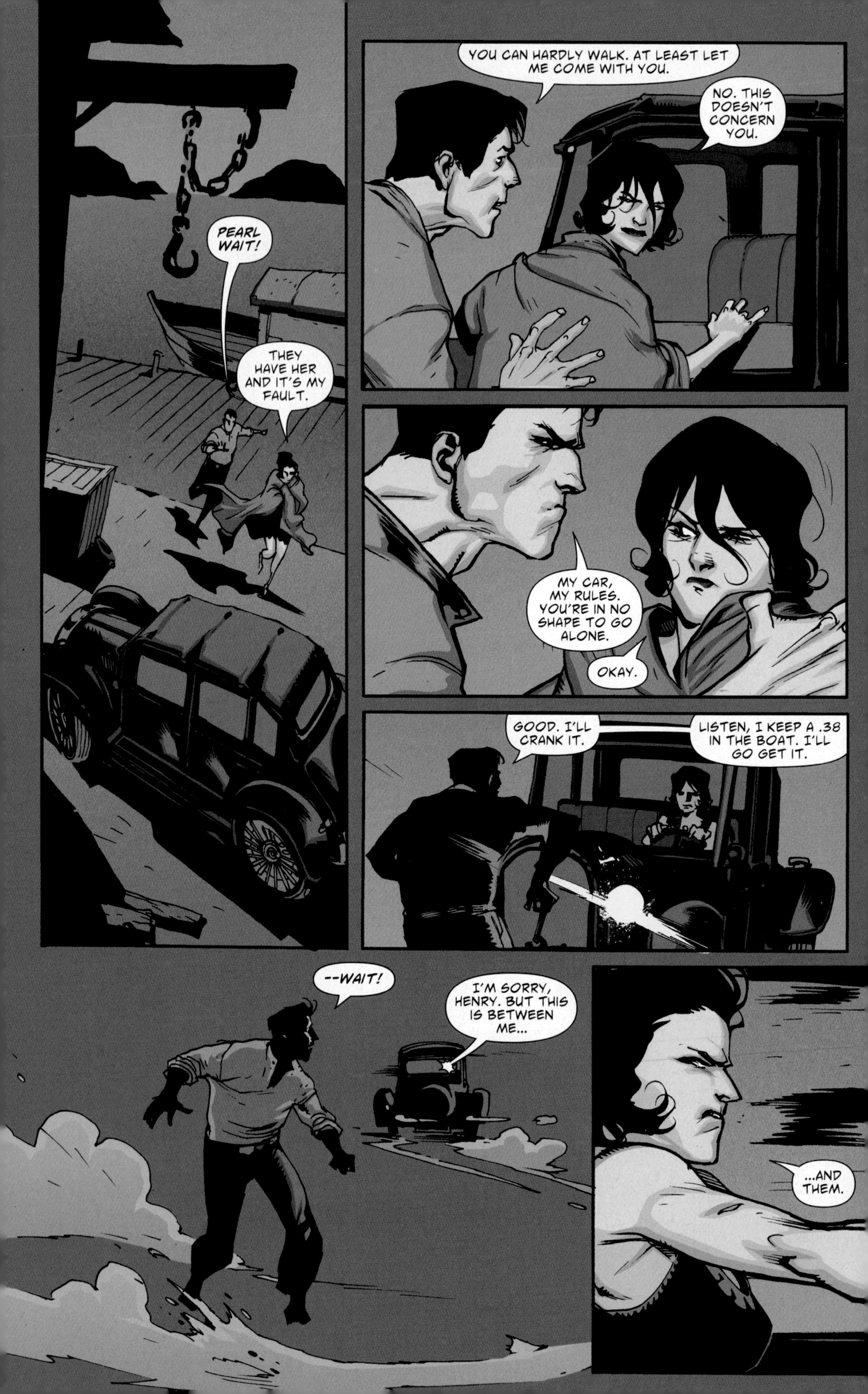
PEARL WAIT!
THEY HAVE HER AND IT'S MY FAULT.
YOU CAN HARDLY WALK. AT LEAST LET ME COME WITH YOU.
NO. THIS DOESN'T CONCERN YOU.
MY CAR, MY RULES. YOU'RE IN NO SHAPE TO GO ALONE.
OKAY.
GOOD. I'LL CRANK IT.
LISTEN, I KEEP A .38 IN THE BOAT. I'LL GO GET IT.
--WAIT!
I'M SORRY, HENRY. BUT THIS IS BETWEEN ME...
...AND THEM.

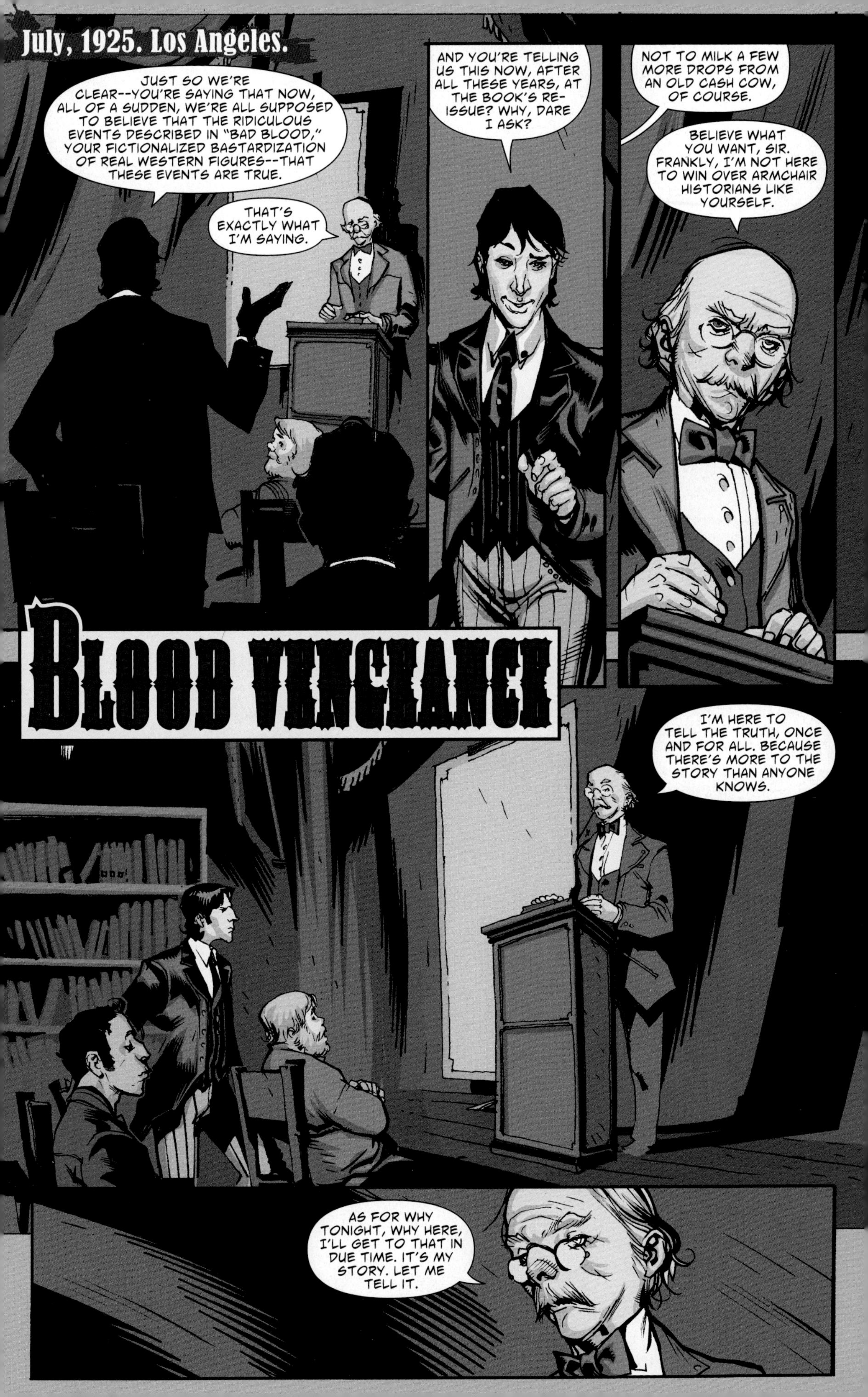
July, 1925. Los Angeles.
JUST SO WE'RE CLEAR--YOU'RE SAYING THAT NOW, ALL OF A SUDDEN, WE'RE ALL SUPPOSED TO BELIEVE THAT THE RIDICULOUS EVENTS DESCRIBED IN "BAD BLOOD," YOUR FICTIONALIZED BASTARDIZATION OF REAL WESTERN FIGURES--THAT THESE EVENTS ARE TRUE.
THAT'S EXACTLY WHAT I'M SAYING.
AND YOU'RE TELLING US THIS NOW, AFTER ALL THESE YEARS, AT THE BOOK'S RE-ISSUE? WHY, DARE I ASK?
NOT TO MILK A FEW MORE DROPS FROM AN OLD CASH COW, OF COURSE.
BELIEVE WHAT YOU WANT, SIR. FRANKLY, I'M NOT HERE TO WIN OVER ARMCHAIR HISTORIANS LIKE YOURSELF.
BLOOD VENGEANCE
I'M HERE TO TELL THE TRUTH, ONCE AND FOR ALL. BECAUSE THERE'S MORE TO THE STORY THAN ANYONE KNOWS.
AS FOR WHY TONIGHT, WHY HERE, I'LL GET TO THAT IN DUE TIME. IT'S MY STORY. LET ME TELL IT.

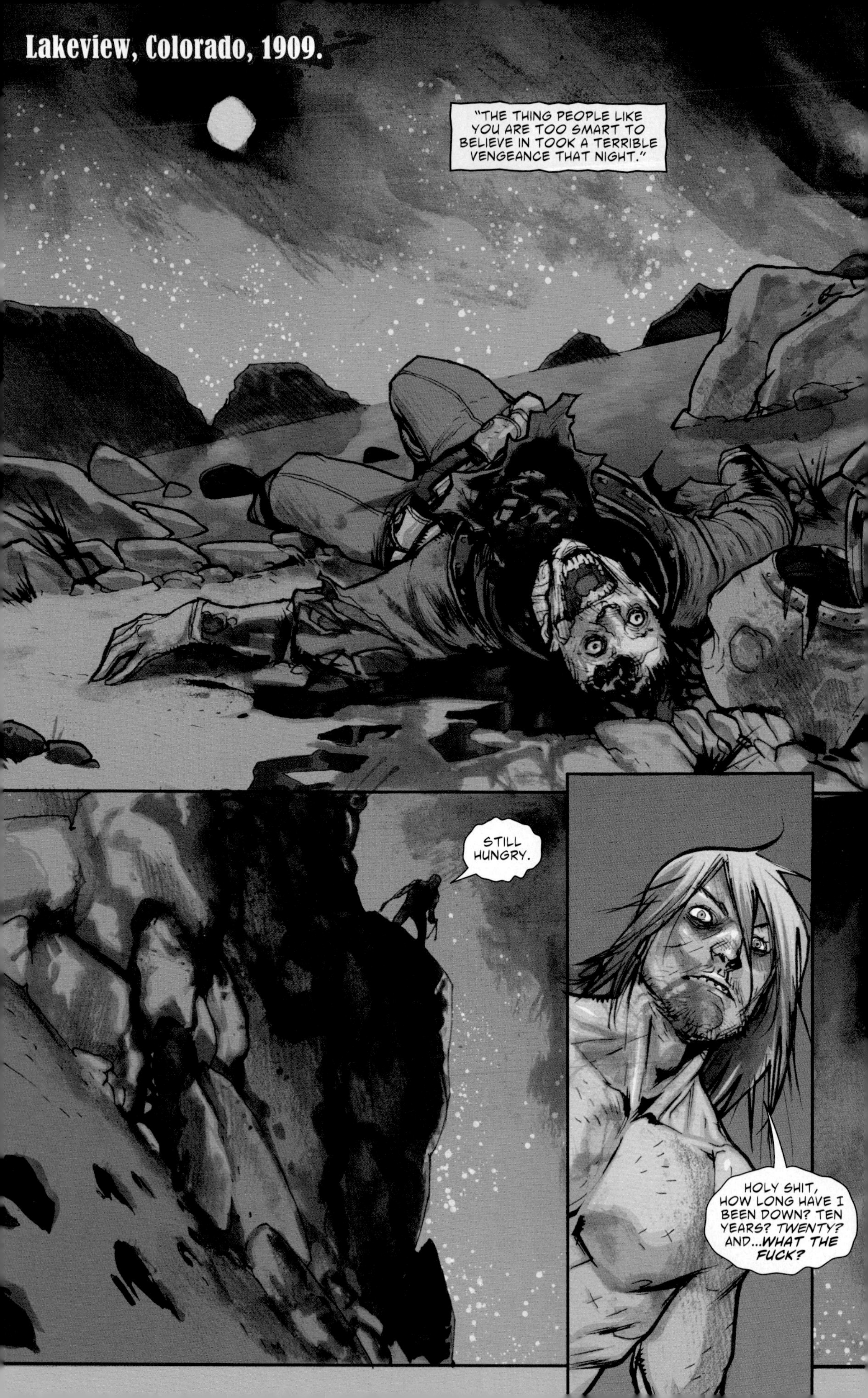
Lakeview, Colorado, 1909.
"THE THING PEOPLE LIKE YOU ARE TOO SMART TO BELIEVE IN TOOK A TERRIBLE VENGEANCE THAT NIGHT."
STILL HUNGRY.
HOLY SHIT, HOW LONG HAVE I BEEN DOWN? TEN YEARS? TWENTY? AND...WHAT THE FUCK?

WELCOME TO LAKEVIEW, EST. 1884

THE HON. HECTOR CAMILLO, MAYOR

"WELCOME, NEIGHBOR! SIT A SPELL!"

THE MAYOR'S A *TACO BENDER?*

THAT AIN'T PROGRESS, THAT'S *INSANITY!*

BARBER

CAMILLO? SAME NAME AS BOOK'S *DEPUTY.* HMMM...

DRUG STORE

WONDER OF THE AGE! *"TELE-PHONE"* YOUR FRIENDS!

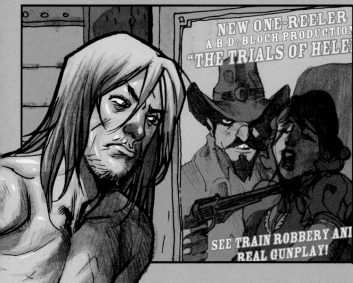

NEW ONE-REELER A B.D. BLOCH PRODUCTION "THE TRIALS OF HELE"

SEE TRAIN ROBBERY AND REAL GUNPLAY!

SOME NEWFANGLED KIND OF *WHOREHOUSE?*... NO...I DON'T KNOW *WHAT* IT IS.

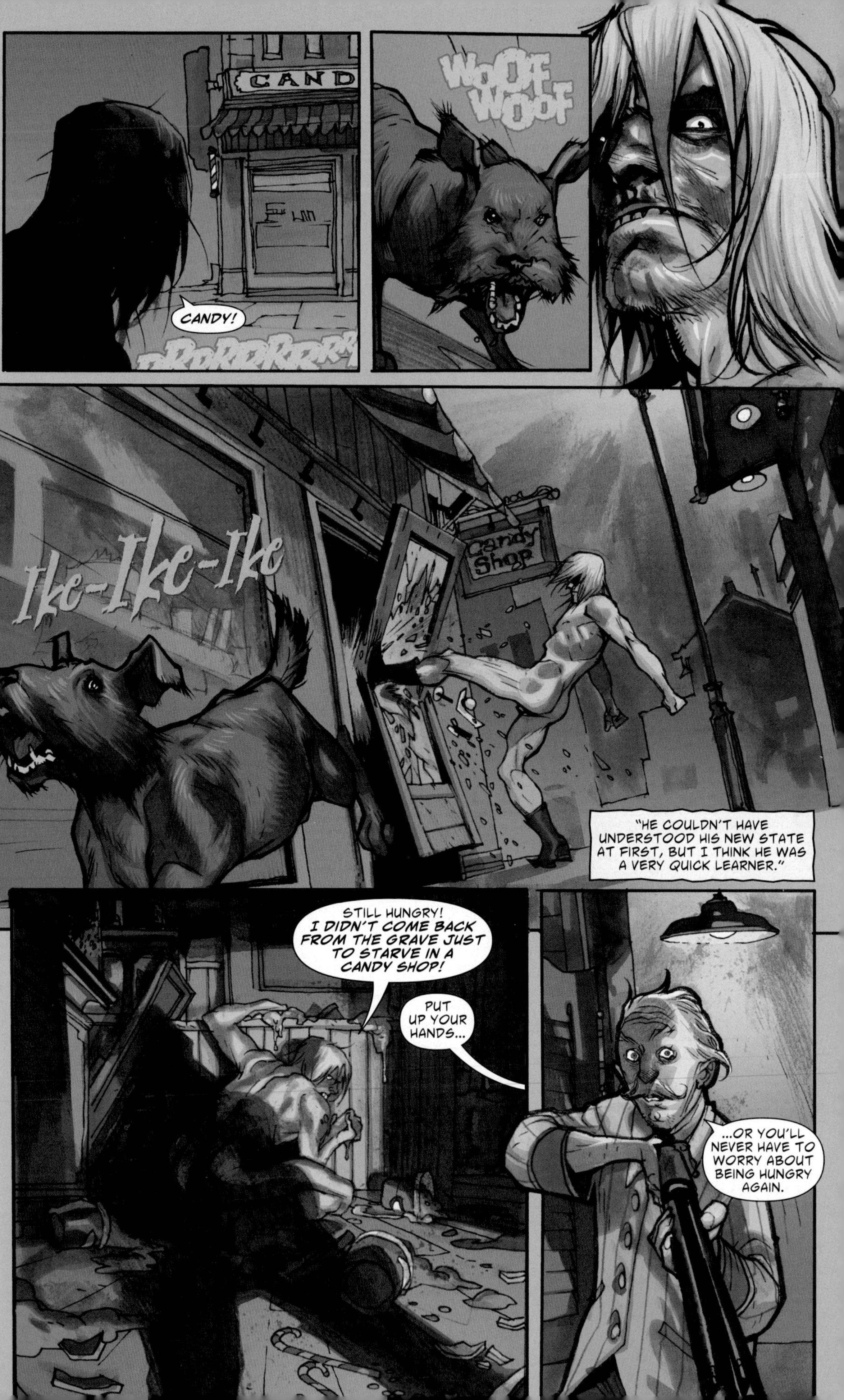
CAND
CANDY!
DRRRRRRRR
WOOF WOOF
Ike-Ike-Ike
Candy Shop
"HE COULDN'T HAVE UNDERSTOOD HIS NEW STATE AT FIRST, BUT I THINK HE WAS A VERY QUICK LEARNER."
STILL HUNGRY! *I DIDN'T COME BACK FROM THE GRAVE JUST TO STARVE IN A CANDY SHOP!*
PUT UP YOUR HANDS...
...OR YOU'LL NEVER HAVE TO WORRY ABOUT BEING HUNGRY AGAIN.

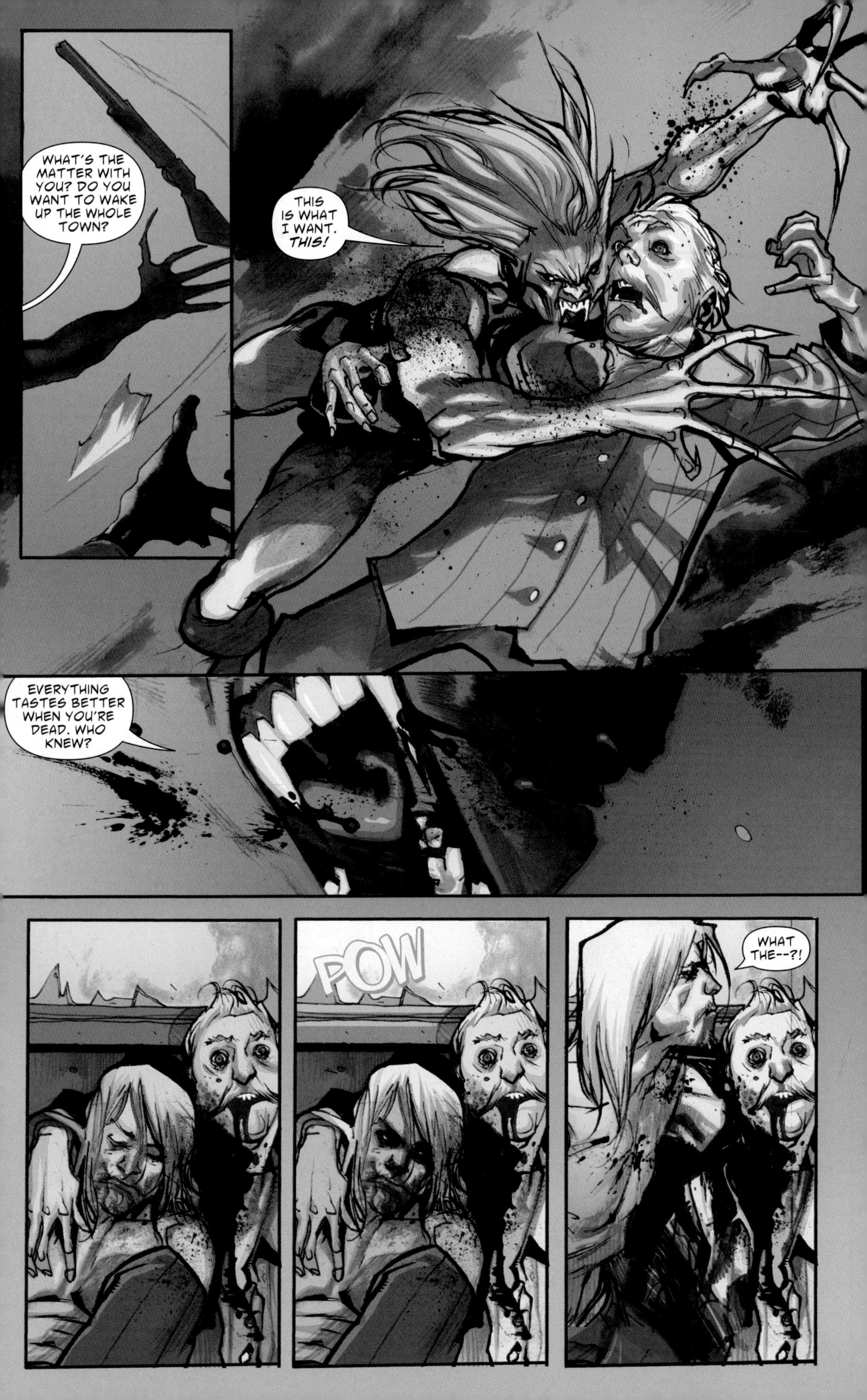
WHAT'S THE MATTER WITH YOU? DO YOU WANT TO WAKE UP THE WHOLE TOWN?
THIS IS WHAT I WANT. *THIS!*
EVERYTHING TASTES BETTER WHEN YOU'RE DEAD. WHO KNEW?
POW
WHAT THE--?!

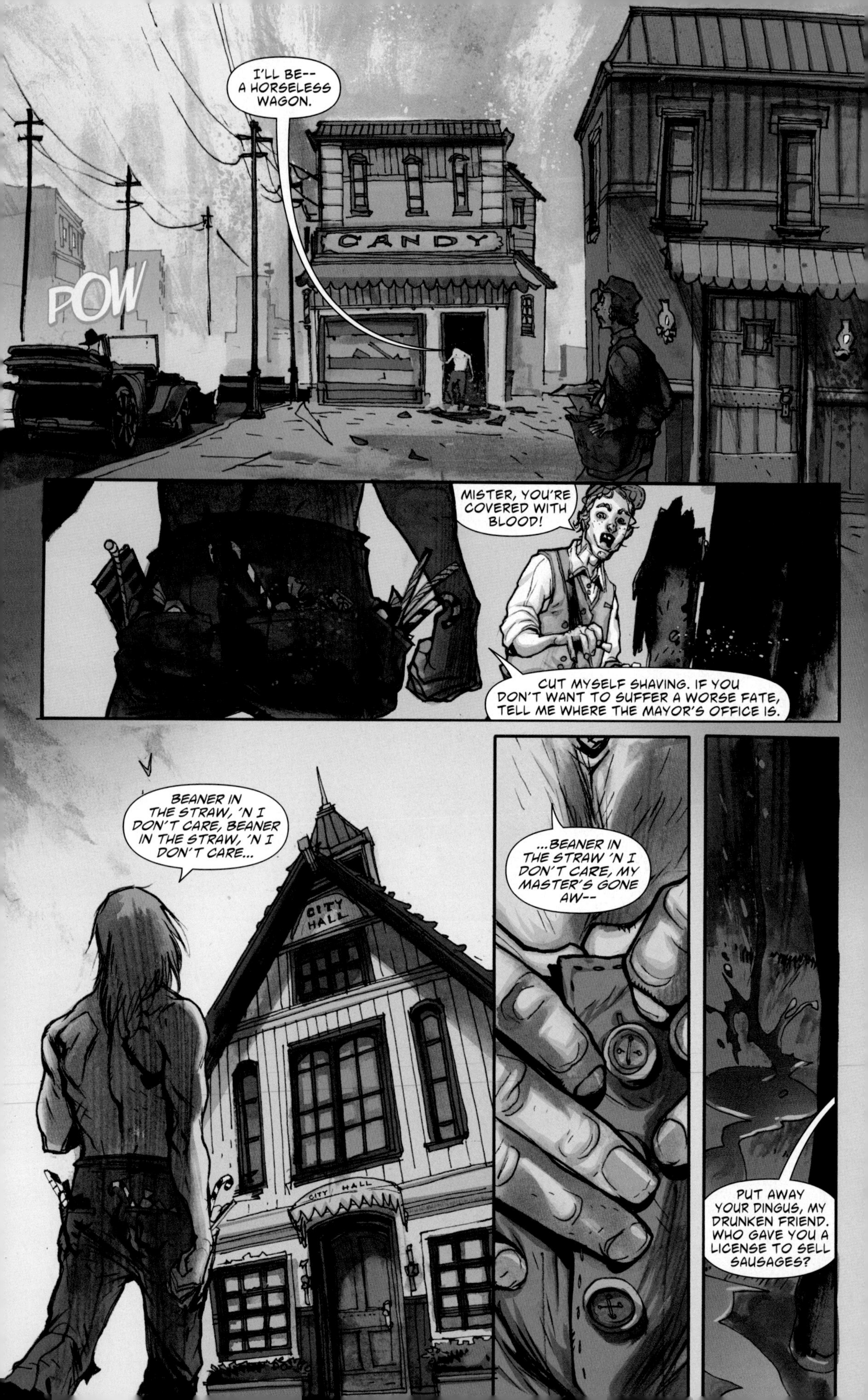
POW
I'LL BE--
A HORSELESS WAGON.
CANDY
MISTER, YOU'RE COVERED WITH BLOOD!
CUT MYSELF SHAVING. IF YOU DON'T WANT TO SUFFER A WORSE FATE, TELL ME WHERE THE MAYOR'S OFFICE IS.
BEANER IN THE STRAW, 'N I DON'T CARE, BEANER IN THE STRAW, 'N I DON'T CARE...
CITY HALL
CITY HALL
...BEANER IN THE STRAW 'N I DON'T CARE, MY MASTER'S GONE AW--
PUT AWAY YOUR DINGUS, MY DRUNKEN FRIEND. WHO GAVE YOU A LICENSE TO SELL SAUSAGES?

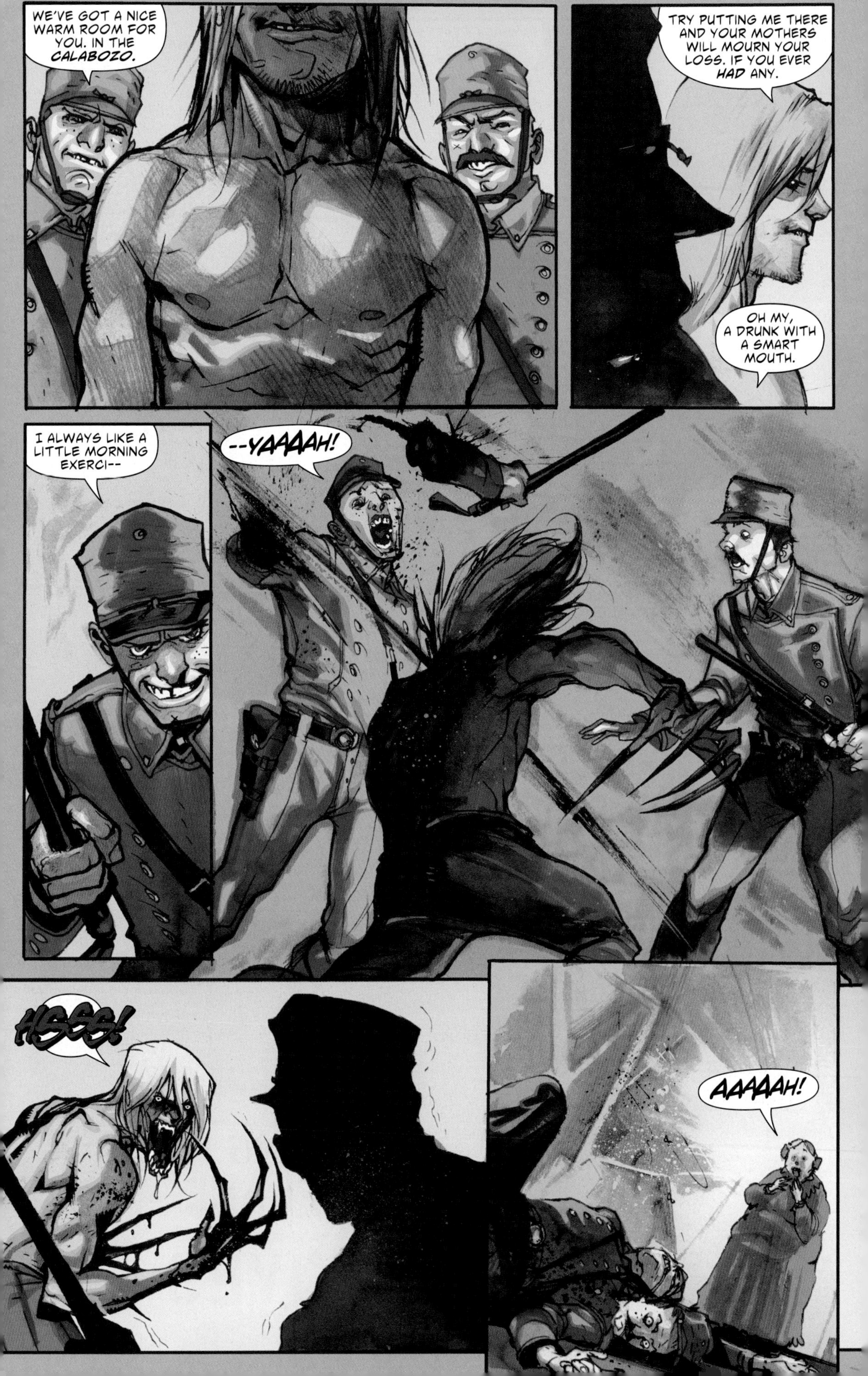
WE'VE GOT A NICE WARM ROOM FOR YOU. IN THE CALABOZO.
TRY PUTTING ME THERE AND YOUR MOTHERS WILL MOURN YOUR LOSS. IF YOU EVER HAD ANY.
OH MY, A DRUNK WITH A SMART MOUTH.
I ALWAYS LIKE A LITTLE MORNING EXERCI--
--YAAAAH!
HSSS!
AAAAAH!

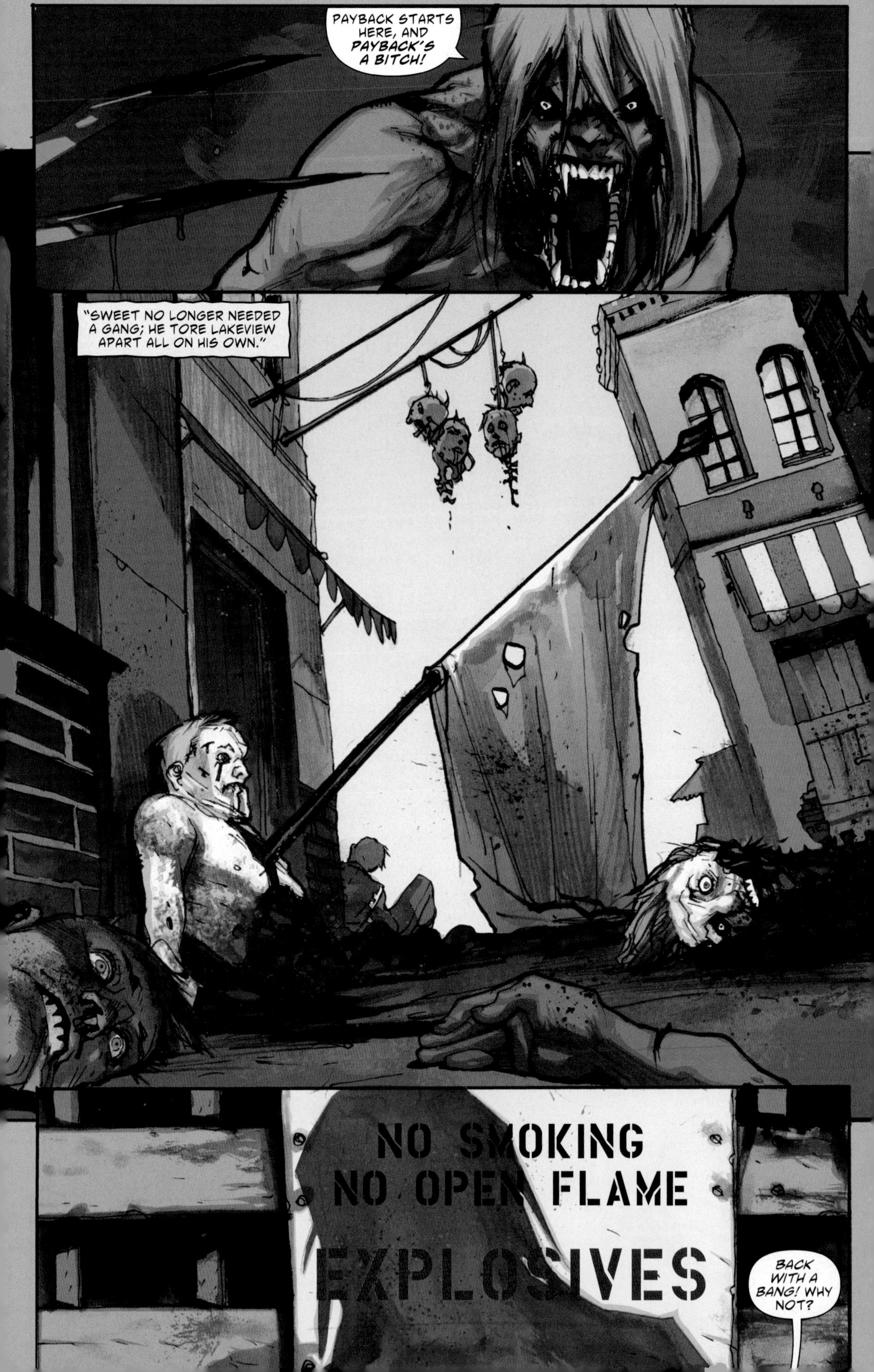
PAYBACK STARTS HERE, AND PAYBACK'S A BITCH!
"SWEET NO LONGER NEEDED A GANG; HE TORE LAKEVIEW APART ALL ON HIS OWN."
NO SMOKING
NO OPEN FLAME
EXPLOSIVES
BACK WITH A BANG! WHY NOT?

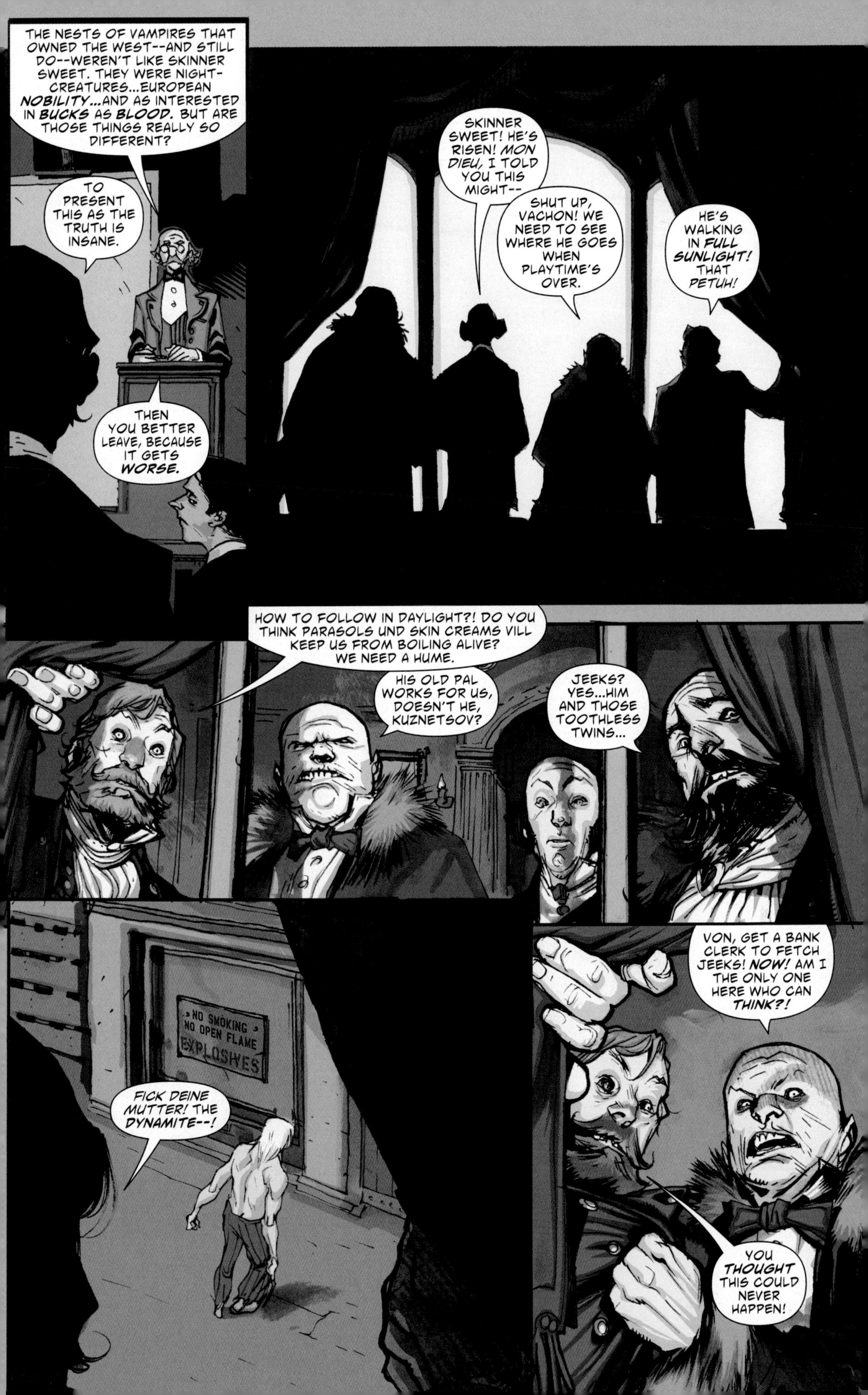
THE NESTS OF VAMPIRES THAT OWNED THE WEST--AND STILL DO--WEREN'T LIKE SKINNER SWEET. THEY WERE NIGHT-CREATURES...EUROPEAN NOBILITY...AND AS INTERESTED IN BUCKS AS BLOOD. BUT ARE THOSE THINGS REALLY SO DIFFERENT?
TO PRESENT THIS AS THE TRUTH IS INSANE.
THEN YOU BETTER LEAVE, BECAUSE IT GETS WORSE.
SKINNER SWEET! HE'S RISEN! MON DIEU, I TOLD YOU THIS MIGHT--
SHUT UP, VACHON! WE NEED TO SEE WHERE HE GOES WHEN PLAYTIME'S OVER.
HE'S WALKING IN FULL SUNLIGHT! THAT PETUH!
HOW TO FOLLOW IN DAYLIGHT?! DO YOU THINK PARASOLS UND SKIN CREAMS VILL KEEP US FROM BOILING ALIVE? WE NEED A HUME.
HIS OLD PAL WORKS FOR US, DOESN'T HE, KUZNETSOV?
JEEKS? YES...HIM AND THOSE TOOTHLESS TWINS...
NO SMOKING
NO OPEN FLAME
EXPLOSIVES
FICK DEINE MUTTER! THE DYNAMITE--!
VON, GET A BANK CLERK TO FETCH JEEKS! NOW! AM I THE ONLY ONE HERE WHO CAN THINK?!
YOU THOUGHT THIS COULD NEVER HAPPEN!

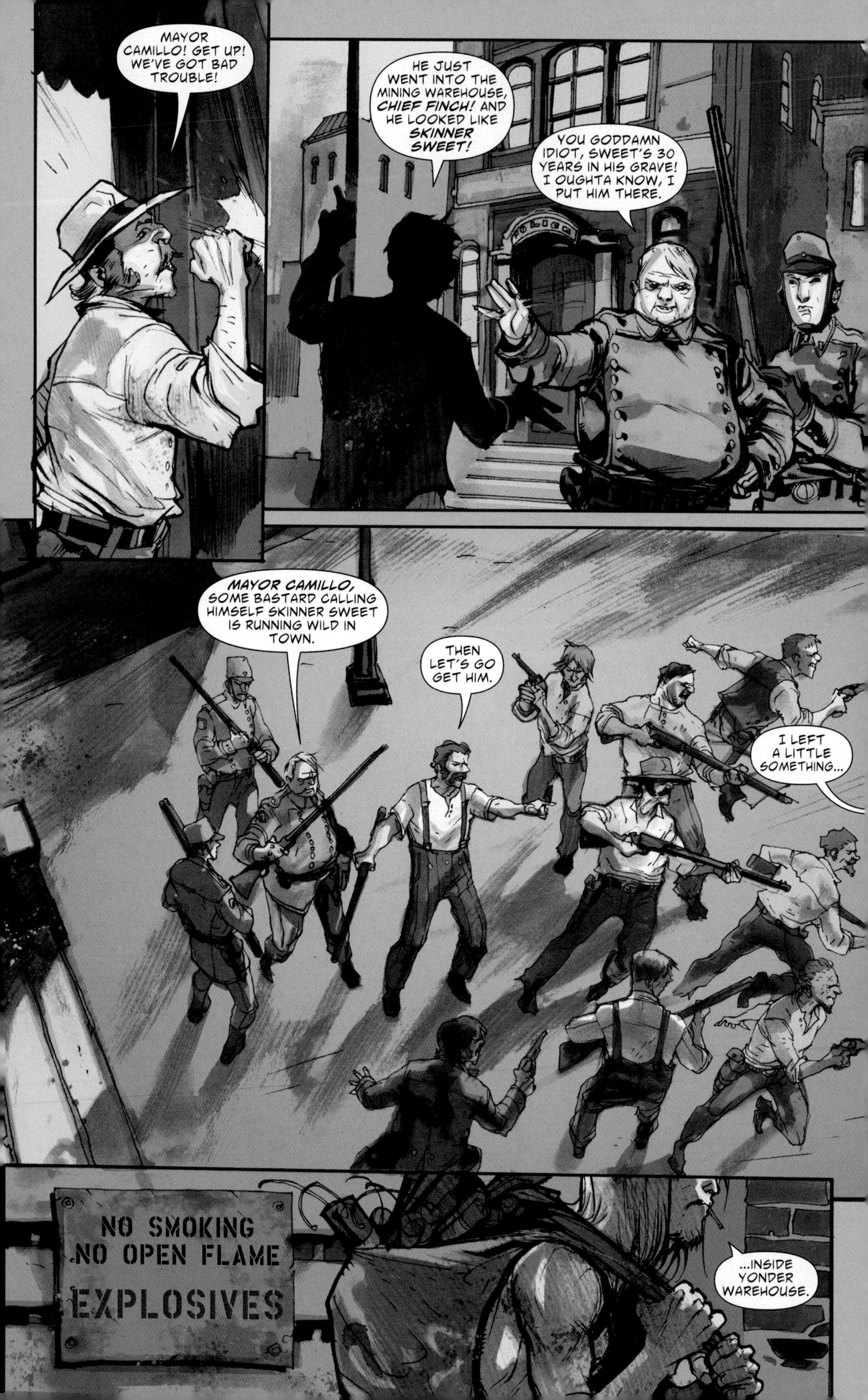
MAYOR CAMILLO! GET UP! WE'VE GOT BAD TROUBLE!
HE JUST WENT INTO THE MINING WAREHOUSE, CHIEF FINCH! AND HE LOOKED LIKE SKINNER SWEET!
YOU GODDAMN IDIOT, SWEET'S 30 YEARS IN HIS GRAVE! I OUGHTA KNOW, I PUT HIM THERE.
MAYOR CAMILLO, SOME BASTARD CALLING HIMSELF SKINNER SWEET IS RUNNING WILD IN TOWN.
THEN LET'S GO GET HIM.
I LEFT A LITTLE SOMETHING...
NO SMOKING
NO OPEN FLAME
EXPLOSIVES
...INSIDE YONDER WAREHOUSE.

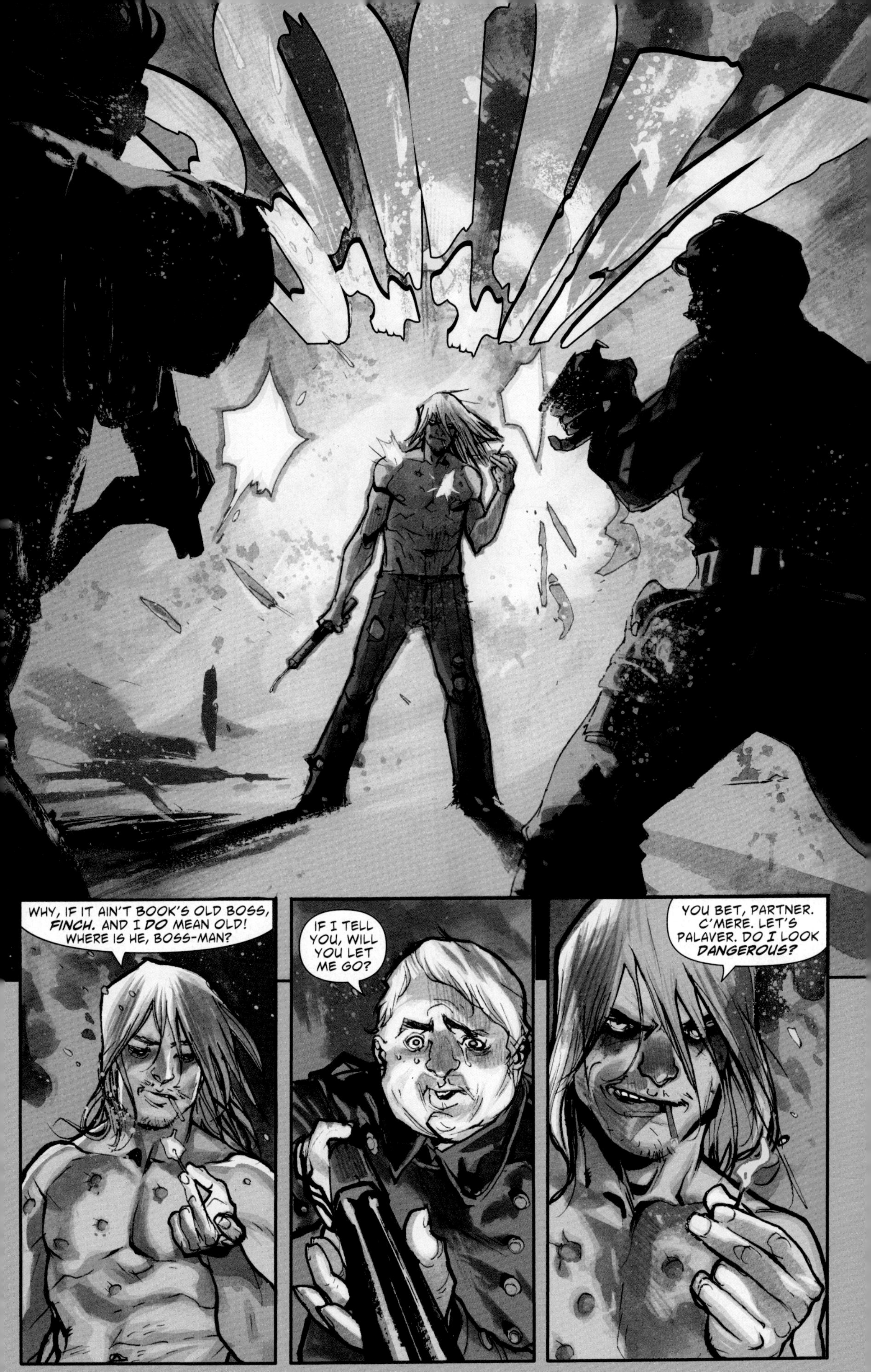
WHY, IF IT AIN'T BOOK'S OLD BOSS, *FINCH.* AND I *DO* MEAN OLD! WHERE IS HE, BOSS-MAN?
IF I TELL YOU, WILL YOU LET ME GO?
YOU BET, PARTNER. C'MERE. LET'S PALAVER. DO I LOOK *DANGEROUS?*

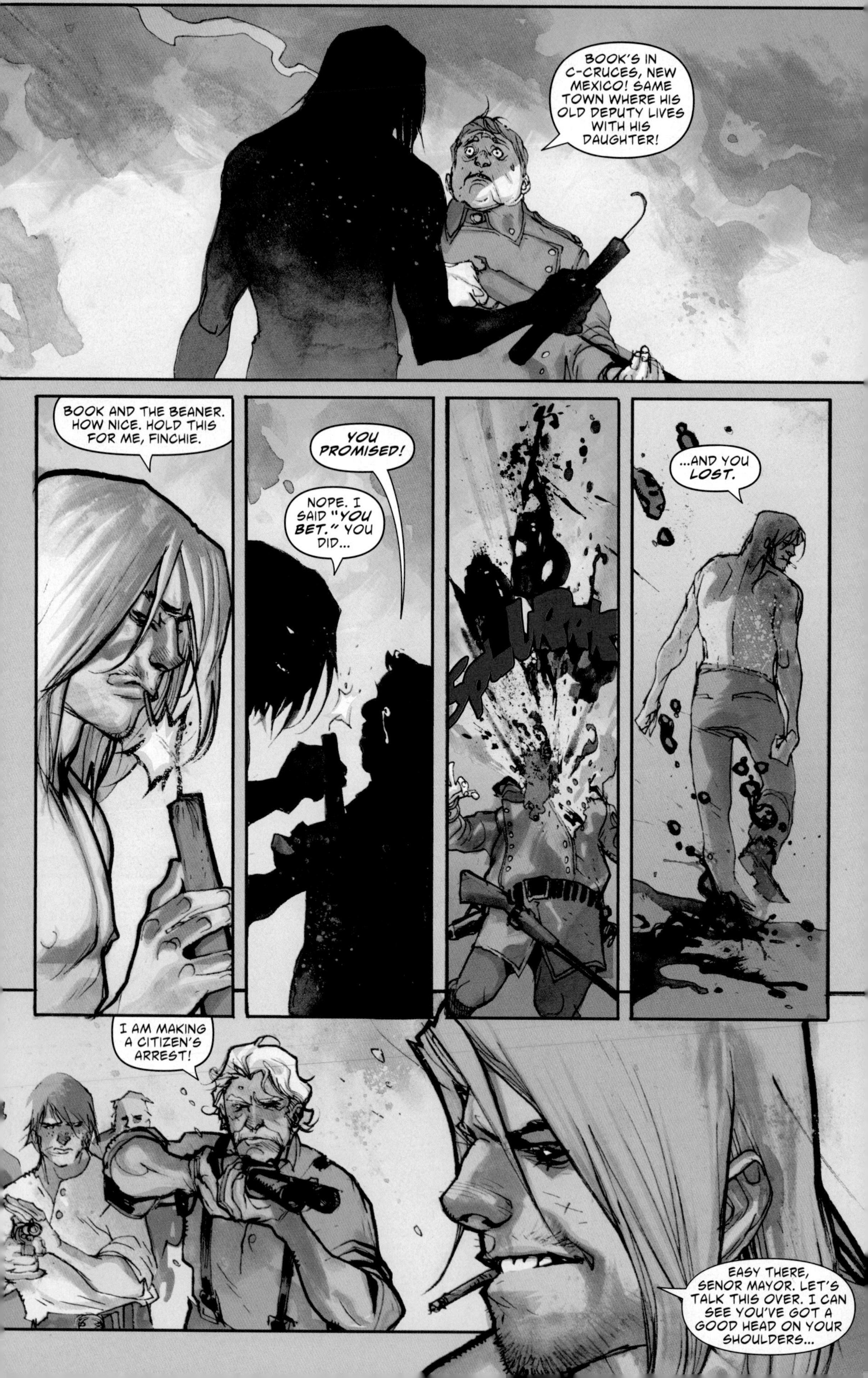
BOOK'S IN C-CRUCES, NEW MEXICO! SAME TOWN WHERE HIS OLD DEPUTY LIVES WITH HIS DAUGHTER!
BOOK AND THE BEANER. HOW NICE. HOLD THIS FOR ME, FINCHIE.
YOU PROMISED!
NOPE. I SAID "YOU BET." YOU DID...
...AND YOU LOST.
I AM MAKING A CITIZEN'S ARREST!
EASY THERE, SENOR MAYOR. LET'S TALK THIS OVER. I CAN SEE YOU'VE GOT A GOOD HEAD ON YOUR SHOULDERS...

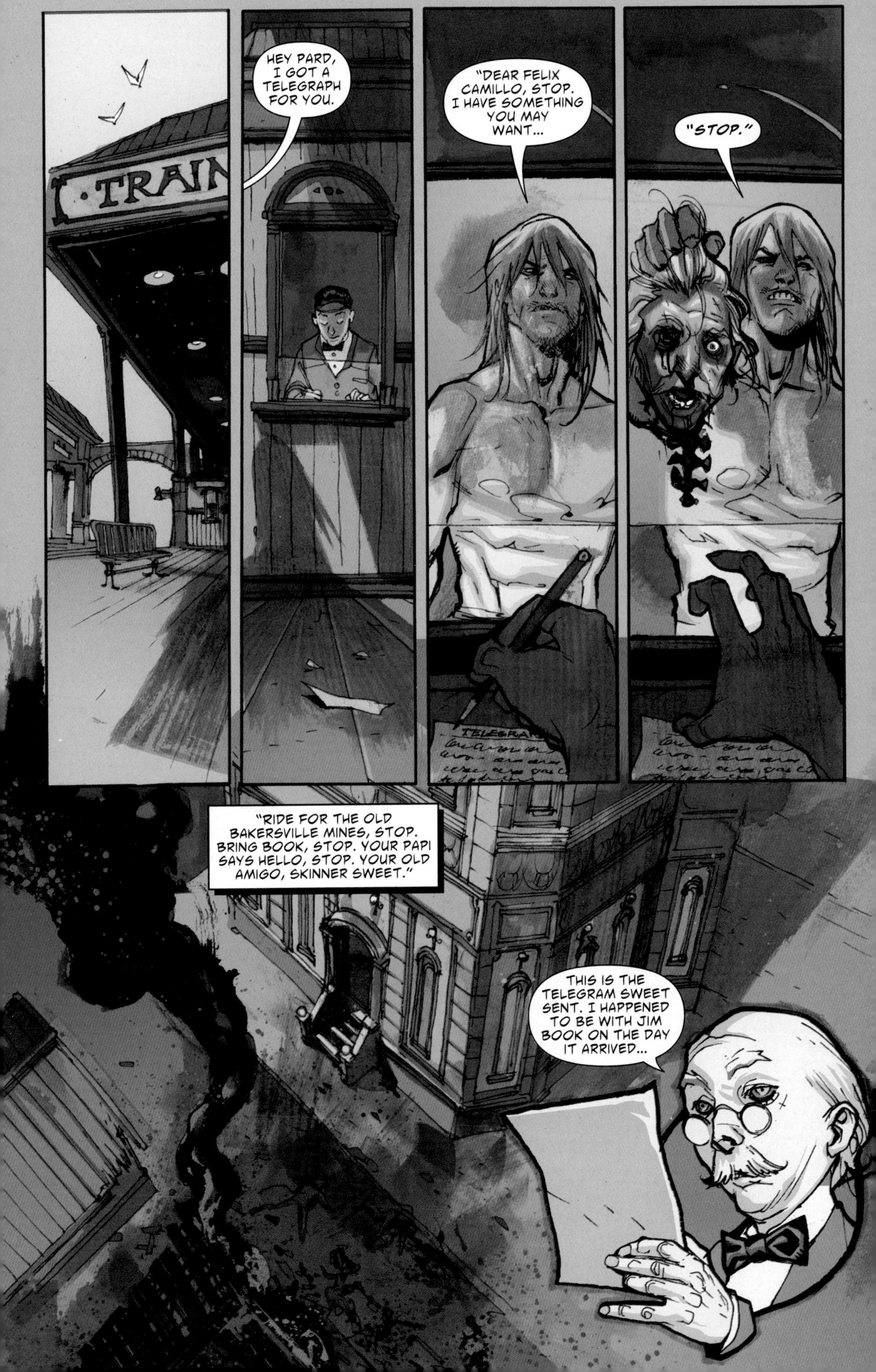
HEY PARD, I GOT A TELEGRAPH FOR YOU.
"DEAR FELIX CAMILLO, STOP. I HAVE SOMETHING YOU MAY WANT...
"STOP."
"RIDE FOR THE OLD BAKERSVILLE MINES, STOP. BRING BOOK, STOP. YOUR PAPI SAYS HELLO, STOP. YOUR OLD AMIGO, SKINNER SWEET."
THIS IS THE TELEGRAM SWEET SENT. I HAPPENED TO BE WITH JIM BOOK ON THE DAY IT ARRIVED...

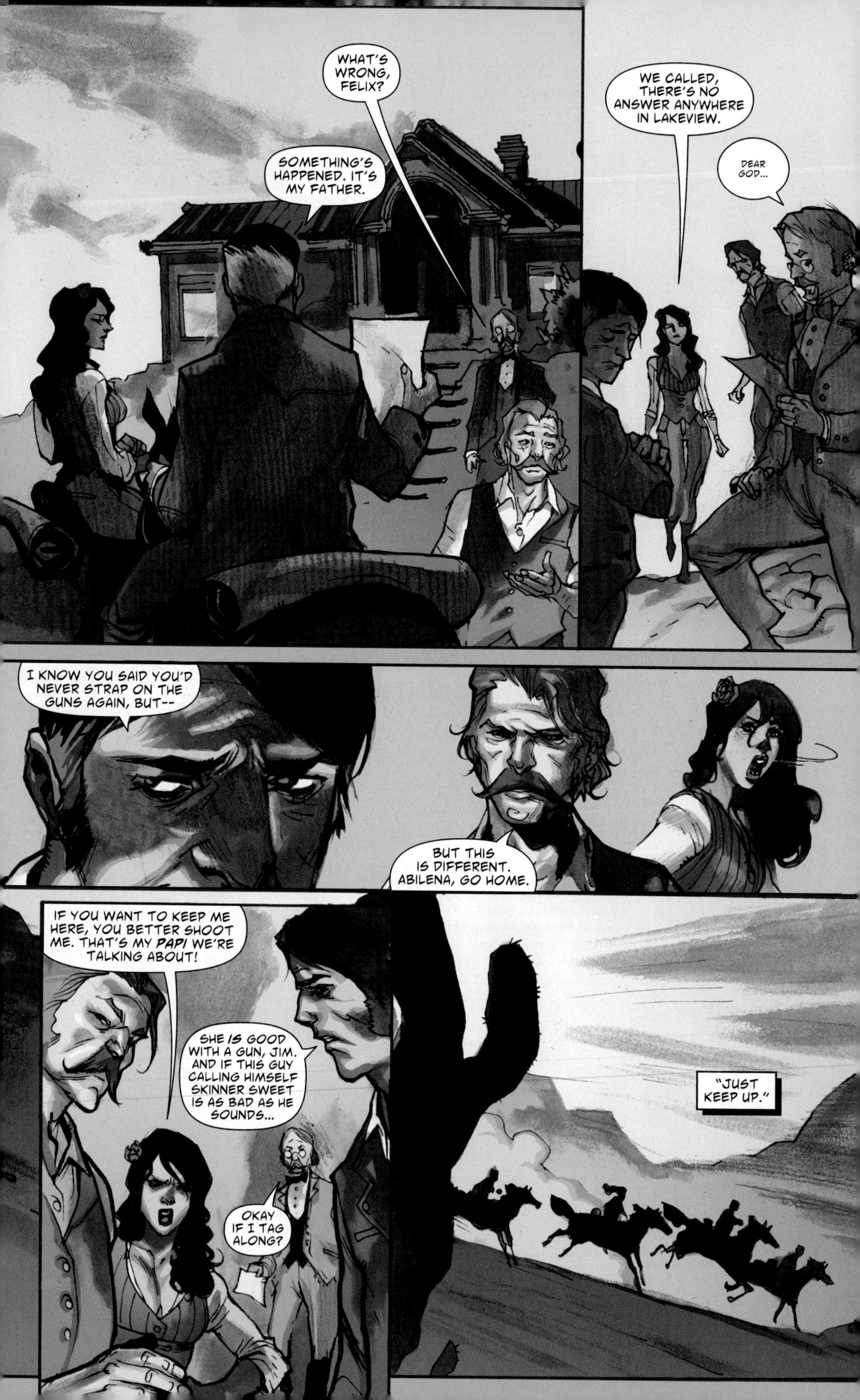
WHAT'S WRONG, FELIX?
SOMETHING'S HAPPENED. IT'S MY FATHER.
WE CALLED, THERE'S NO ANSWER ANYWHERE IN LAKEVIEW.
DEAR GOD...
I KNOW YOU SAID YOU'D NEVER STRAP ON THE GUNS AGAIN, BUT--
BUT THIS IS DIFFERENT. ABILENA, GO HOME.
IF YOU WANT TO KEEP ME HERE, YOU BETTER SHOOT ME. THAT'S MY *PAPI* WE'RE TALKING ABOUT!
SHE *IS* GOOD WITH A GUN, JIM. AND IF THIS GUY CALLING HIMSELF SKINNER SWEET IS AS BAD AS HE SOUNDS...
OKAY IF I TAG ALONG?
"JUST KEEP UP."

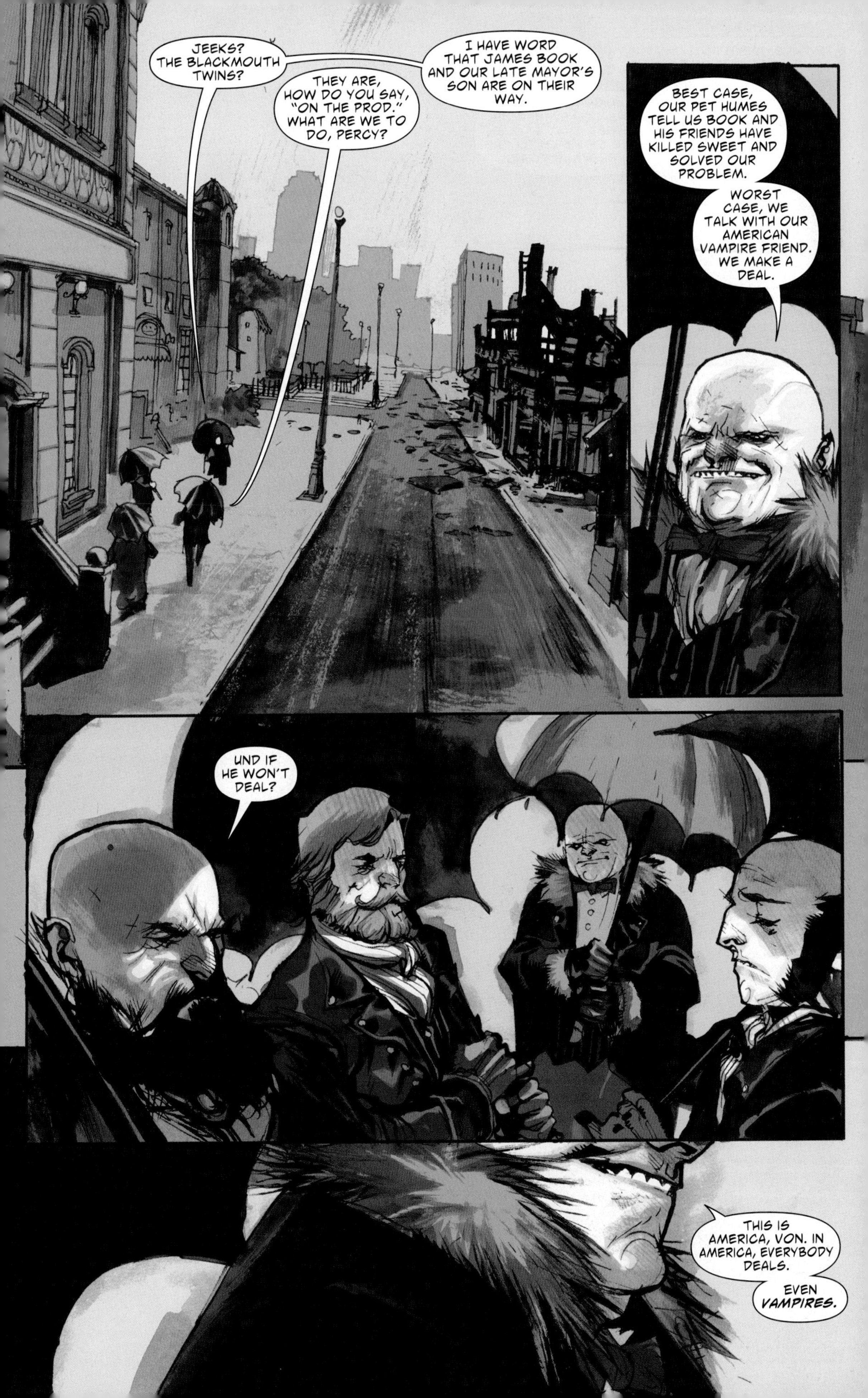
JEEKS? THE BLACKMOUTH TWINS?
I HAVE WORD THAT JAMES BOOK AND OUR LATE MAYOR'S SON ARE ON THEIR WAY.
THEY ARE, HOW DO YOU SAY, "ON THE PROD." WHAT ARE WE TO DO, PERCY?
BEST CASE, OUR PET HUMES TELL US BOOK AND HIS FRIENDS HAVE KILLED SWEET AND SOLVED OUR PROBLEM.
WORST CASE, WE TALK WITH OUR AMERICAN VAMPIRE FRIEND. WE MAKE A DEAL.
UND IF HE WON'T DEAL?
THIS IS AMERICA, VON. IN AMERICA, EVERYBODY DEALS.
EVEN VAMPIRES.

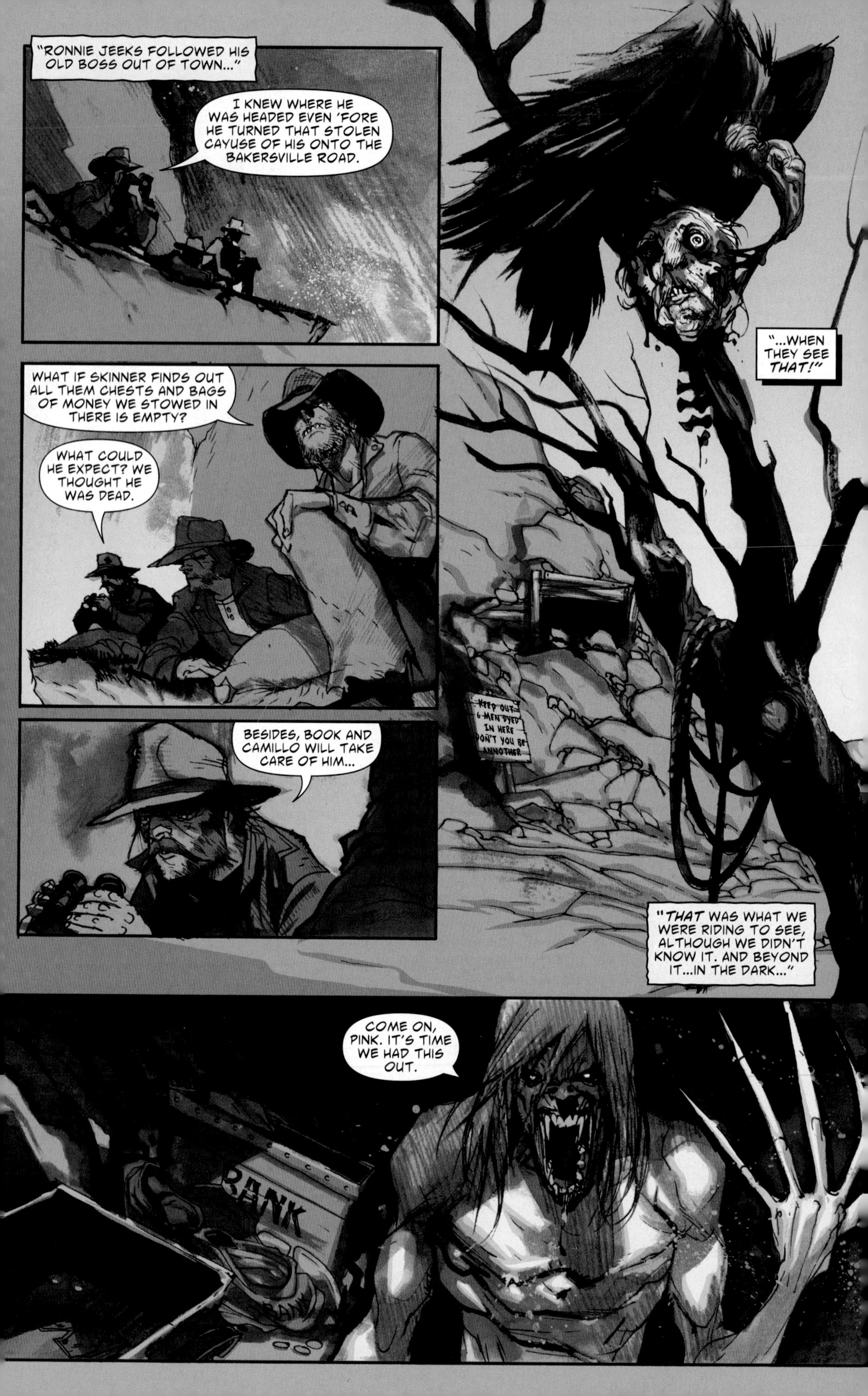
"RONNIE JEEKS FOLLOWED HIS OLD BOSS OUT OF TOWN..."
I KNEW WHERE HE WAS HEADED EVEN 'FORE HE TURNED THAT STOLEN CAYUSE OF HIS ONTO THE BAKERSVILLE ROAD.
WHAT IF SKINNER FINDS OUT ALL THEM CHESTS AND BAGS OF MONEY WE STOWED IN THERE IS EMPTY?
WHAT COULD HE EXPECT? WE THOUGHT HE WAS DEAD.
BESIDES, BOOK AND CAMILLO WILL TAKE CARE OF HIM...
"...WHEN THEY SEE THAT!"
KEEP OUT 6 MEN DYED IN HERE DON'T YOU BE ANNOTHER
"THAT WAS WHAT WE WERE RIDING TO SEE, ALTHOUGH WE DIDN'T KNOW IT. AND BEYOND IT...IN THE DARK..."
COME ON, PINK. IT'S TIME WE HAD THIS OUT.
BANK

Chapter Four

Double Exposure
Scott Snyder Writer

One Drop of Blood
Stephen King Writer

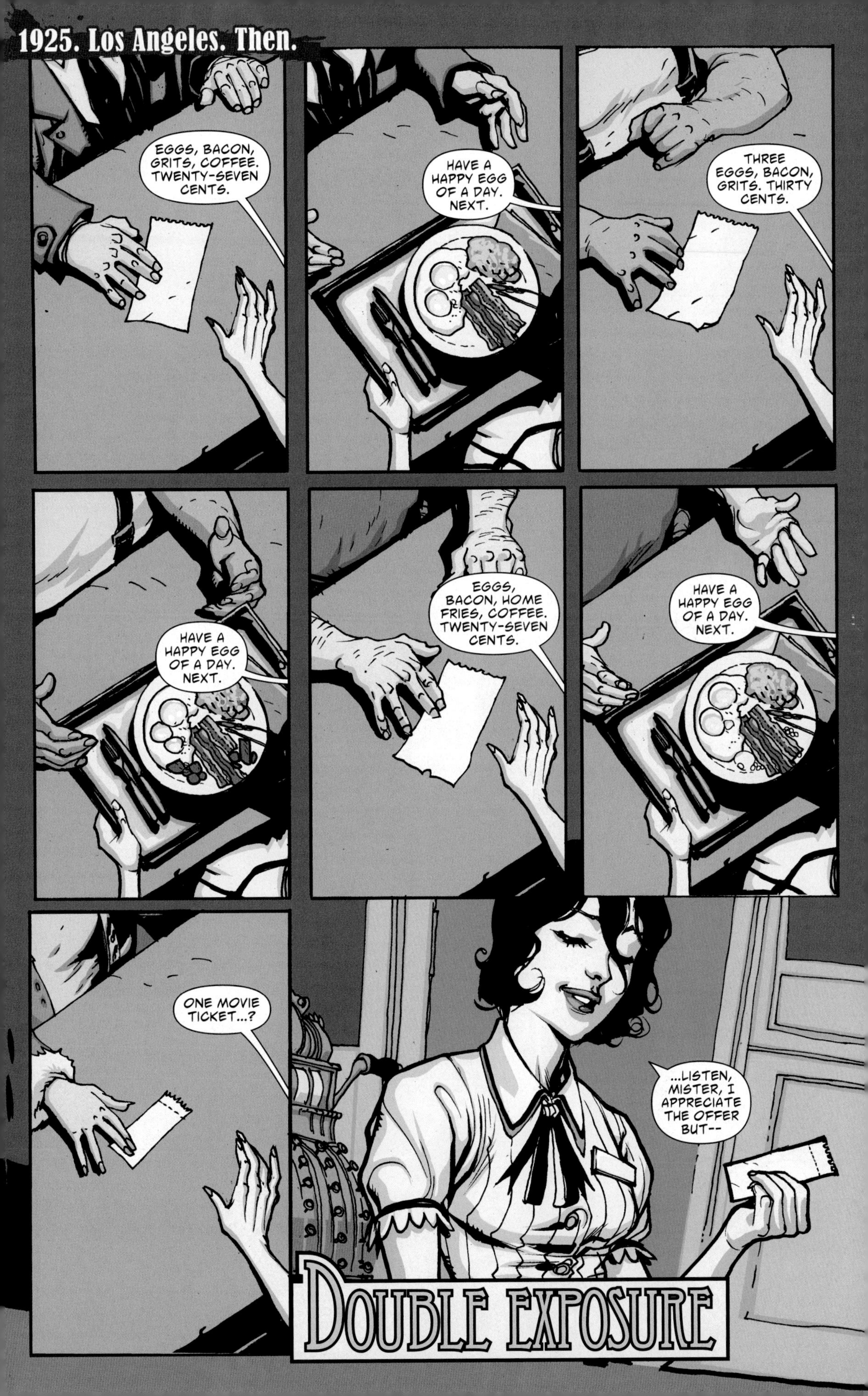
1925. Los Angeles. Then.
EGGS, BACON, GRITS, COFFEE. TWENTY-SEVEN CENTS.
HAVE A HAPPY EGG OF A DAY. NEXT.
THREE EGGS, BACON, GRITS. THIRTY CENTS.
HAVE A HAPPY EGG OF A DAY. NEXT.
EGGS, BACON, HOME FRIES, COFFEE. TWENTY-SEVEN CENTS.
HAVE A HAPPY EGG OF A DAY. NEXT.
ONE MOVIE TICKET...?
...LISTEN, MISTER, I APPRECIATE THE OFFER BUT--
DOUBLE EXPOSURE

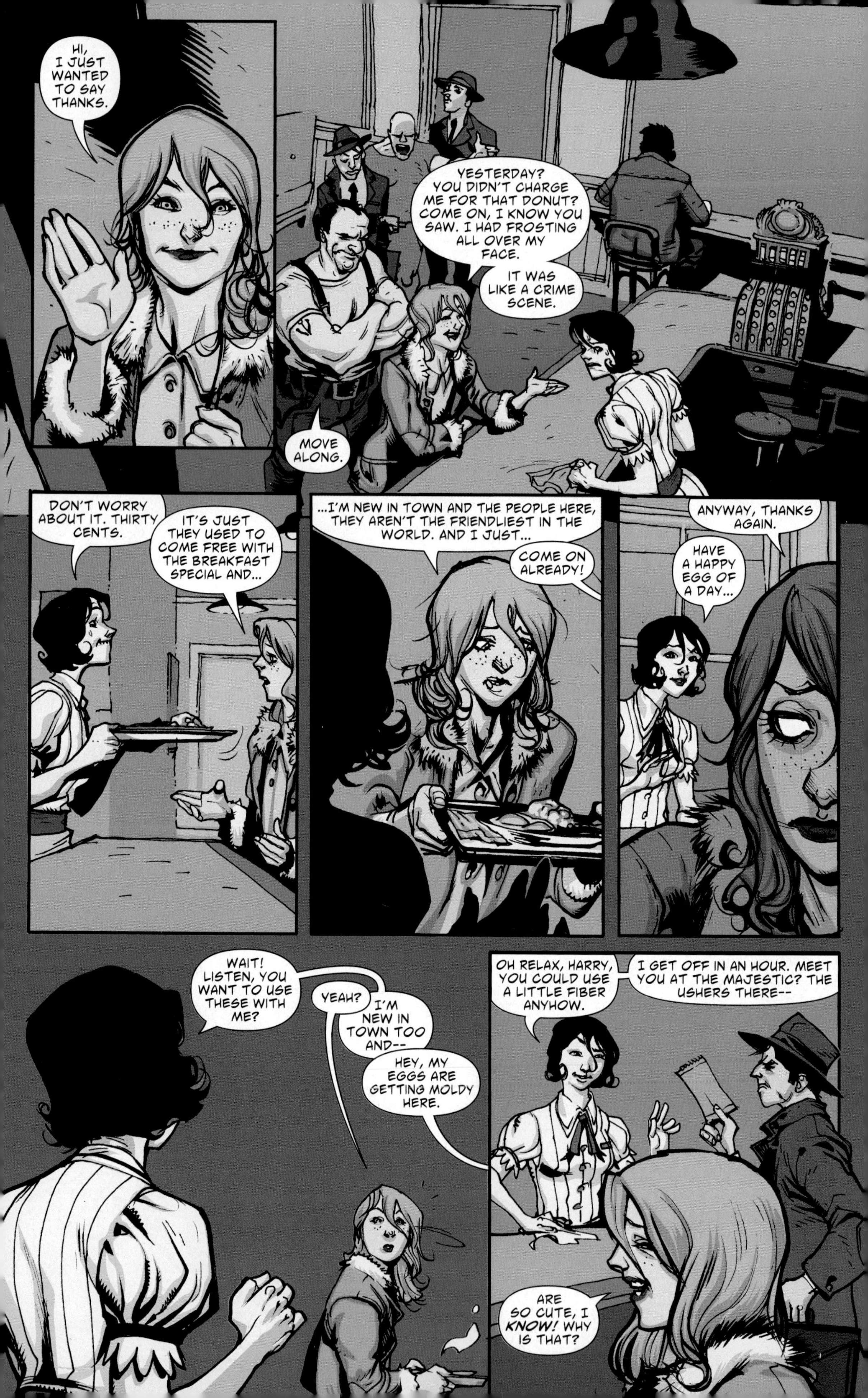
HI, I JUST WANTED TO SAY THANKS.
YESTERDAY? YOU DIDN'T CHARGE ME FOR THAT DONUT? COME ON, I KNOW YOU SAW. I HAD FROSTING ALL OVER MY FACE.
IT WAS LIKE A CRIME SCENE.
MOVE ALONG.
DON'T WORRY ABOUT IT. THIRTY CENTS.
IT'S JUST THEY USED TO COME FREE WITH THE BREAKFAST SPECIAL AND...
...I'M NEW IN TOWN AND THE PEOPLE HERE, THEY AREN'T THE FRIENDLIEST IN THE WORLD. AND I JUST...
COME ON ALREADY!
ANYWAY, THANKS AGAIN.
HAVE A HAPPY EGG OF A DAY...
WAIT! LISTEN, YOU WANT TO USE THESE WITH ME?
YEAH?
I'M NEW IN TOWN TOO AND--
HEY, MY EGGS ARE GETTING MOLDY HERE.
OH RELAX, HARRY, YOU COULD USE A LITTLE FIBER ANYHOW.
I GET OFF IN AN HOUR. MEET YOU AT THE MAJESTIC? THE USHERS THERE--
ARE SO CUTE, I KNOW! WHY IS THAT?

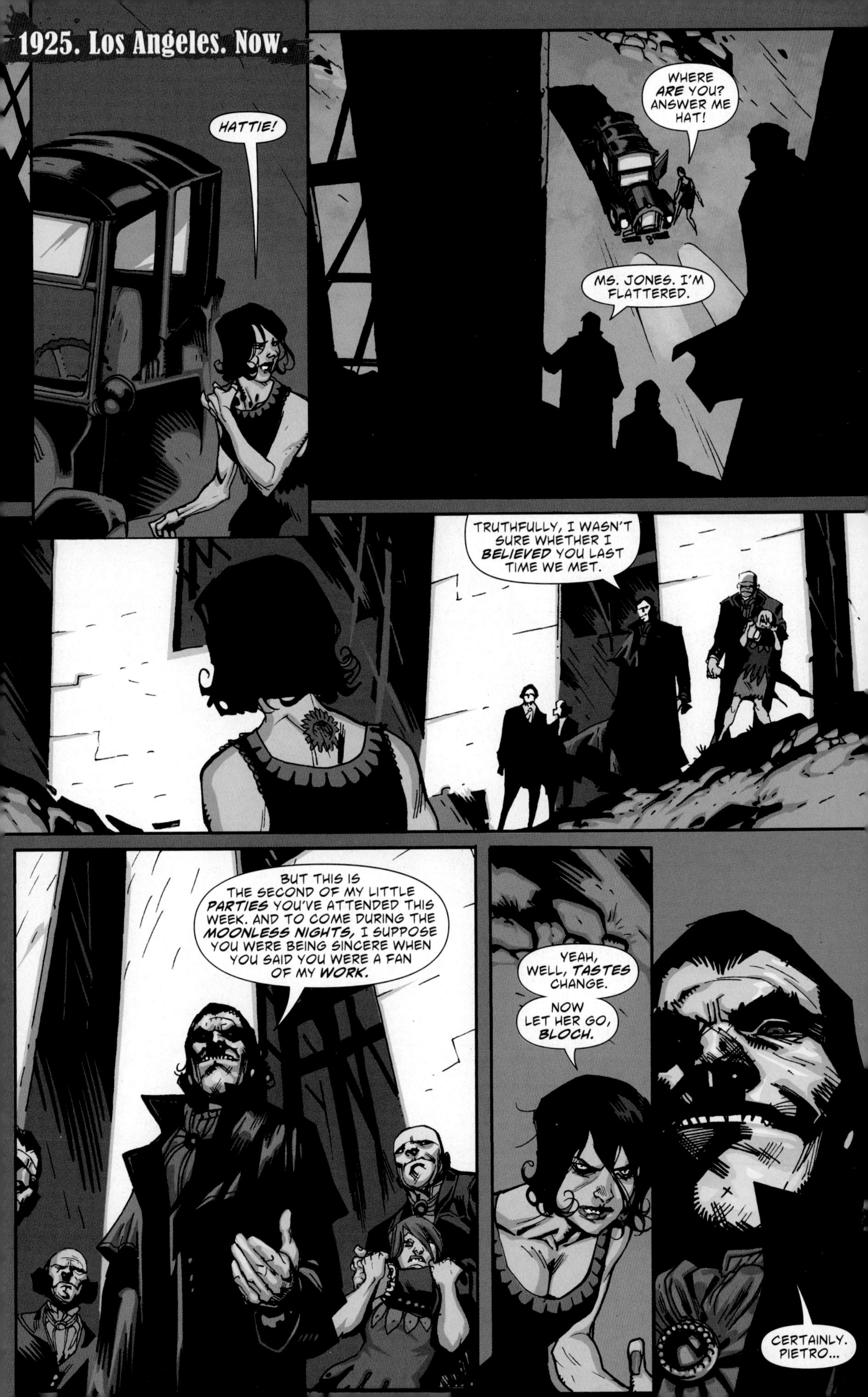
1925. Los Angeles. Now.
HATTIE!
WHERE ARE YOU? ANSWER ME HAT!
MS. JONES. I'M FLATTERED.
TRUTHFULLY, I WASN'T SURE WHETHER I BELIEVED YOU LAST TIME WE MET.
BUT THIS IS THE SECOND OF MY LITTLE PARTIES YOU'VE ATTENDED THIS WEEK. AND TO COME DURING THE MOONLESS NIGHTS, I SUPPOSE YOU WERE BEING SINCERE WHEN YOU SAID YOU WERE A FAN OF MY WORK.
YEAH, WELL, TASTES CHANGE.
NOW LET HER GO, BLOCH.
CERTAINLY. PIETRO...

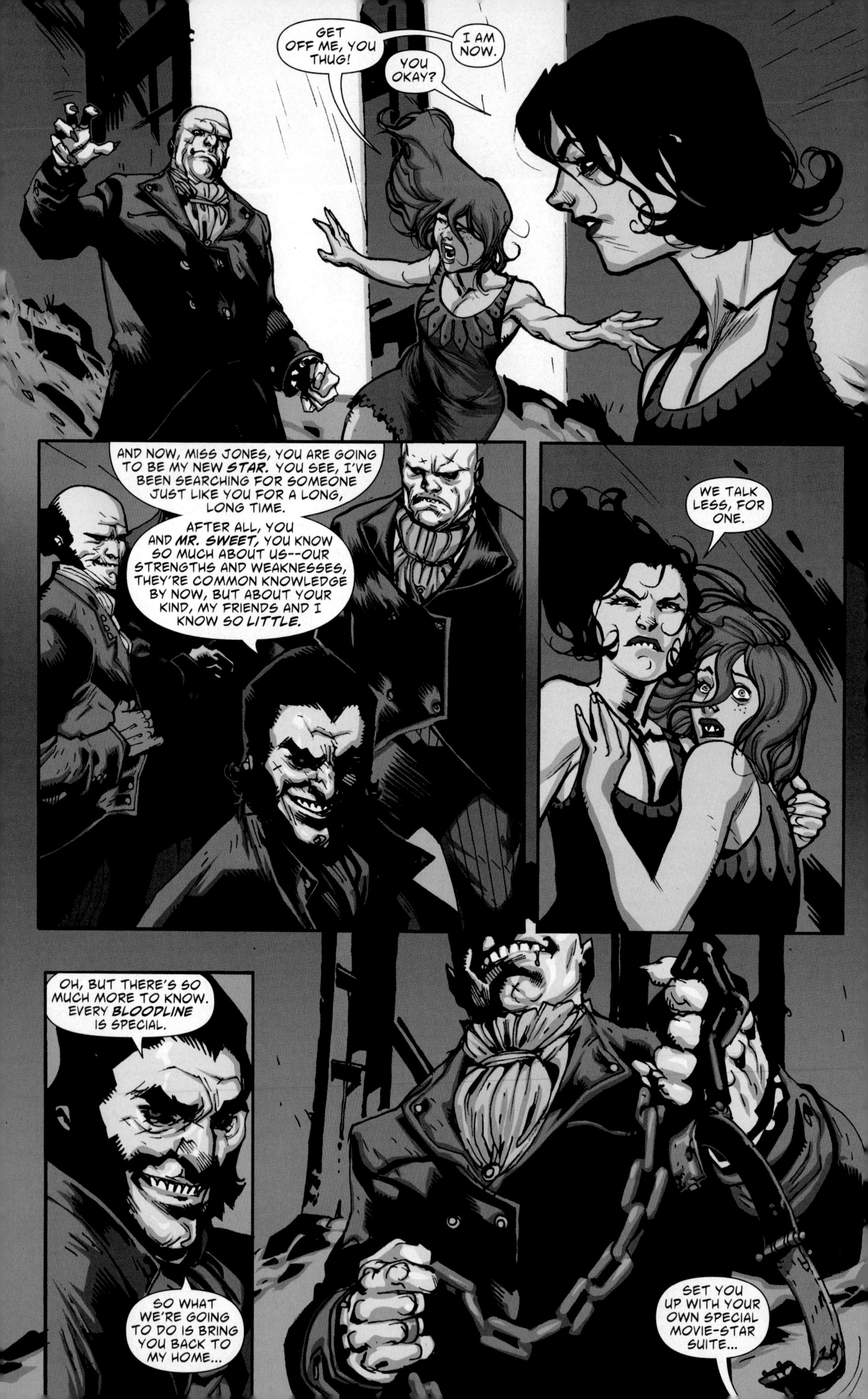
GET OFF ME, YOU THUG!
YOU OKAY?
I AM NOW.
AND NOW, MISS JONES, YOU ARE GOING TO BE MY NEW STAR. YOU SEE, I'VE BEEN SEARCHING FOR SOMEONE JUST LIKE YOU FOR A LONG, LONG TIME.
AFTER ALL, YOU AND MR. SWEET, YOU KNOW SO MUCH ABOUT US--OUR STRENGTHS AND WEAKNESSES, THEY'RE COMMON KNOWLEDGE BY NOW, BUT ABOUT YOUR KIND, MY FRIENDS AND I KNOW SO LITTLE.
WE TALK LESS, FOR ONE.
OH, BUT THERE'S SO MUCH MORE TO KNOW. EVERY BLOODLINE IS SPECIAL.
SO WHAT WE'RE GOING TO DO IS BRING YOU BACK TO MY HOME...
SET YOU UP WITH YOUR OWN SPECIAL MOVIE-STAR SUITE...

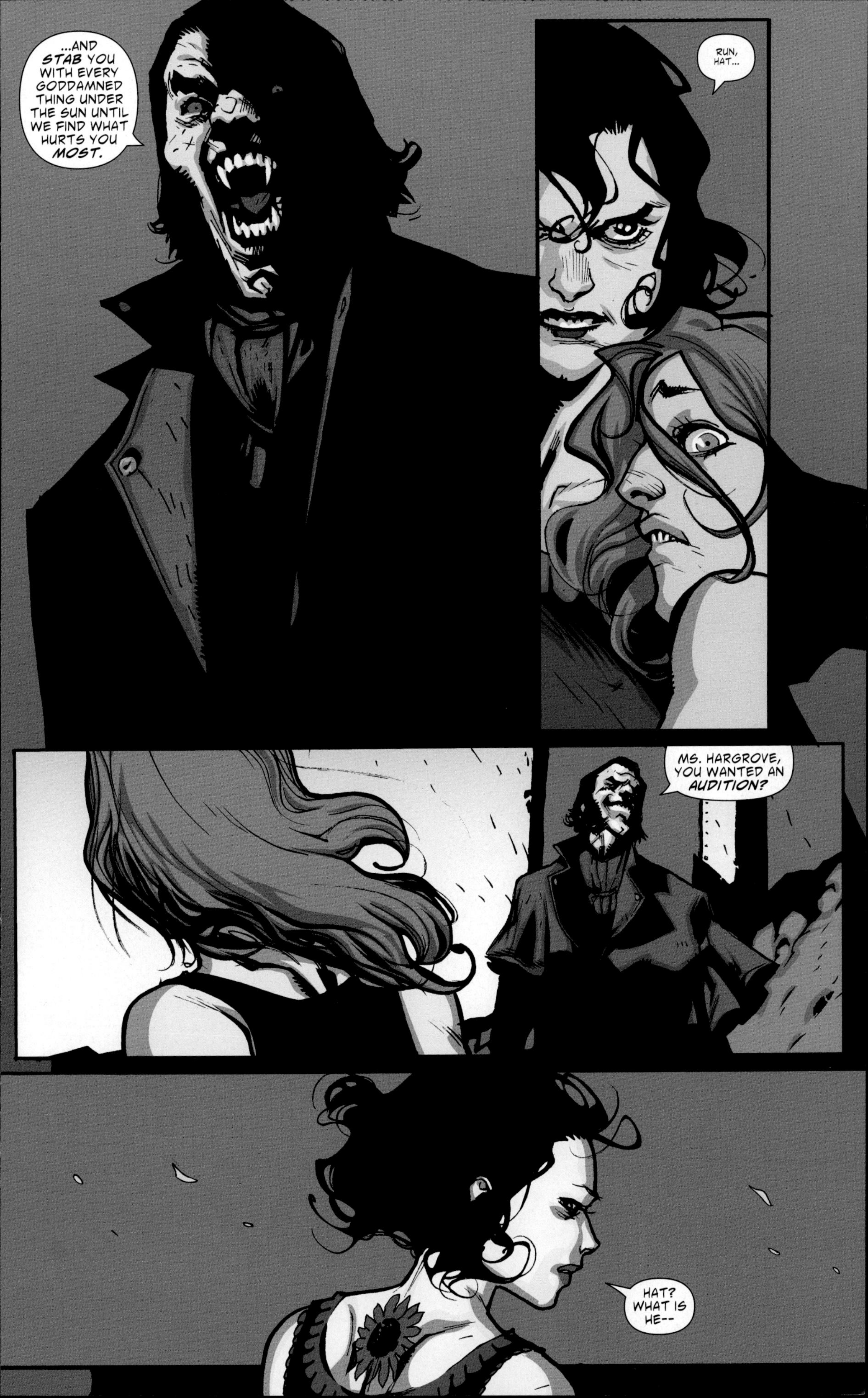
...AND STAB YOU WITH EVERY GODDAMNED THING UNDER THE SUN UNTIL WE FIND WHAT HURTS YOU MOST.
RUN, HAT...
MS. HARGROVE, YOU WANTED AN AUDITION?
HAT? WHAT IS HE--

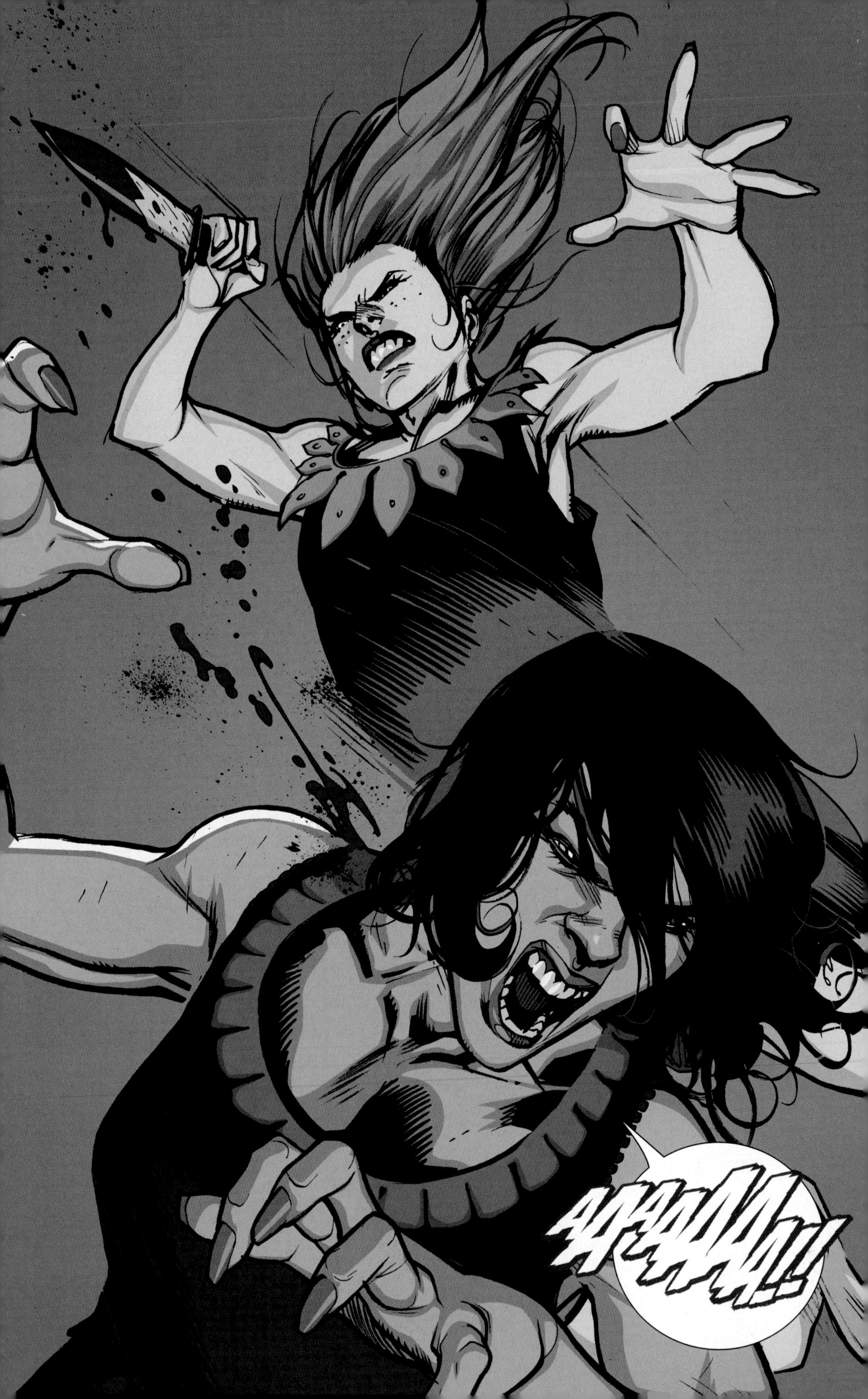
AAAAAA!!

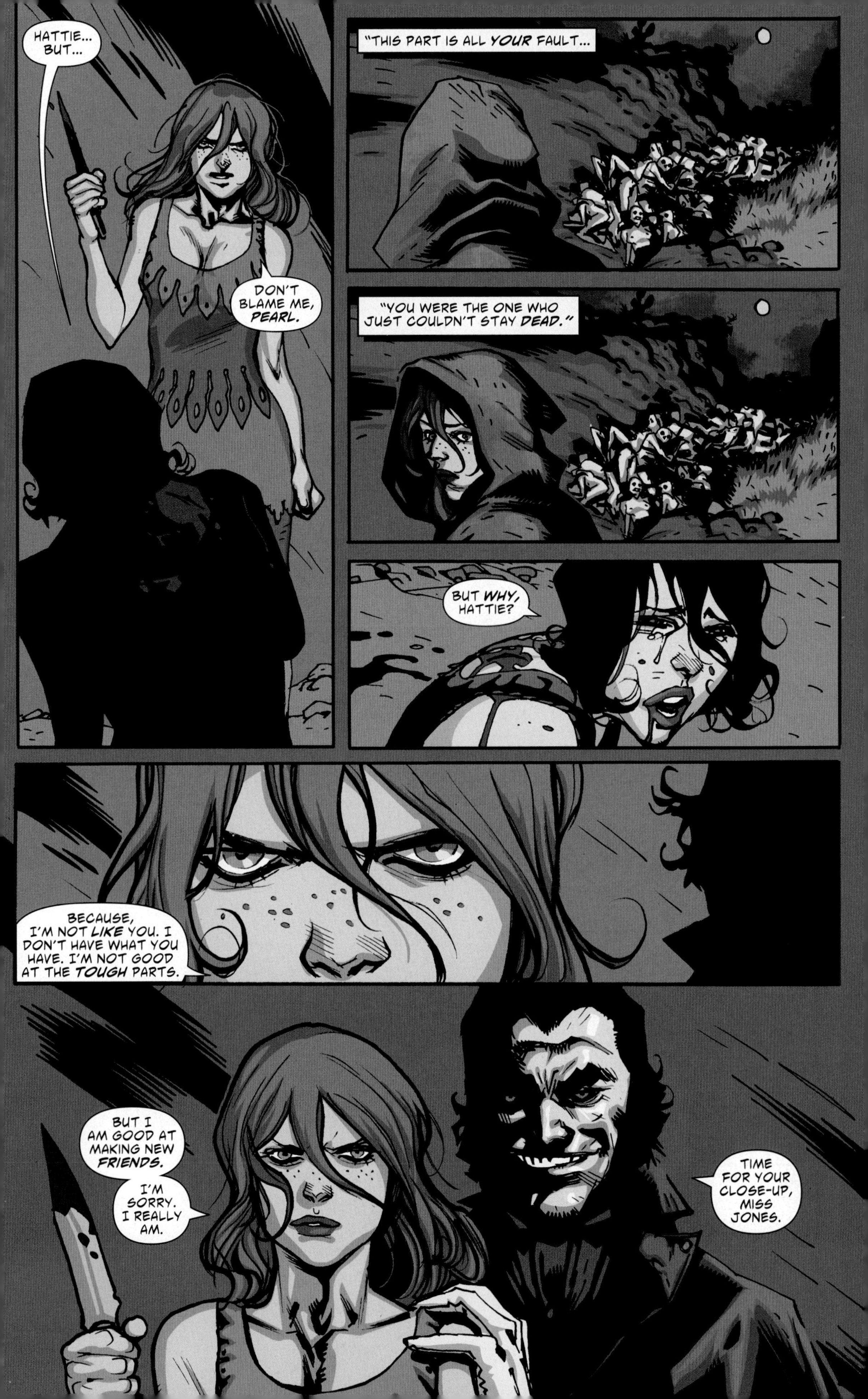
HATTIE... BUT...
DON'T BLAME ME, PEARL.
"THIS PART IS ALL YOUR FAULT...
"YOU WERE THE ONE WHO JUST COULDN'T STAY DEAD."
BUT WHY, HATTIE?
BECAUSE, I'M NOT LIKE YOU. I DON'T HAVE WHAT YOU HAVE. I'M NOT GOOD AT THE TOUGH PARTS.
BUT I AM GOOD AT MAKING NEW FRIENDS.
I'M SORRY. I REALLY AM.
TIME FOR YOUR CLOSE-UP, MISS JONES.

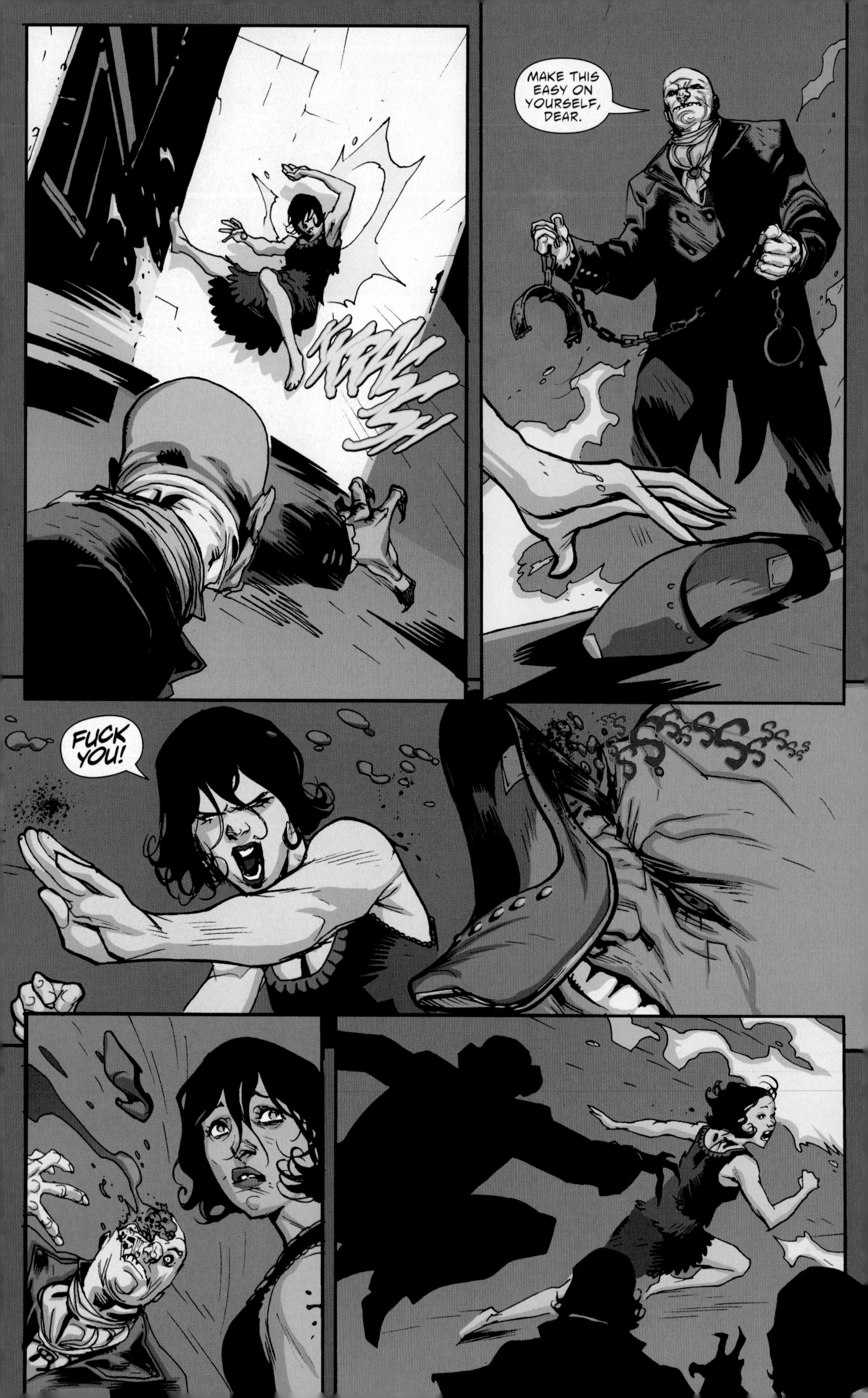
KRAASH
MAKE THIS EASY ON YOURSELF, DEAR.
FUCK YOU!
SSSSSS

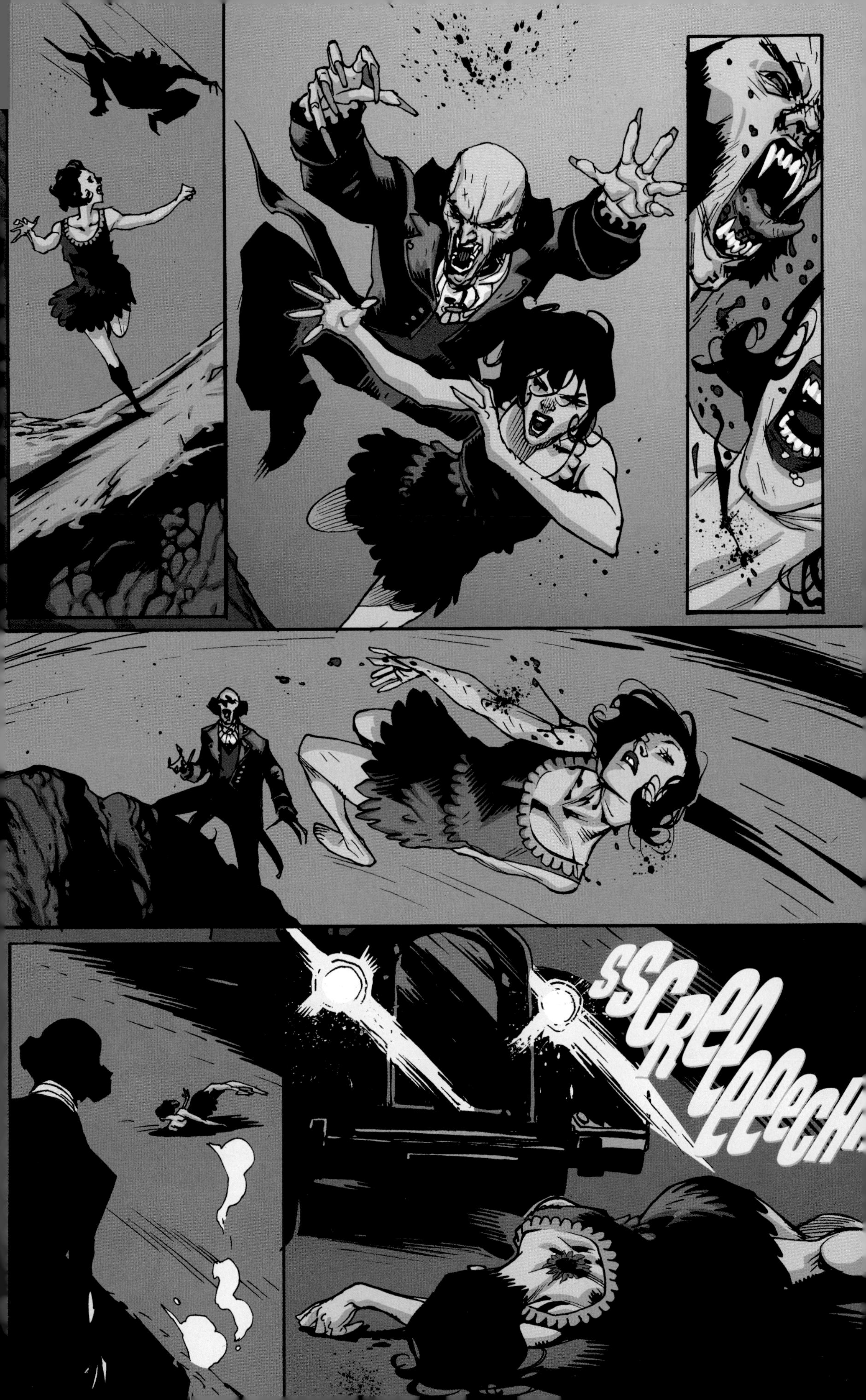
SSCREEEEEEECH!

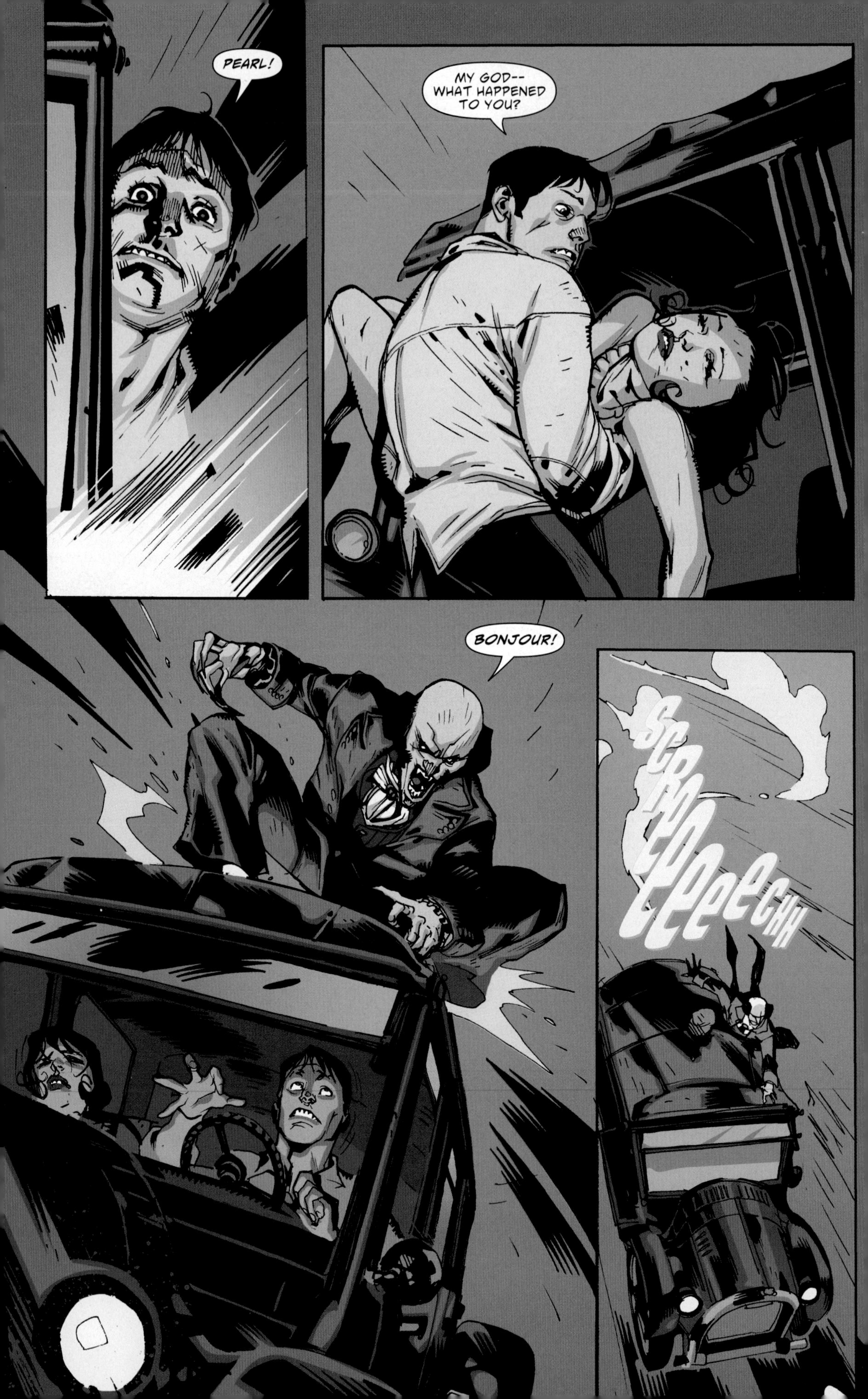
PEARL!
MY GOD-- WHAT HAPPENED TO YOU?
BONJOUR!
SCREEEEEECHH

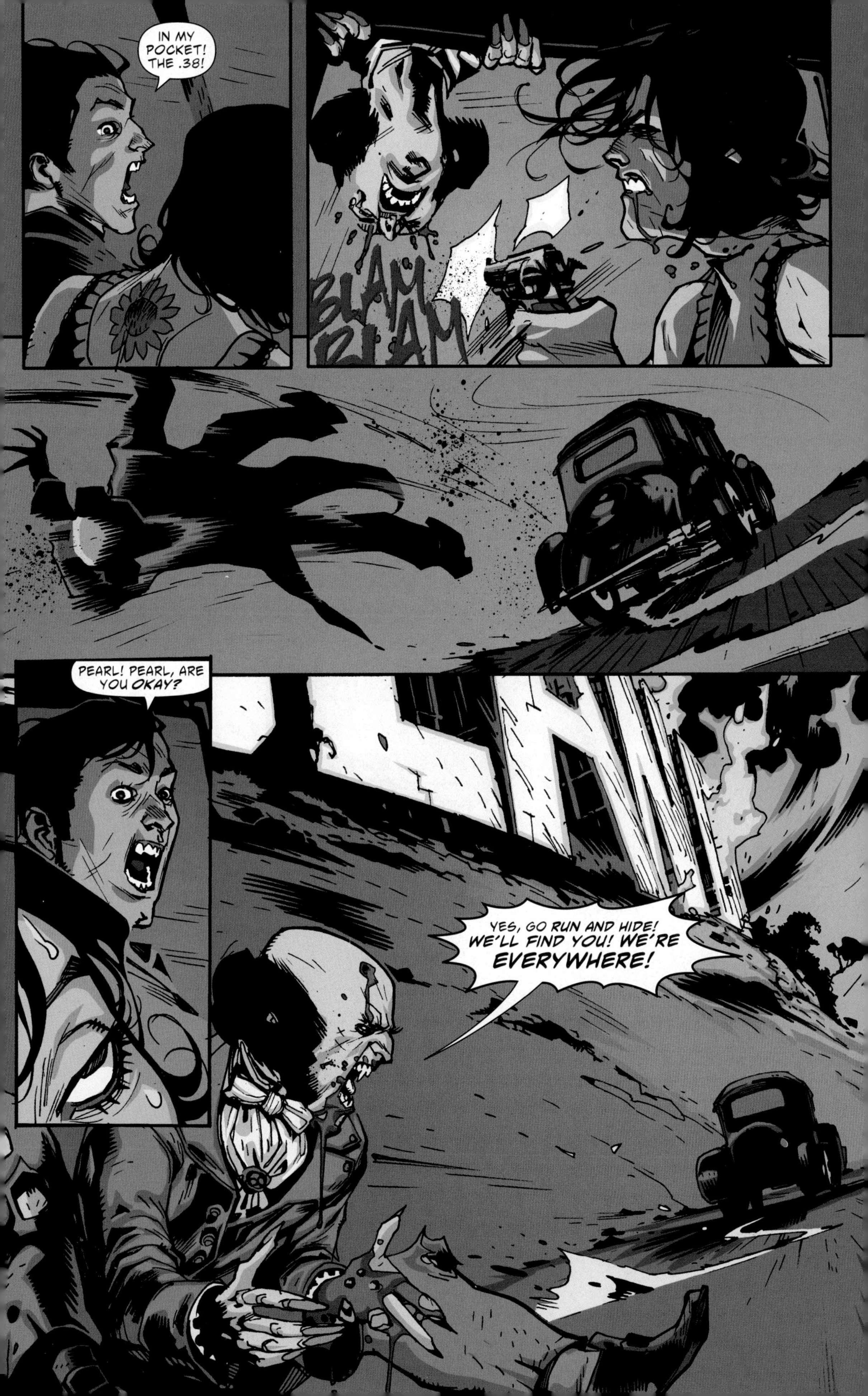
IN MY POCKET! THE .38!
BLAM
BLAM
PEARL! PEARL, ARE YOU OKAY?
YES, GO RUN AND HIDE! WE'LL FIND YOU! WE'RE EVERYWHERE!

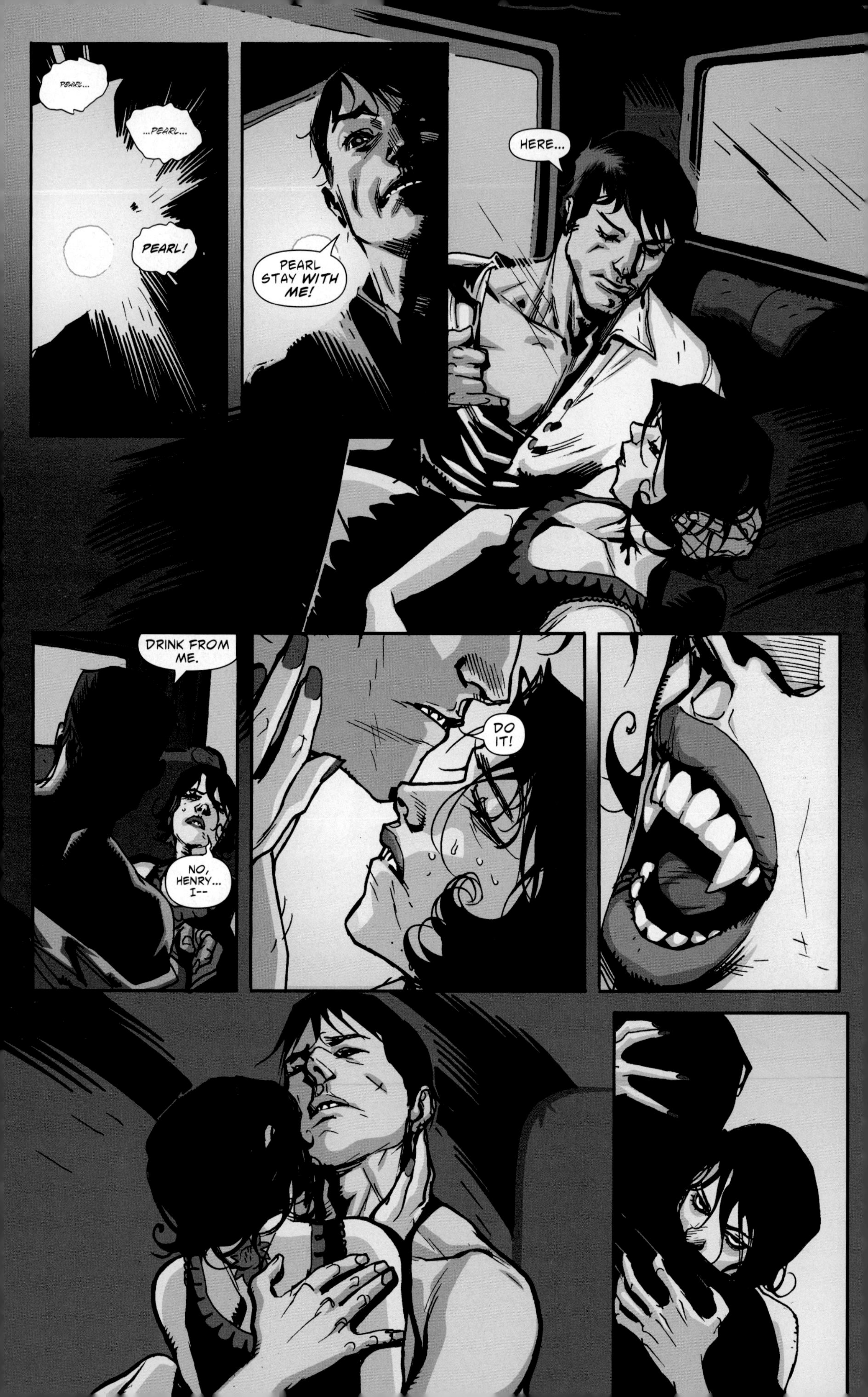
PEARL...
...PEARL...
PEARL!
PEARL STAY WITH ME!
HERE...
DRINK FROM ME.
NO, HENRY... I--
DO IT!

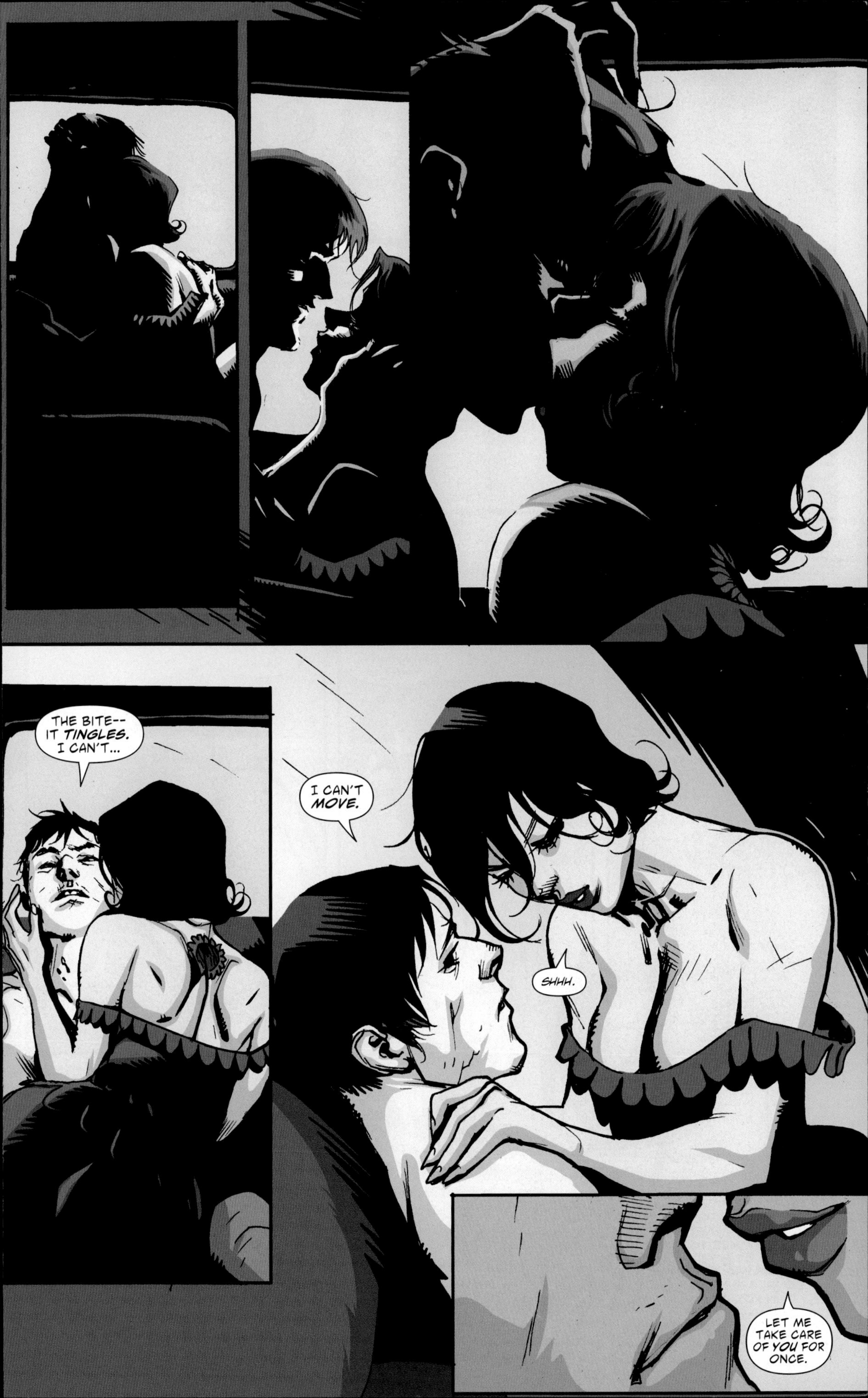
THE BITE-- IT TINGLES. I CAN'T...
I CAN'T MOVE.
SHHH.
LET ME TAKE CARE OF YOU FOR ONCE.

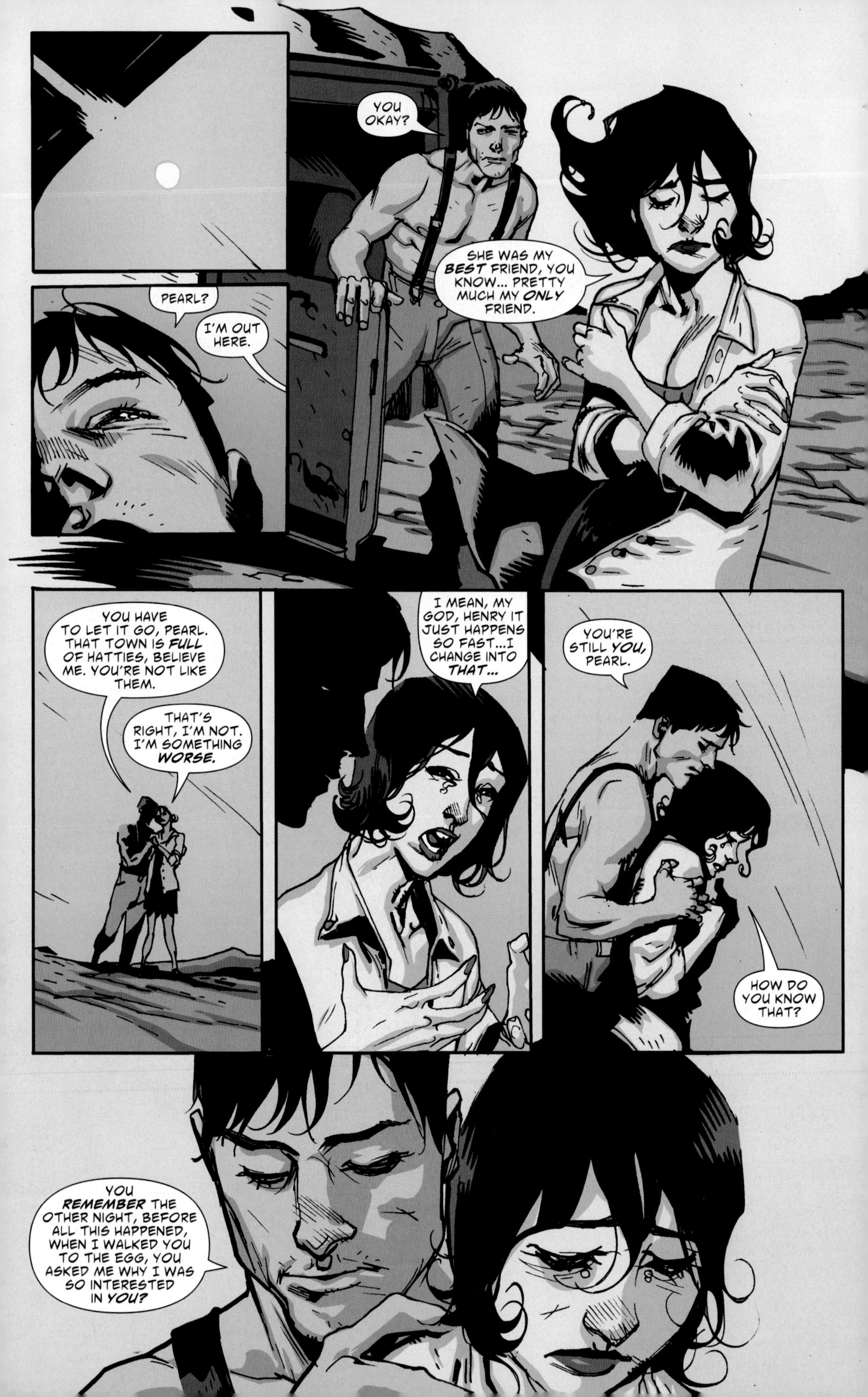
YOU OKAY?
PEARL?
I'M OUT HERE.
SHE WAS MY BEST FRIEND, YOU KNOW... PRETTY MUCH MY ONLY FRIEND.
YOU HAVE TO LET IT GO, PEARL. THAT TOWN IS FULL OF HATTIES, BELIEVE ME. YOU'RE NOT LIKE THEM.
THAT'S RIGHT, I'M NOT. I'M SOMETHING WORSE.
I MEAN, MY GOD, HENRY IT JUST HAPPENS SO FAST...I CHANGE INTO THAT...
YOU'RE STILL YOU, PEARL.
HOW DO YOU KNOW THAT?
YOU REMEMBER THE OTHER NIGHT, BEFORE ALL THIS HAPPENED, WHEN I WALKED YOU TO THE EGG, YOU ASKED ME WHY I WAS SO INTERESTED IN YOU?

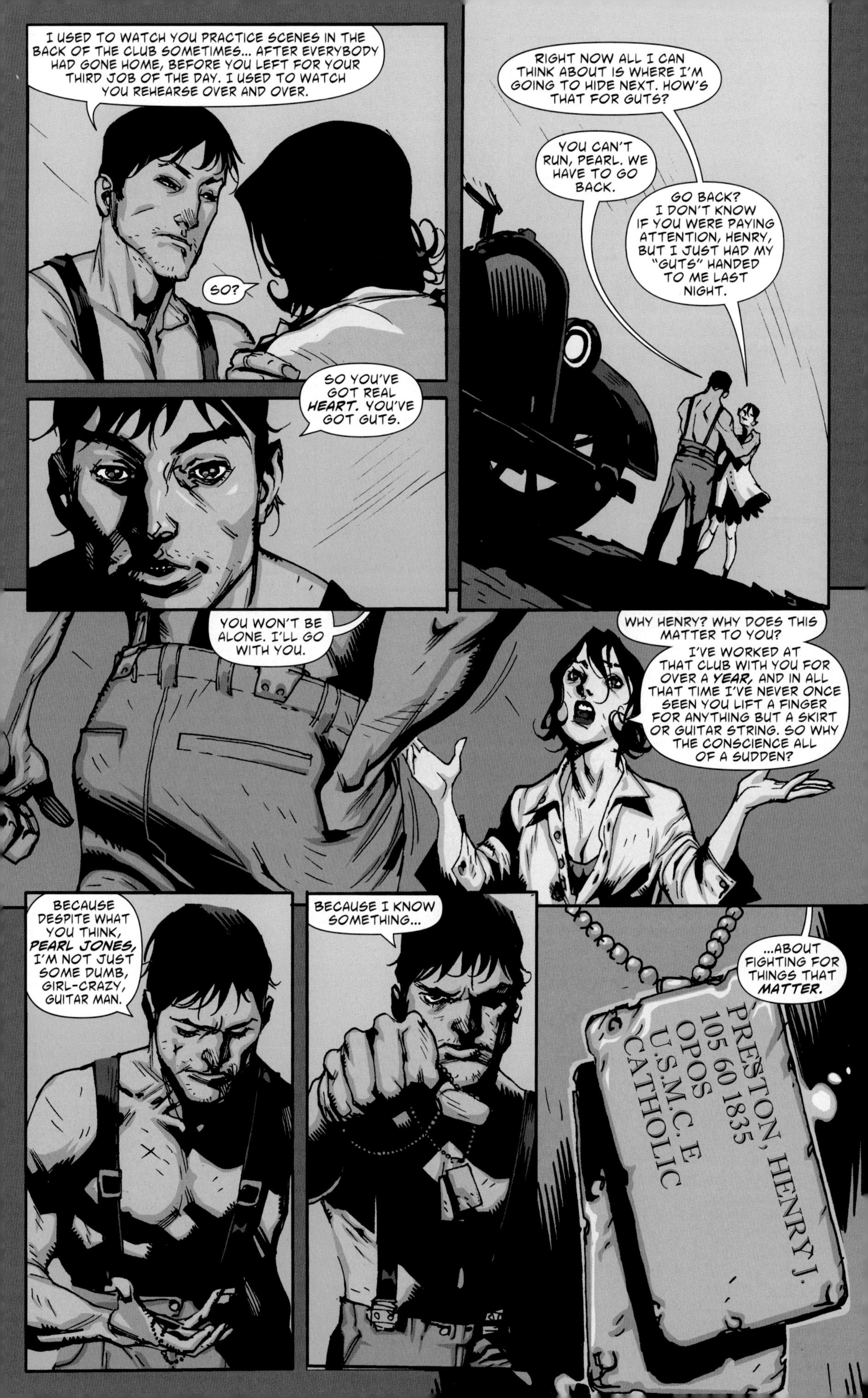
I USED TO WATCH YOU PRACTICE SCENES IN THE BACK OF THE CLUB SOMETIMES... AFTER EVERYBODY HAD GONE HOME, BEFORE YOU LEFT FOR YOUR THIRD JOB OF THE DAY. I USED TO WATCH YOU REHEARSE OVER AND OVER.
SO?
SO YOU'VE GOT REAL HEART. YOU'VE GOT GUTS.
RIGHT NOW ALL I CAN THINK ABOUT IS WHERE I'M GOING TO HIDE NEXT. HOW'S THAT FOR GUTS?
YOU CAN'T RUN, PEARL. WE HAVE TO GO BACK.
GO BACK? I DON'T KNOW IF YOU WERE PAYING ATTENTION, HENRY, BUT I JUST HAD MY "GUTS" HANDED TO ME LAST NIGHT.
YOU WON'T BE ALONE. I'LL GO WITH YOU.
WHY HENRY? WHY DOES THIS MATTER TO YOU?
I'VE WORKED AT THAT CLUB WITH YOU FOR OVER A YEAR, AND IN ALL THAT TIME I'VE NEVER ONCE SEEN YOU LIFT A FINGER FOR ANYTHING BUT A SKIRT OR GUITAR STRING. SO WHY THE CONSCIENCE ALL OF A SUDDEN?
BECAUSE DESPITE WHAT YOU THINK, PEARL JONES, I'M NOT JUST SOME DUMB, GIRL-CRAZY, GUITAR MAN.
BECAUSE I KNOW SOMETHING...
...ABOUT FIGHTING FOR THINGS THAT MATTER.
PRESTON, HENRY J.
105 60 1835
OPOS
U.S.M.C.E
CATHOLIC

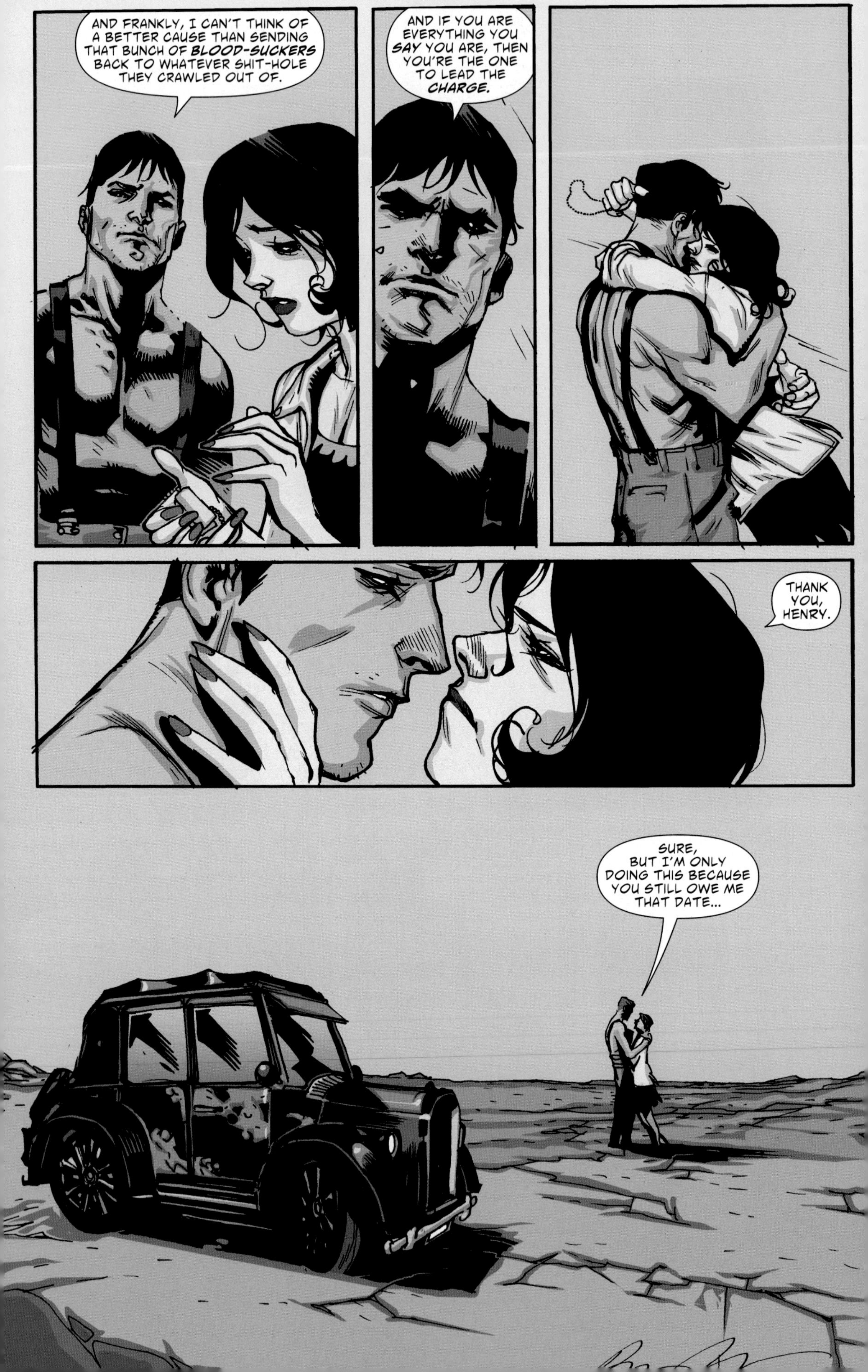
AND FRANKLY, I CAN'T THINK OF A BETTER CAUSE THAN SENDING THAT BUNCH OF BLOOD-SUCKERS BACK TO WHATEVER SHIT-HOLE THEY CRAWLED OUT OF.
AND IF YOU ARE EVERYTHING YOU SAY YOU ARE, THEN YOU'RE THE ONE TO LEAD THE CHARGE.
THANK YOU, HENRY.
SURE, BUT I'M ONLY DOING THIS BECAUSE YOU STILL OWE ME THAT DATE...

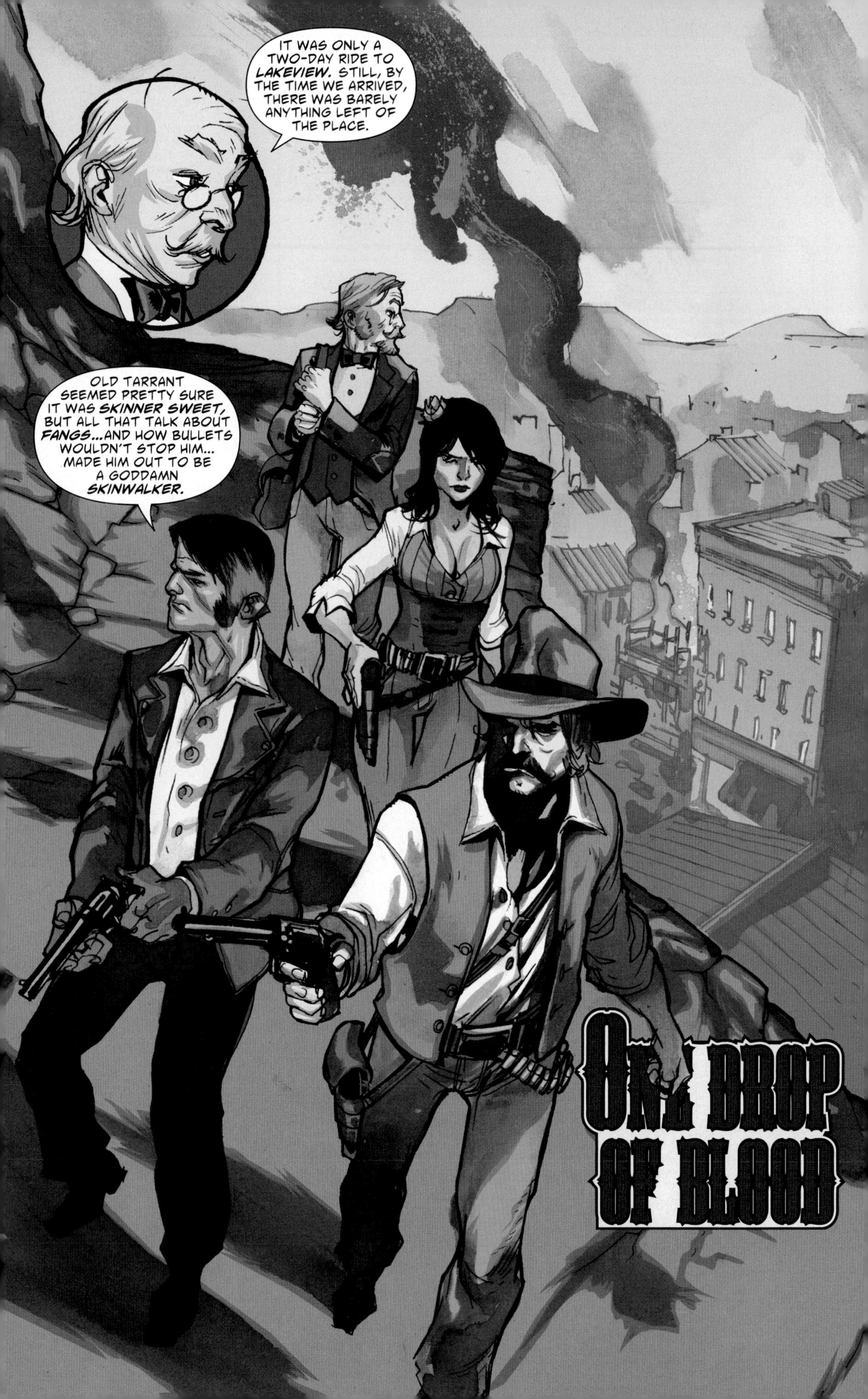
IT WAS ONLY A TWO-DAY RIDE TO LAKEVIEW. STILL, BY THE TIME WE ARRIVED, THERE WAS BARELY ANYTHING LEFT OF THE PLACE.
OLD TARRANT SEEMED PRETTY SURE IT WAS SKINNER SWEET, BUT ALL THAT TALK ABOUT FANGS...AND HOW BULLETS WOULDN'T STOP HIM... MADE HIM OUT TO BE A GODDAMN SKINWALKER.
ONE DROP OF BLOOD

ARE THERE SUCH THINGS?

SOMEONE TOLD ME SO ONCE. I *DIDN'T* LISTEN TO HIM.

JIM, YOU DON'T KNOW HOW MANY TIMES I'VE DOUBTED WHAT I SAW THAT DAY.

NOW THAT'S A LIE IF *I* EVER HEARD ONE. BESIDES, I STOOD NEXT TO PERCY MYSELF. SENT A *SHIVER* THROUGH ME WHEN THE MAN TOOK MY HAND.

BEEN THINKING IT OVER THE LAST COUPLE DAYS, AND IT'S *NOT* THAT I DIDN'T BELIEVE YOU, WILL. IT'S THAT I JUST *DIDN'T CARE.* SO LONG AS SWEET WAS DEAD, IT DIDN'T MATTER TO ME IF THE DEVIL HIMSELF DID THE DEED.

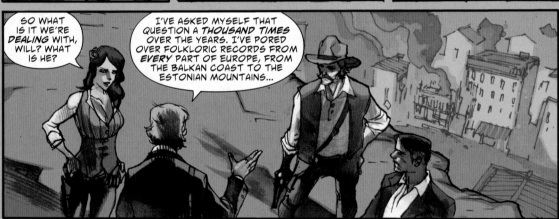

SO WHAT IS IT WE'RE *DEALING* WITH, WILL? WHAT IS HE?

I'VE ASKED MYSELF THAT QUESTION A *THOUSAND TIMES* OVER THE YEARS. I'VE PORED OVER FOLKLORIC RECORDS FROM *EVERY* PART OF EUROPE, FROM THE BALKAN COAST TO THE ESTONIAN MOUNTAINS...

AND WHAT I'VE COME TO BELIEVE IS THAT MR. PERCY IS WHAT WAS REFERRED TO IN THE OLD WORLD AS A *WAMPYR.*

A WHAT?

A VAMPIRE.

A BEING *INFECTED* WITH AN *ANCIENT EVIL,* RISEN FROM THE GRAVE TO FEED ON THE LIFE BLOOD OF THE LIVING UNDER COVER OF DARKNESS. THE INFECTION IS COMMUNICATED THROUGH THE *BLOOD.*

I IMAGINE SOME MEASURE OF PERCY'S BLOOD MUST HAVE GOTTEN INTO SWEET'S WOUNDS BEFORE SWEET PASSED.

BUT WHAT I CAN'T FIGURE OUT IS...

...VAMPIRES...BY ALL ACCOUNTS THEY ONLY WALK BY NIGHT. IF SWEET IS A VAMPIRE, HOW WAS HE ABLE TO TAKE LAKEVIEW IN FULL SUNLIGHT?

I ONLY WANT TO KNOW *ONE THING,* WILL...

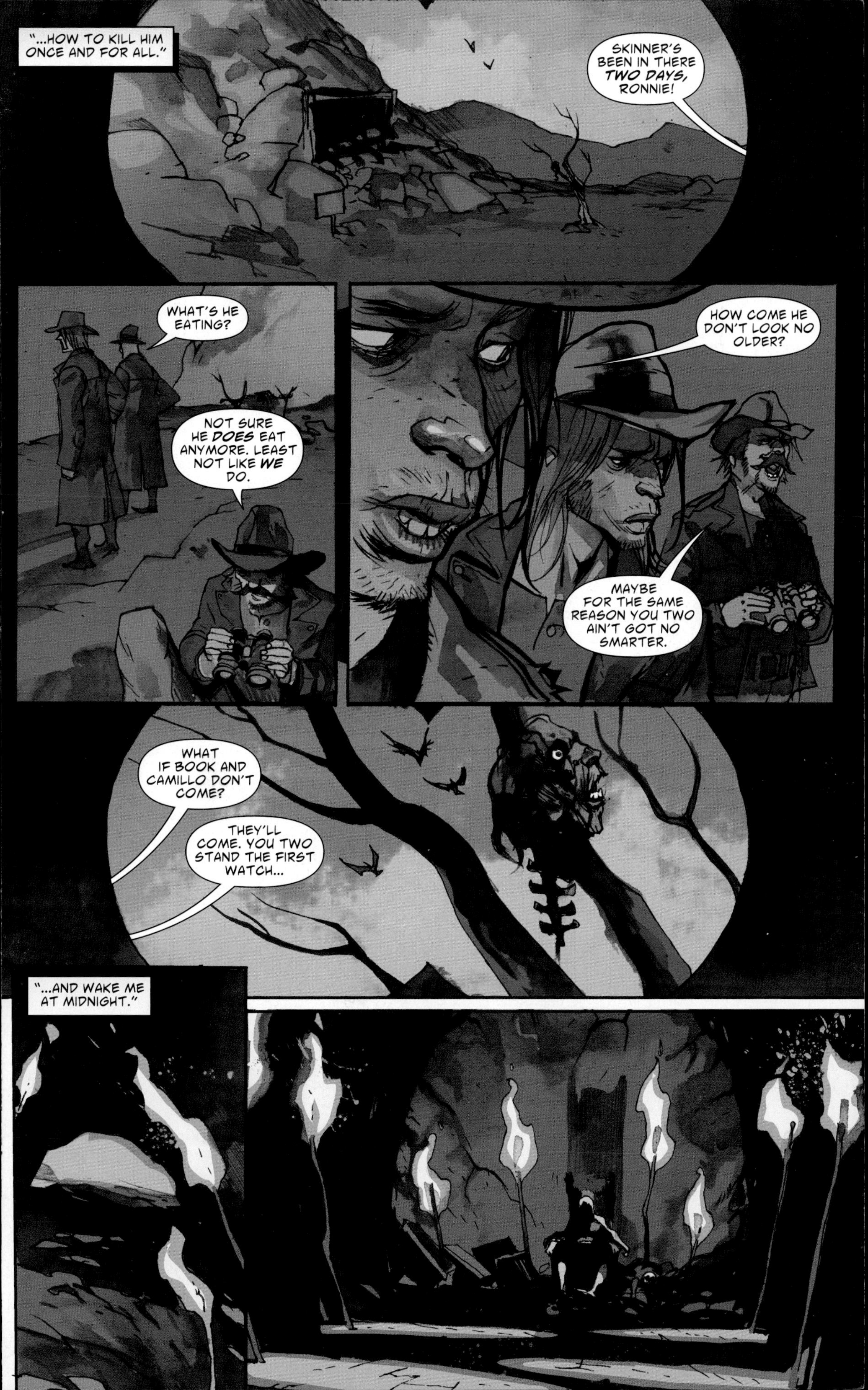
"...HOW TO KILL HIM ONCE AND FOR ALL."
SKINNER'S BEEN IN THERE TWO DAYS, RONNIE!
WHAT'S HE EATING?
NOT SURE HE DOES EAT ANYMORE. LEAST NOT LIKE WE DO.
HOW COME HE DON'T LOOK NO OLDER?
MAYBE FOR THE SAME REASON YOU TWO AIN'T GOT NO SMARTER.
WHAT IF BOOK AND CAMILLO DON'T COME?
THEY'LL COME. YOU TWO STAND THE FIRST WATCH...
"...AND WAKE ME AT MIDNIGHT."

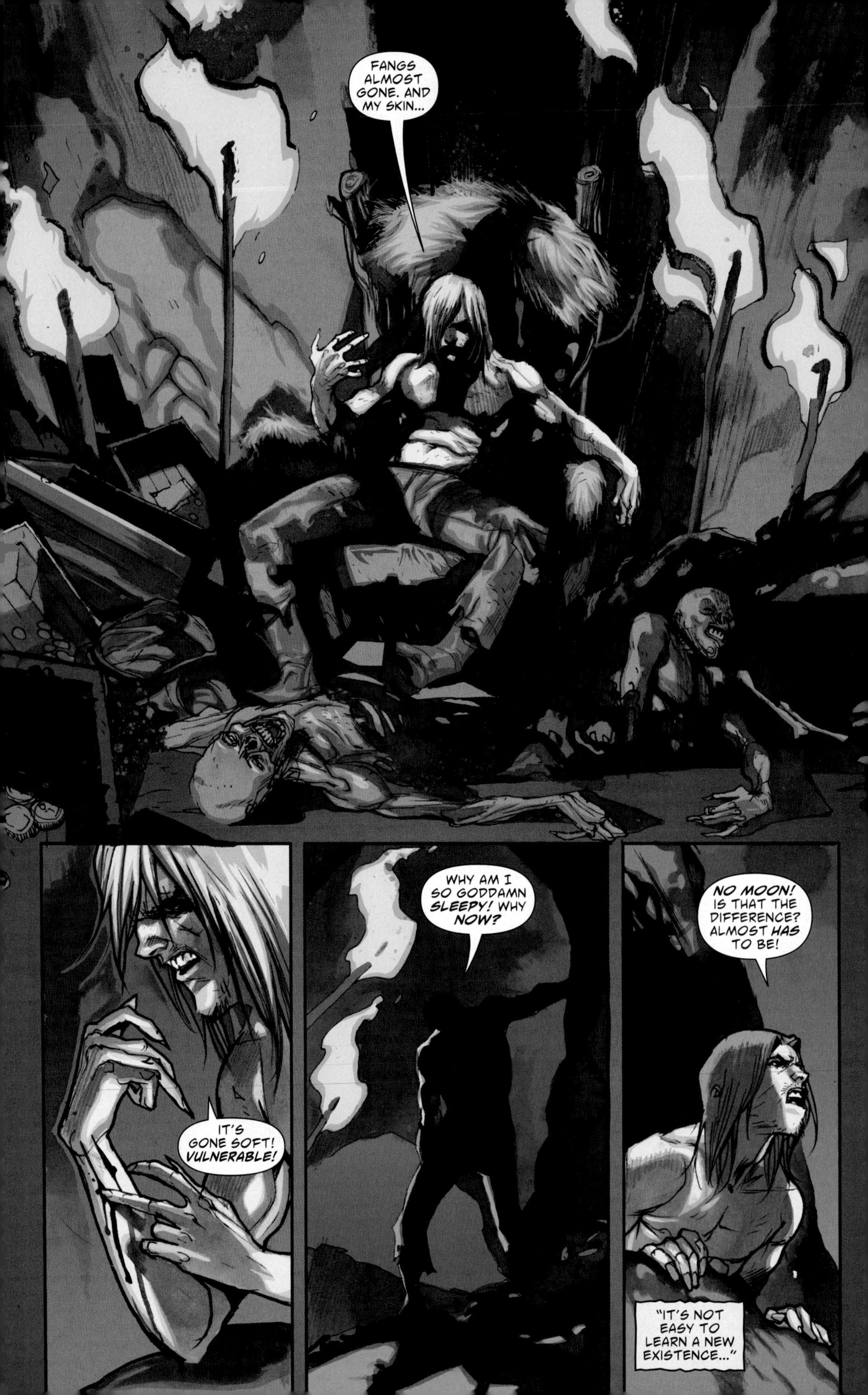
FANGS ALMOST GONE. AND MY SKIN...
IT'S GONE SOFT! VULNERABLE!
WHY AM I SO GODDAMN SLEEPY! WHY NOW?
NO MOON! IS THAT THE DIFFERENCE? ALMOST HAS TO BE!
"IT'S NOT EASY TO LEARN A NEW EXISTENCE..."

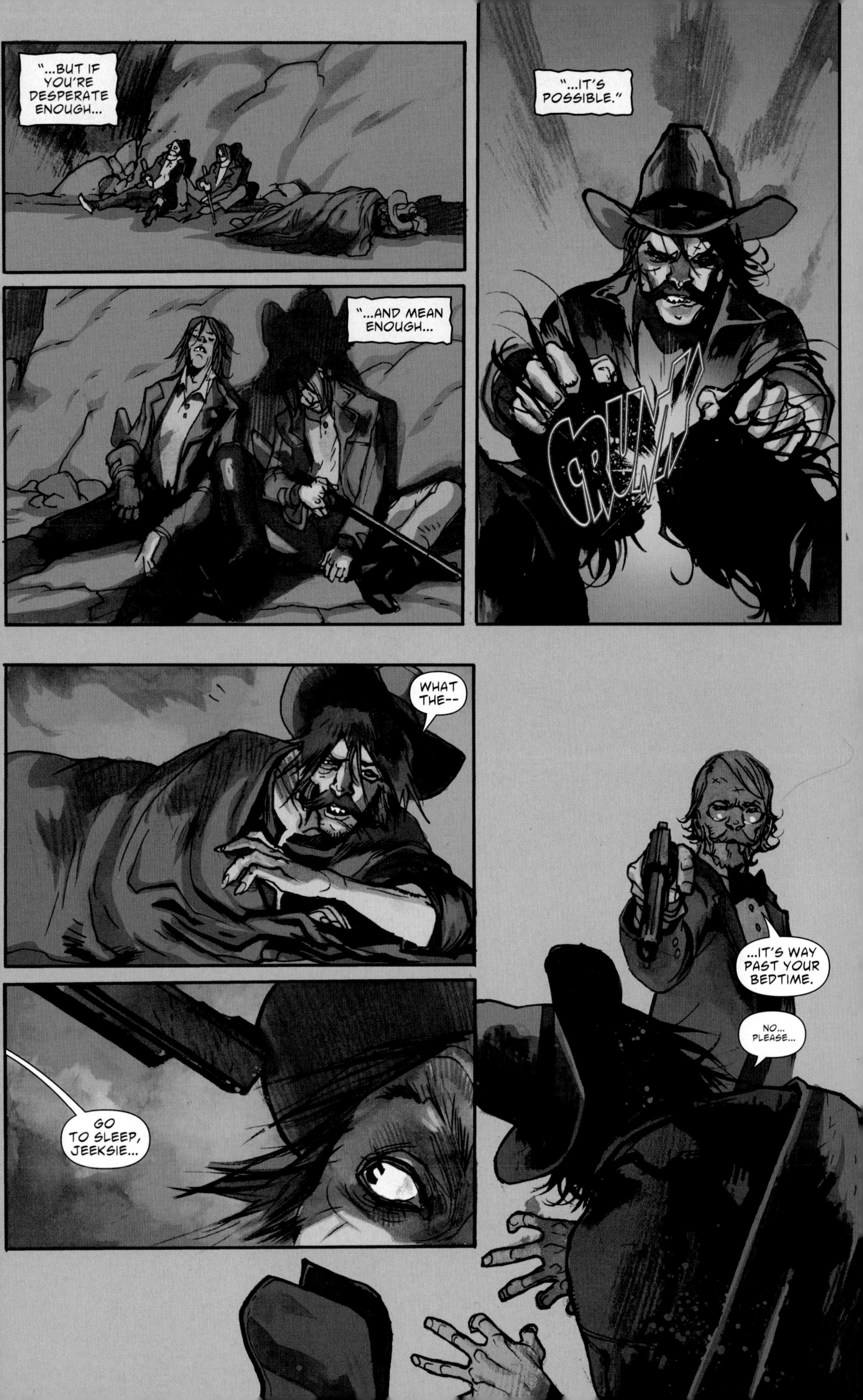
"...BUT IF YOU'RE DESPERATE ENOUGH...
"...AND MEAN ENOUGH...
"...IT'S POSSIBLE."
GRUNK
WHAT THE--
GO TO SLEEP, JEEKSIE...
...IT'S WAY PAST YOUR BEDTIME.
NO... PLEASE...

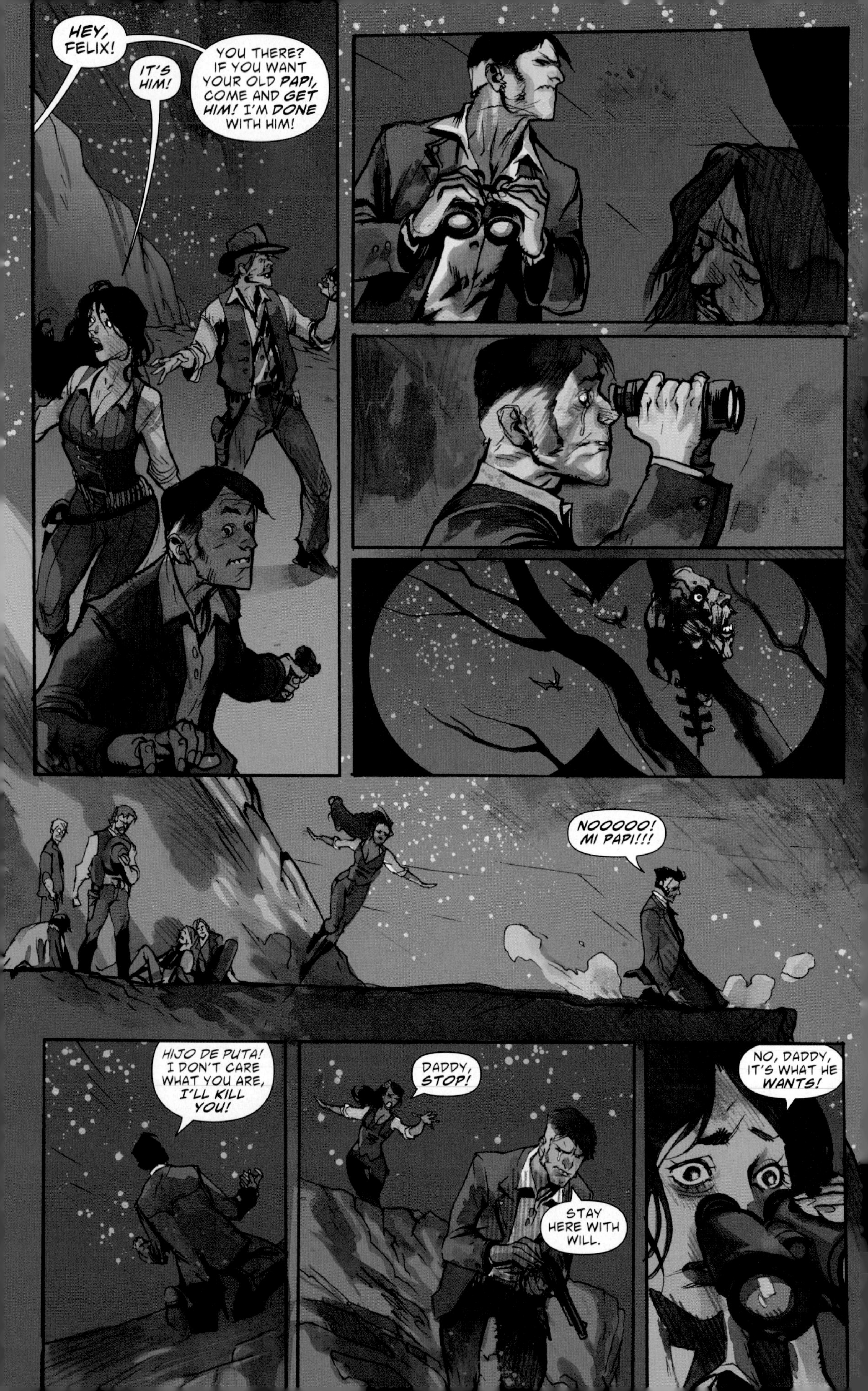
HEY, FELIX!
IT'S HIM!
YOU THERE? IF YOU WANT YOUR OLD PAPI, COME AND GET HIM! I'M DONE WITH HIM!
NOOOOO! MI PAPI!!!
HIJO DE PUTA! I DON'T CARE WHAT YOU ARE, I'LL KILL YOU!
DADDY, STOP!
STAY HERE WITH WILL.
NO, DADDY, IT'S WHAT HE WANTS!

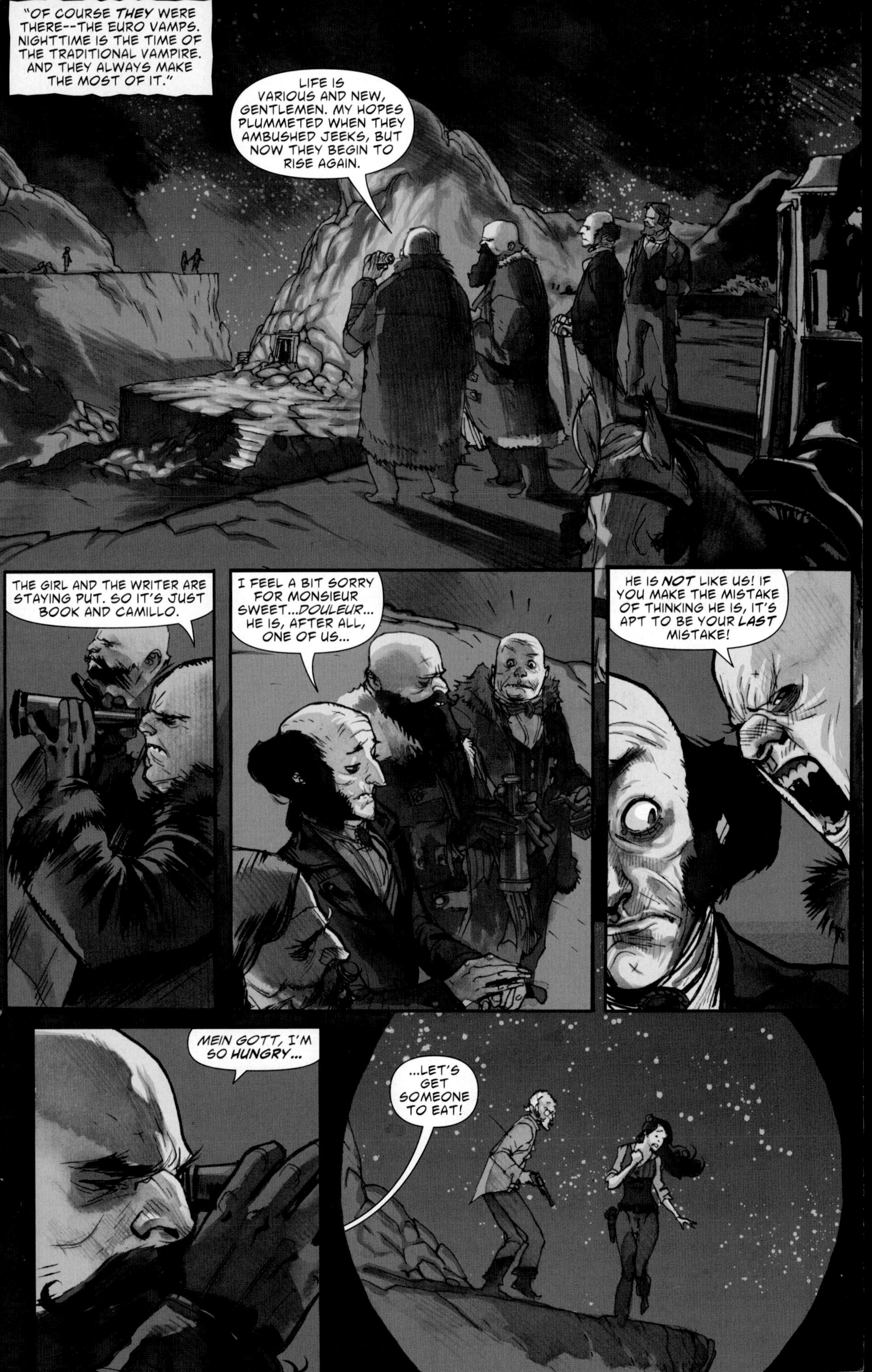
"OF COURSE THEY WERE THERE--THE EURO VAMPS. NIGHTTIME IS THE TIME OF THE TRADITIONAL VAMPIRE. AND THEY ALWAYS MAKE THE MOST OF IT."
LIFE IS VARIOUS AND NEW, GENTLEMEN. MY HOPES PLUMMETED WHEN THEY AMBUSHED JEEKS, BUT NOW THEY BEGIN TO RISE AGAIN.
THE GIRL AND THE WRITER ARE STAYING PUT. SO IT'S JUST BOOK AND CAMILLO.
I FEEL A BIT SORRY FOR MONSIEUR SWEET...DOULEUR... HE IS, AFTER ALL, ONE OF US...
HE IS NOT LIKE US! IF YOU MAKE THE MISTAKE OF THINKING HE IS, IT'S APT TO BE YOUR LAST MISTAKE!
MEIN GOTT, I'M SO HUNGRY...
...LET'S GET SOMEONE TO EAT!

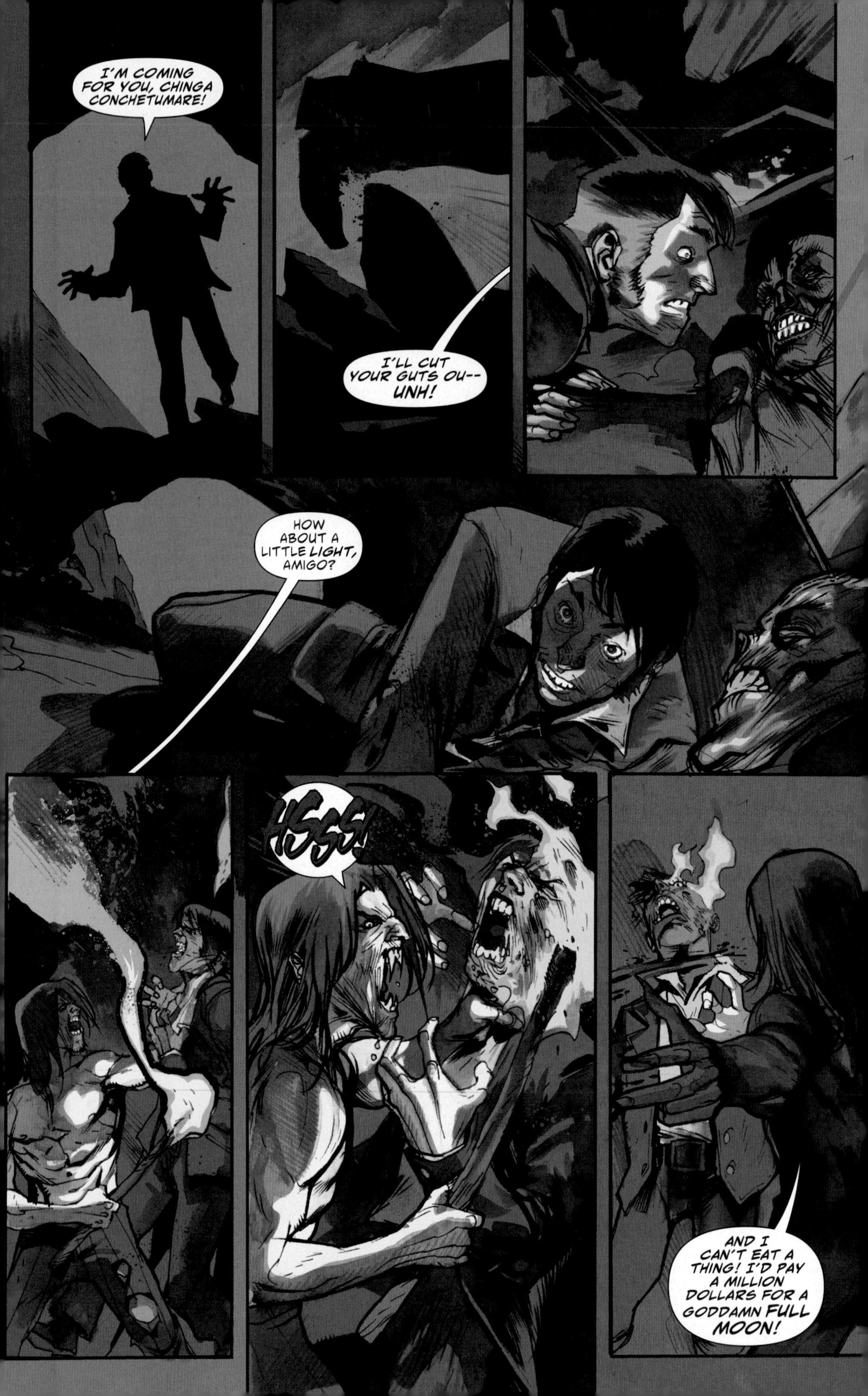
I'M COMING FOR YOU, CHINGA CONCHETUMARE!
I'LL CUT YOUR GUTS OU-- UNH!
HOW ABOUT A LITTLE LIGHT, AMIGO?
HSSS!
AND I CAN'T EAT A THING! I'D PAY A MILLION DOLLARS FOR A GODDAMN FULL MOON!

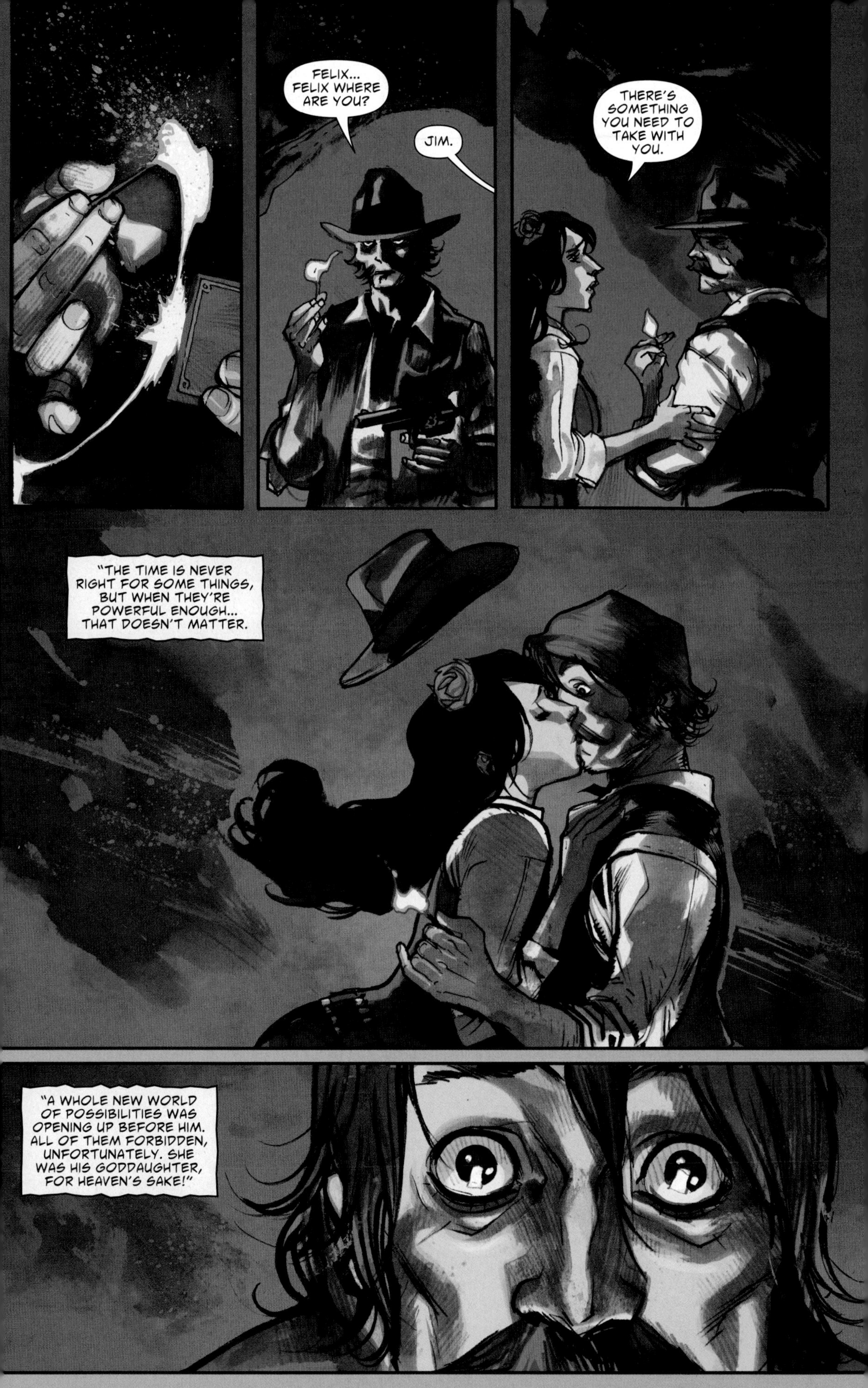
FELIX... FELIX WHERE ARE YOU?
JIM.
THERE'S SOMETHING YOU NEED TO TAKE WITH YOU.
"THE TIME IS NEVER RIGHT FOR SOME THINGS, BUT WHEN THEY'RE POWERFUL ENOUGH... THAT DOESN'T MATTER.
"A WHOLE NEW WORLD OF POSSIBILITIES WAS OPENING UP BEFORE HIM. ALL OF THEM FORBIDDEN, UNFORTUNATELY. SHE WAS HIS GODDAUGHTER, FOR HEAVEN'S SAKE!"

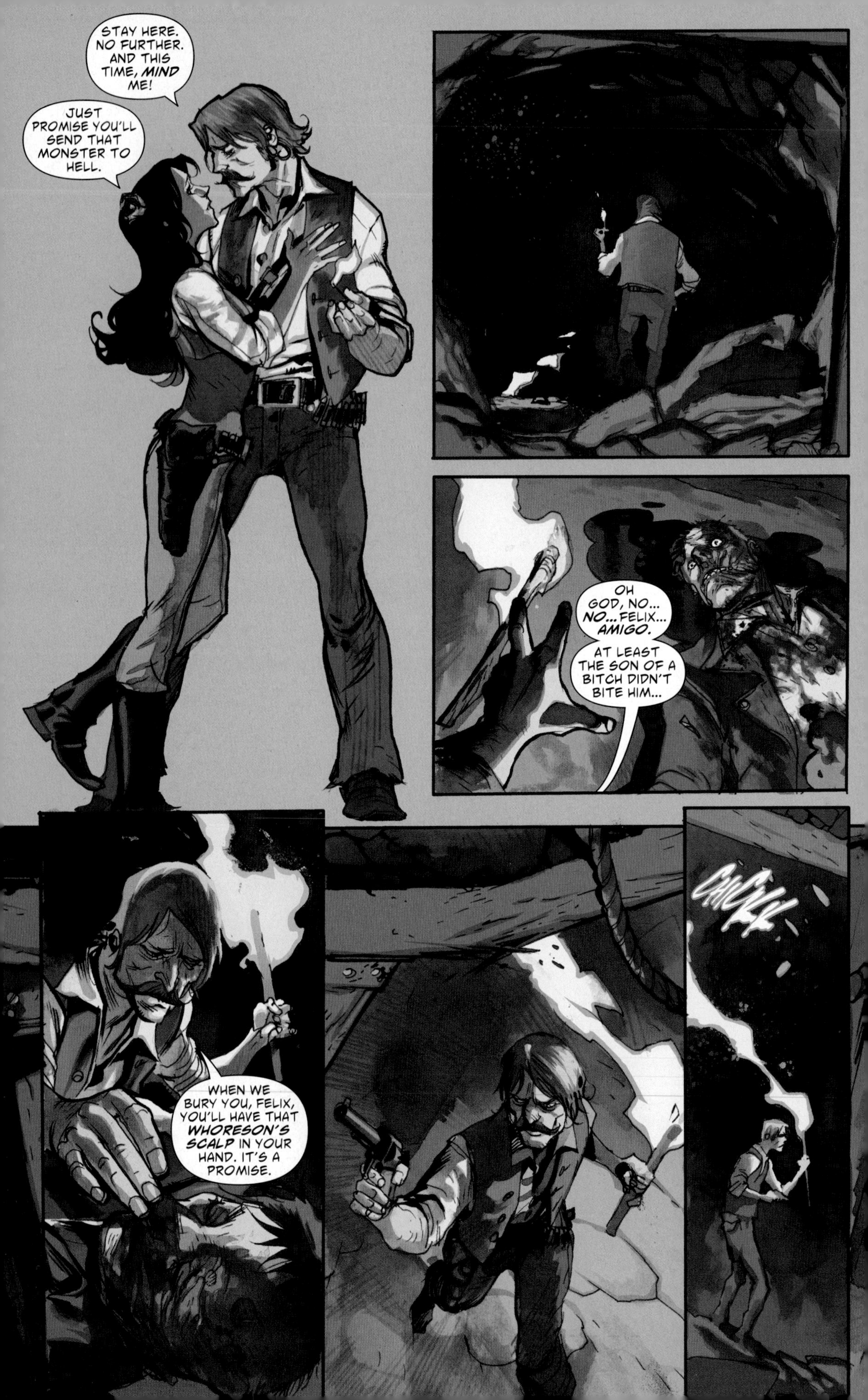
STAY HERE. NO FURTHER. AND THIS TIME, MIND ME!
JUST PROMISE YOU'LL SEND THAT MONSTER TO HELL.
OH GOD, NO... NO... FELIX... AMIGO.
AT LEAST THE SON OF A BITCH DIDN'T BITE HIM...
WHEN WE BURY YOU, FELIX, YOU'LL HAVE THAT WHORESON'S SCALP IN YOUR HAND. IT'S A PROMISE.
CHICK

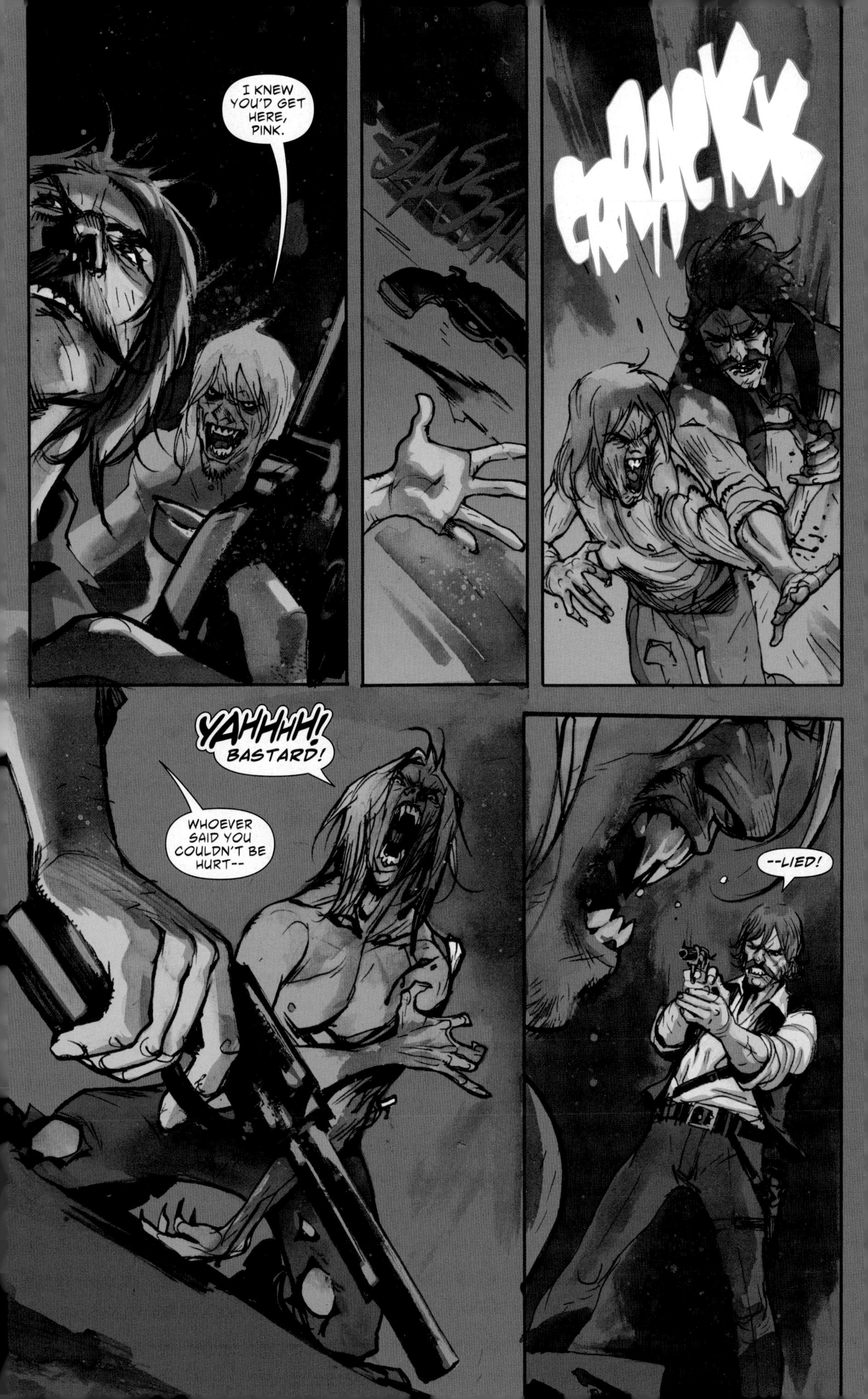
I KNEW YOU'D GET HERE, PINK.
YAHHHH! BASTARD!
WHOEVER SAID YOU COULDN'T BE HURT--
--LIED!

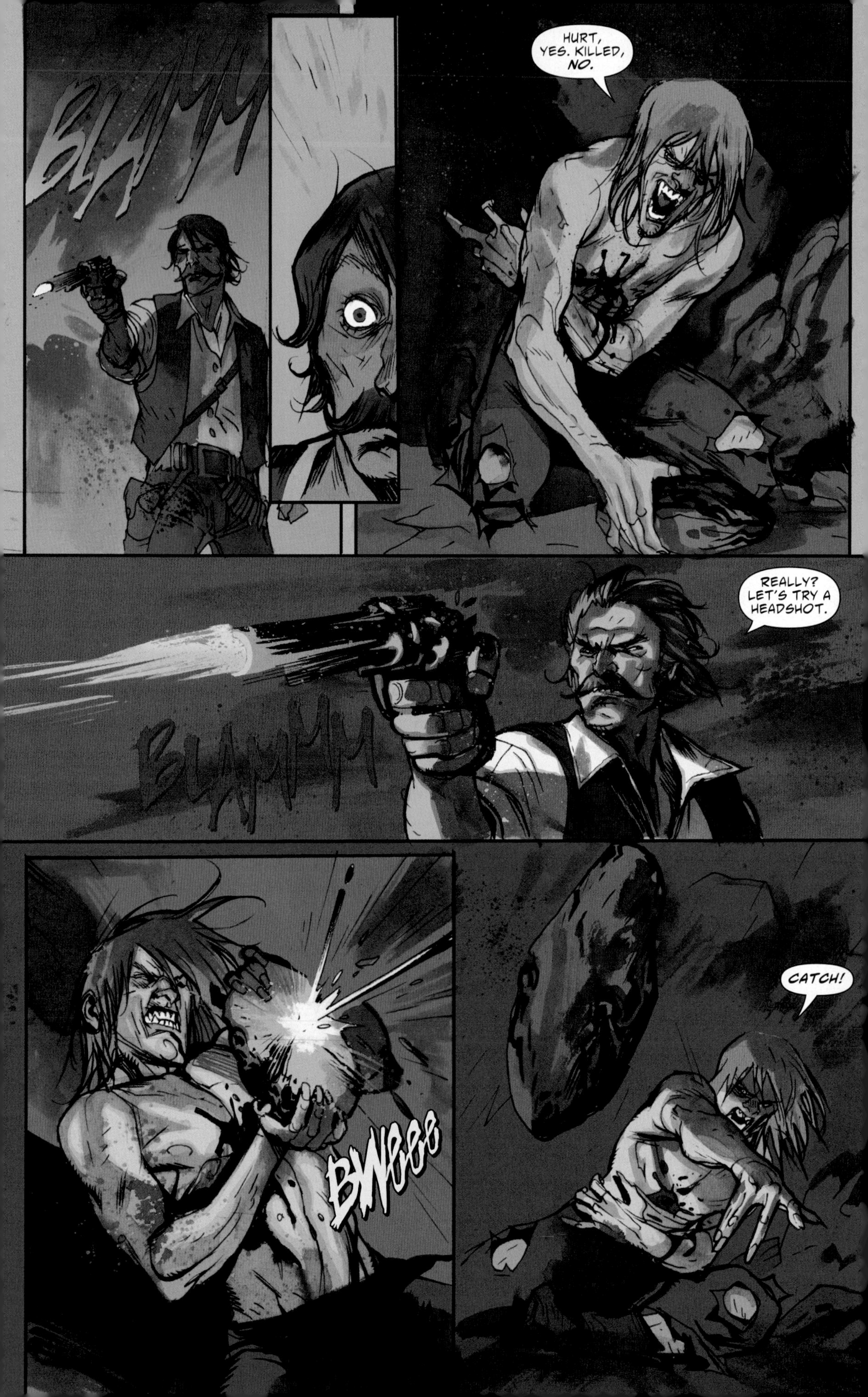
BLAMM
HURT, YES. KILLED, NO.
REALLY? LET'S TRY A HEADSHOT.
BLAMMM
BWEEE
CATCH!

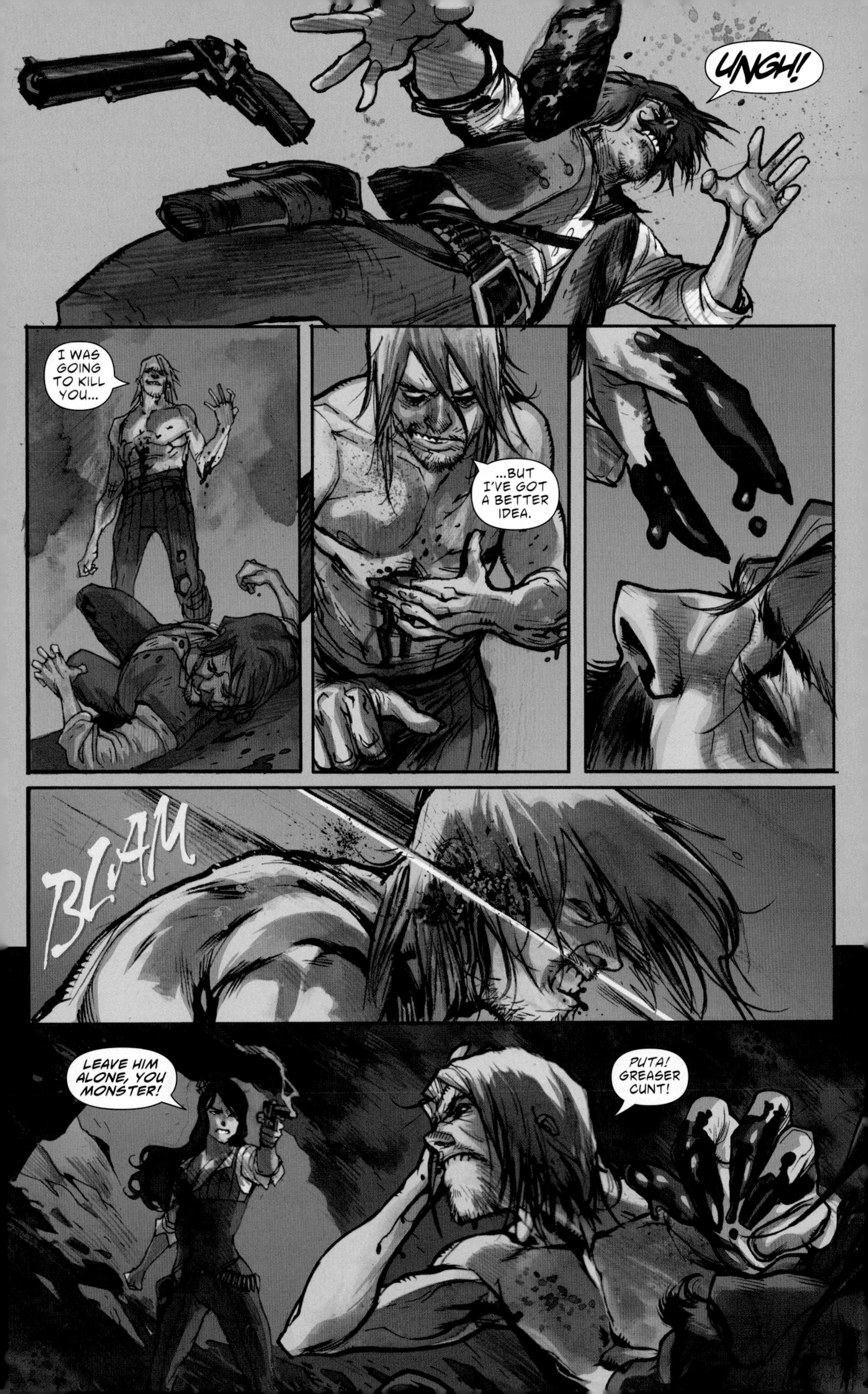
UNGH!
I WAS GOING TO KILL YOU...
...BUT I'VE GOT A BETTER IDEA.
BLAM
LEAVE HIM ALONE, YOU MONSTER!
PUTA! GREASER CUNT!

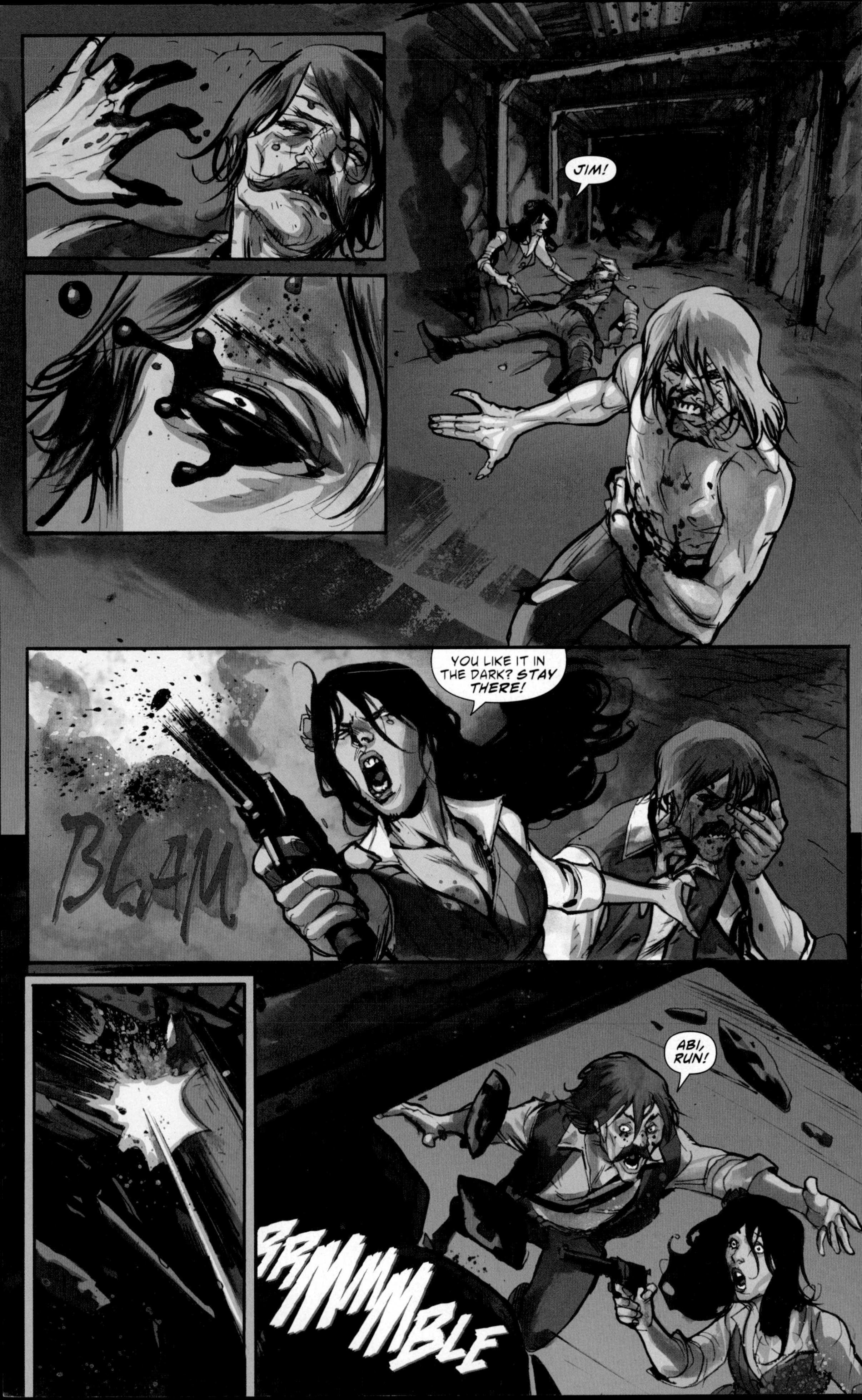
JIM!
YOU LIKE IT IN THE DARK? STAY THERE!
BLAM
ABI, RUN!
RRMMMBLE

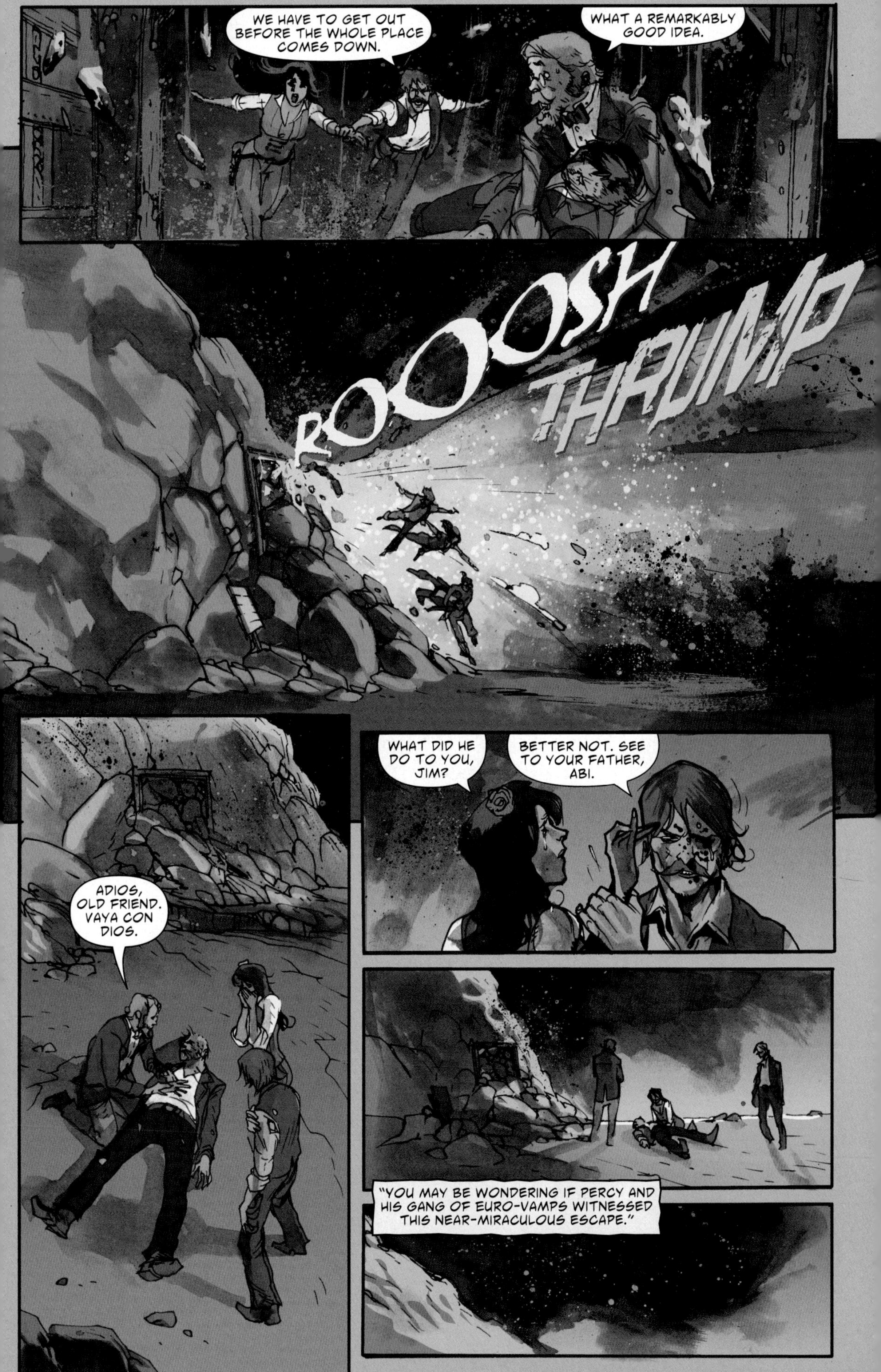
WE HAVE TO GET OUT BEFORE THE WHOLE PLACE COMES DOWN.
WHAT A REMARKABLY GOOD IDEA.
ROOOOSH
THRUMP
ADIOS, OLD FRIEND. VAYA CON DIOS.
WHAT DID HE DO TO YOU, JIM?
BETTER NOT. SEE TO YOUR FATHER, ABI.
"YOU MAY BE WONDERING IF PERCY AND HIS GANG OF EURO-VAMPS WITNESSED THIS NEAR-MIRACULOUS ESCAPE."

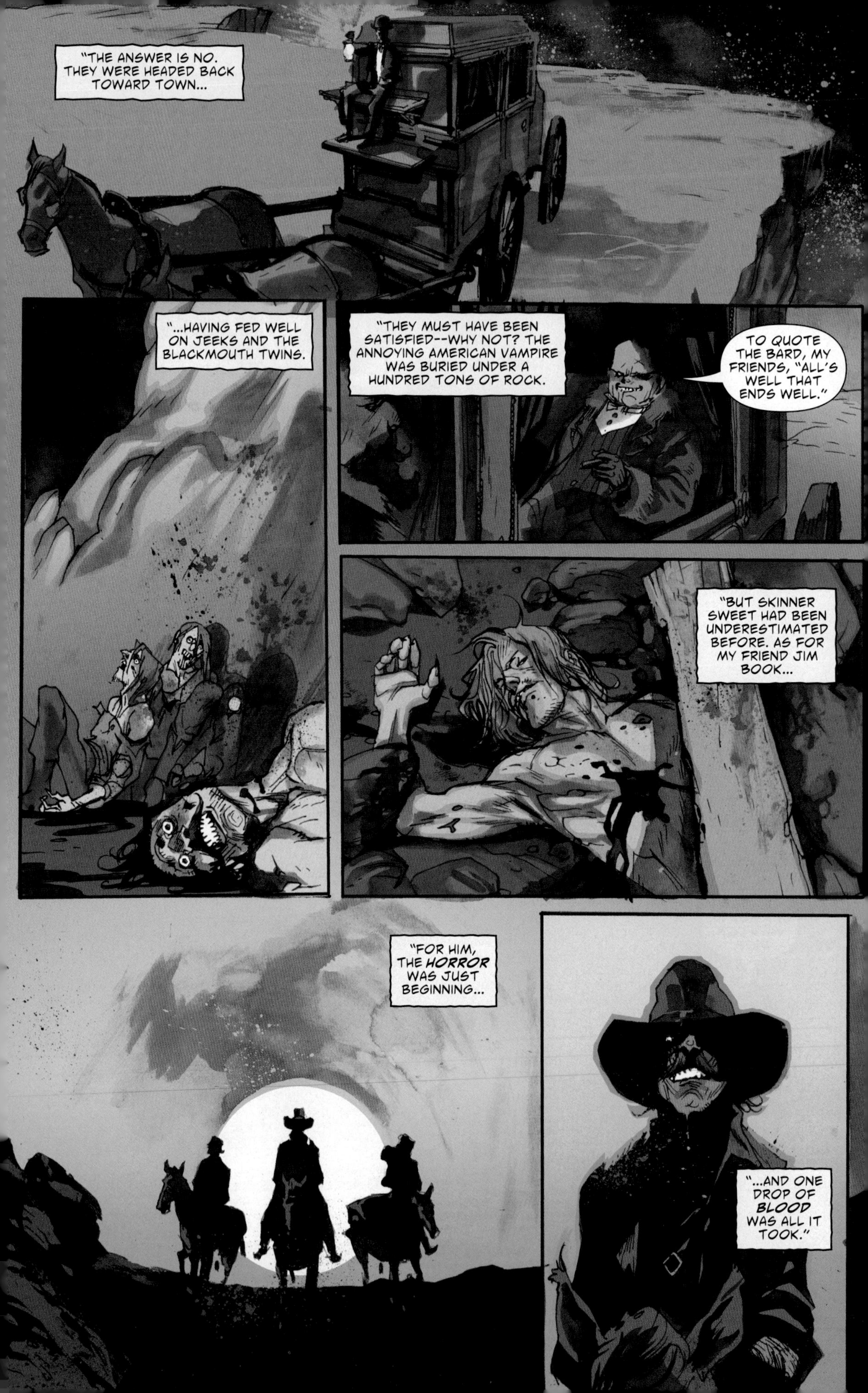
"THE ANSWER IS NO. THEY WERE HEADED BACK TOWARD TOWN...
"...HAVING FED WELL ON JEEKS AND THE BLACKMOUTH TWINS.
"THEY MUST HAVE BEEN SATISFIED--WHY NOT? THE ANNOYING AMERICAN VAMPIRE WAS BURIED UNDER A HUNDRED TONS OF ROCK.
TO QUOTE THE BARD, MY FRIENDS, "ALL'S WELL THAT ENDS WELL."
"BUT SKINNER SWEET HAD BEEN UNDERESTIMATED BEFORE. AS FOR MY FRIEND JIM BOOK...
"FOR HIM, THE *HORROR* WAS JUST BEGINNING...
"...AND ONE DROP OF *BLOOD* WAS ALL IT TOOK."

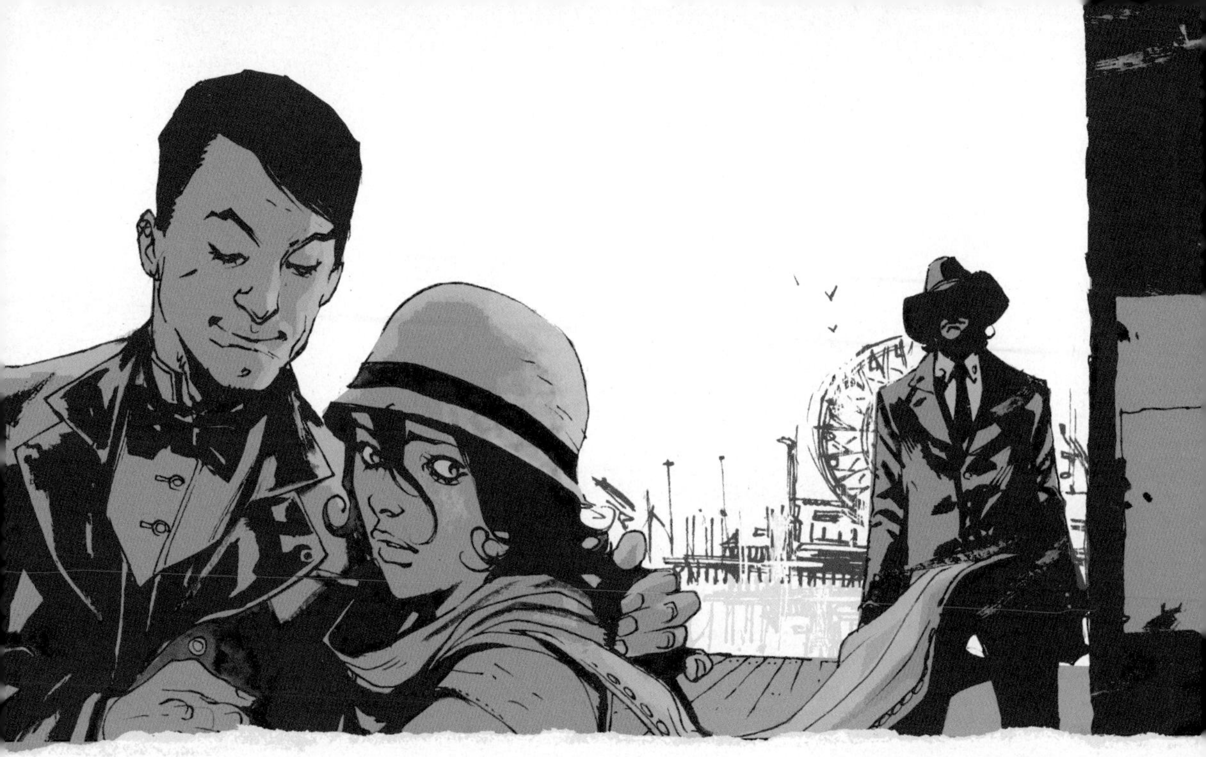

Chapter Five

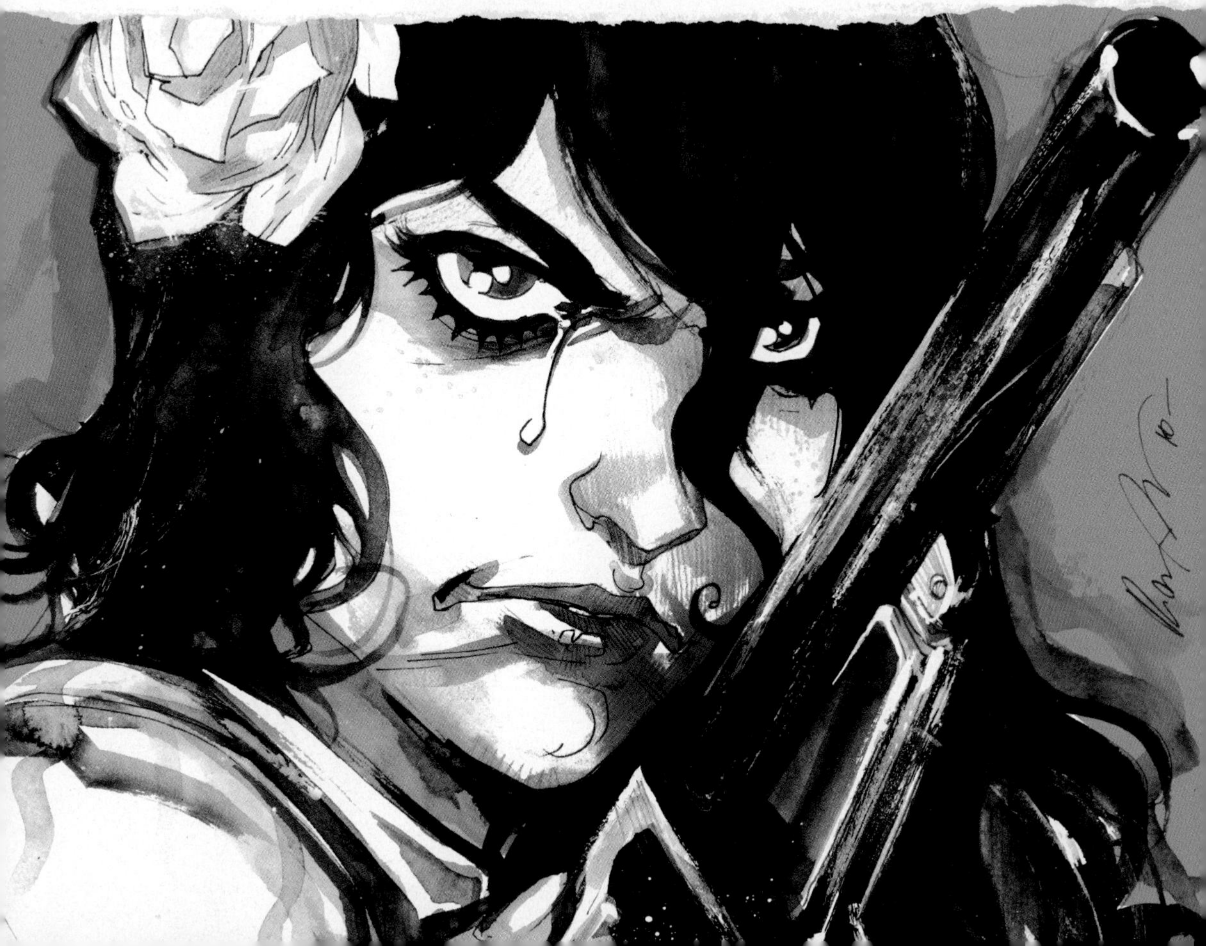

Curtain Call

Scott Snyder Writer

If Thy Right Hand
Offend Thee...

Stephen King Writer

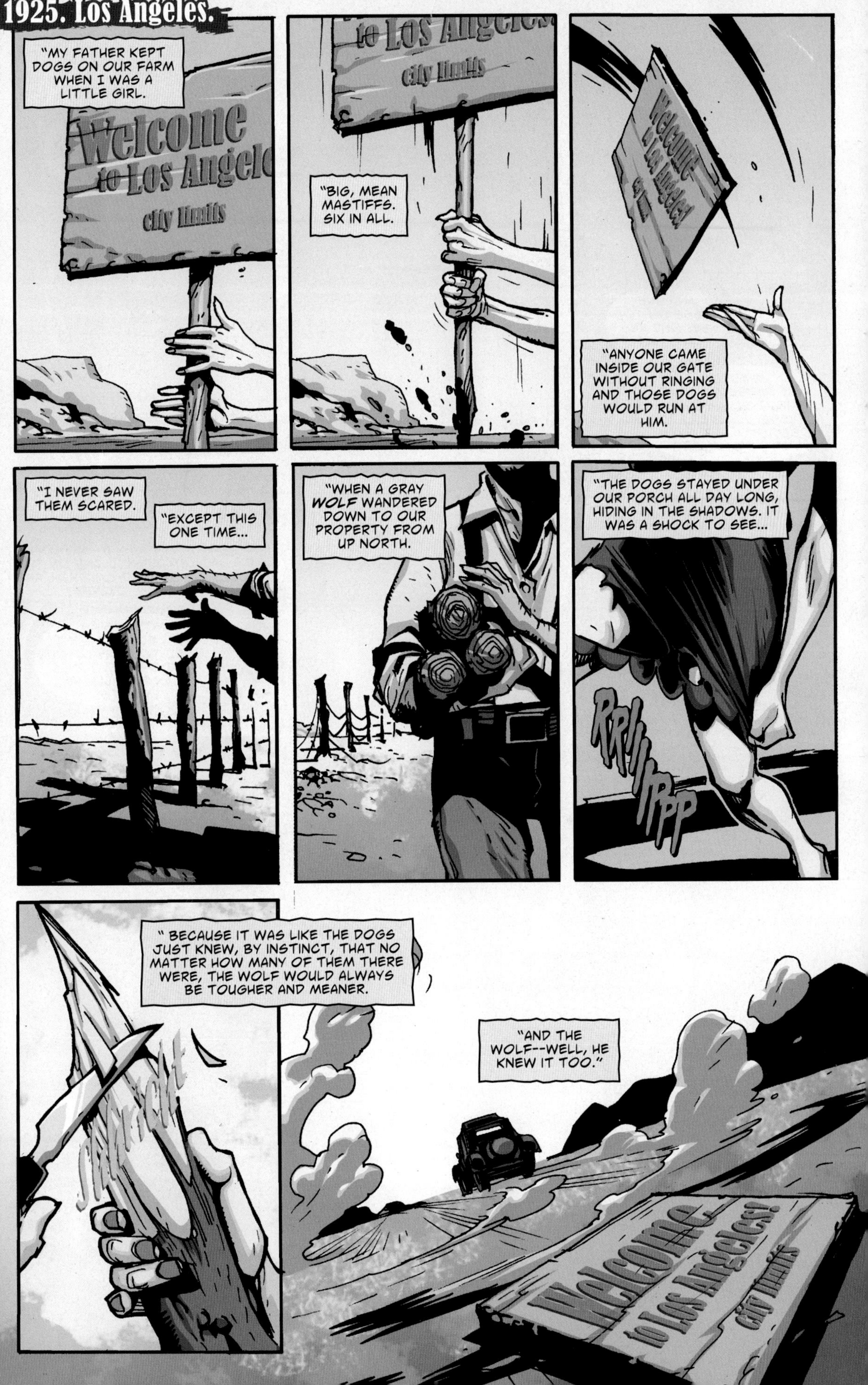
1925. Los Angeles.
"MY FATHER KEPT DOGS ON OUR FARM WHEN I WAS A LITTLE GIRL.
Welcome to Los Angeles city limits
"BIG, MEAN MASTIFFS. SIX IN ALL.
"ANYONE CAME INSIDE OUR GATE WITHOUT RINGING AND THOSE DOGS WOULD RUN AT HIM.
"I NEVER SAW THEM SCARED.
"EXCEPT THIS ONE TIME...
"WHEN A GRAY WOLF WANDERED DOWN TO OUR PROPERTY FROM UP NORTH.
"THE DOGS STAYED UNDER OUR PORCH ALL DAY LONG, HIDING IN THE SHADOWS. IT WAS A SHOCK TO SEE...
" BECAUSE IT WAS LIKE THE DOGS JUST KNEW, BY INSTINCT, THAT NO MATTER HOW MANY OF THEM THERE WERE, THE WOLF WOULD ALWAYS BE TOUGHER AND MEANER.
"AND THE WOLF--WELL, HE KNEW IT TOO."
Welcome to Los Angeles! city limits

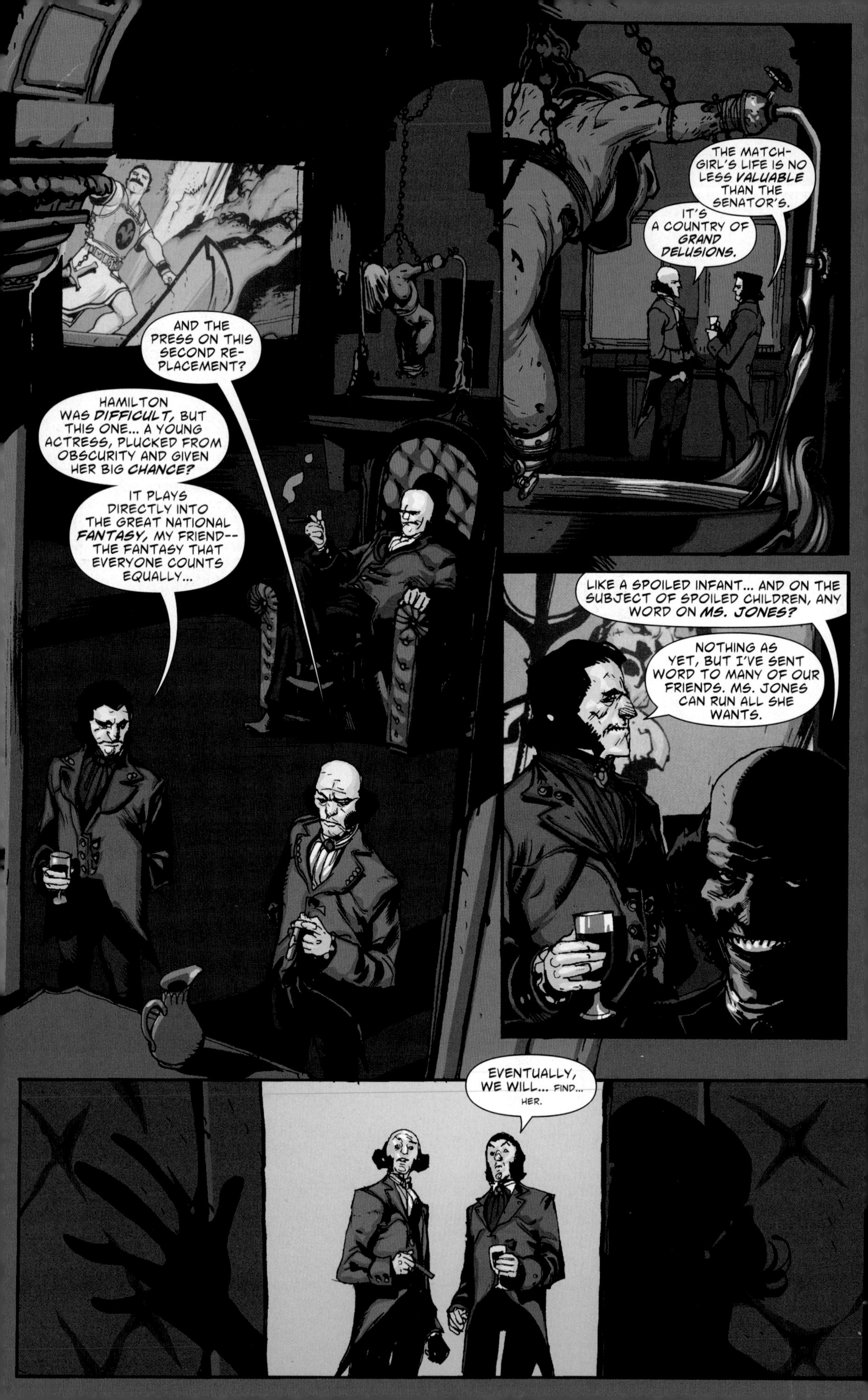
AND THE PRESS ON THIS SECOND REPLACEMENT?
HAMILTON WAS DIFFICULT, BUT THIS ONE... A YOUNG ACTRESS, PLUCKED FROM OBSCURITY AND GIVEN HER BIG CHANCE?
IT PLAYS DIRECTLY INTO THE GREAT NATIONAL FANTASY, MY FRIEND-- THE FANTASY THAT EVERYONE COUNTS EQUALLY...
THE MATCH-GIRL'S LIFE IS NO LESS VALUABLE THAN THE SENATOR'S.
IT'S A COUNTRY OF GRAND DELUSIONS.
LIKE A SPOILED INFANT... AND ON THE SUBJECT OF SPOILED CHILDREN, ANY WORD ON MS. JONES?
NOTHING AS YET, BUT I'VE SENT WORD TO MANY OF OUR FRIENDS. MS. JONES CAN RUN ALL SHE WANTS.
EVENTUALLY, WE WILL... FIND... HER.

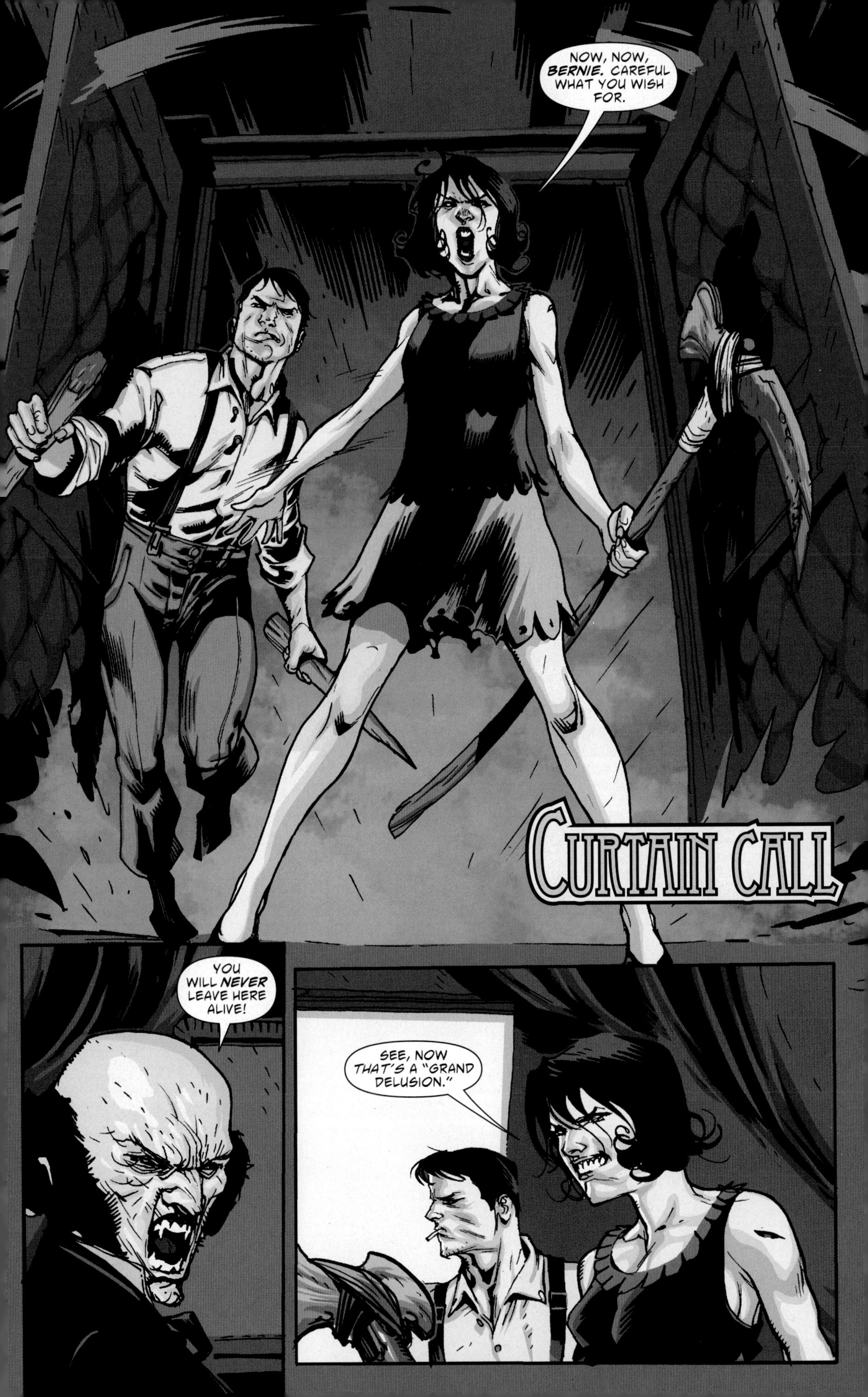
NOW, NOW, BERNIE. CAREFUL WHAT YOU WISH FOR.
CURTAIN CALL
YOU WILL NEVER LEAVE HERE ALIVE!
SEE, NOW THAT'S A "GRAND DELUSION."

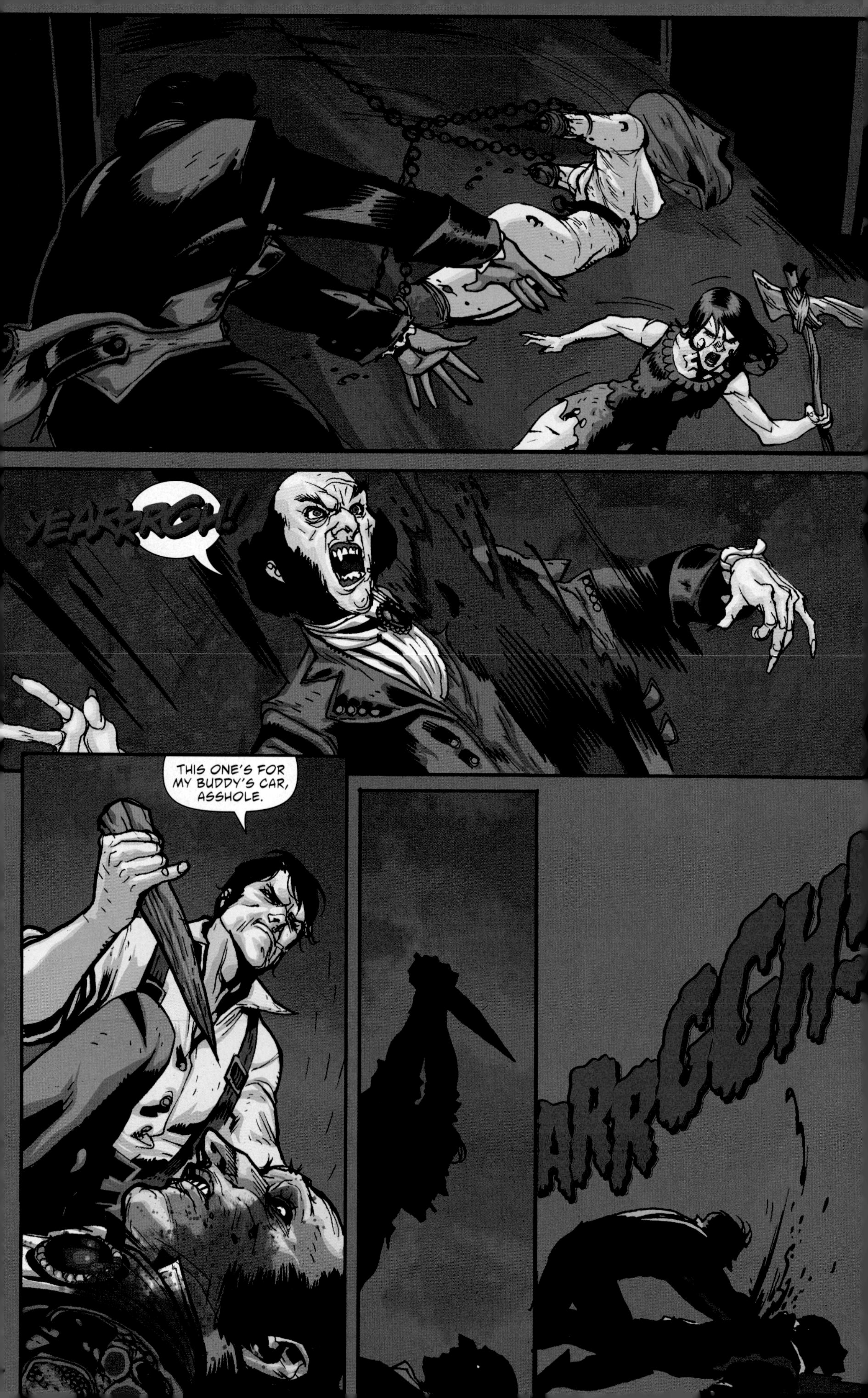
YEARRRGH!
THIS ONE'S FOR MY BUDDY'S CAR, ASSHOLE.
ARRGGH!

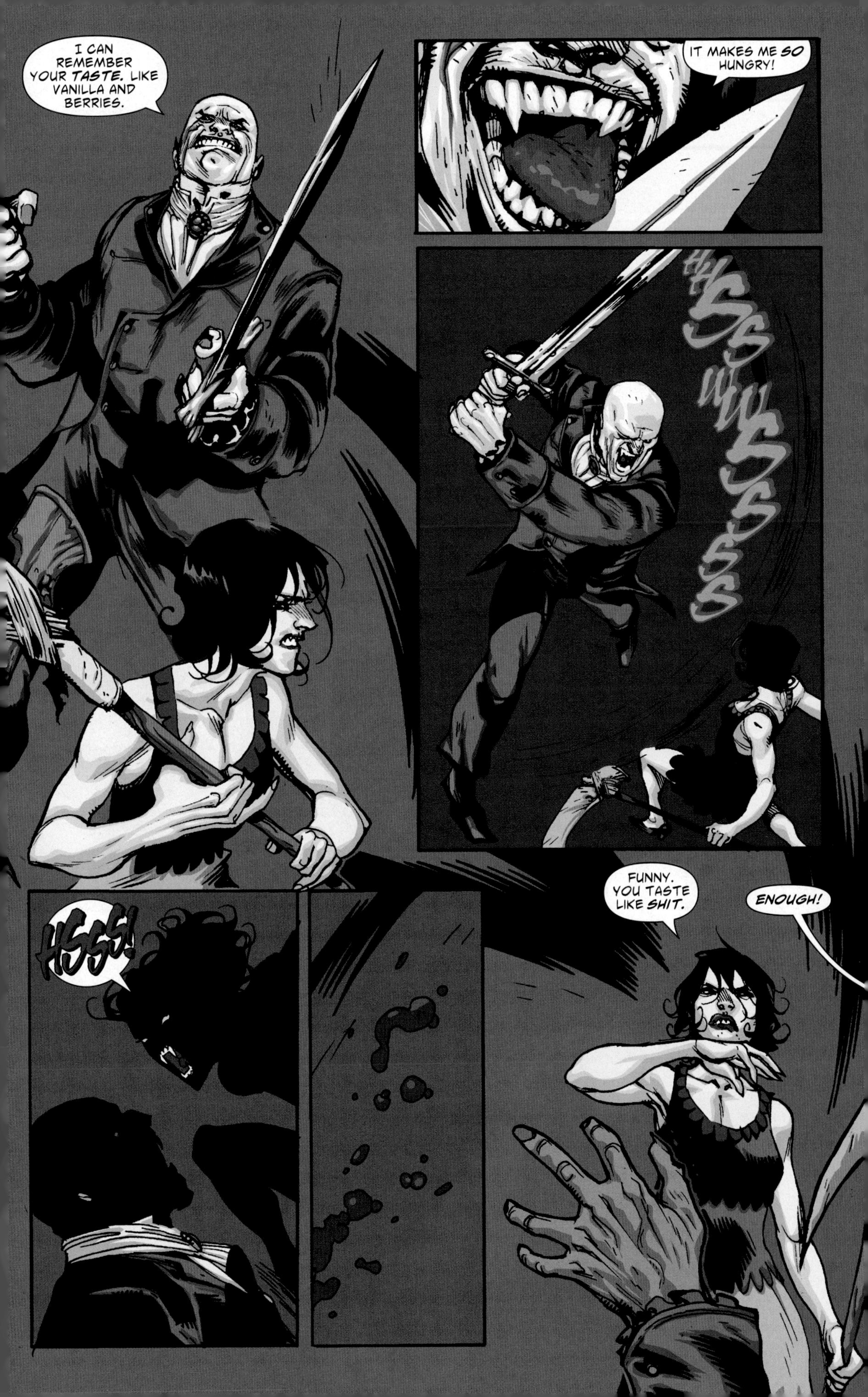
I CAN REMEMBER YOUR *TASTE*. LIKE VANILLA AND BERRIES.
IT MAKES ME *SO* HUNGRY!
HSSWWSSSSS
HSSS!
FUNNY. YOU TASTE LIKE *SHIT*.
ENOUGH!

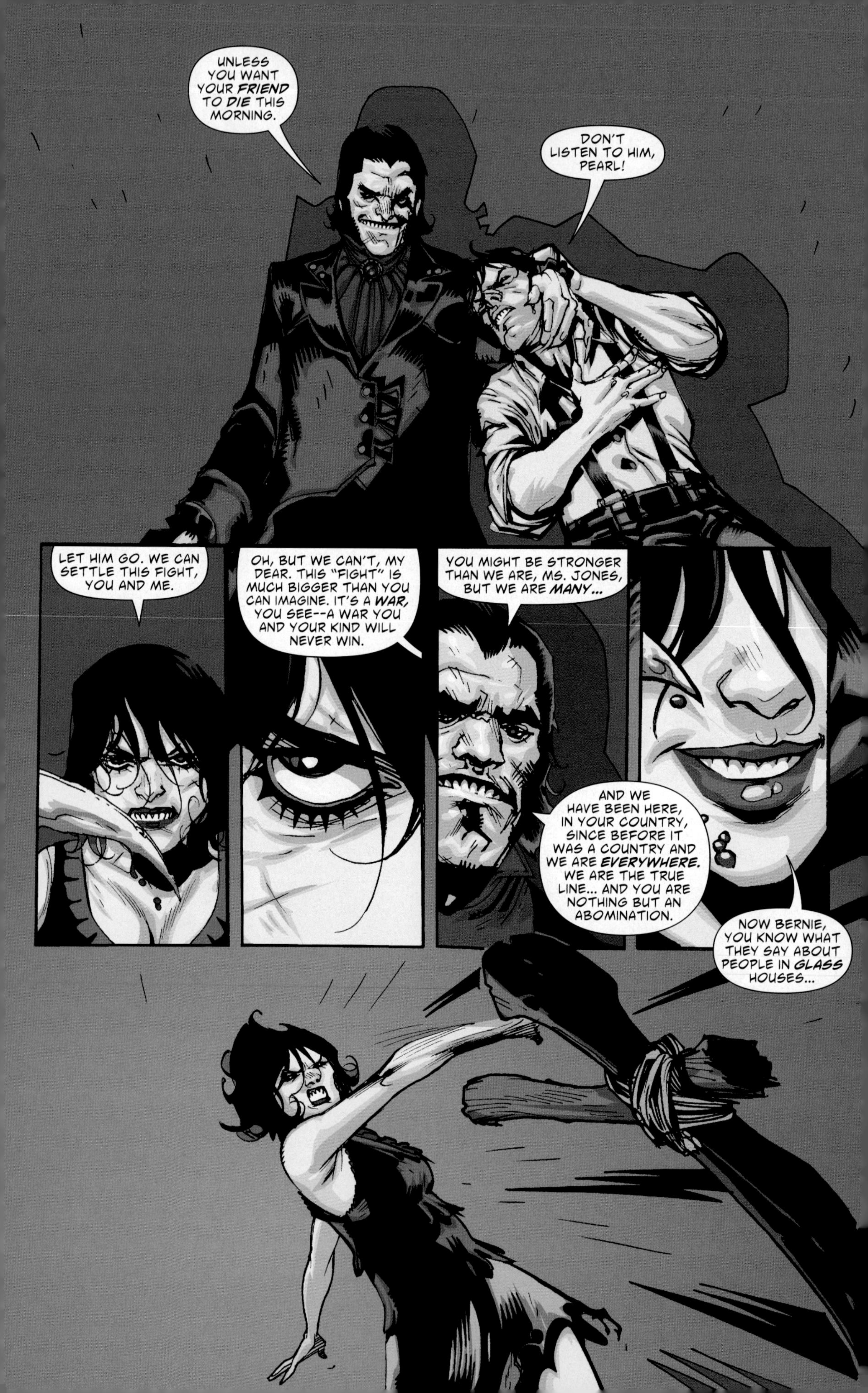
UNLESS YOU WANT YOUR FRIEND TO DIE THIS MORNING.
DON'T LISTEN TO HIM, PEARL!
LET HIM GO. WE CAN SETTLE THIS FIGHT, YOU AND ME.
OH, BUT WE CAN'T, MY DEAR. THIS "FIGHT" IS MUCH BIGGER THAN YOU CAN IMAGINE. IT'S A WAR, YOU SEE--A WAR YOU AND YOUR KIND WILL NEVER WIN.
YOU MIGHT BE STRONGER THAN WE ARE, MS. JONES, BUT WE ARE MANY...
AND WE HAVE BEEN HERE, IN YOUR COUNTRY, SINCE BEFORE IT WAS A COUNTRY AND WE ARE EVERYWHERE. WE ARE THE TRUE LINE... AND YOU ARE NOTHING BUT AN ABOMINATION.
NOW BERNIE, YOU KNOW WHAT THEY SAY ABOUT PEOPLE IN GLASS HOUSES...

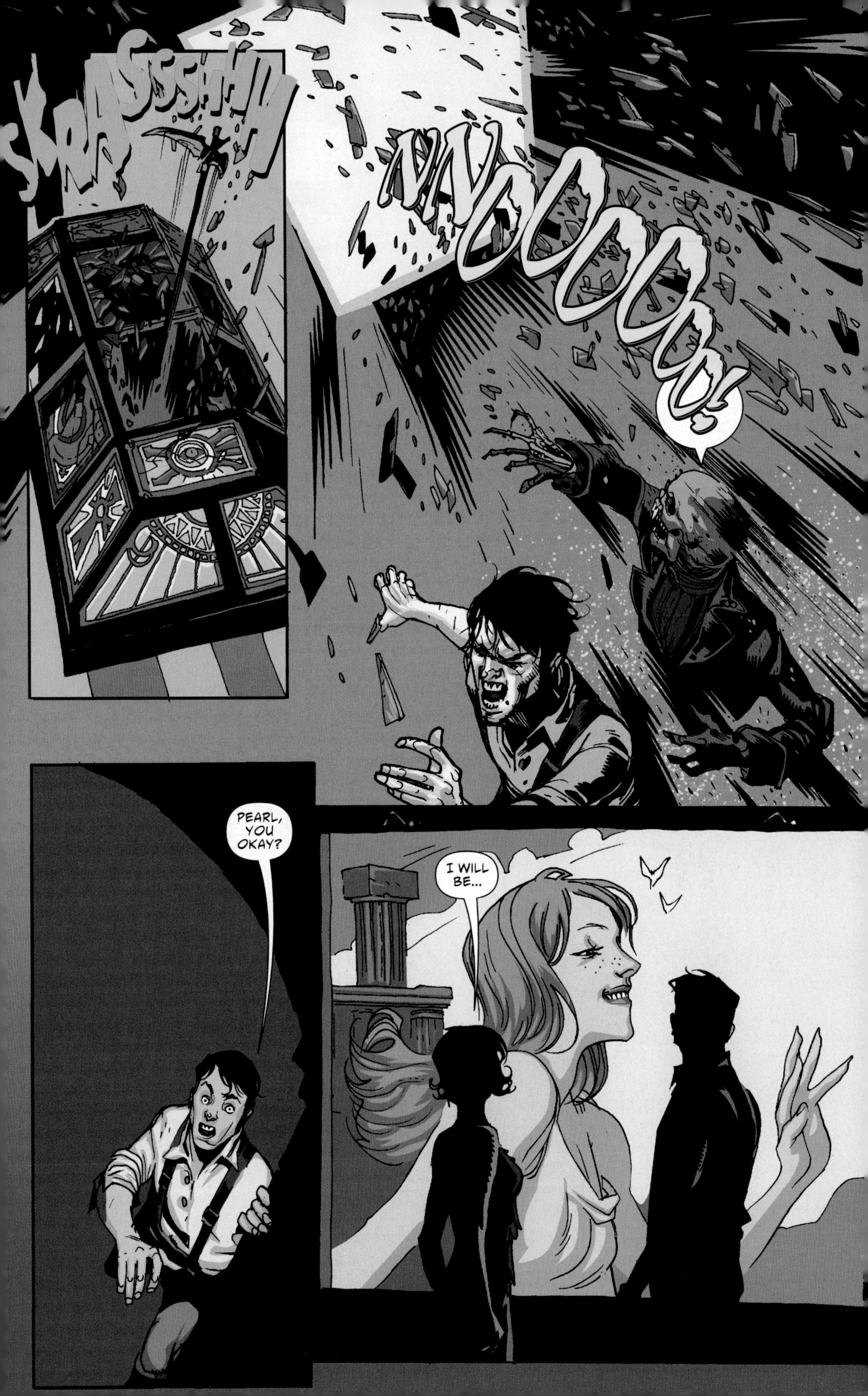
SKRASSSSHH!
NNOOOOOO!
PEARL, YOU OKAY?
I WILL BE...

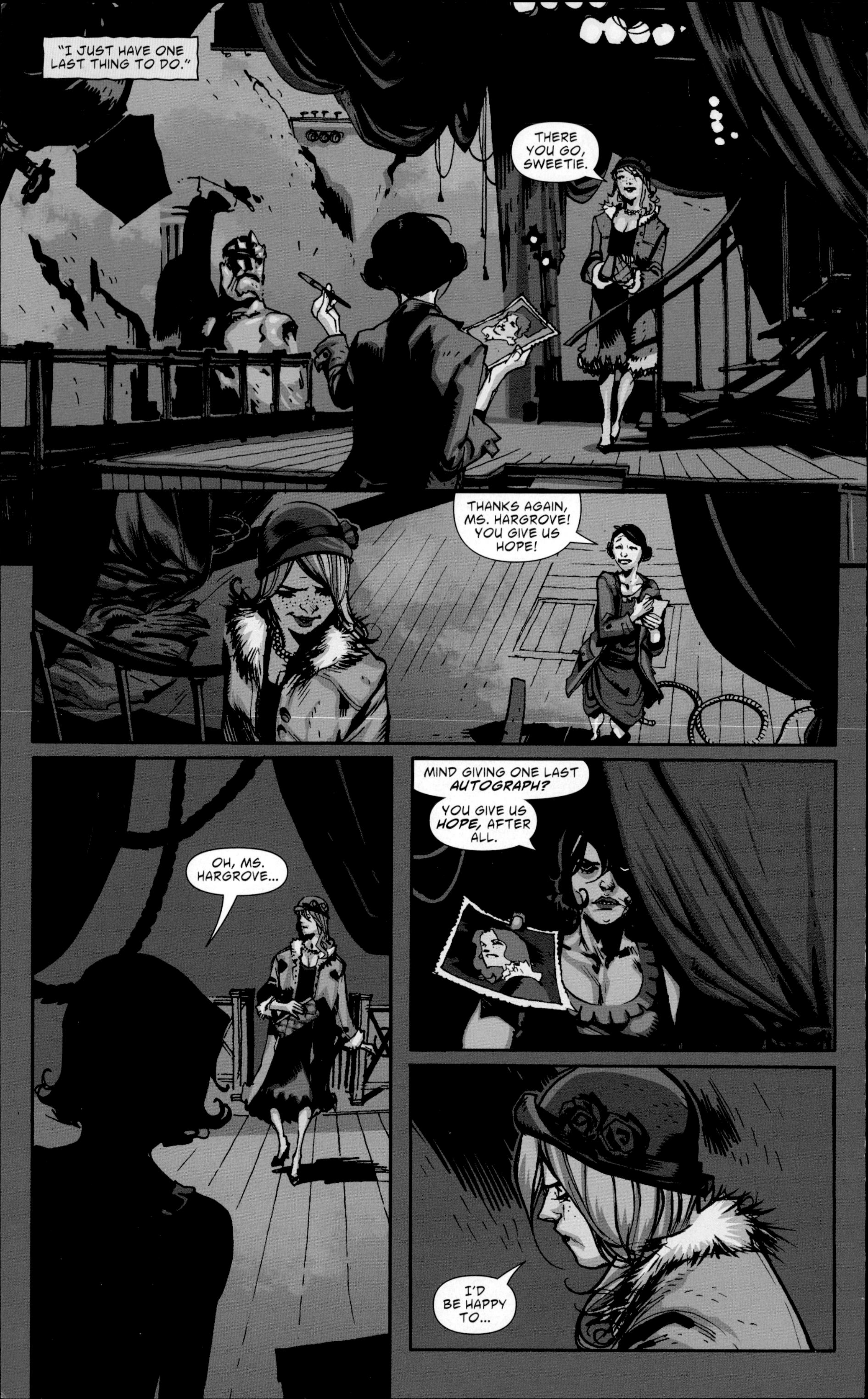
"I JUST HAVE ONE LAST THING TO DO."
THERE YOU GO, SWEETIE.
THANKS AGAIN, MS. HARGROVE! YOU GIVE US HOPE!
OH, MS. HARGROVE...
MIND GIVING ONE LAST AUTOGRAPH?
YOU GIVE US HOPE, AFTER ALL.
I'D BE HAPPY TO...

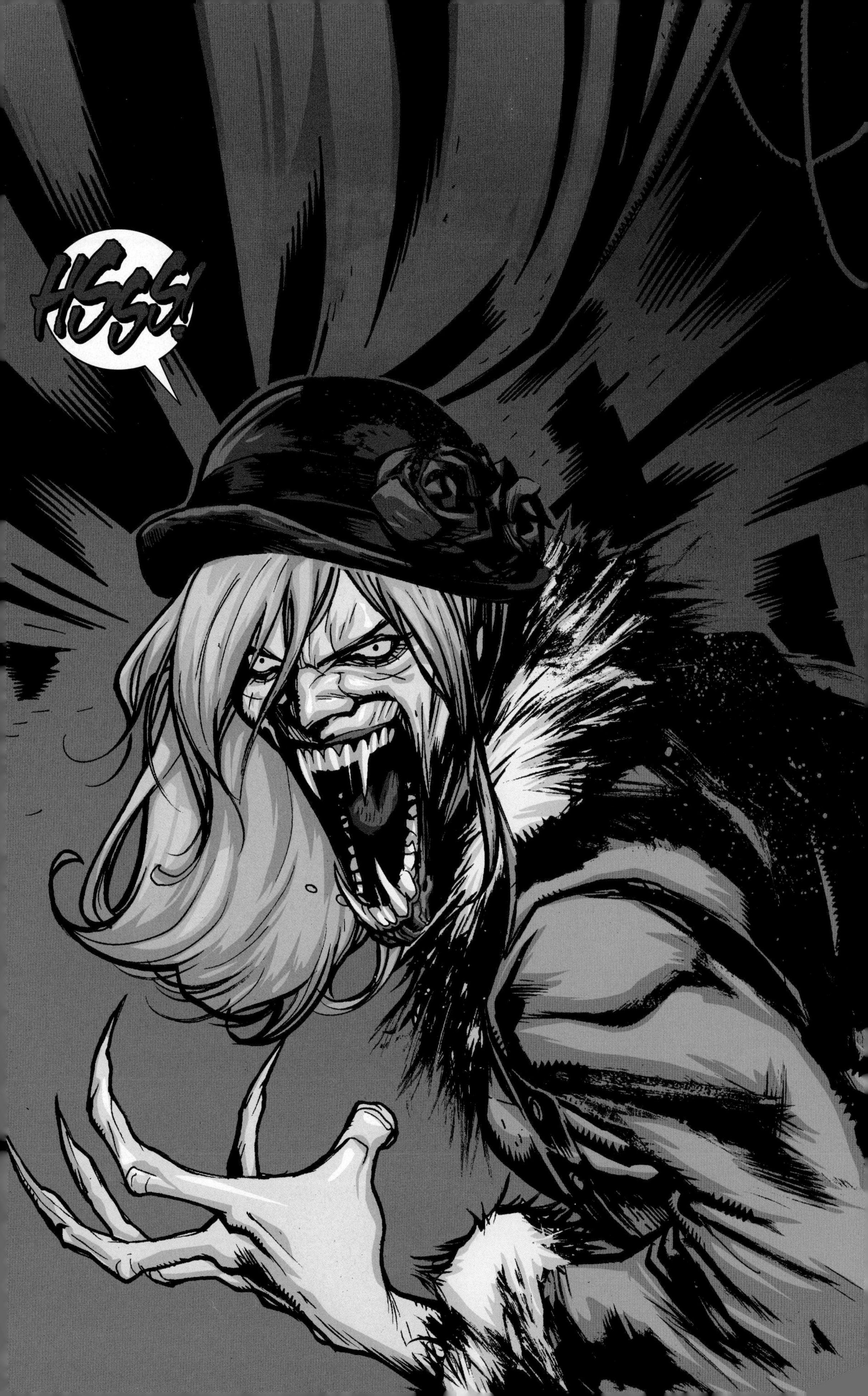
HSSS!

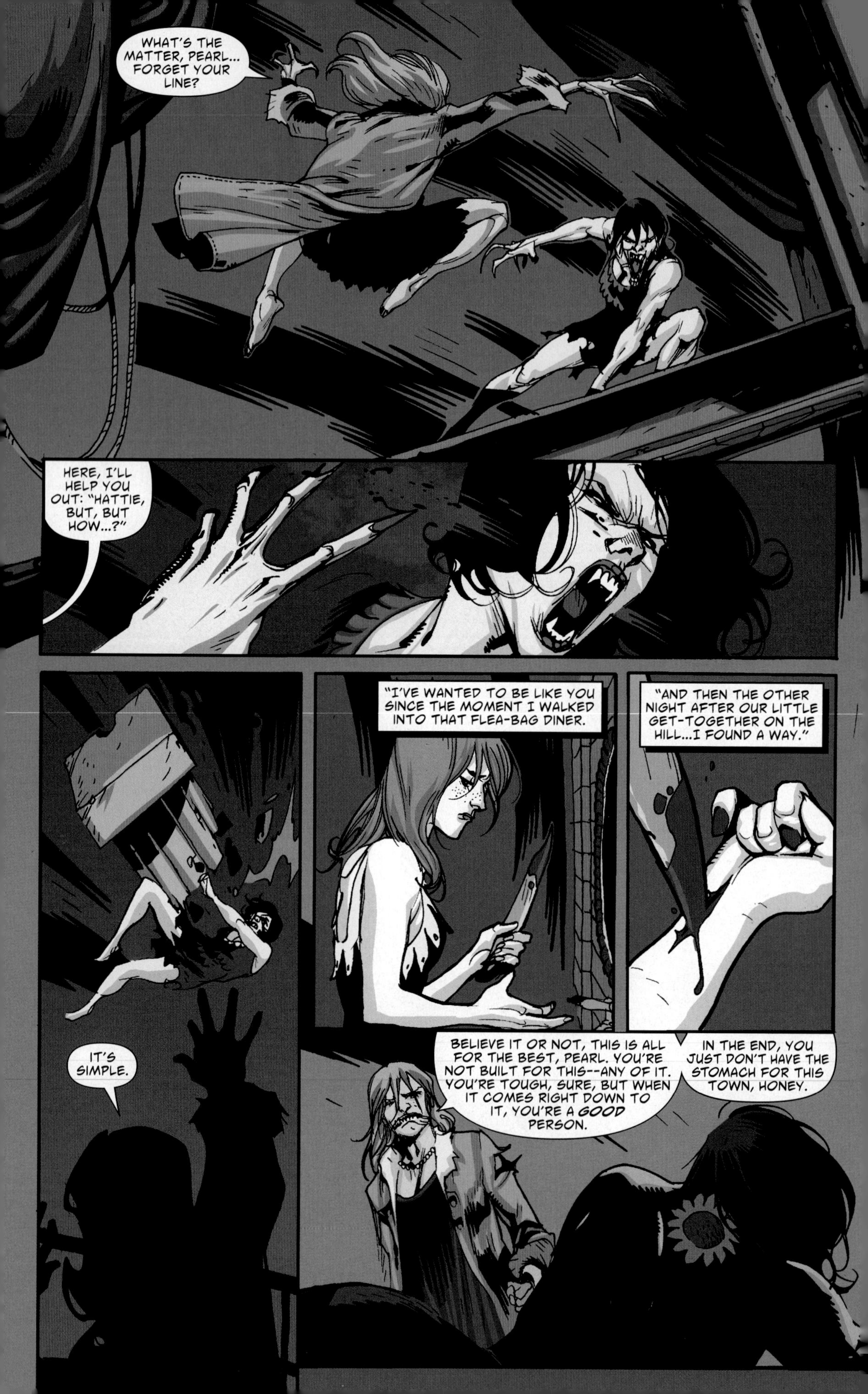
WHAT'S THE MATTER, PEARL... FORGET YOUR LINE?
HERE, I'LL HELP YOU OUT: "HATTIE, BUT, BUT HOW...?"
"I'VE WANTED TO BE LIKE YOU SINCE THE MOMENT I WALKED INTO THAT FLEA-BAG DINER.
"AND THEN THE OTHER NIGHT AFTER OUR LITTLE GET-TOGETHER ON THE HILL...I FOUND A WAY."
IT'S SIMPLE.
BELIEVE IT OR NOT, THIS IS ALL FOR THE BEST, PEARL. YOU'RE NOT BUILT FOR THIS--ANY OF IT. YOU'RE TOUGH, SURE, BUT WHEN IT COMES RIGHT DOWN TO IT, YOU'RE A *GOOD* PERSON.
IN THE END, YOU JUST DON'T HAVE THE STOMACH FOR THIS TOWN, HONEY.

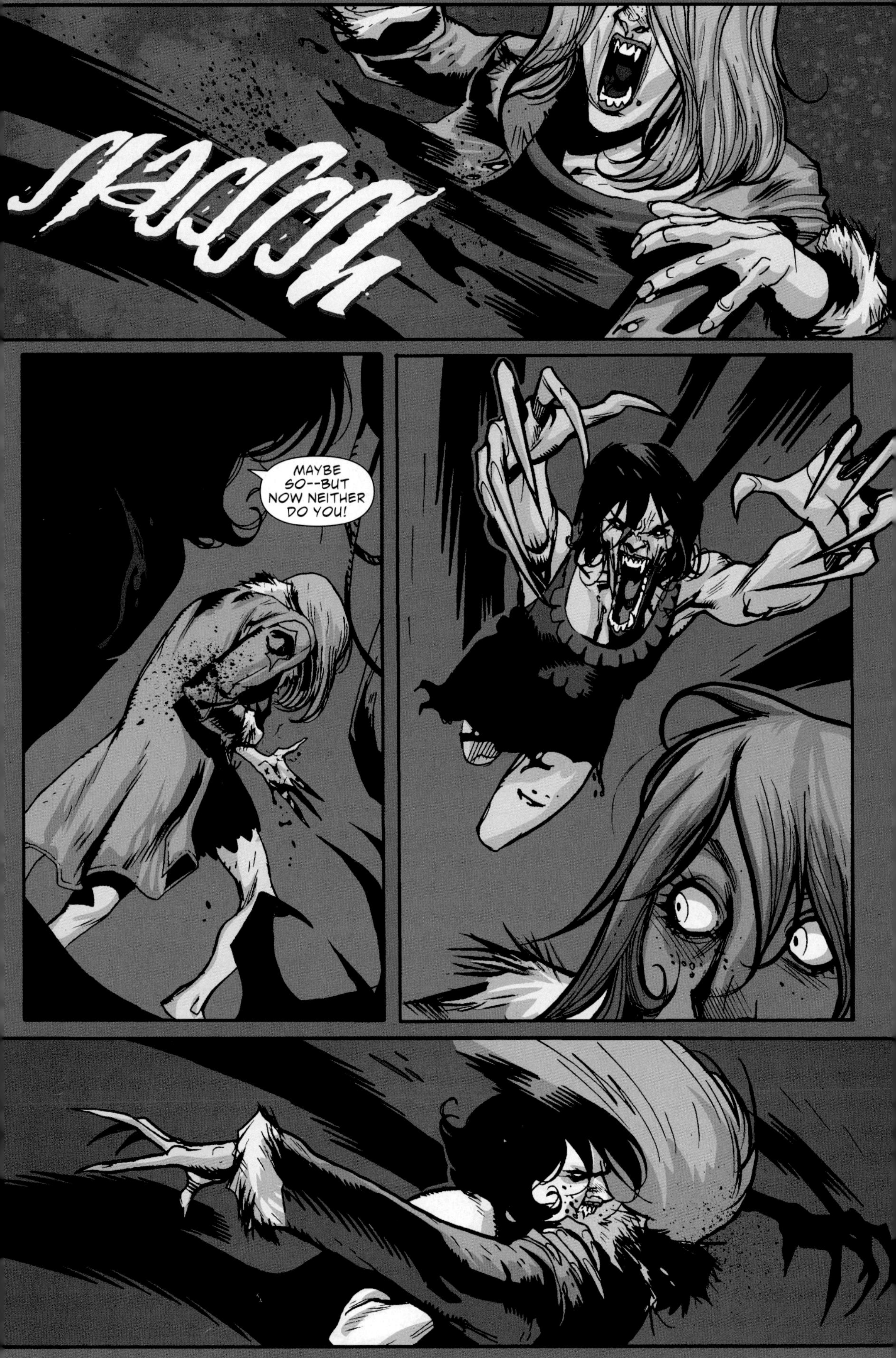
MAYBE SO--BUT NOW NEITHER DO YOU!

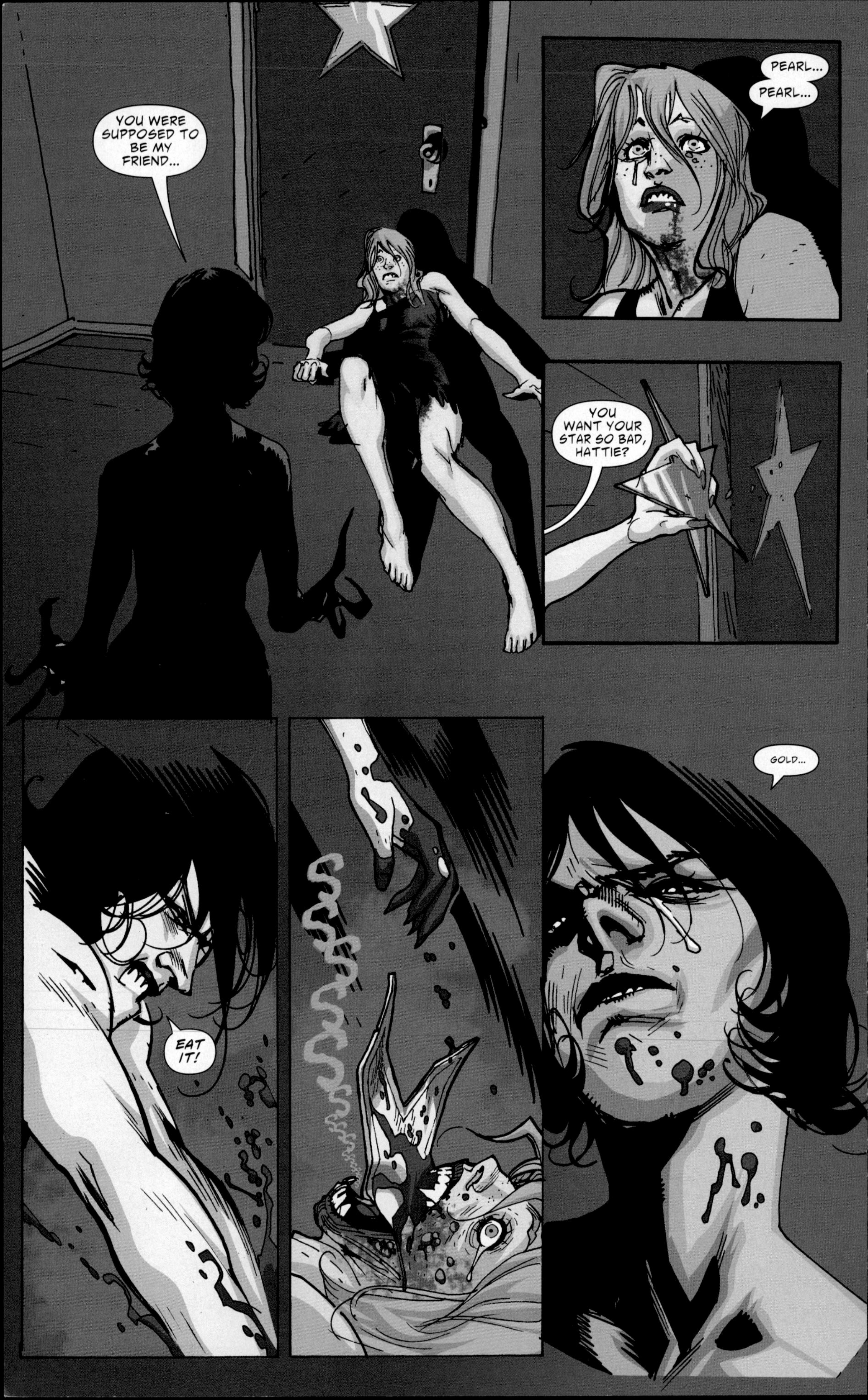
YOU WERE SUPPOSED TO BE MY FRIEND...
PEARL...
PEARL...
YOU WANT YOUR STAR SO BAD, HATTIE?
EAT IT!
GOLD...

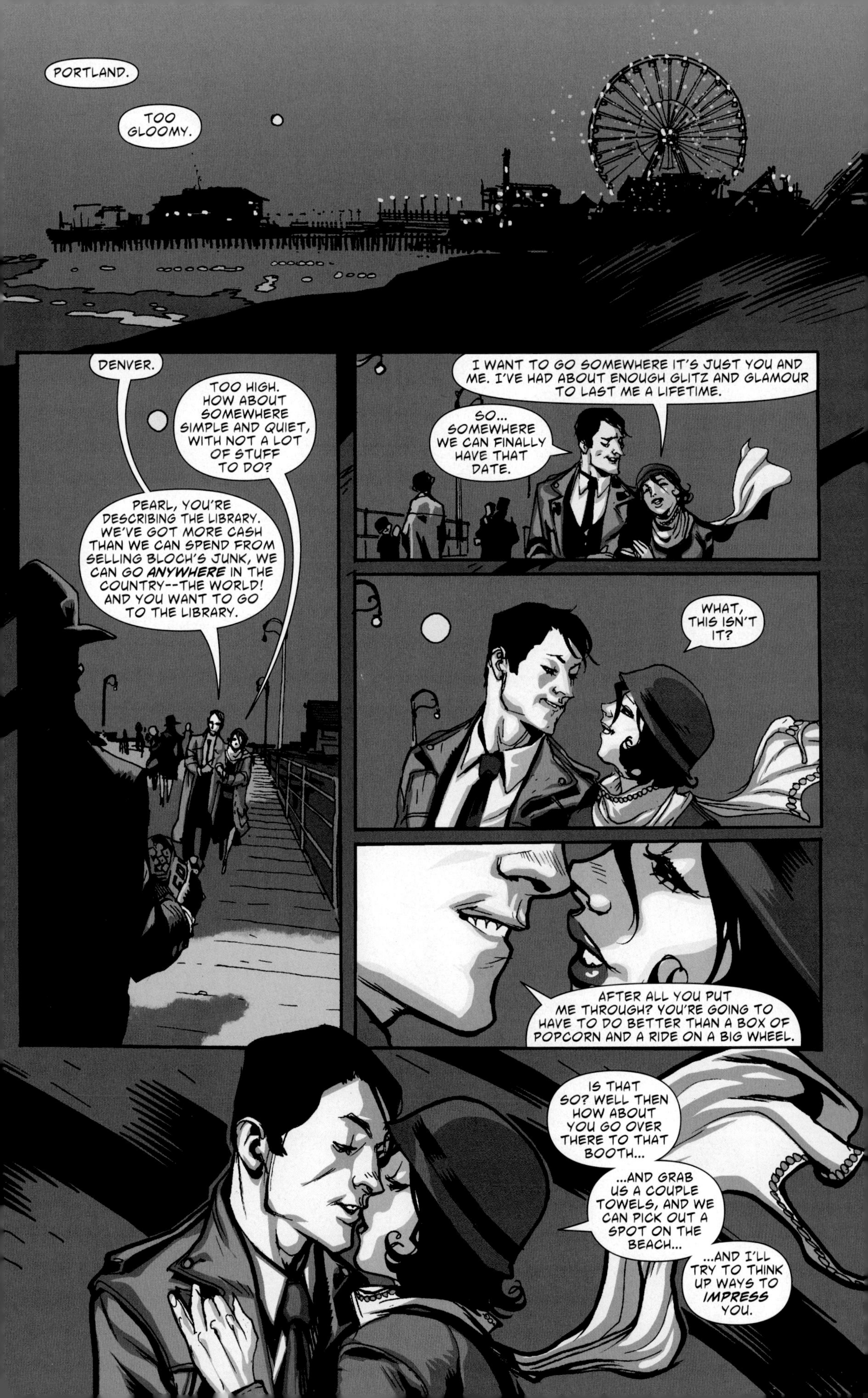
PORTLAND.
TOO GLOOMY.
DENVER.
TOO HIGH. HOW ABOUT SOMEWHERE SIMPLE AND QUIET, WITH NOT A LOT OF STUFF TO DO?
PEARL, YOU'RE DESCRIBING THE LIBRARY. WE'VE GOT MORE CASH THAN WE CAN SPEND FROM SELLING BLOCH'S JUNK, WE CAN GO *ANYWHERE* IN THE COUNTRY--THE WORLD! AND YOU WANT TO GO TO THE LIBRARY.
I WANT TO GO SOMEWHERE IT'S JUST YOU AND ME. I'VE HAD ABOUT ENOUGH GLITZ AND GLAMOUR TO LAST ME A LIFETIME.
SO... SOMEWHERE WE CAN FINALLY HAVE THAT DATE.
WHAT, THIS ISN'T IT?
AFTER ALL YOU PUT ME THROUGH? YOU'RE GOING TO HAVE TO DO BETTER THAN A BOX OF POPCORN AND A RIDE ON A BIG WHEEL.
IS THAT SO? WELL THEN HOW ABOUT YOU GO OVER THERE TO THAT BOOTH...
...AND GRAB US A COUPLE TOWELS, AND WE CAN PICK OUT A SPOT ON THE BEACH...
...AND I'LL TRY TO THINK UP WAYS TO *IMPRESS* YOU.

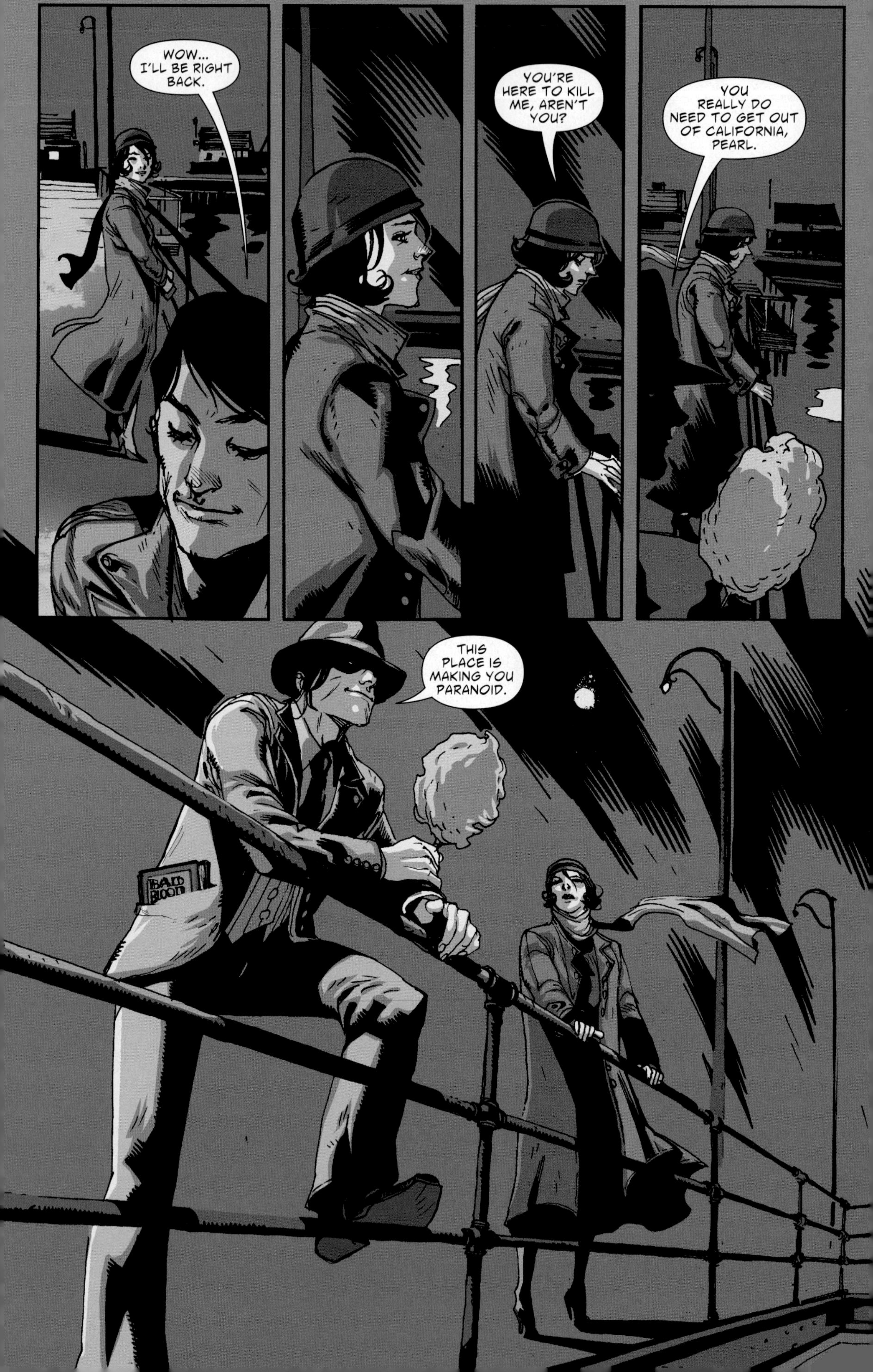
WOW... I'LL BE RIGHT BACK.
YOU'RE HERE TO KILL ME, AREN'T YOU?
YOU REALLY DO NEED TO GET OUT OF CALIFORNIA, PEARL.
THIS PLACE IS MAKING YOU PARANOID.
BAD BLOOD

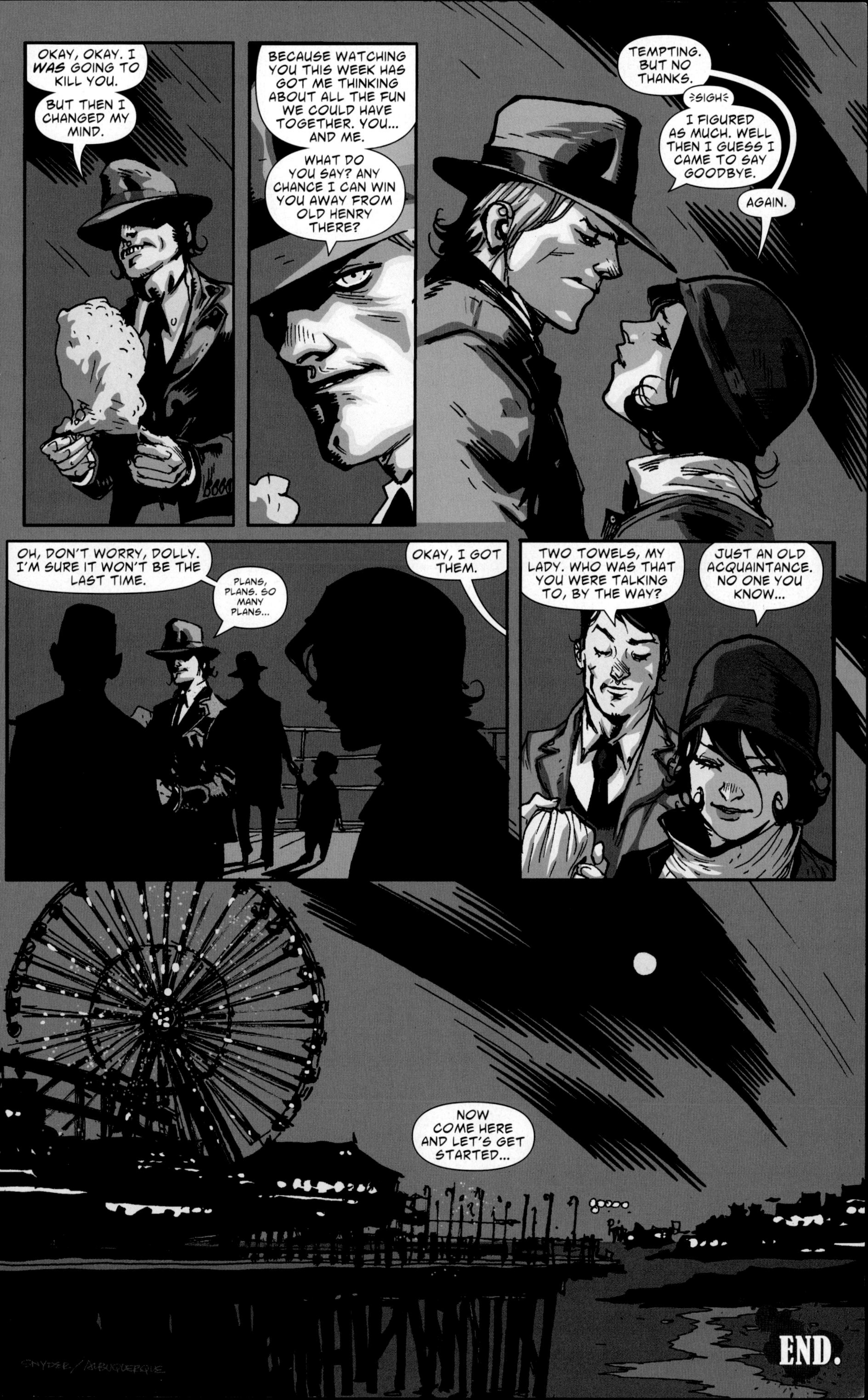
OKAY, OKAY. I WAS GOING TO KILL YOU.
BUT THEN I CHANGED MY MIND.
BECAUSE WATCHING YOU THIS WEEK HAS GOT ME THINKING ABOUT ALL THE FUN WE COULD HAVE TOGETHER. YOU... AND ME.
WHAT DO YOU SAY? ANY CHANCE I CAN WIN YOU AWAY FROM OLD HENRY THERE?
TEMPTING. BUT NO THANKS.
SIGH
I FIGURED AS MUCH. WELL THEN I GUESS I CAME TO SAY GOODBYE.
AGAIN.
OH, DON'T WORRY, DOLLY. I'M SURE IT WON'T BE THE LAST TIME.
PLANS, PLANS. SO MANY PLANS...
OKAY, I GOT THEM.
TWO TOWELS, MY LADY. WHO WAS THAT YOU WERE TALKING TO, BY THE WAY?
JUST AN OLD ACQUAINTANCE. NO ONE YOU KNOW...
NOW COME HERE AND LET'S GET STARTED...
END.

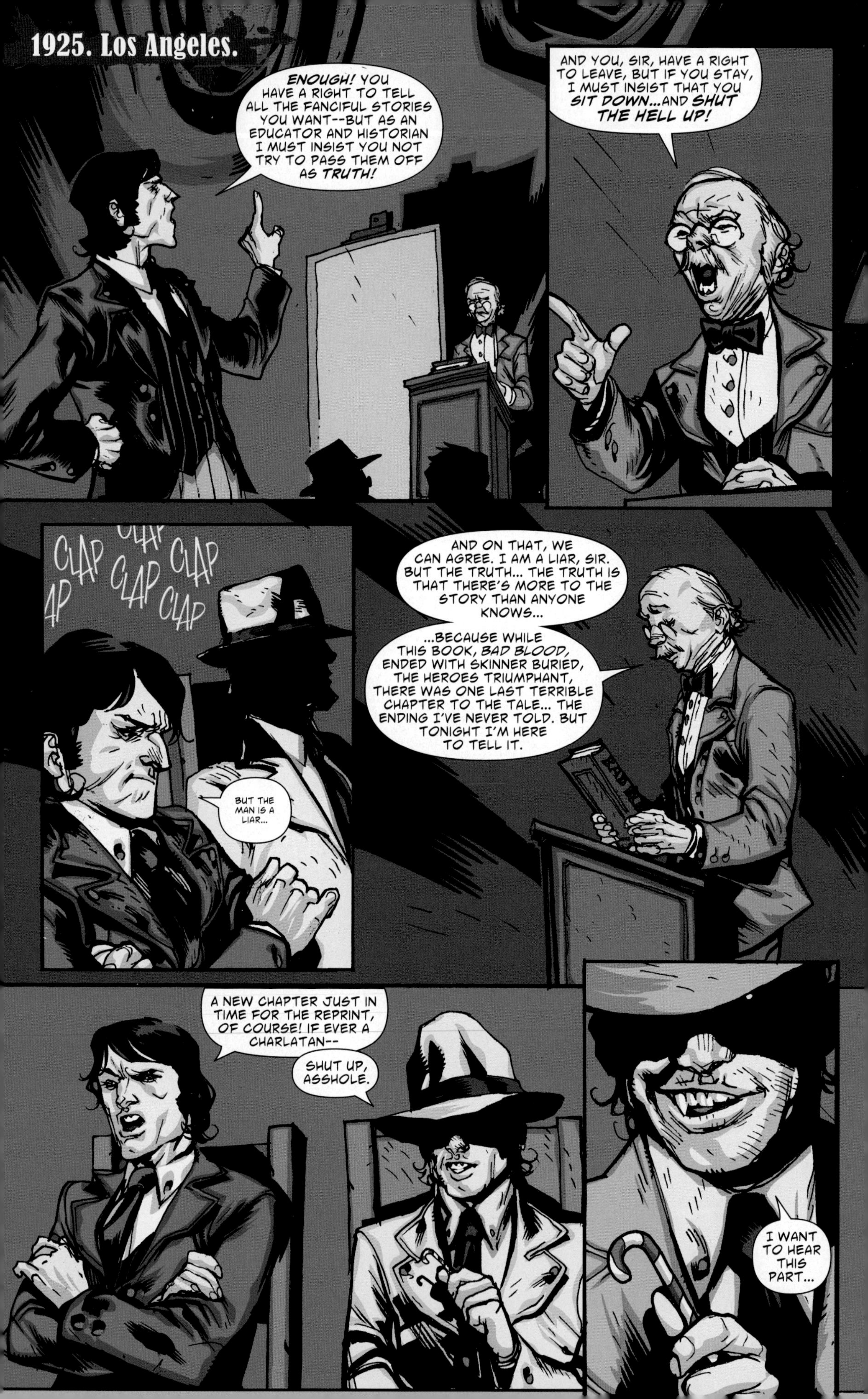
1925. Los Angeles.
ENOUGH! YOU HAVE A RIGHT TO TELL ALL THE FANCIFUL STORIES YOU WANT--BUT AS AN EDUCATOR AND HISTORIAN I MUST INSIST YOU NOT TRY TO PASS THEM OFF AS TRUTH!
AND YOU, SIR, HAVE A RIGHT TO LEAVE, BUT IF YOU STAY, I MUST INSIST THAT YOU SIT DOWN...AND SHUT THE HELL UP!
CLAP CLAP CLAP CLAP CLAP CLAP
BUT THE MAN IS A LIAR...
AND ON THAT, WE CAN AGREE. I AM A LIAR, SIR. BUT THE TRUTH... THE TRUTH IS THAT THERE'S MORE TO THE STORY THAN ANYONE KNOWS...
...BECAUSE WHILE THIS BOOK, BAD BLOOD, ENDED WITH SKINNER BURIED, THE HEROES TRIUMPHANT, THERE WAS ONE LAST TERRIBLE CHAPTER TO THE TALE... THE ENDING I'VE NEVER TOLD. BUT TONIGHT I'M HERE TO TELL IT.
A NEW CHAPTER JUST IN TIME FOR THE REPRINT, OF COURSE! IF EVER A CHARLATAN--
SHUT UP, ASSHOLE.
I WANT TO HEAR THIS PART...

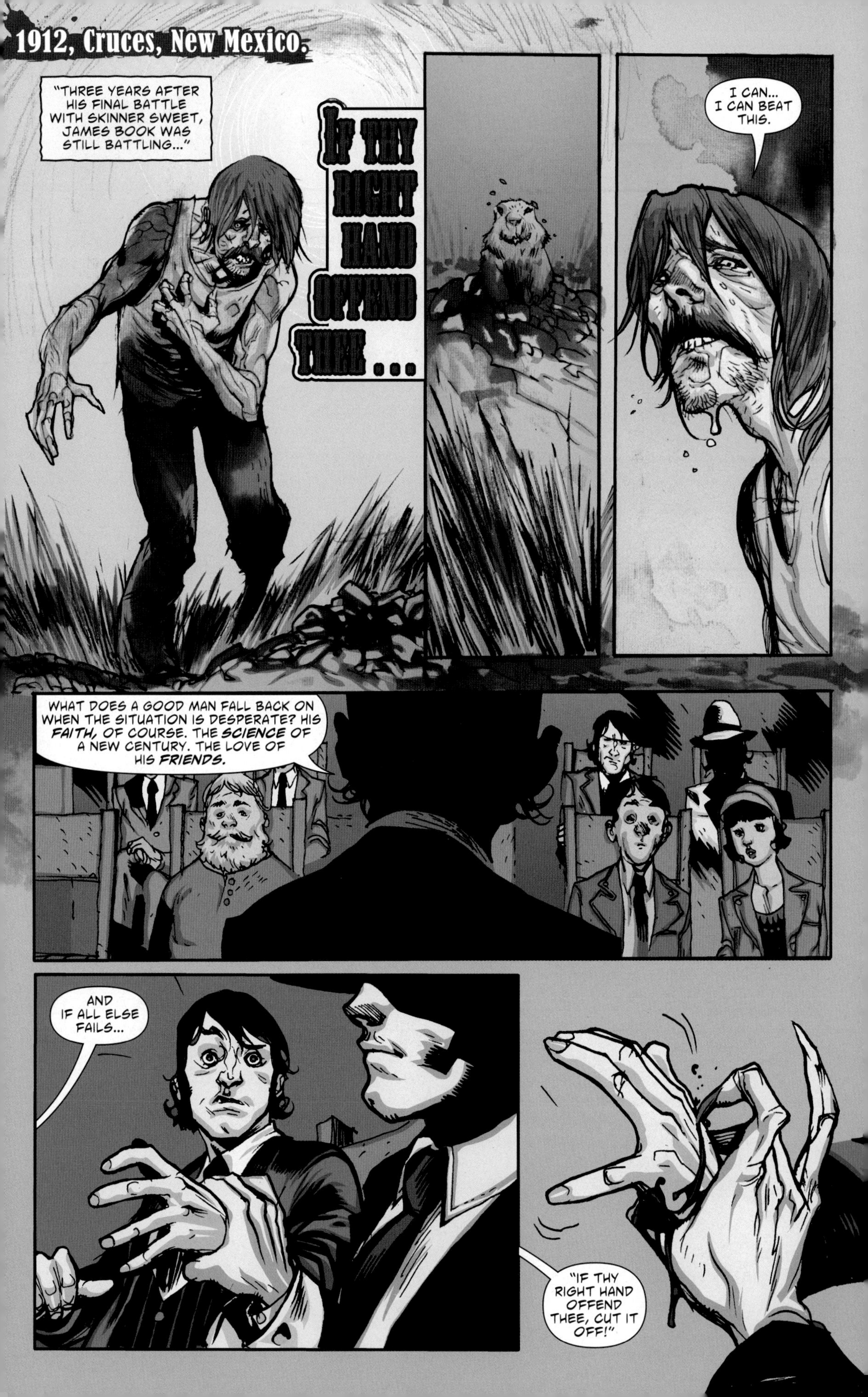
1912, Cruces, New Mexico.
"THREE YEARS AFTER HIS FINAL BATTLE WITH SKINNER SWEET, JAMES BOOK WAS STILL BATTLING..."
IF THY RIGHT HAND OFFEND THEE...
I CAN... I CAN BEAT THIS.
WHAT DOES A GOOD MAN FALL BACK ON WHEN THE SITUATION IS DESPERATE? HIS *FAITH,* OF COURSE. THE *SCIENCE* OF A NEW CENTURY. THE LOVE OF HIS *FRIENDS.*
AND IF ALL ELSE FAILS...
"IF THY RIGHT HAND OFFEND THEE, CUT IT OFF!"

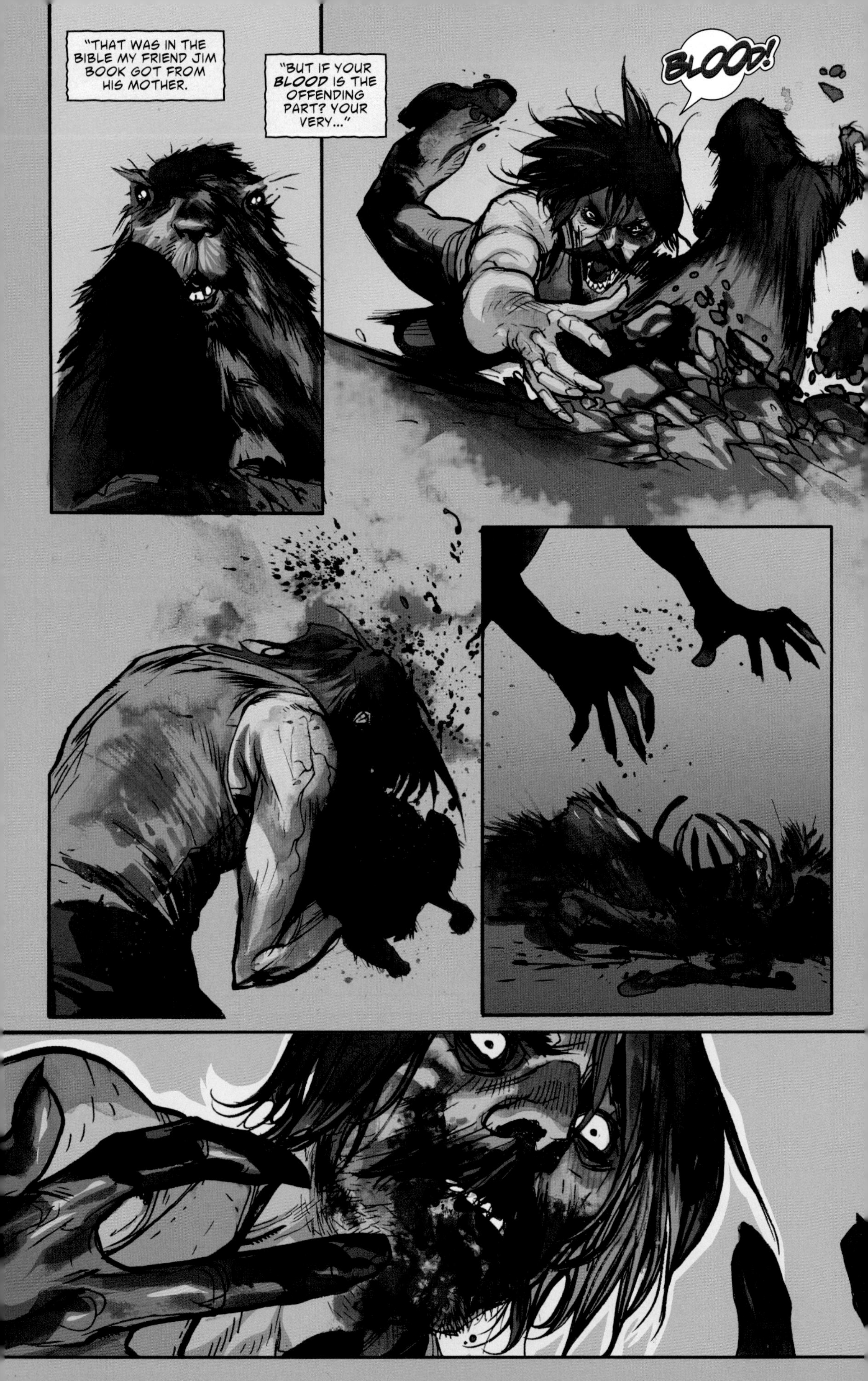
"THAT WAS IN THE BIBLE MY FRIEND JIM BOOK GOT FROM HIS MOTHER.
"BUT IF YOUR *BLOOD* IS THE OFFENDING PART? YOUR VERY..."
BLOOD!

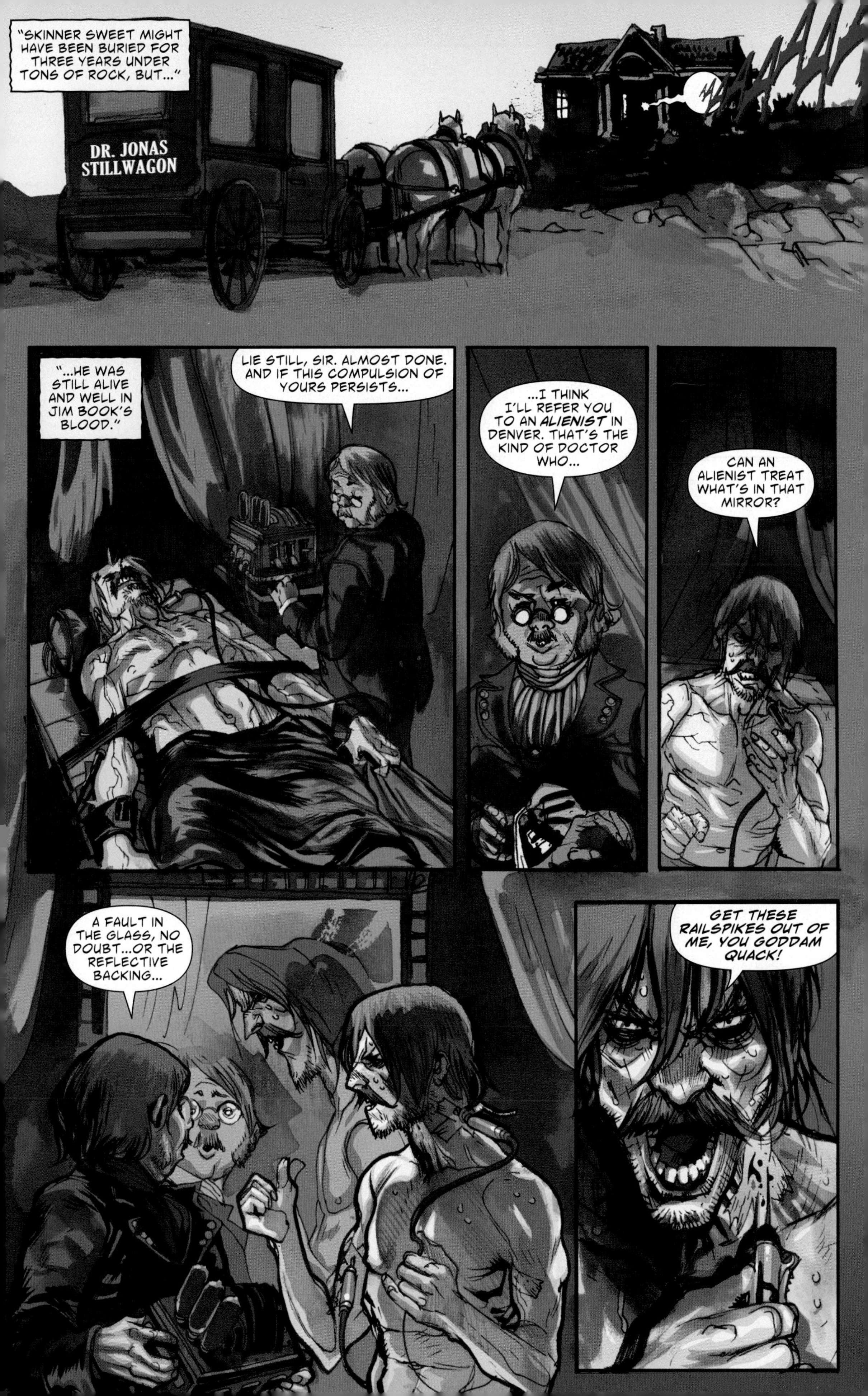
"SKINNER SWEET MIGHT HAVE BEEN BURIED FOR THREE YEARS UNDER TONS OF ROCK, BUT..."
DR. JONAS STILLWAGON
"...HE WAS STILL ALIVE AND WELL IN JIM BOOK'S BLOOD."
LIE STILL, SIR. ALMOST DONE. AND IF THIS COMPULSION OF YOURS PERSISTS...
...I THINK I'LL REFER YOU TO AN *ALIENIST* IN DENVER. THAT'S THE KIND OF DOCTOR WHO...
CAN AN ALIENIST TREAT WHAT'S IN THAT MIRROR?
A FAULT IN THE GLASS, NO DOUBT...OR THE REFLECTIVE BACKING...
GET THESE RAILSPIKES OUT OF ME, YOU GODDAM QUACK!

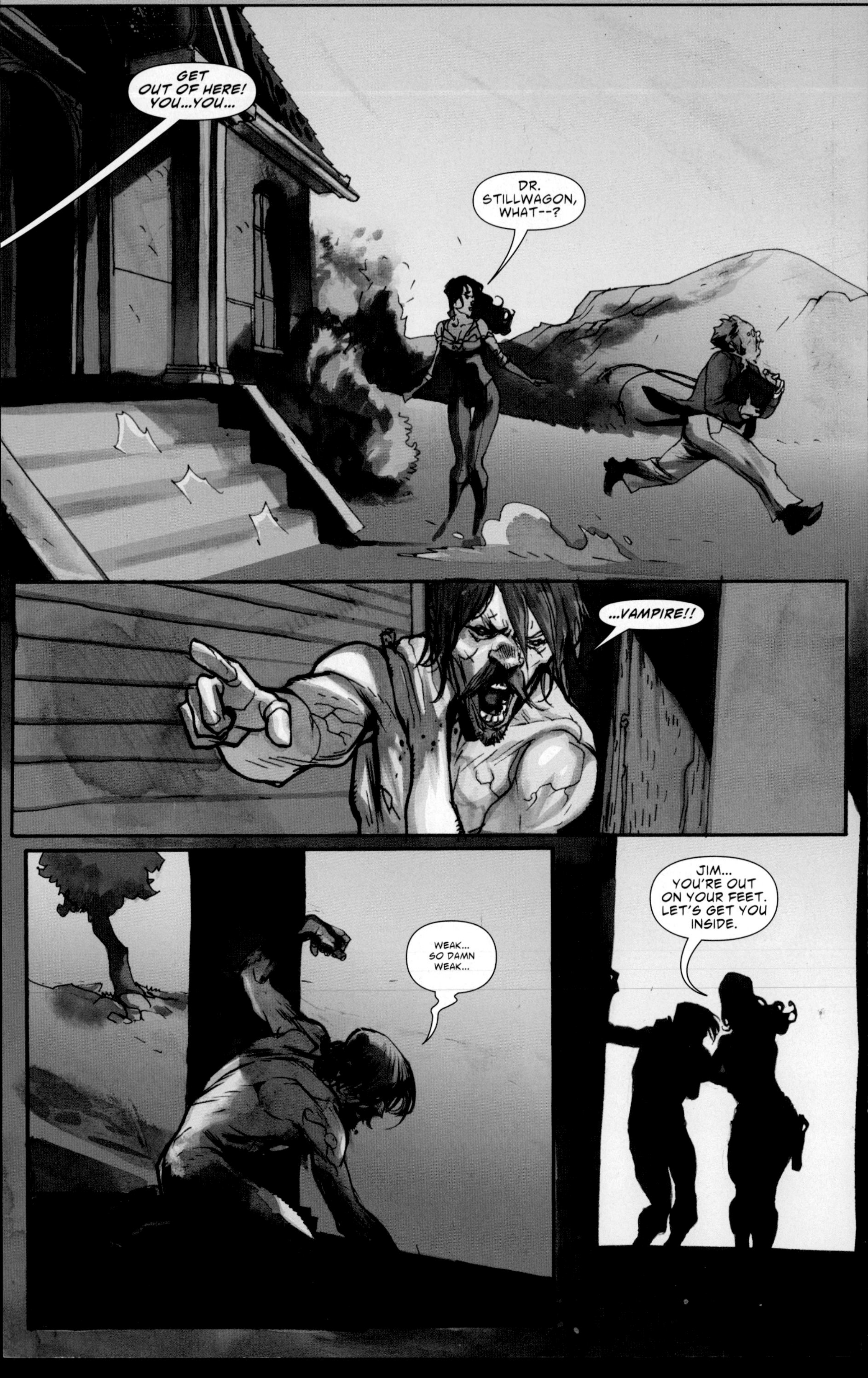
GET OUT OF HERE! YOU...YOU...
DR. STILLWAGON, WHAT--?
...VAMPIRE!!
WEAK... SO DAMN WEAK...
JIM... YOU'RE OUT ON YOUR FEET. LET'S GET YOU INSIDE.

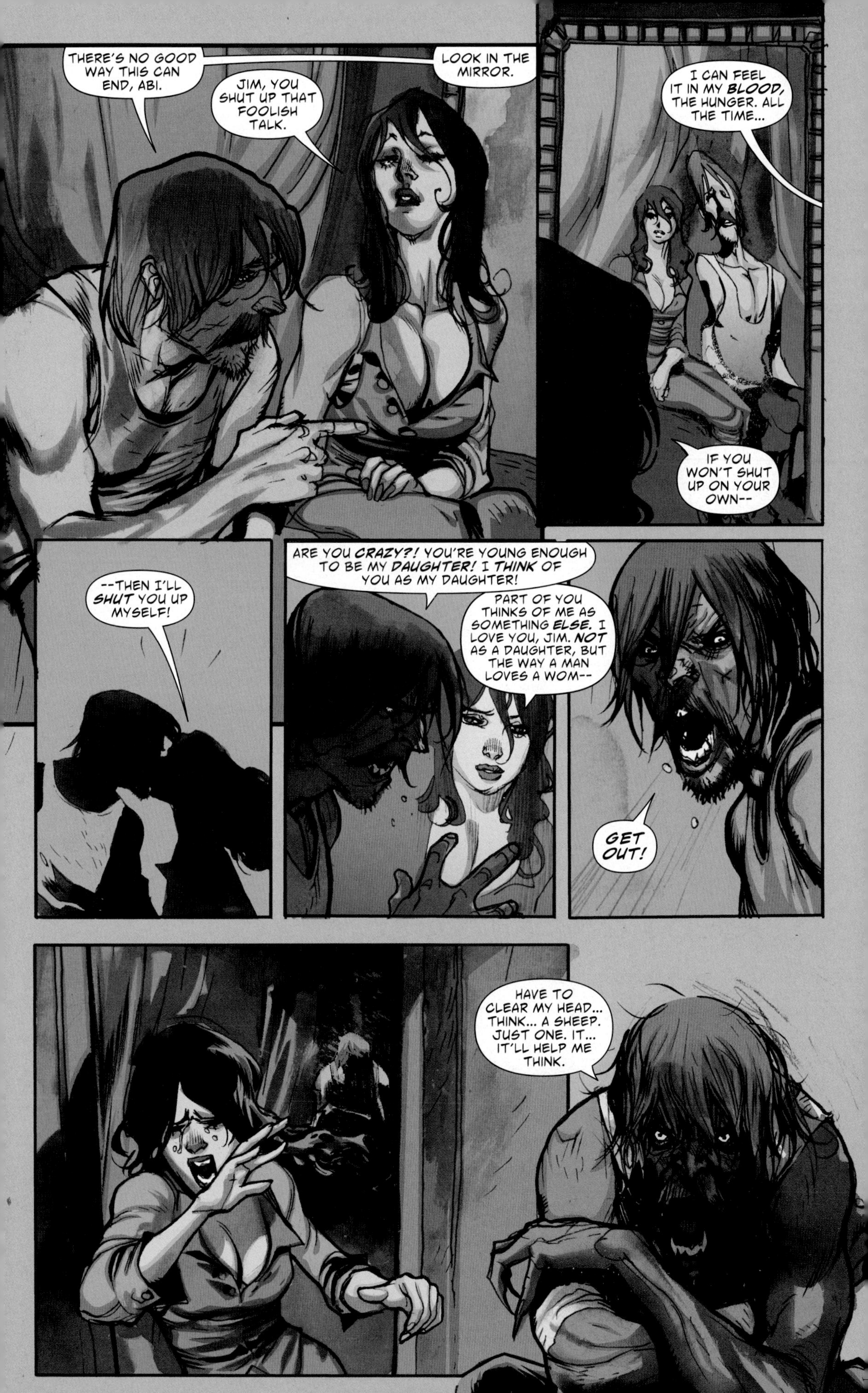
THERE'S NO GOOD WAY THIS CAN END, ABI.
JIM, YOU SHUT UP THAT FOOLISH TALK.
LOOK IN THE MIRROR.
I CAN FEEL IT IN MY BLOOD, THE HUNGER. ALL THE TIME...
IF YOU WON'T SHUT UP ON YOUR OWN--
--THEN I'LL SHUT YOU UP MYSELF!
ARE YOU CRAZY?! YOU'RE YOUNG ENOUGH TO BE MY DAUGHTER! I THINK OF YOU AS MY DAUGHTER!
PART OF YOU THINKS OF ME AS SOMETHING ELSE. I LOVE YOU, JIM. NOT AS A DAUGHTER, BUT THE WAY A MAN LOVES A WOM--
GET OUT!
HAVE TO CLEAR MY HEAD... THINK... A SHEEP. JUST ONE. IT... IT'LL HELP ME THINK.

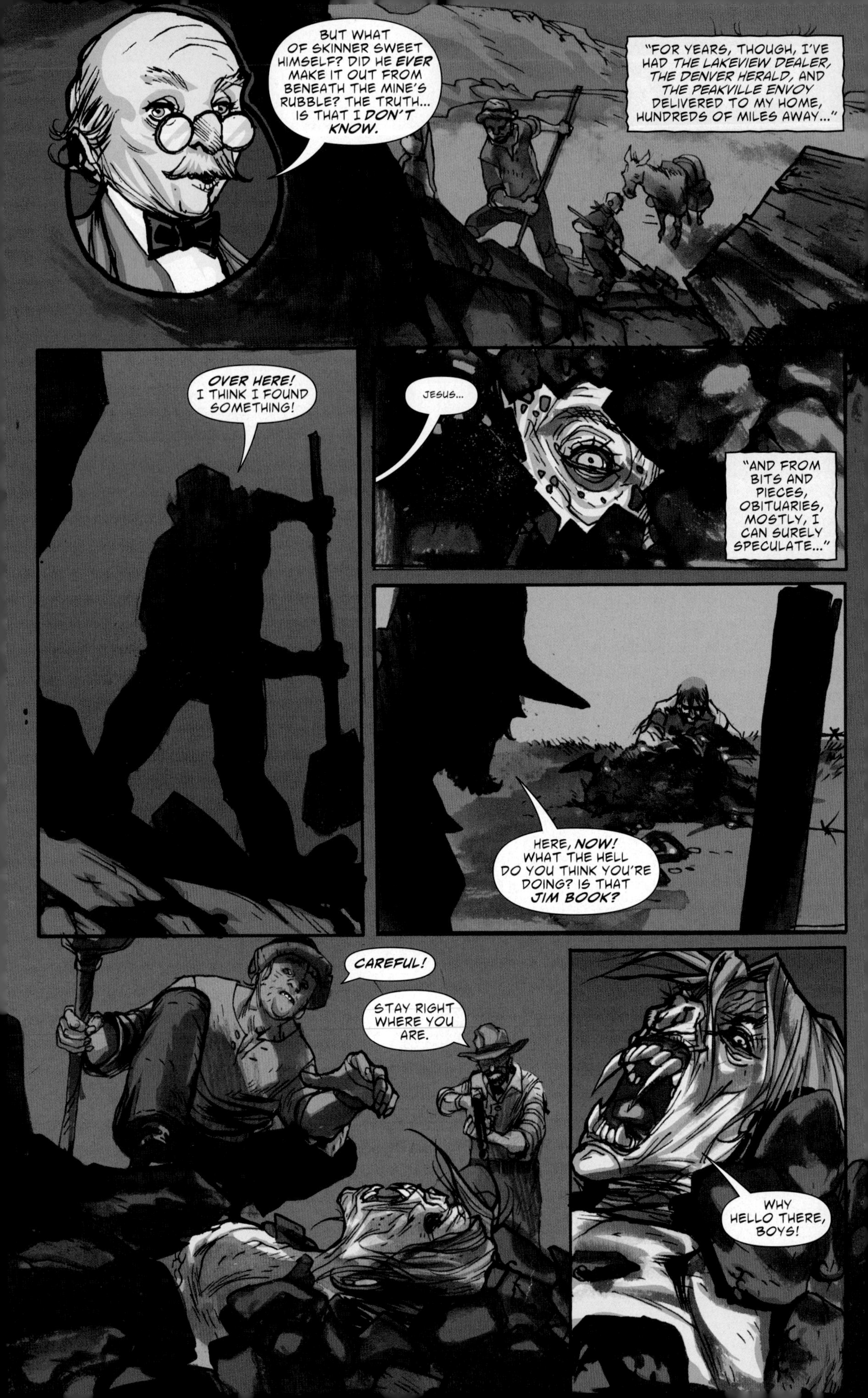
BUT WHAT OF SKINNER SWEET HIMSELF? DID HE EVER MAKE IT OUT FROM BENEATH THE MINE'S RUBBLE? THE TRUTH... IS THAT I DON'T KNOW.
"FOR YEARS, THOUGH, I'VE HAD THE LAKEVIEW DEALER, THE DENVER HERALD, AND THE PEAKVILLE ENVOY DELIVERED TO MY HOME, HUNDREDS OF MILES AWAY..."
OVER HERE! I THINK I FOUND SOMETHING!
JESUS...
"AND FROM BITS AND PIECES, OBITUARIES, MOSTLY, I CAN SURELY SPECULATE..."
HERE, NOW! WHAT THE HELL DO YOU THINK YOU'RE DOING? IS THAT JIM BOOK?
CAREFUL!
STAY RIGHT WHERE YOU ARE.
WHY HELLO THERE, BOYS!

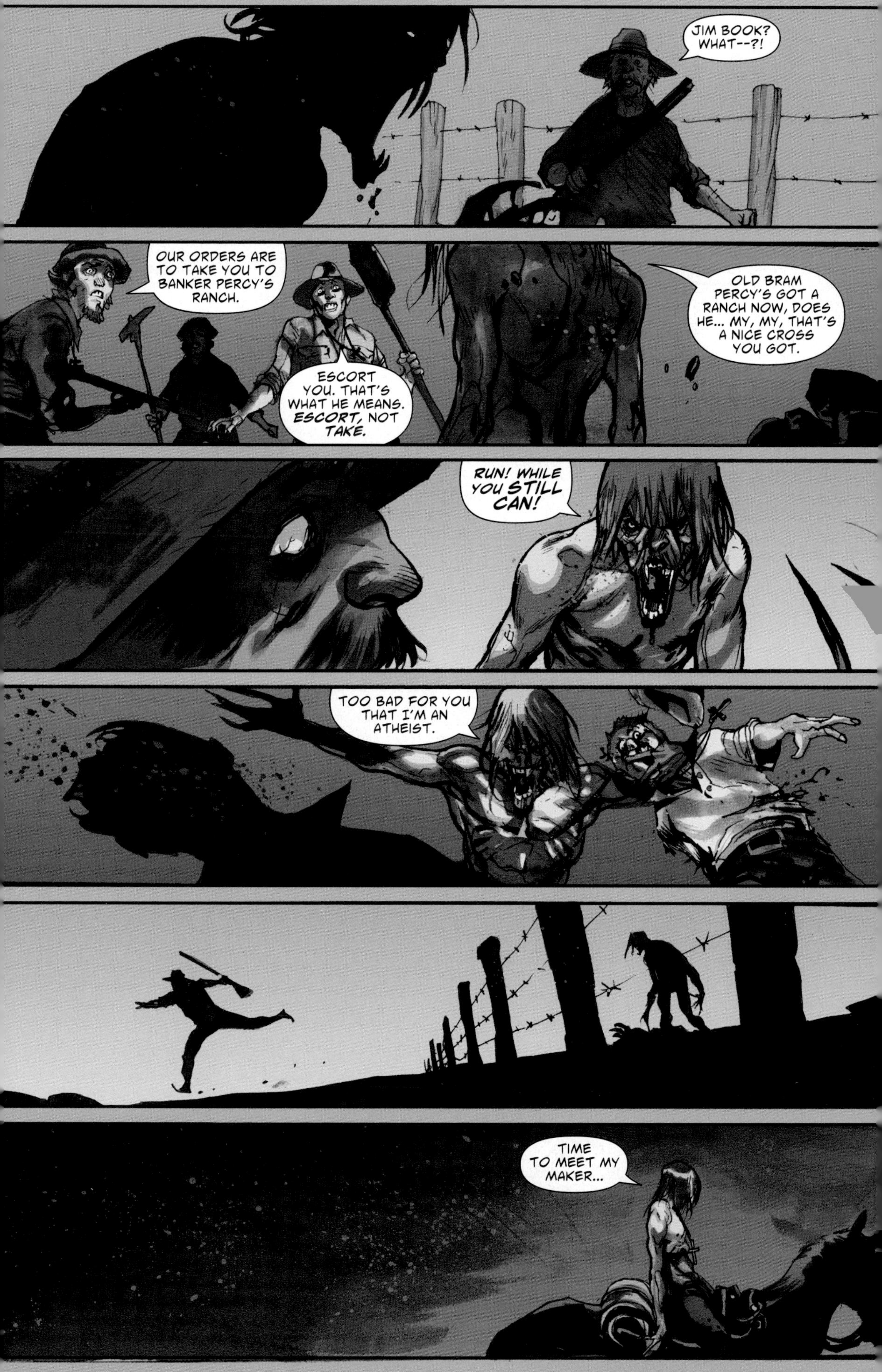
JIM BOOK? WHAT--?!
OUR ORDERS ARE TO TAKE YOU TO BANKER PERCY'S RANCH.
ESCORT YOU. THAT'S WHAT HE MEANS. ESCORT, NOT TAKE.
OLD BRAM PERCY'S GOT A RANCH NOW, DOES HE... MY, MY, THAT'S A NICE CROSS YOU GOT.
RUN! WHILE YOU STILL CAN!
TOO BAD FOR YOU THAT I'M AN ATHEIST.
TIME TO MEET MY MAKER...

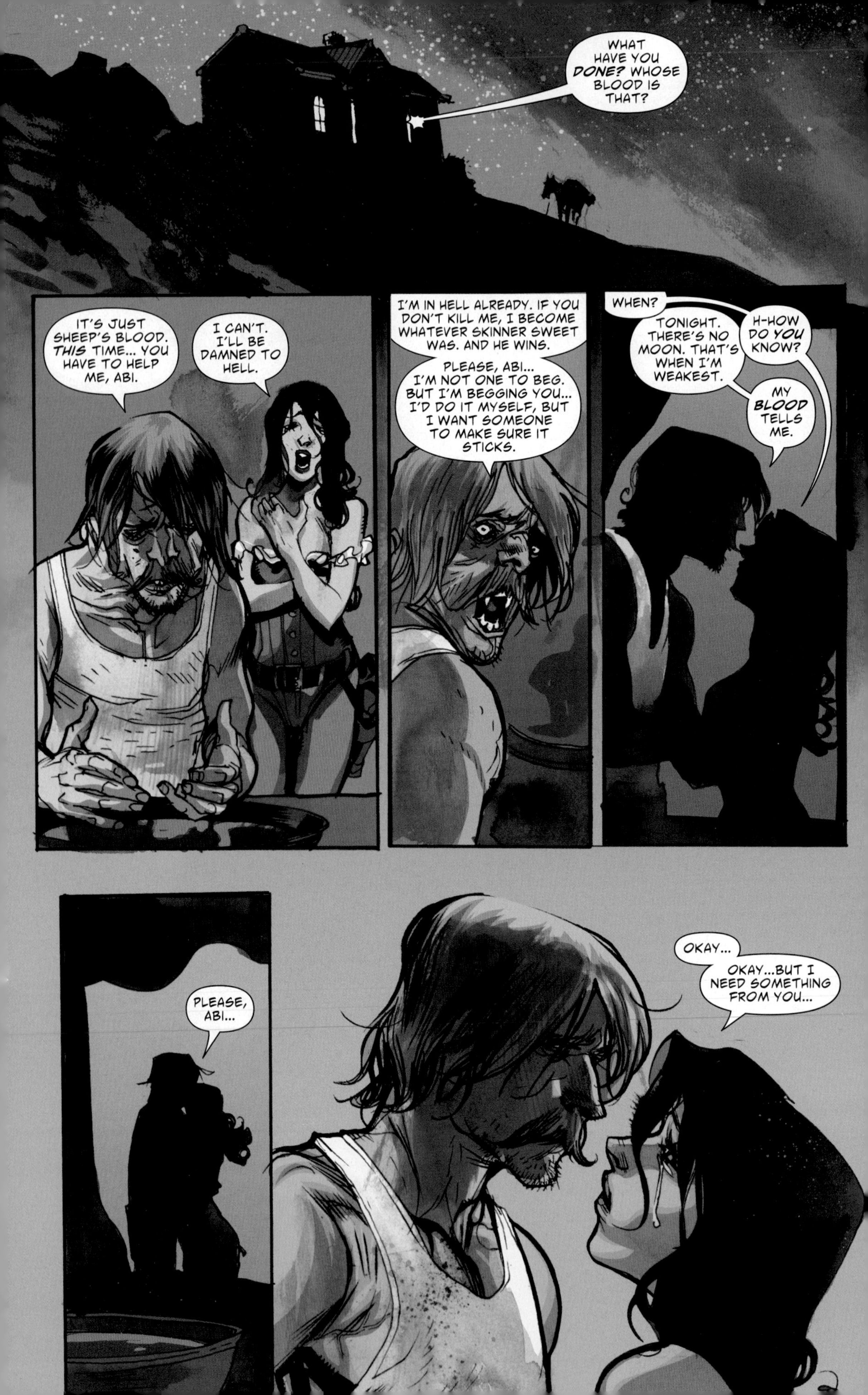
WHAT HAVE YOU DONE? WHOSE BLOOD IS THAT?
IT'S JUST SHEEP'S BLOOD. THIS TIME... YOU HAVE TO HELP ME, ABI.
I CAN'T. I'LL BE DAMNED TO HELL.
I'M IN HELL ALREADY. IF YOU DON'T KILL ME, I BECOME WHATEVER SKINNER SWEET WAS. AND HE WINS.
PLEASE, ABI... I'M NOT ONE TO BEG. BUT I'M BEGGING YOU... I'D DO IT MYSELF, BUT I WANT SOMEONE TO MAKE SURE IT STICKS.
WHEN?
TONIGHT. THERE'S NO MOON. THAT'S WHEN I'M WEAKEST.
H-HOW DO YOU KNOW?
MY BLOOD TELLS ME.
PLEASE, ABI...
OKAY...
OKAY...BUT I NEED SOMETHING FROM YOU...

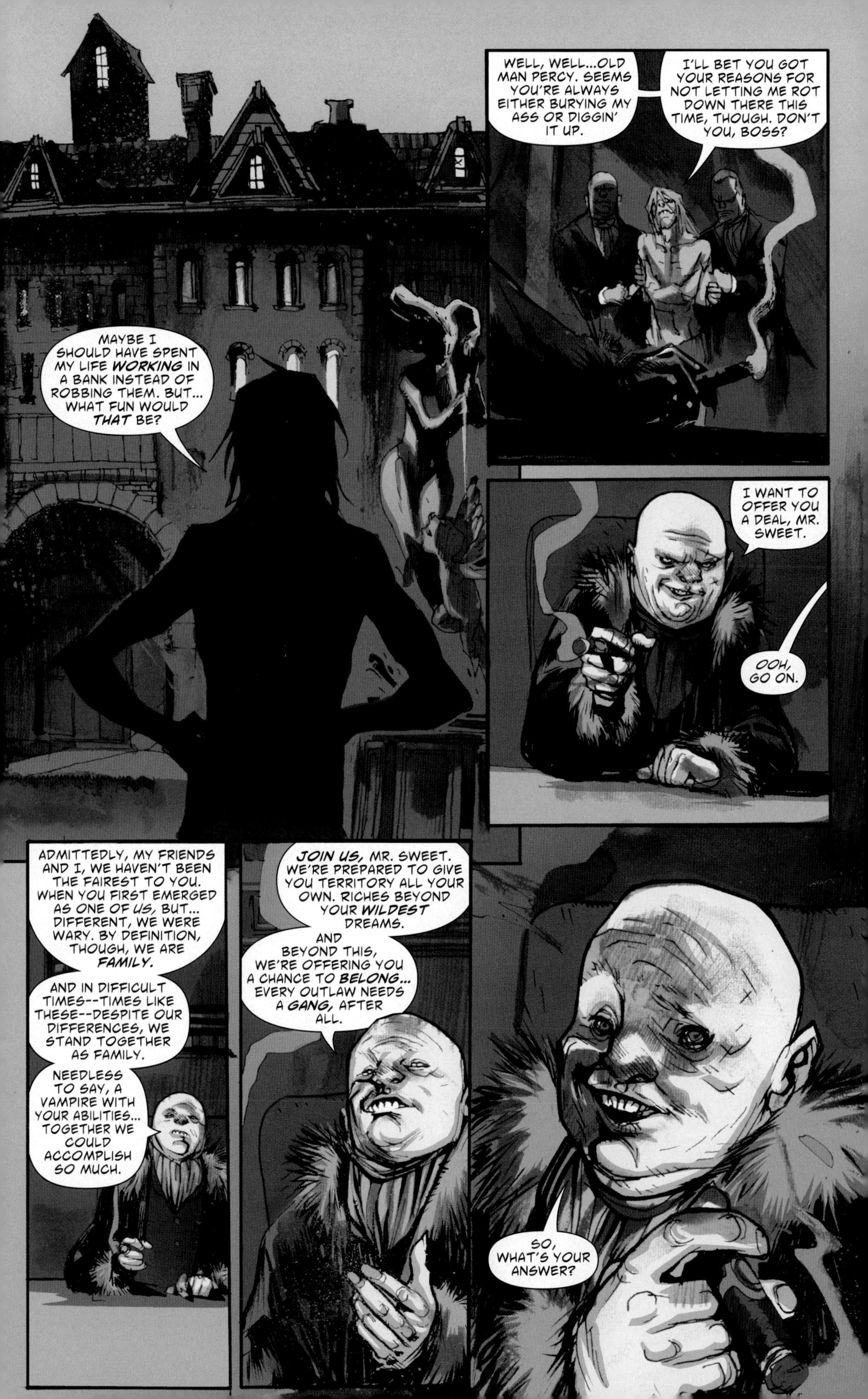
MAYBE I SHOULD HAVE SPENT MY LIFE WORKING IN A BANK INSTEAD OF ROBBING THEM. BUT... WHAT FUN WOULD THAT BE?
WELL, WELL...OLD MAN PERCY. SEEMS YOU'RE ALWAYS EITHER BURYING MY ASS OR DIGGIN' IT UP.
I'LL BET YOU GOT YOUR REASONS FOR NOT LETTING ME ROT DOWN THERE THIS TIME, THOUGH. DON'T YOU, BOSS?
I WANT TO OFFER YOU A DEAL, MR. SWEET.
OOH, GO ON.
ADMITTEDLY, MY FRIENDS AND I, WE HAVEN'T BEEN THE FAIREST TO YOU. WHEN YOU FIRST EMERGED AS ONE OF US, BUT... DIFFERENT, WE WERE WARY. BY DEFINITION, THOUGH, WE ARE FAMILY.
AND IN DIFFICULT TIMES--TIMES LIKE THESE--DESPITE OUR DIFFERENCES, WE STAND TOGETHER AS FAMILY.
NEEDLESS TO SAY, A VAMPIRE WITH YOUR ABILITIES... TOGETHER WE COULD ACCOMPLISH SO MUCH.
JOIN US, MR. SWEET. WE'RE PREPARED TO GIVE YOU TERRITORY ALL YOUR OWN. RICHES BEYOND YOUR WILDEST DREAMS.
AND BEYOND THIS, WE'RE OFFERING YOU A CHANCE TO BELONG... EVERY OUTLAW NEEDS A GANG, AFTER ALL.
SO, WHAT'S YOUR ANSWER?

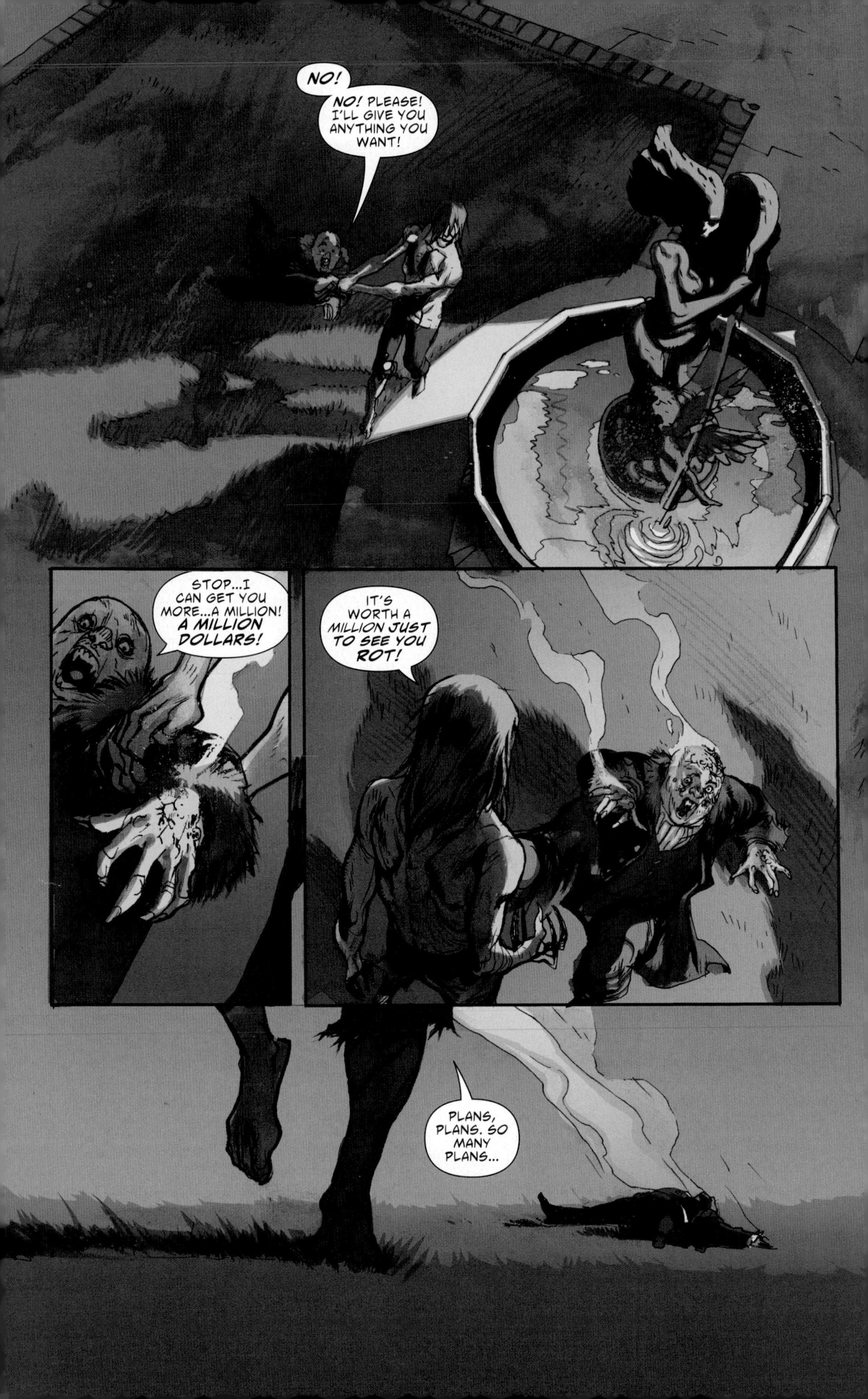
NO!
NO! PLEASE! I'LL GIVE YOU ANYTHING YOU WANT!
STOP...I CAN GET YOU MORE...A MILLION! A MILLION DOLLARS!
IT'S WORTH A MILLION JUST TO SEE YOU ROT!
PLANS, PLANS. SO MANY PLANS...

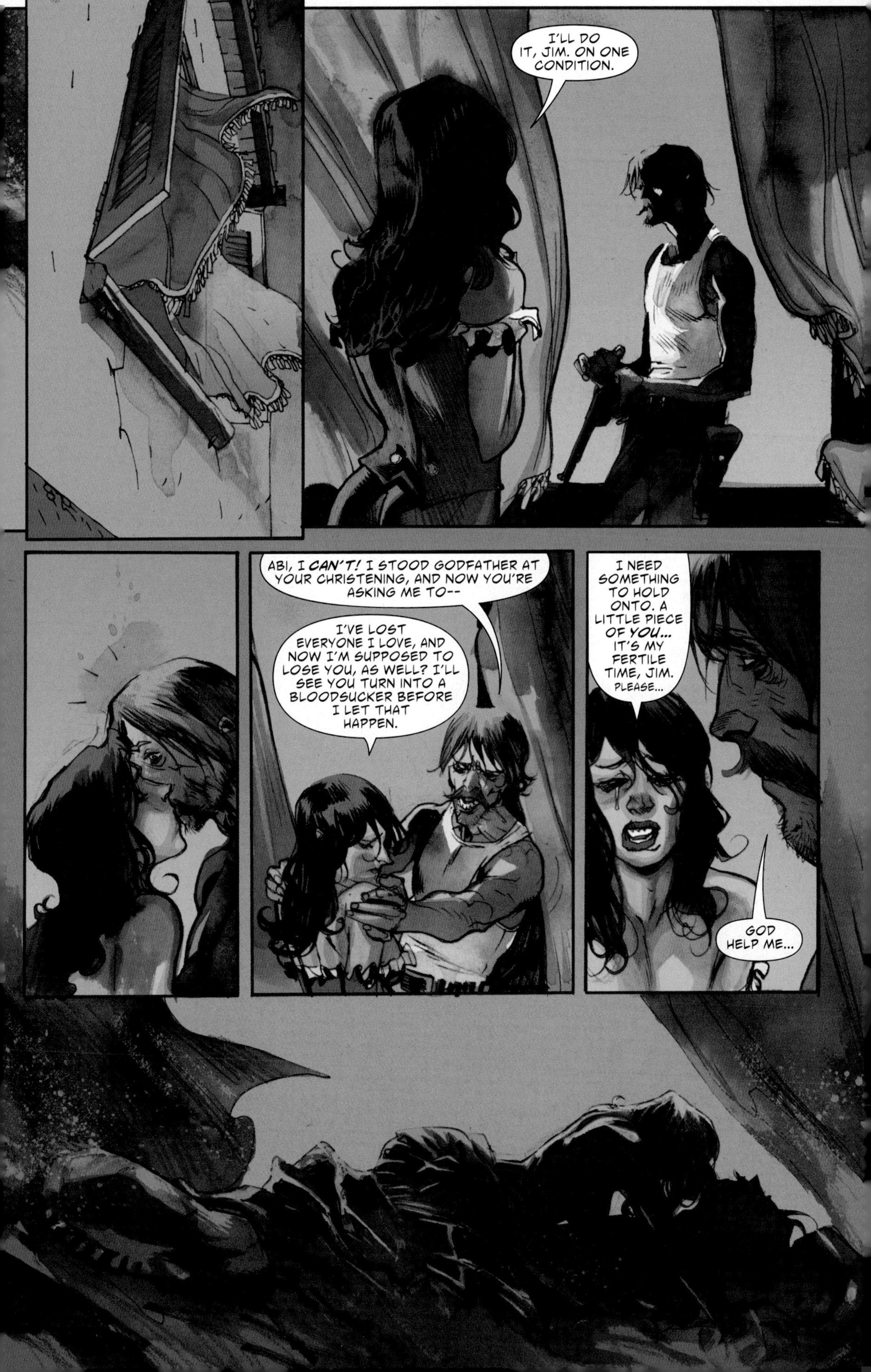
I'LL DO IT, JIM. ON ONE CONDITION.
ABI, I CAN'T! I STOOD GODFATHER AT YOUR CHRISTENING, AND NOW YOU'RE ASKING ME TO--
I'VE LOST EVERYONE I LOVE, AND NOW I'M SUPPOSED TO LOSE YOU, AS WELL? I'LL SEE YOU TURN INTO A BLOODSUCKER BEFORE I LET THAT HAPPEN.
I NEED SOMETHING TO HOLD ONTO. A LITTLE PIECE OF YOU... IT'S MY FERTILE TIME, JIM. PLEASE...
GOD HELP ME...

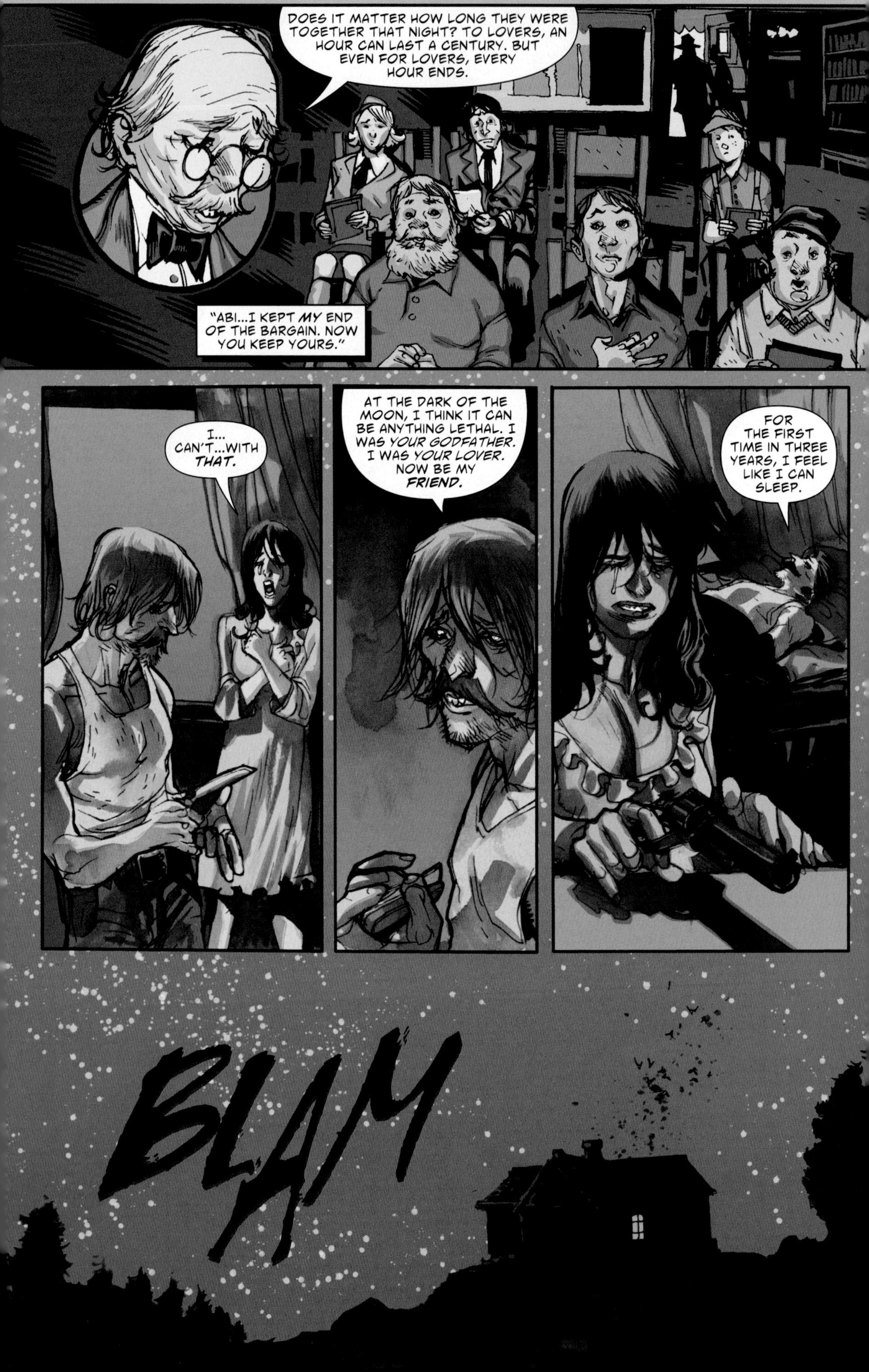
DOES IT MATTER HOW LONG THEY WERE TOGETHER THAT NIGHT? TO LOVERS, AN HOUR CAN LAST A CENTURY. BUT EVEN FOR LOVERS, EVERY HOUR ENDS.
"ABI...I KEPT MY END OF THE BARGAIN. NOW YOU KEEP YOURS."
I... CAN'T...WITH THAT.
AT THE DARK OF THE MOON, I THINK IT CAN BE ANYTHING LETHAL. I WAS YOUR GODFATHER. I WAS YOUR LOVER. NOW BE MY FRIEND.
FOR THE FIRST TIME IN THREE YEARS, I FEEL LIKE I CAN SLEEP.
BLAM

"A YEAR LATER, ABILENA FINALLY LEFT THE HOME SHE'D SHARED WITH JAMES BOOK AND HEADED WEST."

FELIX
CAMILLO
EVERY MAN HE
MET CALLED
HIM FRIEND
1839-1909

JAMES
ELDRED BOOK
LAWMAN
1852-1912
SOLA VIRTUS INVICTA

NGUM

GHTER

855
1880

D UNTIL
ECTION

COME ON, BABY GIRL, LET'S GO.

MIND IF I TAG ALONG?

JUST KEEP UP.

"AND NOW THE STORY IS DONE..."

EARLIER, THOUGH, ONE OF YOU ASKED ME WHY NOW. WHY COME HERE TONIGHT, AFTER ALL THESE YEARS OF LYING, AND FINALLY TELL THE TRUTH?

I SAID BEFORE THAT IT'S ALL ABOUT TIME. AND I'VE BEEN AROUND ENOUGH DEATH TO KNOW WHEN MY OWN TIME IS DRAWING NEAR... AS WELL AS ANY CITY DOCTOR AT LEAST.

SO I'M HERE TONIGHT BECAUSE I WANT IT TO BE KNOWN, BY ALL OF YOU... THAT THERE ARE *MONSTERS* OUT THERE. *REAL MONSTERS* THAT WALK THE ROADS AND RAILS OF THIS COUNTRY.

BUT THERE ARE ALSO HEROES... MEN WHO EMBODY THE BEST WE HAVE TO OFFER. MEN LIKE MY FRIEND, *JAMES BOOK*... WHO WAS MORE OF A HERO THAN ANY CHARACTER I COULD EVER DREAM UP.

BECAUSE SKINNER SWEET DIDN'T WIN, YOU UNDERSTAND? JAMES BOOK *NEVER* BUCKLED, *NEVER* GAVE IN. HE WENT TO HIS GRAVE *EVERY BIT* THE *HERO* I KNEW...

...AND IF YOU ALL NEED A HAPPY ENDING, THAT'S THE *BEST* I CAN DO.

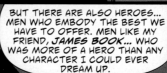

NOW...I'LL BE HAPPY TO SIGN BOOKS FOR THOSE WHO WANT THEM.

WAIT! WHAT HAPPENED TO ABILENA?

AND THE BABY! WHAT ABOUT THE BABY?

THOSE ARE NOT *MY* STORIES TO TELL.

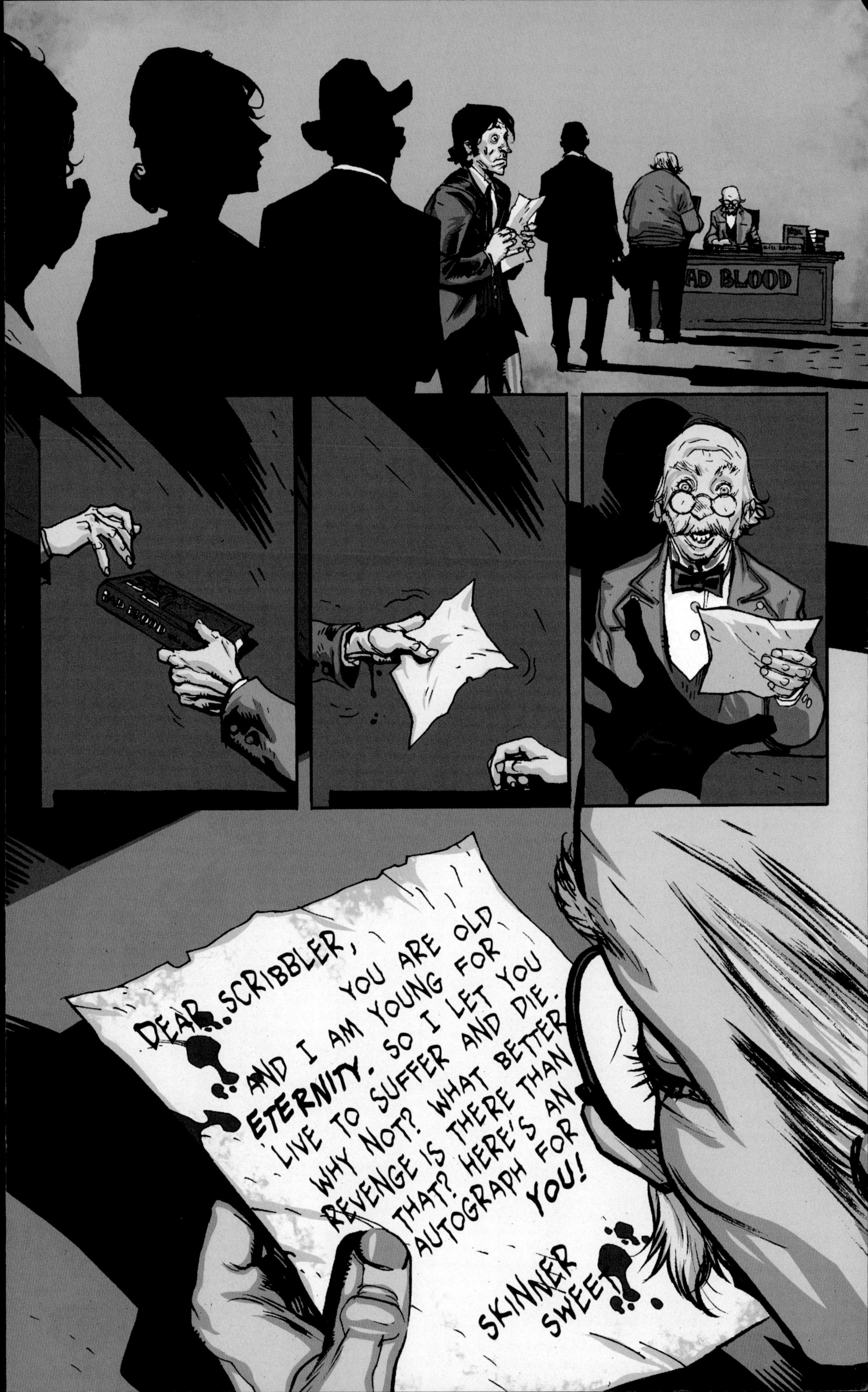

AD BLOOD
DEAR SCRIBBLER,
AND I AM YOU ARE OLD
ETERNITY. SO I LET YOU
LIVE TO SUFFER AND DIE.
WHY NOT? WHAT BETTER
REVENGE IS THERE THAN
THAT? HERE'S AN
AUTOGRAPH FOR
YOU!
SKINNER
SWEET

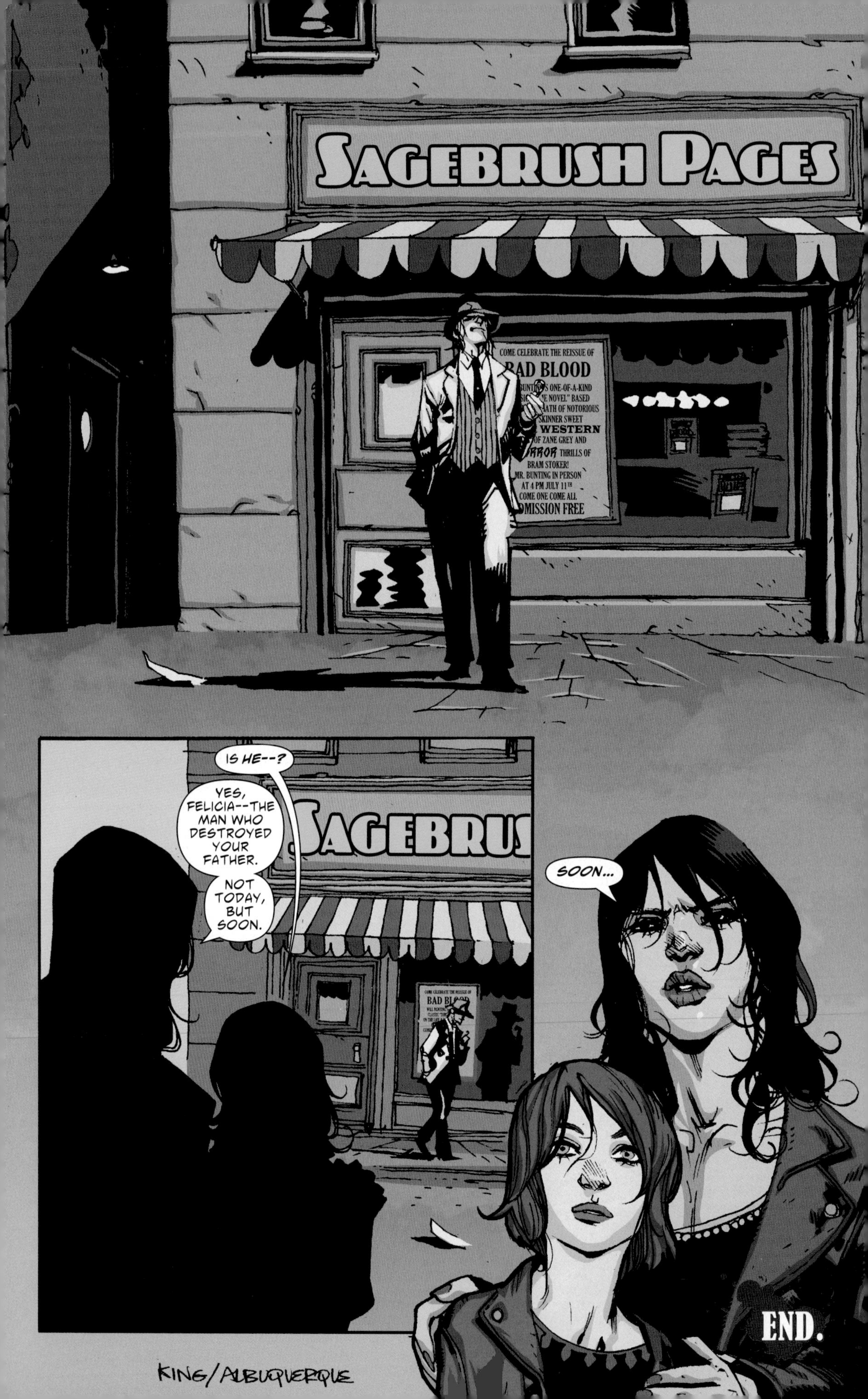
SAGEBRUSH PAGES
COME CELEBRATE THE REISSUE OF
BAD BLOOD
SKINNER SWEET
WESTERN
OF ZANE GREY AND
THRILLS OF
BRAM STOKER!
MR. BUNTING IN PERSON
AT 4 PM JULY 11TH
COME ONE COME ALL.
IS HE--?
YES, FELICIA--THE MAN WHO DESTROYED YOUR FATHER.
NOT TODAY, BUT SOON.
SOON...
END.
KING/ALBUQUERQUE

AFTERWORD
by Scott Snyder

On January 19th of this year, I got an email from Rafael Albuquerque that made me pause. The email had a page attached, but this was nothing new – we were neck-deep in issue two just then and Rafa had been mailing pages fast and furious all month. What made me hesitate was the subject line on the email:

"He's free!"

I didn't need to check the attachment to know what page had arrived. This would be page thirty-one, a splash that Rafa had been building toward for days: the splash page that shows Skinner busting out of that water-logged coffin, grinning in the watery darkness while that unfortunate diver recoils in terror. Skinner, unleashed, free and hungry and headed for the surface.

And so, yes, I'll admit I hesitated a minute before opening the page. More than anything I felt excited – I knew Rafa's page (like all his pages) would be better than anything I could have imagined. And even more than this, I was excited to see Skinner reborn as an American Vampire, to meet him all over again.

But part of me was afraid, too – afraid to open that page and see Skinner and look him straight in his yellow eyes.

Because the fact of the matter is that I'd come up with the idea for Skinner Sweet – this vampire outlaw with a new set of powers and weaknesses – a long time ago. Not just a year or two earlier, but several years. When I look through my notebooks from 2003, even 2002, I can find mentions of him: sketches, and dark, fun details. Most of the time, I'm good about putting pen to paper when I have an idea. I'm not a writer who lets an idea sit for a long time. When an idea excites me, I might spend a few weeks figuring it through a bit before diving in, but I'm talking a matter of weeks, not months, and certainly not years…

So yes, I felt a little afraid to face Skinner that day. Because I was the one who'd kept him locked up for so long. Sure, Book and Felix and the gang (and vampire Percy) might have laid him low, but if anyone was responsible for keeping him down there, in the dark murk where unrealized ideas live, it was me.

So why had I done it? Why hadn't I raised him from his watery grave earlier?

The honest-to-Elvis truth is that I tried. I thought of working up Skinner's story as a screenplay, and later as a novel. But nothing made sense… because his story was simply too big, too sprawling. And so Skinner stayed down there, waiting, waiting… Until one day in the late summer of 2008, after doing a few one-shots, I got the chance to pitch original project ideas to Mark Doyle at Vertigo… And when that happened, I could practically hear Skinner knocking around in his coffin, getting ready for the lid to open… Because I knew, sitting across from Mark in that pizzeria, that I finally had my venue: Skinner's was a story that could ONLY be a comic.

But I couldn't do it alone. Unleashing Skinner upon the world has been wholly a team effort — and so a huge thanks goes to my very own gang of monster outlaws: Rafael, Mark, and Steve. Mark, who believed in the series from day one. Rafael… what else is there to say about Rafa, except that he's the artist I've always dreamed of working with? He's brilliant, ferocious, and wholly invested in the series. The amazing Dave McCaig, who gives Rafa's art such striking color. Steve Wands, our great letterer. Will Dennis, the best "guy behind the guy" in comics. And our gang's wonderfully supportive and twisted den-mother, Karen Berger, who's encouraged us to do our best (and subsequently our worst) with these characters…

And Steve King… Right now, Steve's introduction to this edition is sitting on my desk. I haven't read it yet (would you read Stephen King's intro if you had to write the afterword?), but one thing I'm sure of is that it will be way, way too modest. Because the truth is that before Steve, Skinner was an idea in my head, a sketch, some notes on a pad; Steve is the one who brought him to vibrant, murderous life on the page. He's given so much to the character of Skinner — charisma and viciousness, a secret personal history. But he's also added a tremendous amount to Pearl's story, to the stories of characters to come, to the whole American Vampire mythology. This series — not just this cycle, but the whole series — is exponentially better for his involvement. So big thanks to Uncle Stevie for TCB.

Of course, I did eventually open page thirty-one. And yes, Skinner's cold, bright eyes did give me a bit of a chill. But I'm hoping there was at least a tiny flash of gratitude there, too. Because by waiting for the chance to do his story as a comic series — a series with Vertigo no less — I feel we've all done right by him.

Because while his is the story of the first American Vampire, it's a story about us, about Americans, about what makes us scary and admirable, monstrous and heroic. It's a giant story, bigger than just Skinner Sweet (sorry, Skinner), and the truth is that we're just getting warmed up. Next cycle we're off to Las Vegas of the 1930s. Then it's on to the turmoil of the 1940s and the great war… We'll explore the origins, too; we'll trace the history of human-vampire relations, as well as the history of vampire evolution itself; we'll discover new species, ancient and modern; learn about vicious interspecies conflict…

The bottom line is that this is the story I've always wanted to tell. And this is how it needs to be told.

So, as Skinner says: Off we go…

Scott Snyder
May, 2010

Issue # 1 Variant by Jim Lee

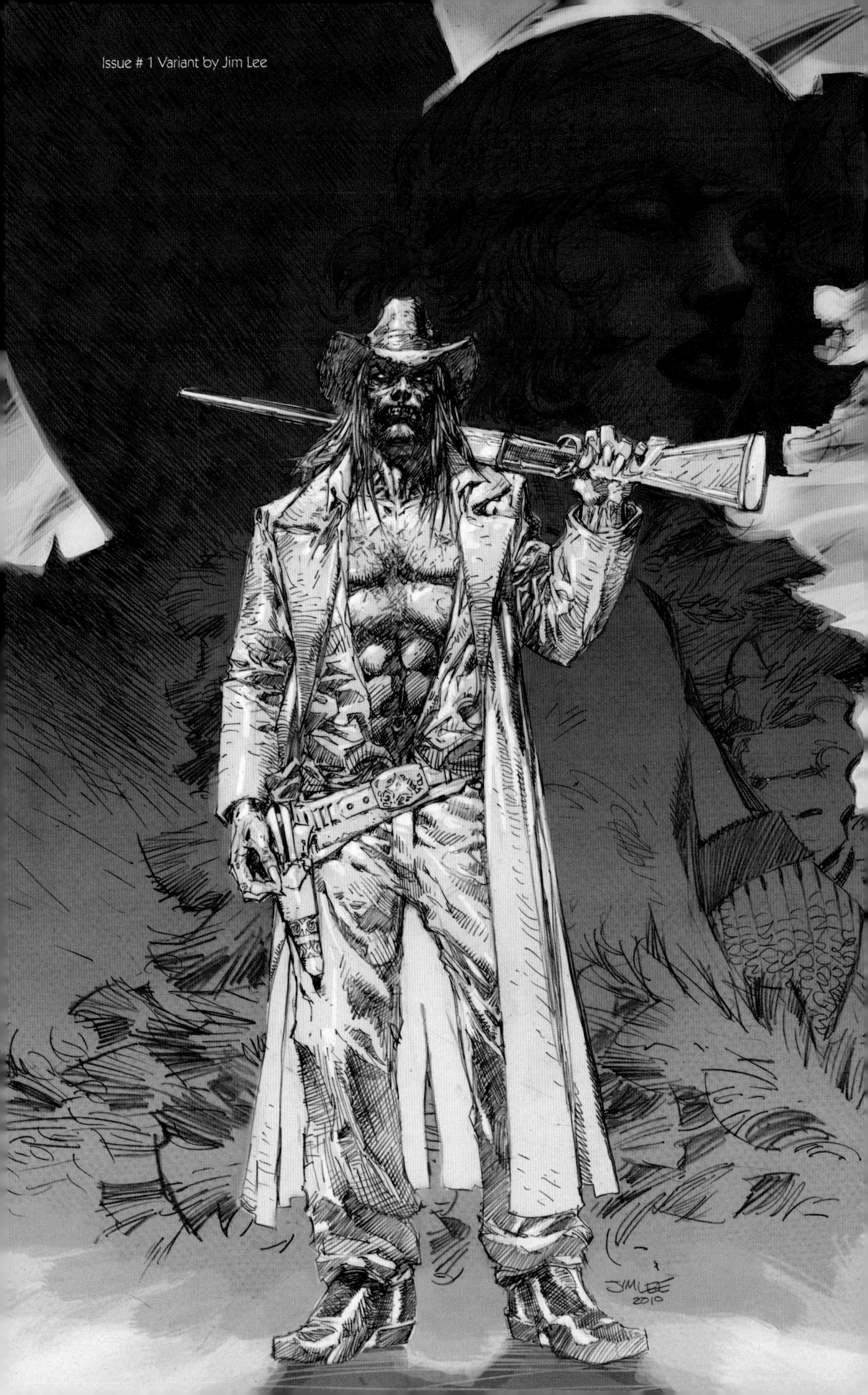
JIM LEE
2010

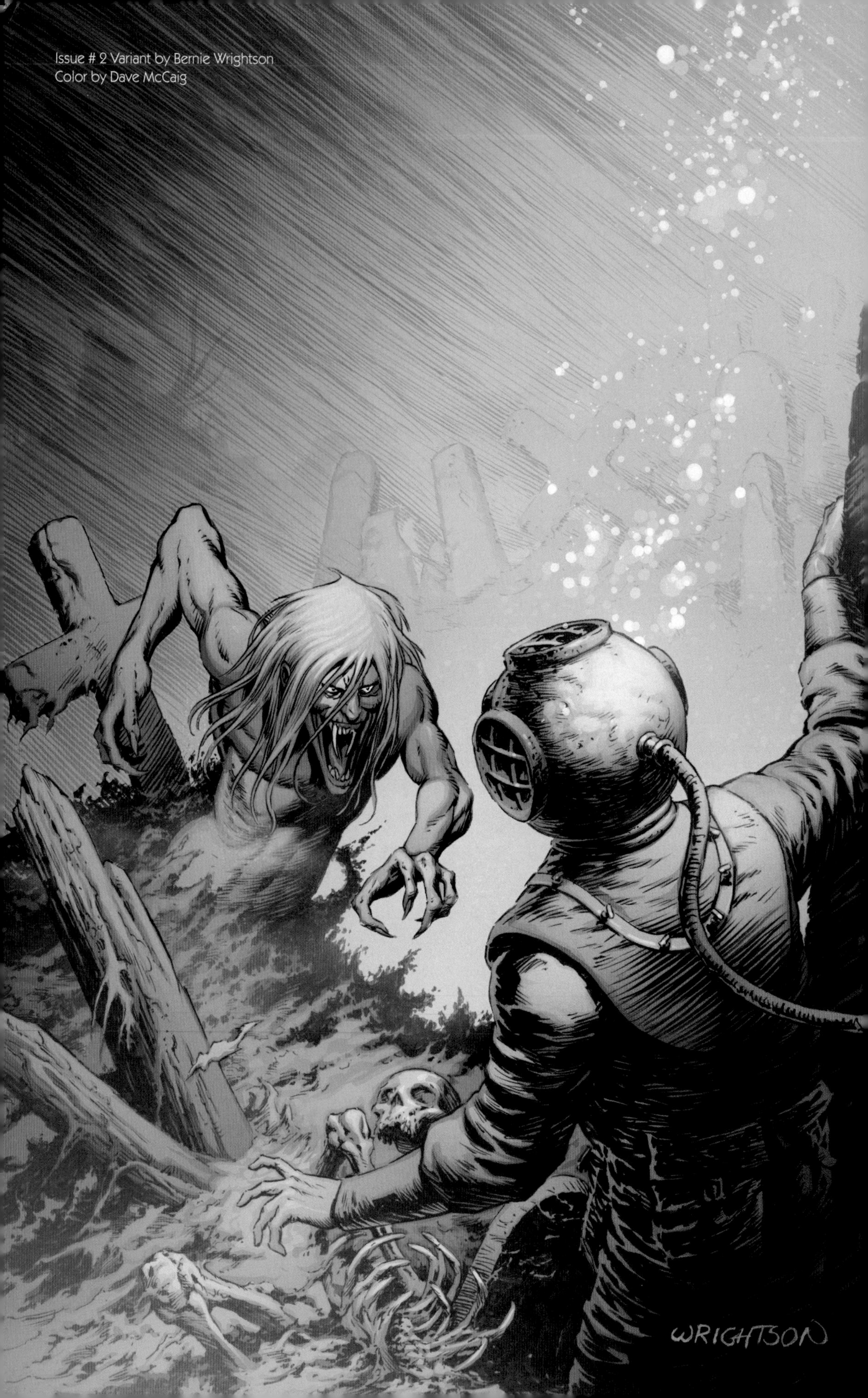
WRIGHTSON

Issue # 2 Variant by Bernie Wrightson
Color by Dave McCaig

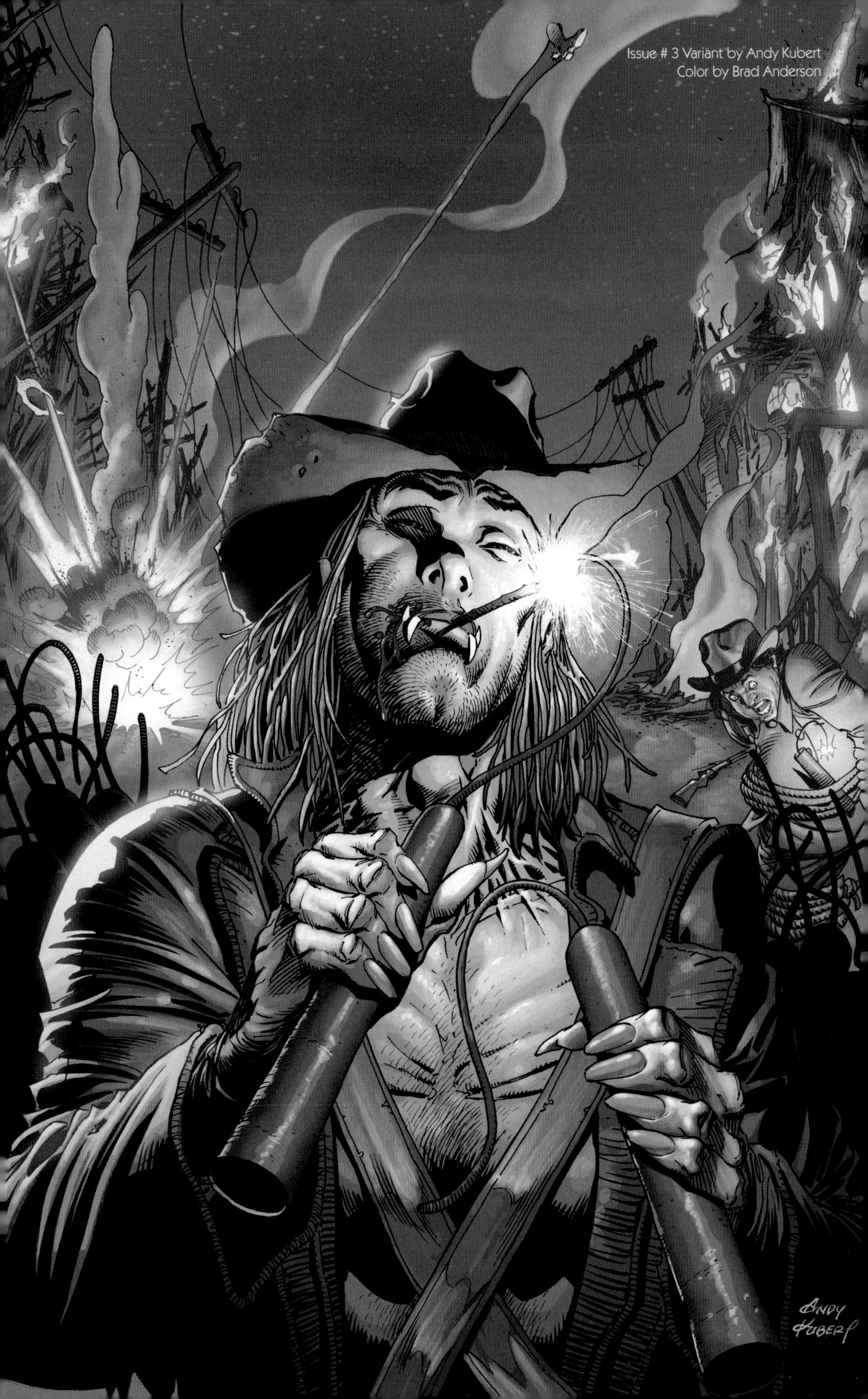
ANDY KUBERT
Issue # 3 Variant by Andy Kubert
Color by Brad Anderson

Issue # 4 Variant by JH Williams III

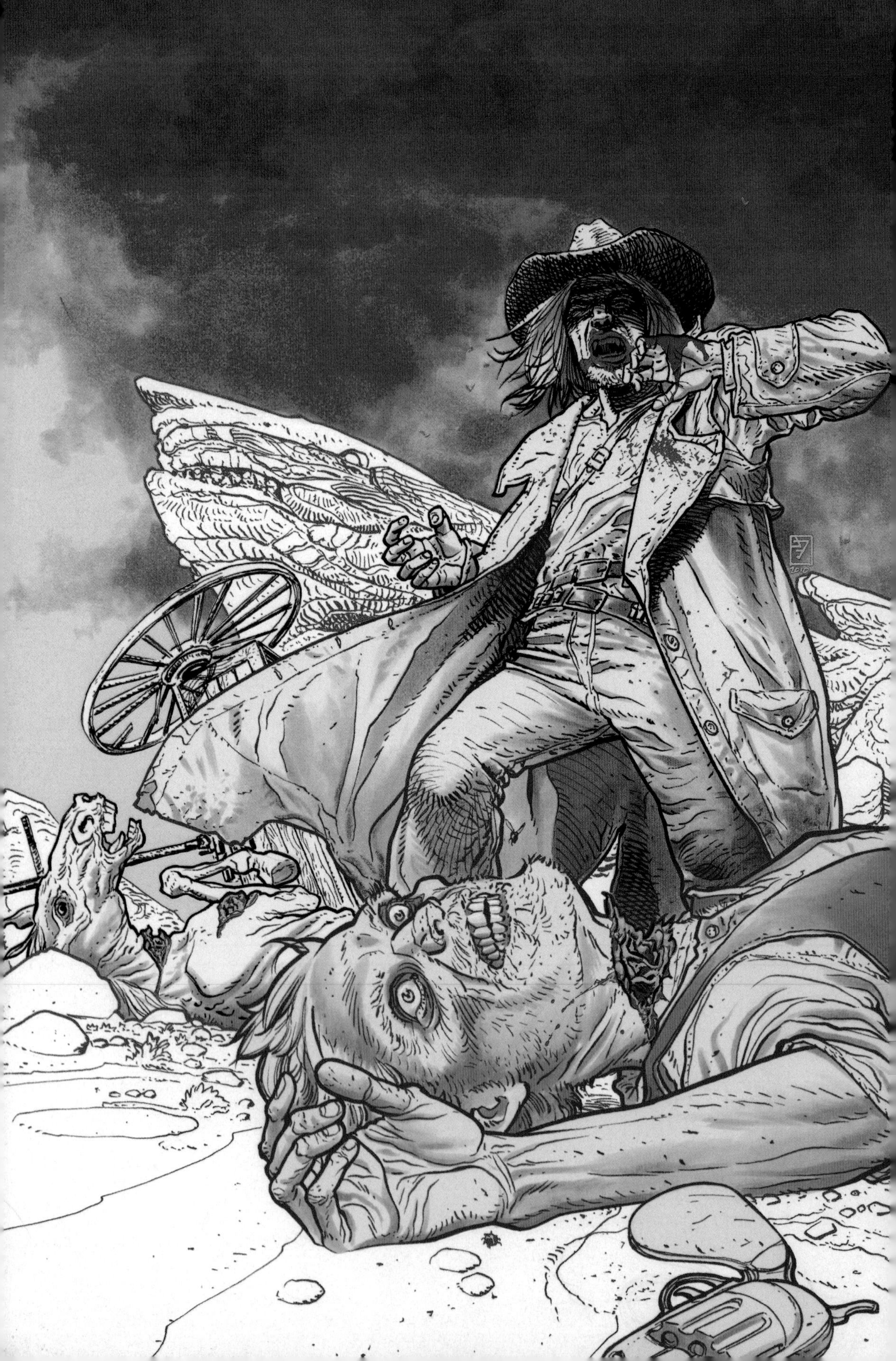

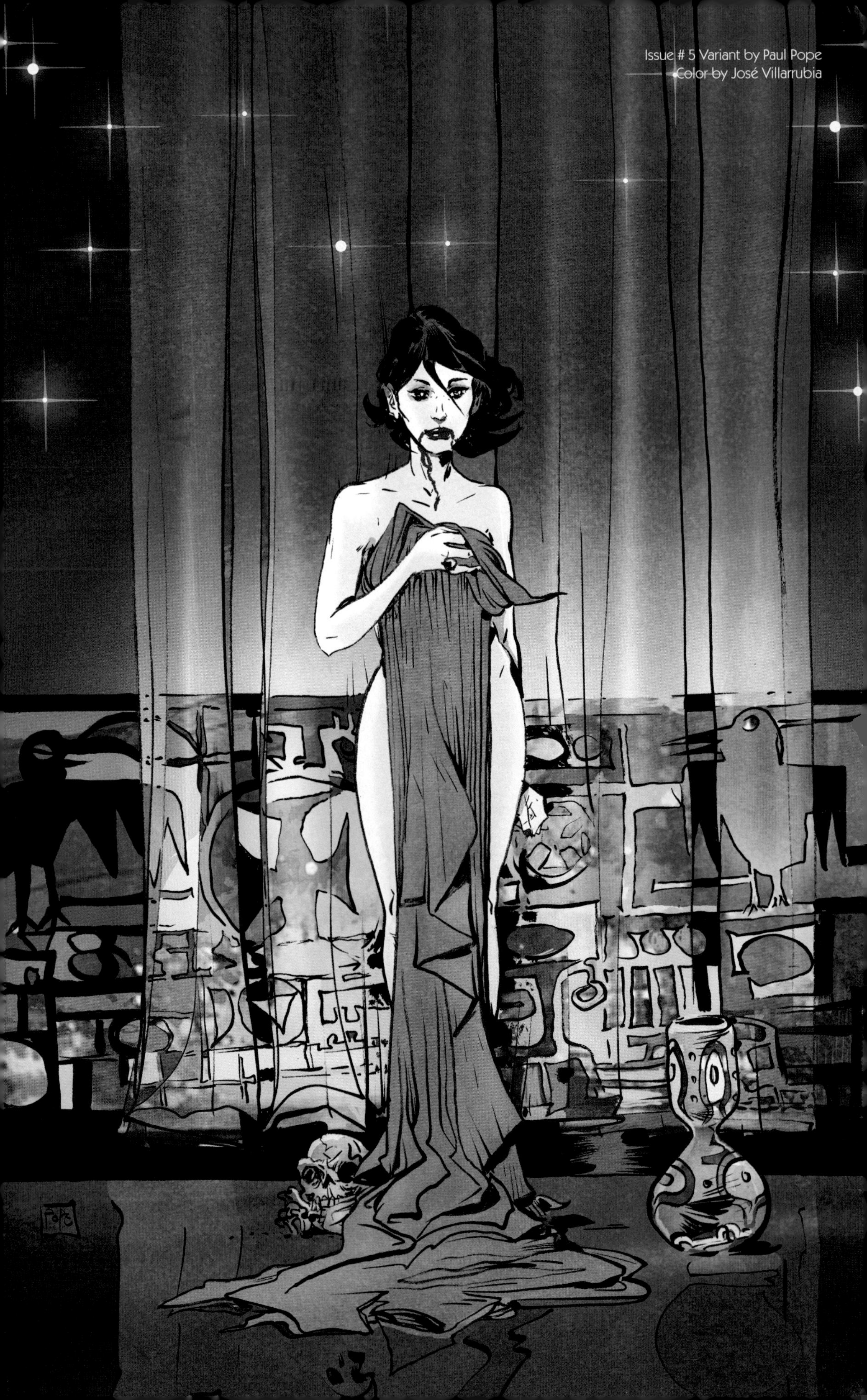

Issue # 5 Variant by Paul Pope
Color by José Villarrubia

The following pages of original script, along with corresponding art, demonstrate the different writing styles and shifting art, from crisp inks for Pearl's story to an ink wash for Skinner's story.

AMERICAN VAMPIRE #1, page 12

By Scott Snyder

PAGE 12:

12.1

Pearl, gathering herself. Skinner, sinking deeper into the chair.

PEARL: [to herself] God, why are the jerks always the cute ones?

PEARL: [to Skinner] Look. Just, don't be here tomorrow. Or I really will call someone.

SKINNER: The sheriff?

12.2

Skinner laughing.

PEARL: The sheriff, exactly. And she'll run you out of town before you know what hit you.

SKINNER: She'll run me out of town, ha ha! You know what? I like you, girlie. You got spunk. So I'll let you in on a little secret…

12.3

Skinner, pretending to whisper.

SKINNER: B.D. Bloch's parties? They ain't any fun at all. No, if I were you, I'd pass on his little jamboree tonight.

PEARL: Wow. And you eavesdrop, too… So I take it you and "B.D." are good friends?

12.4

SKINNER: More like old acquaintances. Actually, I'm just in town to finish a bit of business with the old coot.

SKINNER: And believe me, honey, his get-togethers – bunch of cheese-sniffing Eu-ro-peans drinking with their pinkies out. Why don't you stay here? I'll show you a real party.

12.5

PEARL: Thanks, but I happen to like drinking with my pinkie out.

Hattie appears behind her, surprised and smitten.

HATTIE: Okay, I'm ready to—Ooh. Hi.

12.6

Pearl pulling Hattie away.

PEARL: [to Skinner] Remember what I said about tomorrow.

SKINNER: Suit yourself....

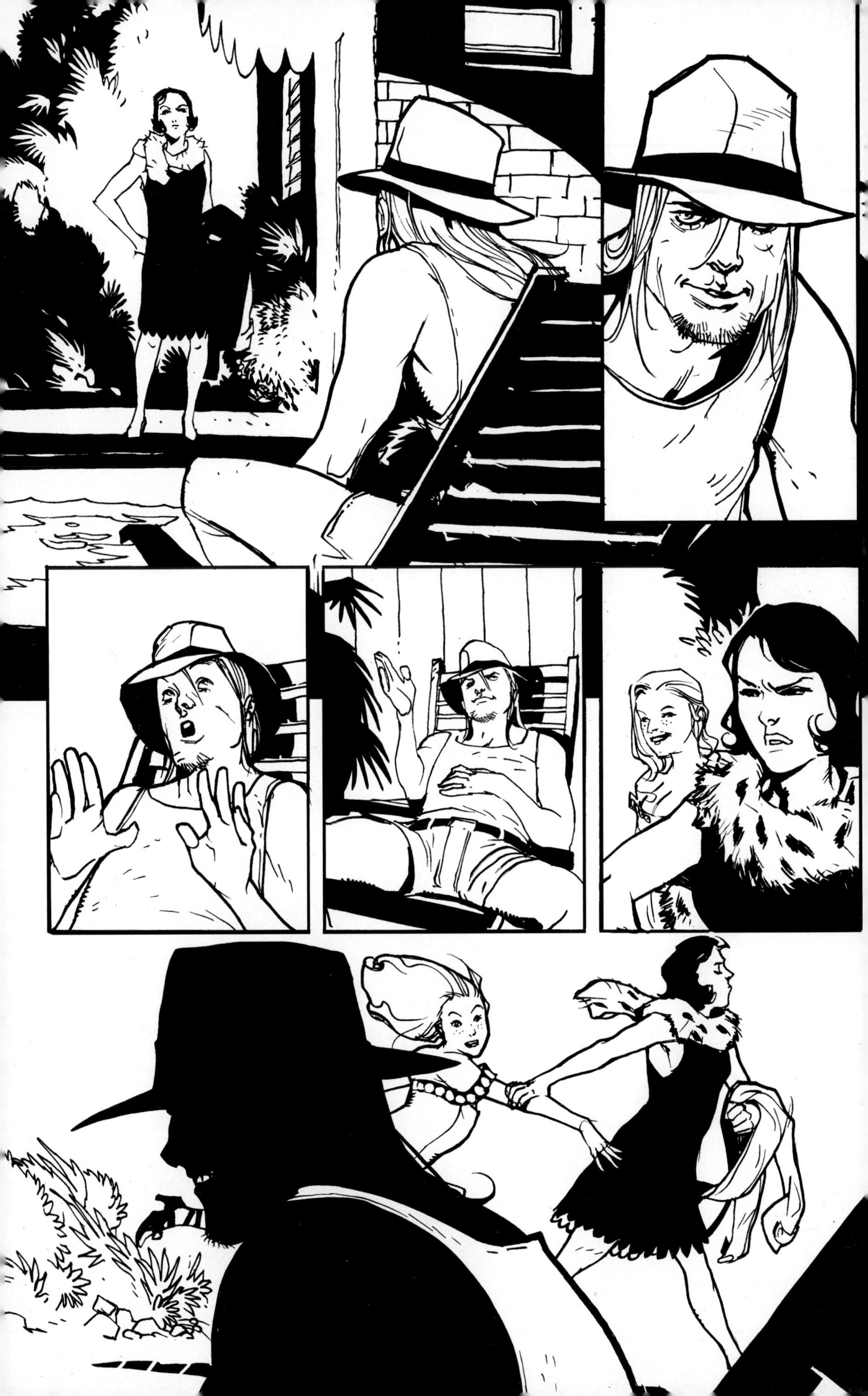

<u>American Vampire #4, page 5</u>
By Scott Snyder

PAGE 5:

5.1
And now Bloch's viciousness is apparent, his grinning, cruel, vampire face — hundreds of years of evil in his eyes.

BLOCH: And stab you with every god damned thing under the sun until we find what hurts you most.

5.2
Pearl, holding Hattie.

PEARL: Run, Hat…

5.3
To Hattie.

BLOCH: Ms. Hargrove, you wanted an audition?

5.4
Pearl, looking over her shoulder at Hattie.

PEARL: Hat? What is he —

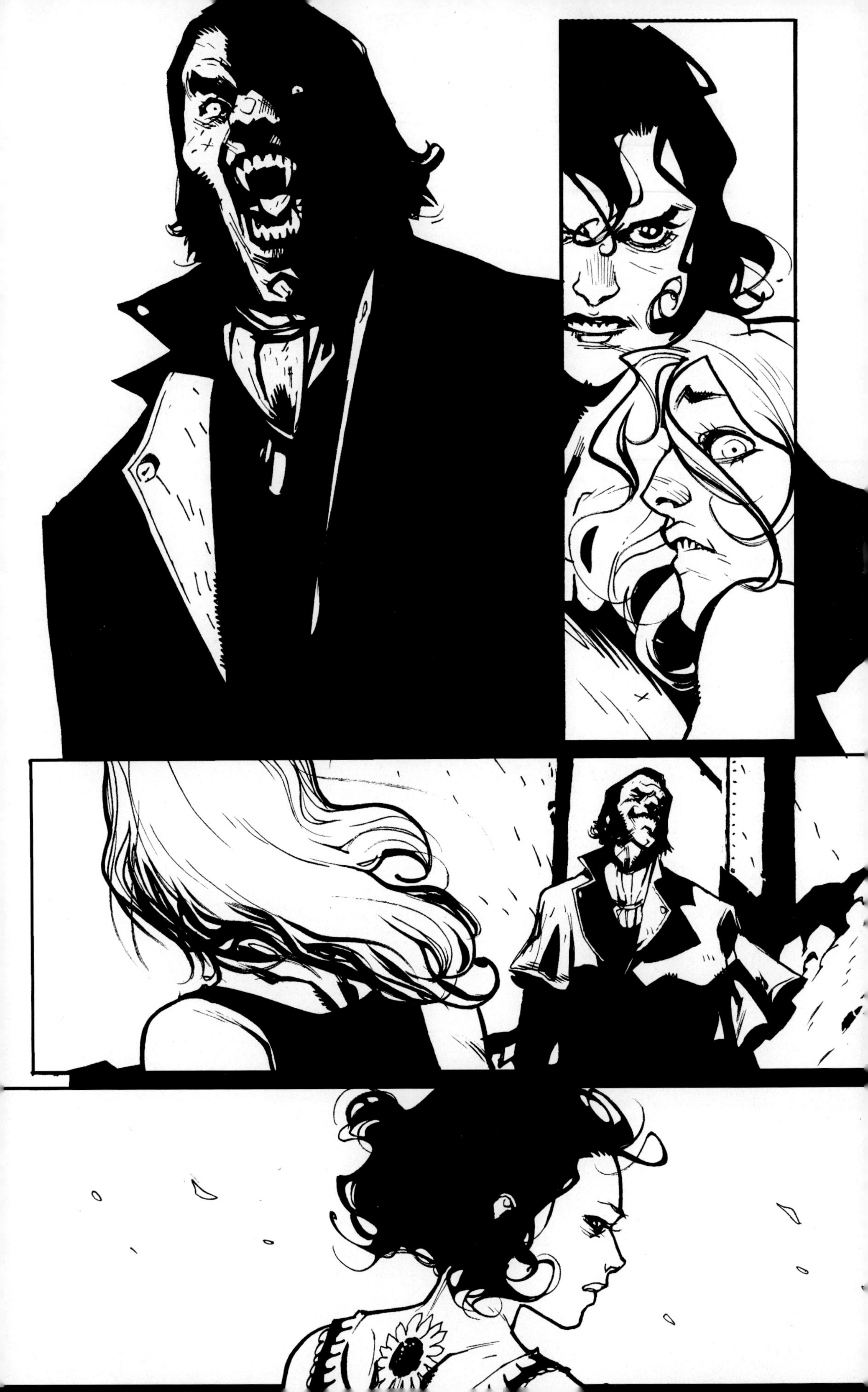

American Vampire #3 page 27
By Stephen King

PAGE TWENTY-SEVEN

Panel One

SKINNER (continues): …inside yonder warehouse.

This is a big panel. Behind SKINNER, the warehouse explodes in a gout of yellow-red flame. Bursts of wooden shrapnel rain down on the warehouse's side of the street. The roof, split into three or four large pieces, is lifting off like a bunch of 4th of July rockets. Townspeople flee from the explosion, screaming.

In the FG, the combined posse is shooting at SKINNER, giving him everything they've got, but SKINNER is unaffected. He pops a wooden match alight with a filthy fingernail.

[The following three panels are in a line across the bottom of the page, below the big panel.]

Panel Two

SKINNER [lighting his cigarillo]: Why, if it ain't Book's old boss. And I do mean old! Where is he, boss-man?

Panel Three

CU on FINCH, and he's scared to death.

FINCH: If I tell you, will you let me go?

Panel Four

SKINNER is holding a bundle of dynamite. He's got the burning tip of his cigarillo less than an inch from the fuse.

SKINNER: You bet, partner. C'mere. Let's palaver. Do I look dangerous?

(You bet he does.)

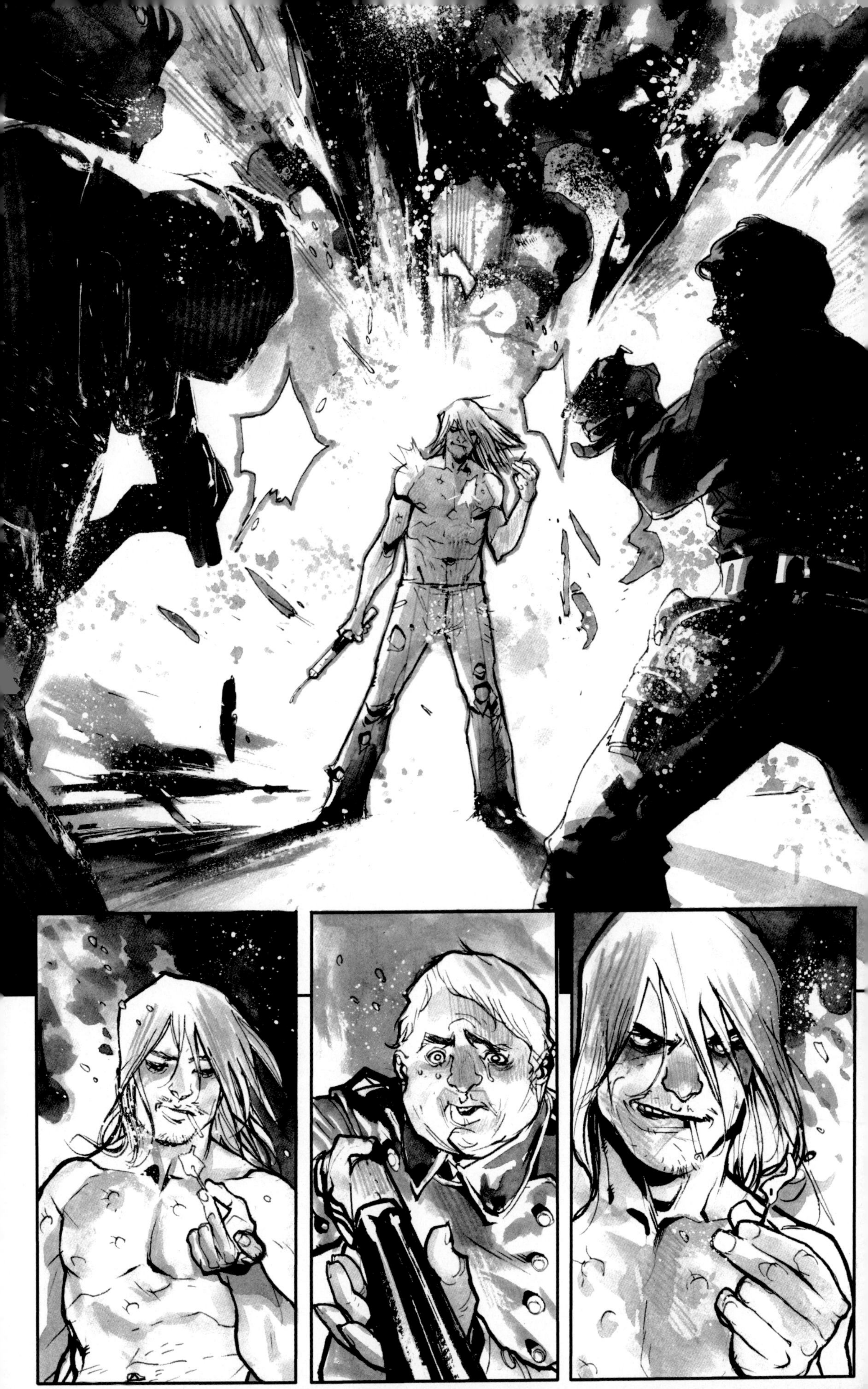

American Vampire #5, page 28
By Stephen King

Panel One

CLOSE on Will — We're back in SAGEBRUSH PAGES. OLD WILL'S head is lowered. He's lost in the past.

WILL: Does it matter how long they were together that night? To lovers, an hour can last a century. But even for lovers, every hour ends.

Panel Two

His audience is lost in his story (some may be in tears). Except…the FUSSY ACADEMIC looks dazed…hypnotized. And the seat next to him is empty. SKINNER'S gone.

VOICE-OVER BOX AT BOTTOM (BOOK): "Abi…I kept my end of the bargain. Now you keep yours."

Panel Three

BOOK'S bedroom. BOOK is holding the straight-razor. ABI (wearing a white shift) is looking at it with horror.

ABI: I…can't…with that.

Panel Four

BOOK (folds the razor shut): At the dark of the moon, I think it can be anything lethal. I was your godfather. I was your lover. Now be my friend.

Panel Five

Tears rolling down her cheeks, she reaches for the holstered .44 on the dresser. BOOK is lying back on his pillow, eyes shut.

BOOK: For the first time in three years, I feel like I can sleep.

Panel Six

The exterior of BOOK'S house, under all those amazing stars. From the window:

SFX: BLAMM!

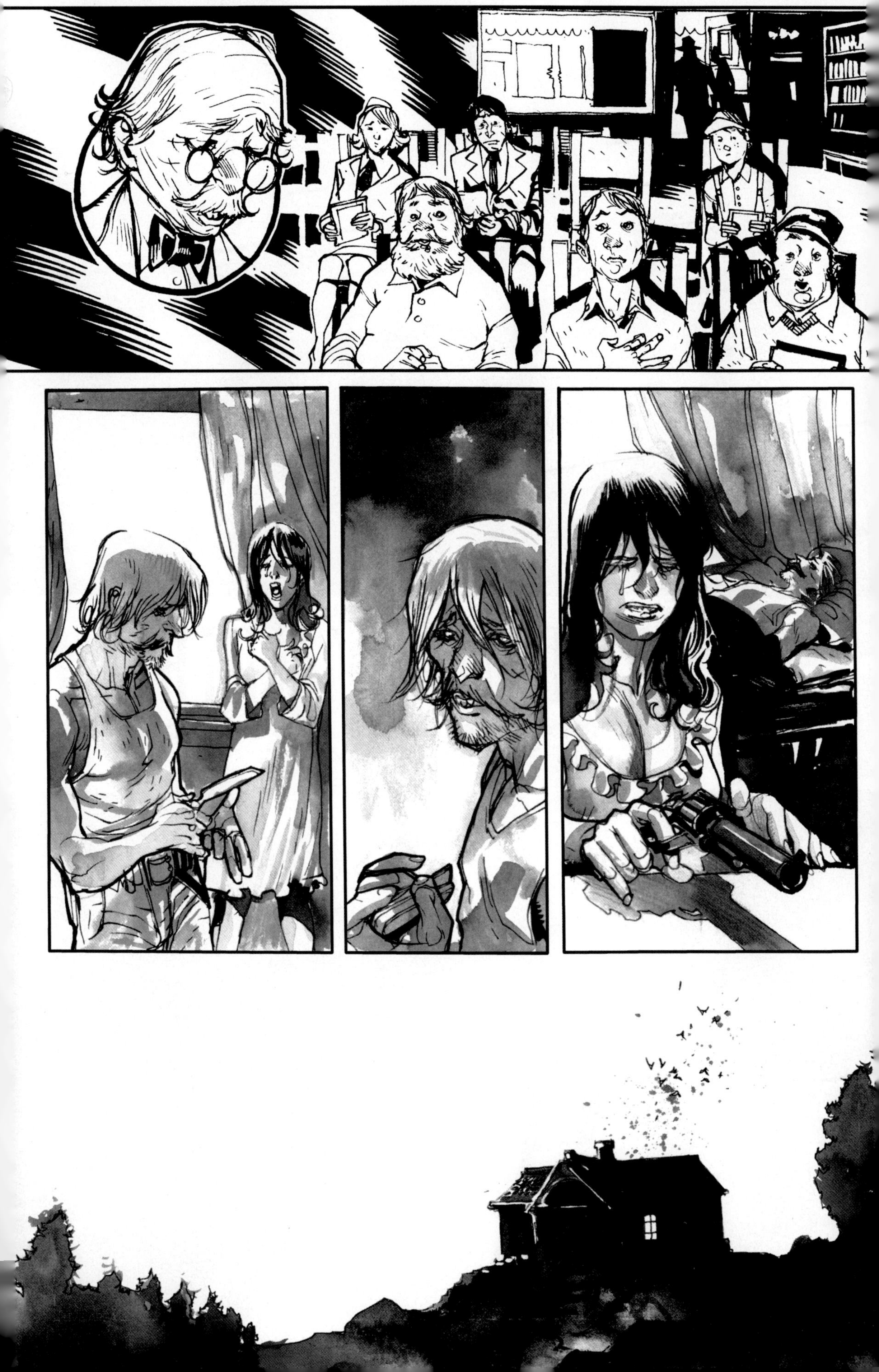

Original cover designs for issues 1 & 2 by Rafael Albuquerque

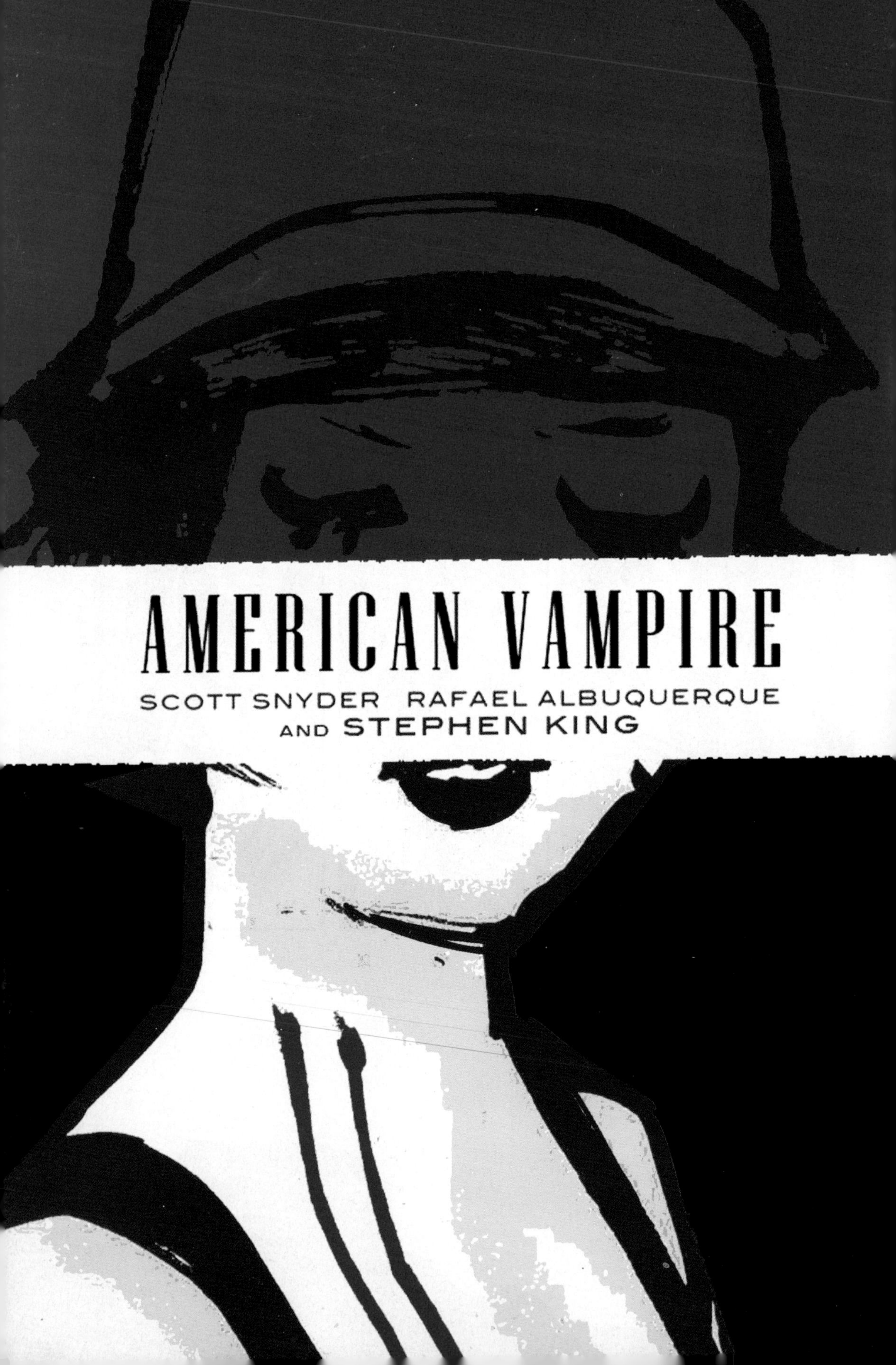
AMERICAN VAMPIRE
SCOTT SNYDER RAFAEL ALBUQUERQUE
AND STEPHEN KING

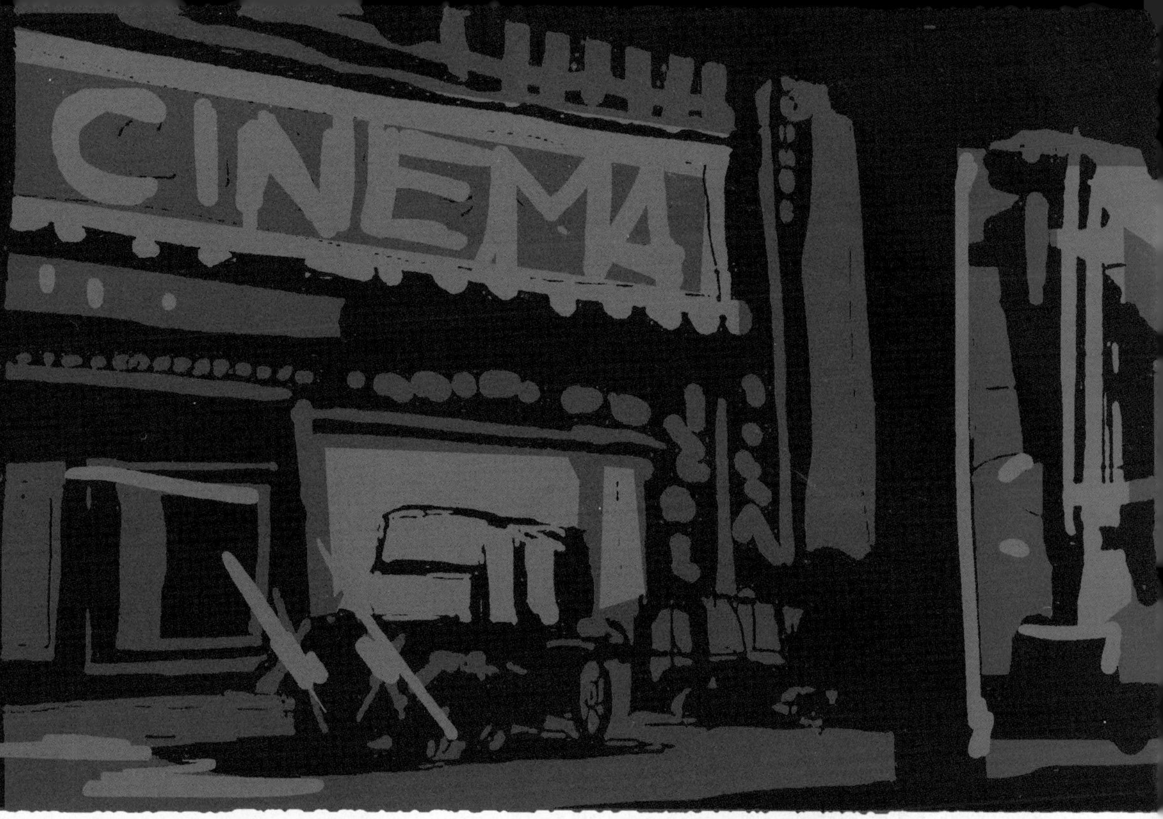
CINEMA

AMERICAN VAMPIRE

SCOTT SNYDER   RAFAEL ALBUQUERQUE
AND STEPHEN KING

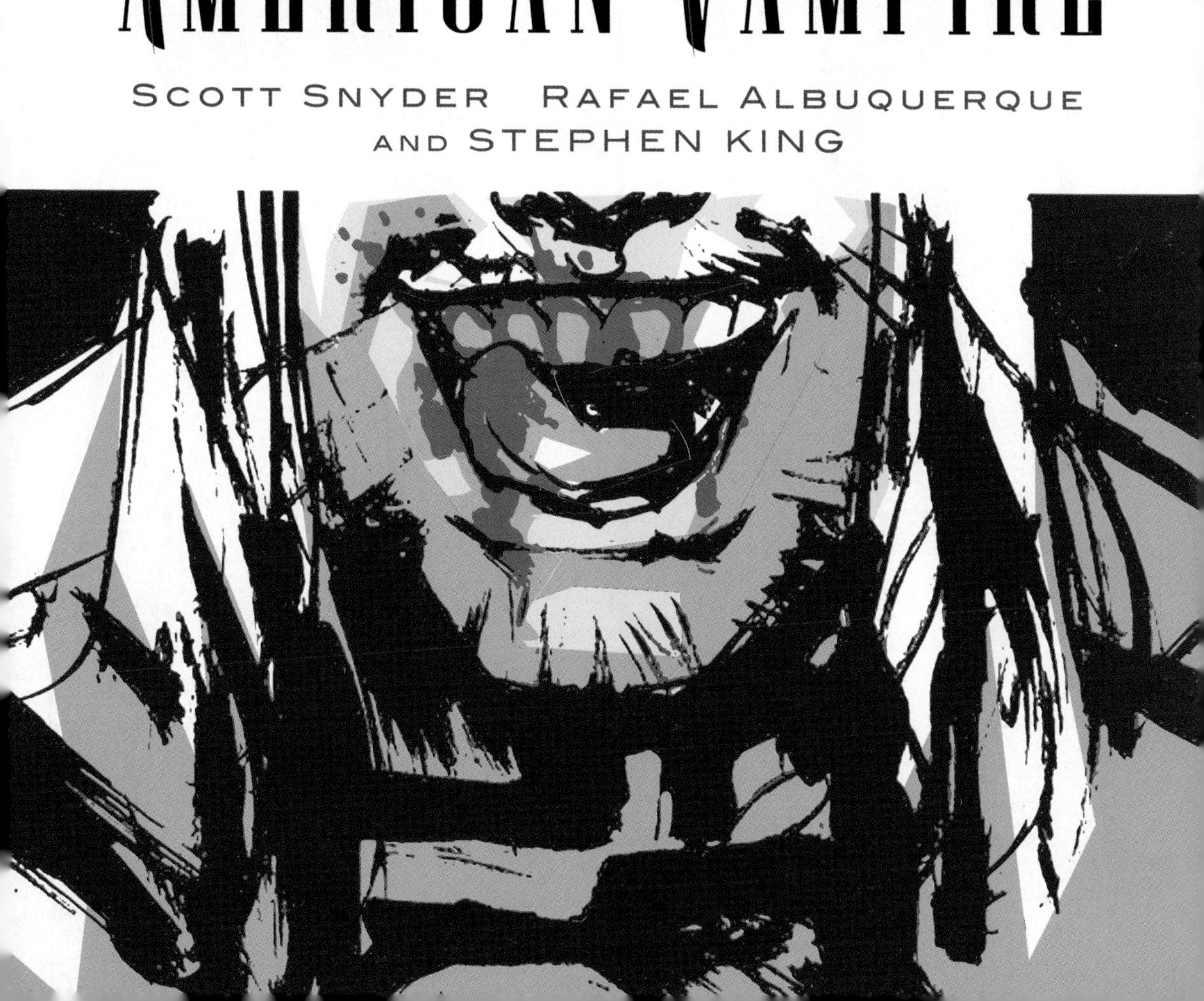

Original sketch of Skinner Sweet
1880s and 1920s version

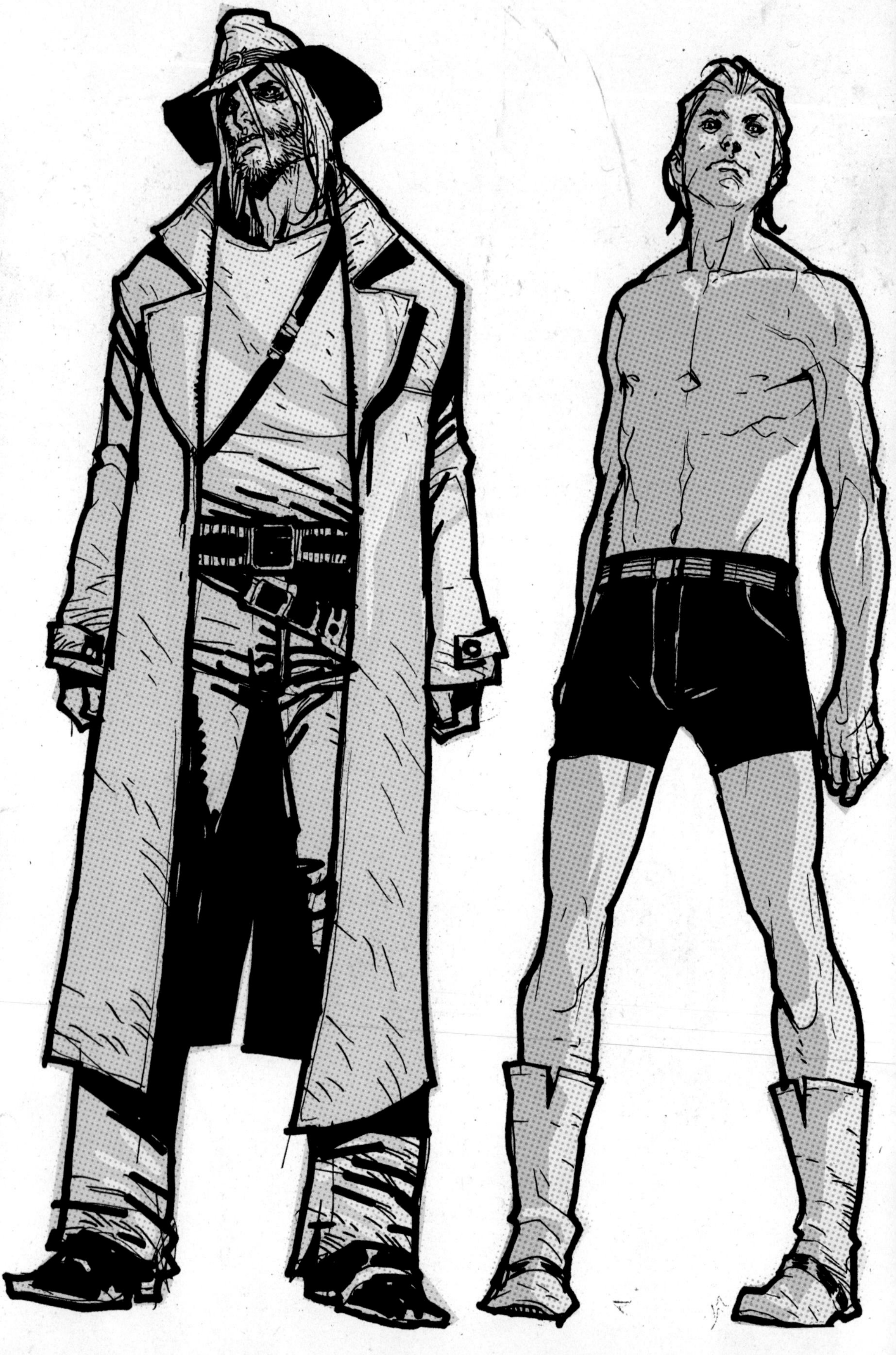

Original sketch for Pearl Jones

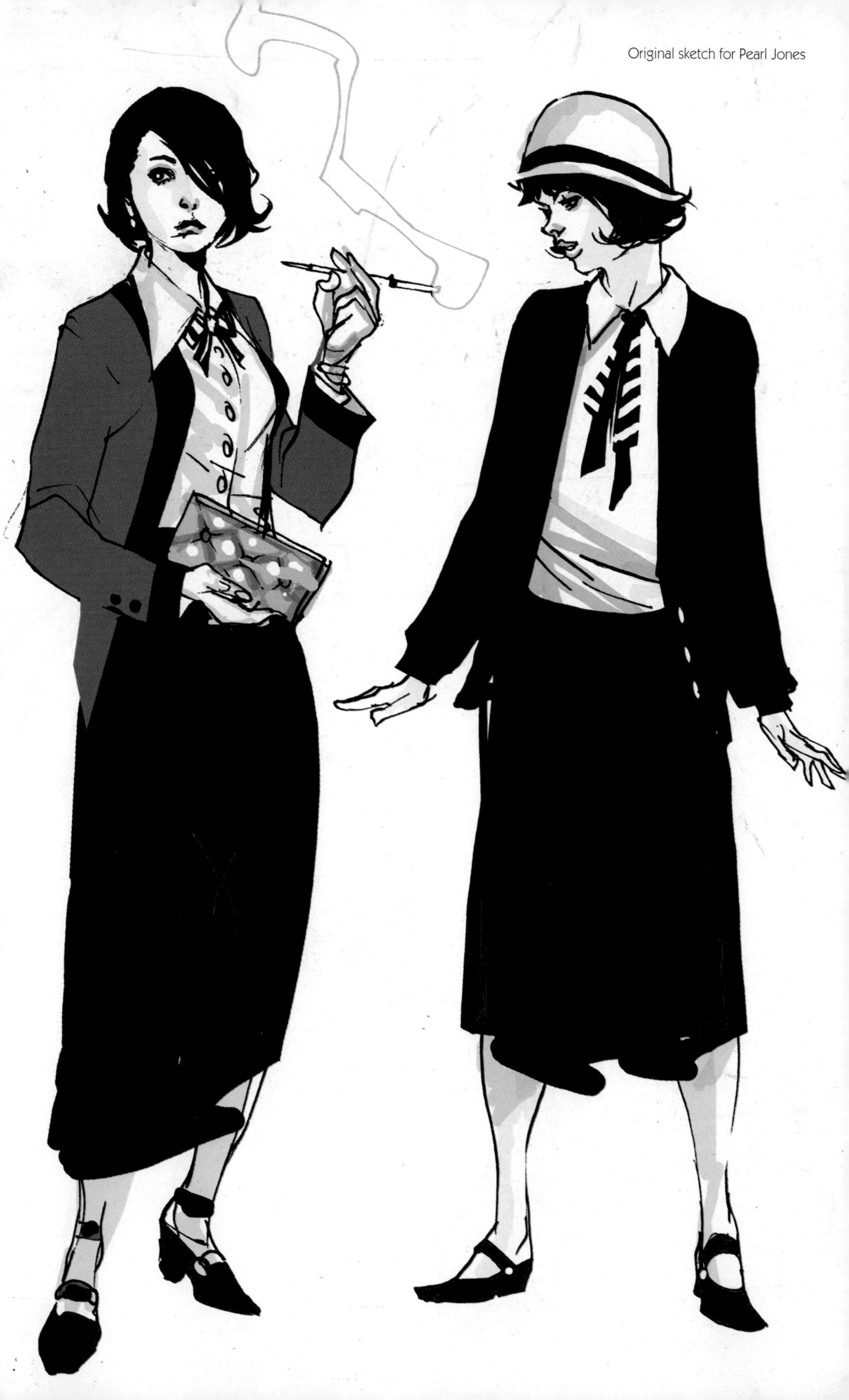

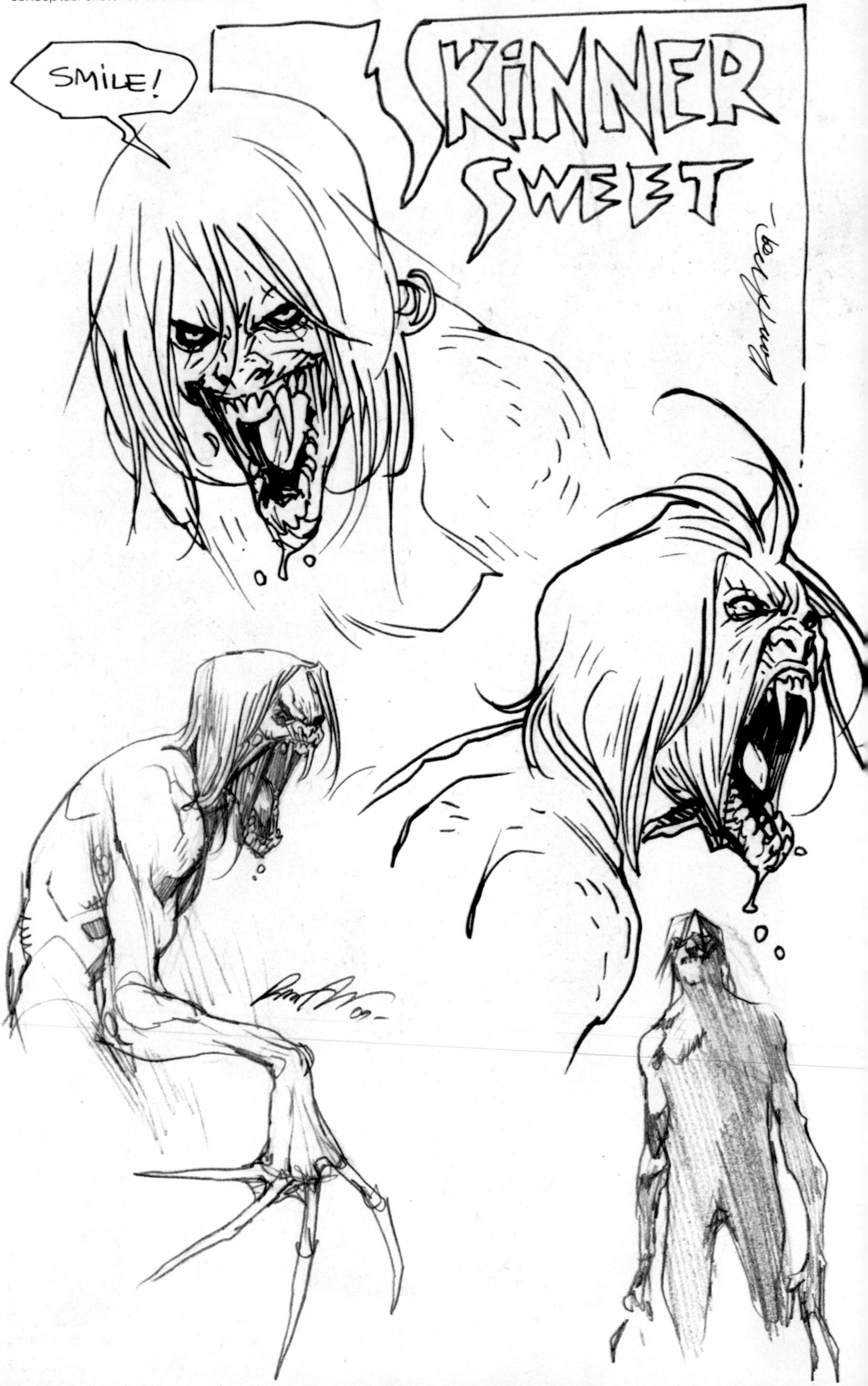
SMILE!
SKINNER SWEET

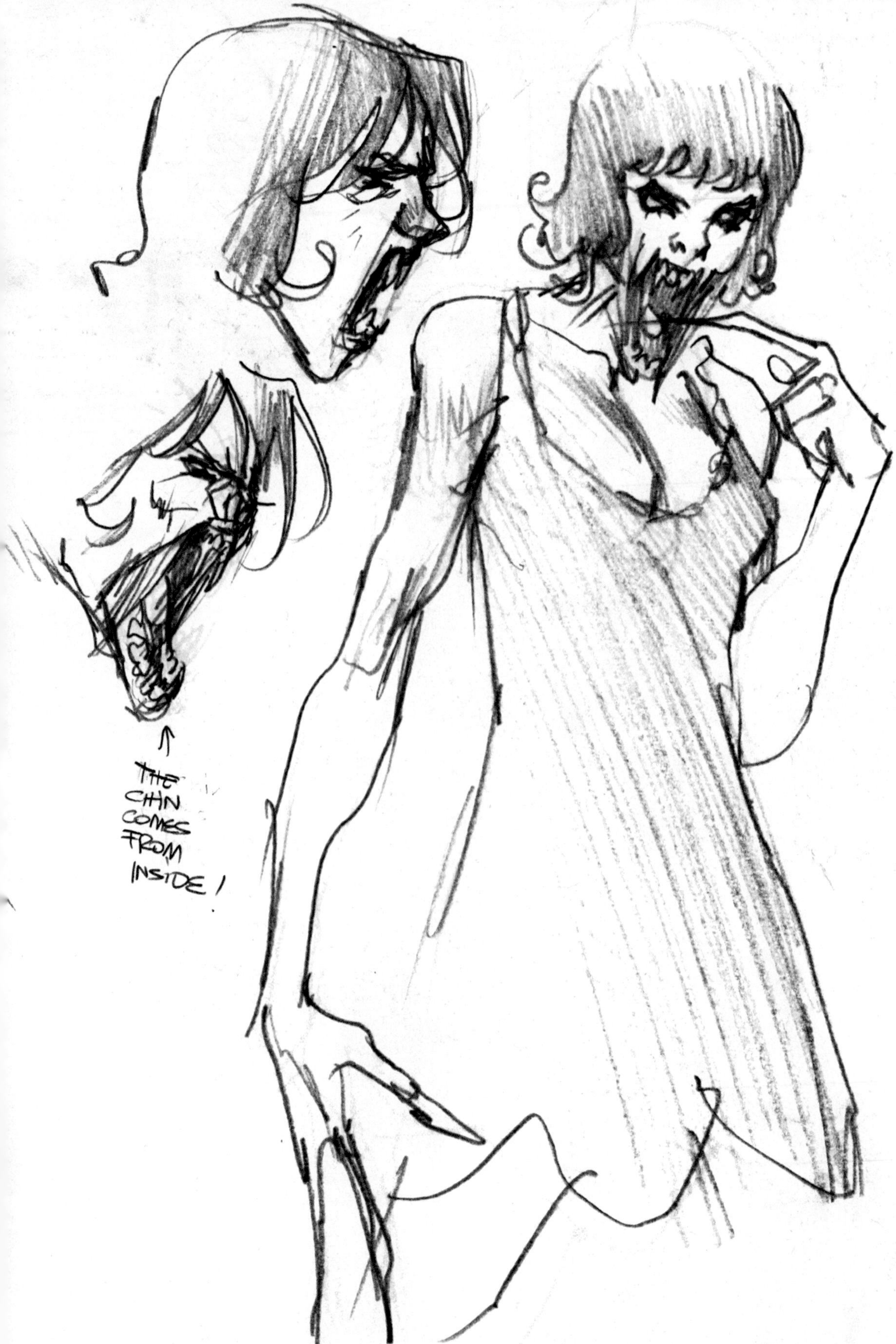
THE CHIN COMES FROM INSIDE!

Conceptual Sketches of Pearl Jones

Original sketch of James Book

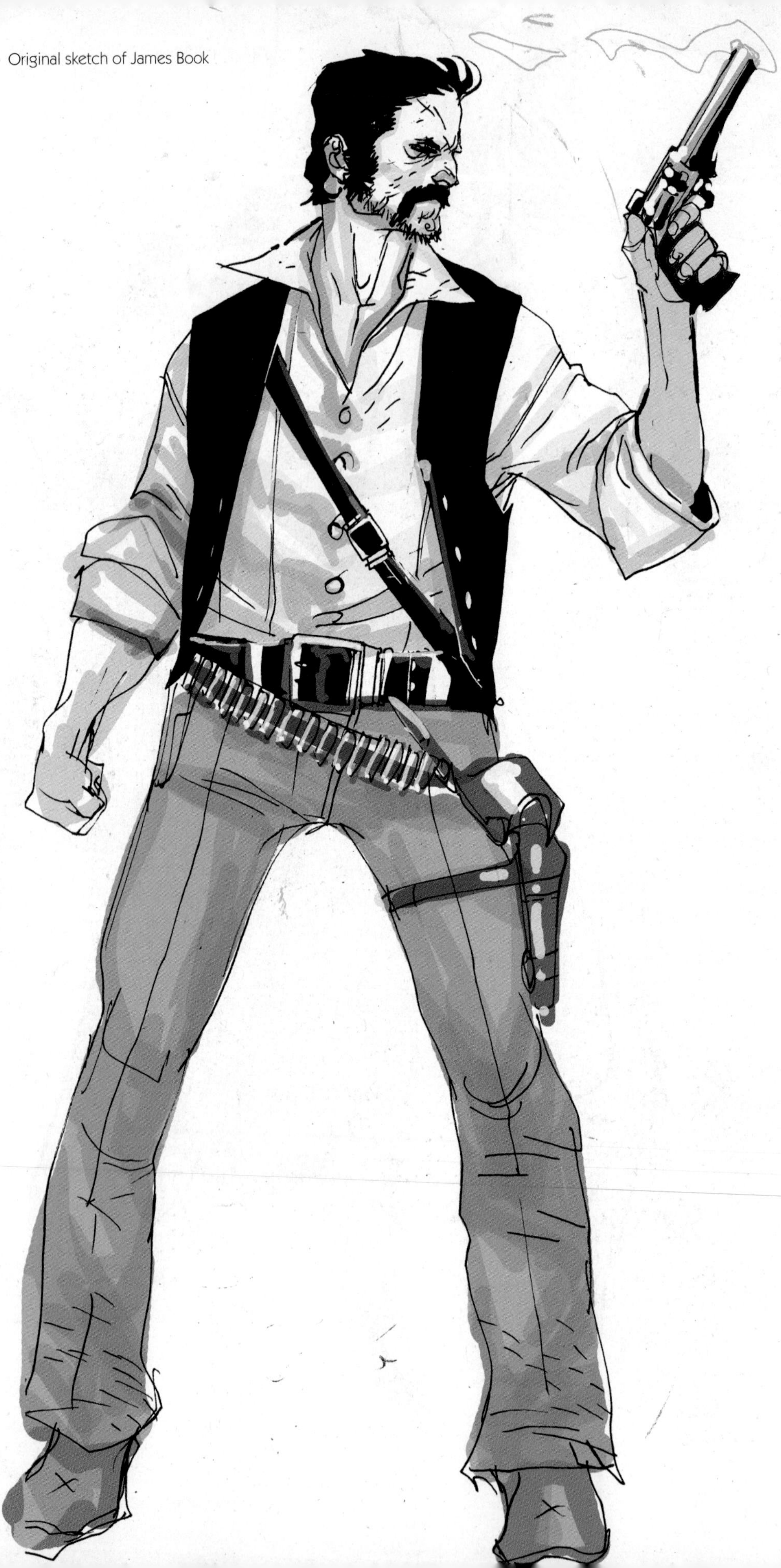

Original sketch of Henry Preston and Percy

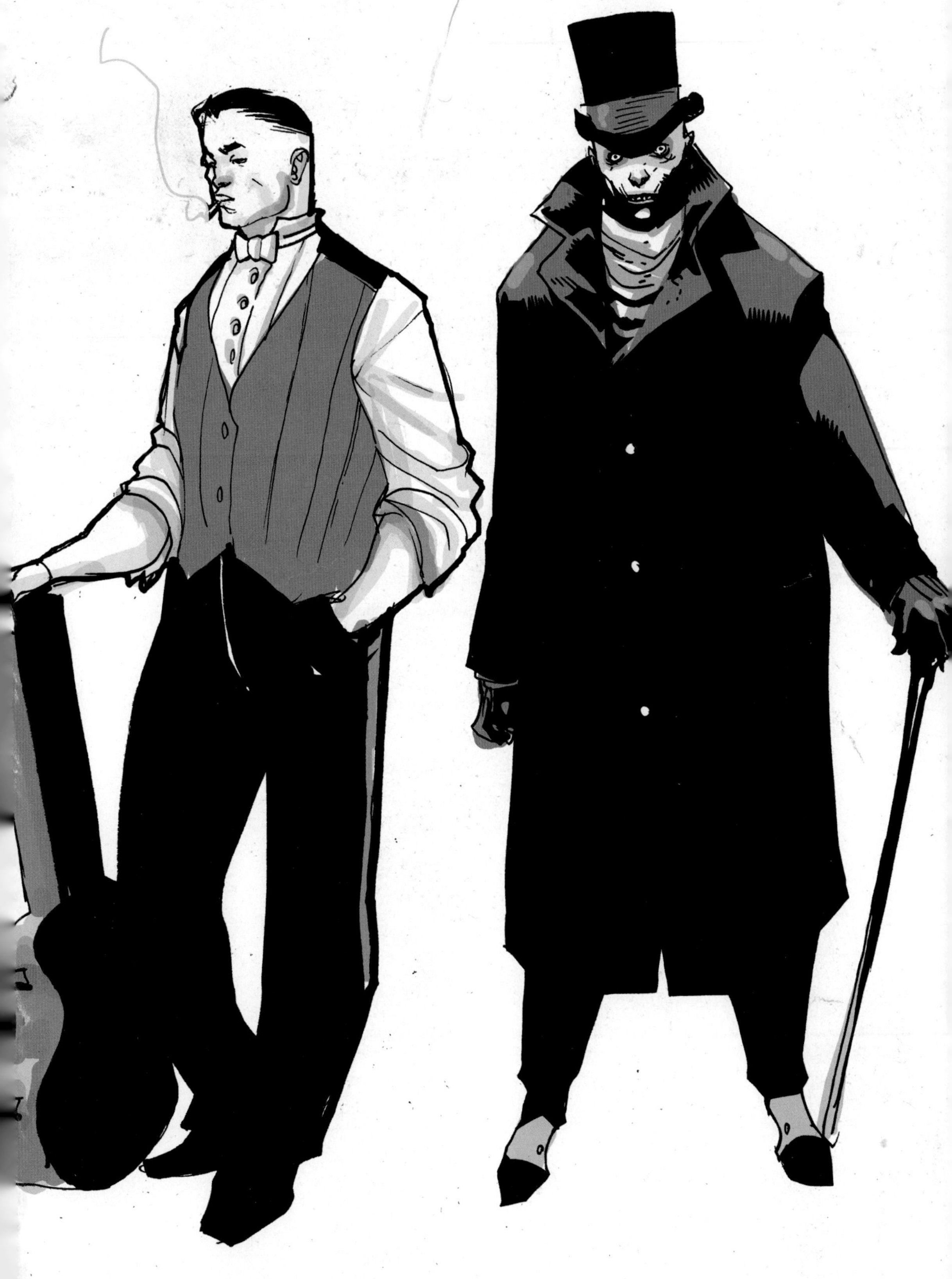

Scott Snyder's first collection of stories, *Voodoo Heart,* was published in 2006 by the Dial Press. He has written for both Marvel and DC, but AMERICAN VAMPIRE is his first creator-owned series. He lives on Long Island with his wife, Jeanie, his son, Jack Presley, and those chicken photos (originals and copies) in the event that Stephen ever acts up.

Rafael Albuquerque was born in Porto Alegre, Brazil. Rafael has been working in the American comic book industry since 2005. Best known for his work on the *Savage Brothers, Blue Beetle* and *Superman/Batman,* he has also worked on the creator-owned graphic novels *Crimeland* (2007) and *Mondo Urbano* (2010).

Stephen King lives in Maine with his wife, the novelist Tabitha King. He has written over 50 books. Although he has been adapted for comics before, AMERICAN VAMPIRE is the first time he's written one himself. He claims it's Scott Snyder's fault. Scott, he says, threatened to send pictures of Steve and the chickens to *The National Enquirer* if he didn't cooperate.